FRESHWATER FISHERY LAW

FRESHWATER FISHERY LAW

William Howarth BA, LLM

Lecturer in Law, University College of Wales, Aberystwyth

Financial Training

First published in Great Britain 1987 by Financial Training Publications Limited, Holland House, 140–144 Freston Road, London W10 6TR

ISBN: 1 85185 030 9

Typeset by Kerrypress Ltd, Luton
Printed by Redwood Burn Ltd, Trowbridge

CONTENTS

1.01 Some general themes in freshwater fishery law   1.02 Methods of fishing under the Salmon and Freshwater Fisheries Act 1975 1.03 Categories of fish under the Salmon and Freshwater Fisheries Act 1975   1.04 Fishing in freshwater and saltwater under the Salmon and Freshwater Fisheries Act 1975 1.05 The ownership of fisheries 1.06 Public fisheries   1.07 Private fisheries   1.08 Presumptions in relation to the ownership of fisheries   1.09 The ownership of water   1.10 The legal distinction between common law and statute law in freshwater fishery law   1.11 The legal distinction between civil wrongs and criminal offences in freshwater fishery law 1.12 Penalties under the Salmon and Freshwater Fisheries Act 1975

2.01 Ancient and modern freshwater fishery law   2.02 Early laws on obstructions to migratory fish   2.03 Early statutes on close seasons   2.04 Early restrictions on improper netting   2.05 Early enactments on the theft of fish   2.06 Early administrative provisions   2.07 The Report of the Commissioners Appointed to Inquire into Salmon Fisheries (1861)   2.08 The Salmon Fishery Act 1861   2.09 The regulation of fishing for freshwater fish   2.10 Twentieth century reforms in freshwater fishery law   2.11 Reforms in fishery administration   2.12 The Salmon and Freshwater Fisheries Act 1975 and other freshwater fisheries legislation

3.01 Three levels of restriction on improper methods of taking fish   3.02 Special provision relating to fish farms   3.03 Part I of the Salmon and Freshwater Fisheries Act 1975   3.04 Prohibited methods of taking fish under s.1 of the Salmon and Freshwater Fisheries Act

exceptions to the offence of causing polluting matter to enter a stream contrary to s.31(1) of the Control of Pollution Act 1974   11.15 Penalties under s.31 of the Control of Pollution Act 1974   11.16 Regulations and byelaws under s.31 of the Control of Pollution Act 1974   11.17 Trade and sewage effluent discharge unde s.32 of the Control of Pollution Act 1974   11.18 Defences and exceptions to the offence of discharging trade or sewage effluent contrary to s.32 of the Control of Pollution Act 1974   11.19 Penalties under s.32 of the Control of Pollution Act 1974   11.20 Sanitary appliances on vessels under s.33 of the Control of Pollution Act 1974   11.21 Discharges permitted by consent under s.34 of the Control of Pollution Act 1974   11.22 Appeals to the Secretary of State   11.23 Deposits and vegetation in streams under s.49 of the Control of Pollution Act 1974   11.24 Miscellaneous statutory provisions 11.25 Diseased animal carcases   11.26 Pollution by gas waste   11.27 Pollution of water supplies   11.28 Radioactive pollution   11.29 Abandoned vehicles and litter

PREFACE

Angling has been a popular craft through the ages, whether for the occasional enthusiast browsing over his line in some shady reach on a river convenient to town, or the fervid angler testing his skill against salmon or trout in the remoteness of . . . a quiet Welsh valley. Never have there been so many fishing publications, mostly profusely illustrated with fish and fly portraits, retailing the varieties of bait, tackle and the best fishing waters and recounting the niceties and methods of catching fish.

However, on turning to the legal side of fishing, it is soon discovered that there is a great lack of literature on the subject. True, one could (if you have a copy) dip into Chapter 6 of Coulson and Forbes on *Waters and Land Drainage* (6th edn) but this is a weighty tome not easily transported from the desk or library and even there the detail is not too profuse. One of the best books devoted entirely to fishery law was *The History and Law of Fisheries* by S.A. and H.S. Moore—but mark the date, 1903. Again, in the wake of the Salmon and Freshwater Fisheries Act 1923, several textbooks were published with annotations on the provisions of the Act, but these books sadly lack a modern edition. A new textbook on fishery law based on the Salmon and Freshwater Fisheries Act 1975, is badly needed.

These are the words of the late A.S. Wisdom, who wrote widely on all aspects of the law relating to water and fisheries, in his posthumous *Aspects of Water Law* (1981 at p.88). The present work attempts to fill the gap that Wisdom perceived.

For the most part the law relating to freshwater fisheries in England and Wales is codified in a single Act: the Salmon and Freshwater Fisheries Act 1975. This Act serves as the skeleton for this book which, after a brief examination of the history of fishery law, follows the order of the six parts of the Act:

Part I—Prohibition of certain modes of taking or destroying fish (ss.1 to 5);
Part II—Obstruction to passage of fish (ss.6 to 18);
Part III—Times of fishing and selling and exporting fish (ss.19 to 24);
Part IV—Fishing licences (ss.25 to 27);
Part V—Administration and enforcement (ss.28 to 37); and
Part VI—Miscellaneous and supplementary (ss.38 to 43).

After examining these areas a step is taken outside the provisions of the Act to look at two other topics which constitute an essential part of the law relating to freshwater fisheries: water pollution and water abstraction. The final chapter considers the changes in the law brought about by the Salmon Act 1986.

It must be noted from the outset that the Salmon and Freshwater Fisheries Act

1975 regulates both fishing for sport and commercial fishing for the types of fish covered by the Act. Correspondingly this book deals with the law relating to both coarse and game angling, and commercial methods of fishing for salmon, trout, freshwater fish and eels. Few readers will be directly concerned with all the topics which are discussed, though all with an involvement with fishing (in the broadest sense) or fishery administration, and their legal advisors, will find an account of the law as it affects them by a selective reading of the text. The overriding object is that this work should provide as complete a discussion of the subject as can be given within the confines of the space available.

It is generally estimated that there are in excess of three million anglers in England and Wales. By a sizeable margin this makes angling the most popular active recreational pursuit in this nation. Given that the great majority of these participants pursue their hobby for enjoyment alone, without commercial motivation, the place of legal regulation is open to question from the beginning. Why should the law have any more place in angling than in golf or football or any other sport?

> There are indeed many arguments for leaving sport free from statutory regulation; a man's pleasure is hardly suitable to be regulated by law and public opinion in sporting matters is, or ought to be, a much more powerful sanction against malpractice than resort to the courts. (Bledisloe Report (1961) p.18.)

The argument for deregulation fails because of a number of features which angling does not share with other sports: the importance of property rights in fisheries, the need to conserve fish stocks from overexploitation and environmental deterioration, and the requirement that fish be protected from illegitimate fishing practices and poaching by force of law. These factors, amongst others, serve to give the activity of angling a legal character which is distinct from all other sports. Hence the angler, unlike other sportsmen and women is bound not only by the rules of his or her sport, but by the extensive and sometimes complex code of legal provisions which this book describes.

In the sphere of commercial fishing the reasons for legal regulation are self-evident. Where the motive for taking fish is to profit by their sale then the incentive is to maximise profit at the expense of fish stocks. There is little doubt that the unrestrained use of netting and trapping methods of taking fish is capable of bringing about the extinction of many kinds of fish. The paradox of modern commercial fishing is that the methods which are used are simply too efficient. Because of this, the need to preserve the resource has to override the market demand for fish in order to secure the survival of fish stocks, and so in turn to ensure the continuation of commercial fishing as a viable enterprise. Almost without exception, the legal rules governing commercial fishing methods discussed in this book are explicable on the basis of the need to reduce the effectiveness of such methods.

The Salmon and Freshwater Fisheries Act 1975 and the other freshwater fishery laws discussed in this book represent a legal attempt to draw a balance between the demands of those who fish, either for sport or for commercial reasons, weighed against the need to conserve fish stocks. I have not resisted the temptation to comment where it has appeared that the balance is unevenly drawn, neither have I refrained from criticism at those points where the law appears to me to be inappropriate, inequitable or incomprehensible. Although not in themselves of any legal authority my hope is that these comments will assist the reader in understanding and evaluating a subject which is as complex as it is fascinating.

In writing this book I have become indebted to a large number of persons and organisations who, at no small amount of inconvenience and expense, have provided me with much of the information used in the research and preparation of this book. I wish to express my gratitude to all who have contributed their knowledge and advice and thereby made this a much better work than it would otherwise have been.

A primary debt is owed to Ron I. Millichamp, formerly Fisheries Officer with the Welsh Water Authority, who has the insight gained through a lifetime's work on the operation and enforcement of the Salmon and Fisheries Acts. His enthusiasm for the subject has been a constant source of encouragement and his experience and willingness to help by suggesting source materials and reading and commenting on an earlier draft have sharpened up my thinking and saved me from innumerable errors. Another valuable contribution of experience and insight came from David C. Gibbs, Divisional Solicitor with the Welsh Water Authority, who read and commented on a draft and drew my attention to a number of central points which would otherwise have been overlooked.

A great deal of the information used in this book has been provided by a large number of bodies who replied to questions and requests for information, often with more help and courtesy than was deserved. These bodies included the 10 water authorities for England and Wales who supplied me with copies of fishery byelaws for their areas, which have provided a valuable source of illustration of fishery regulations. Amongst the 10 water authorities a special appreciation is owed to my local water authority, the Welsh Water Authority, who took the brunt of my enquiries, and particularly to Warwick Ayton, John Gregory and Richard Howell. Other information was provided by: the Ministry of Agriculture, Fisheries and Food where David Wright gave me the benefit of his encyclopaedic knowledge of recent legislative developments; the Department of the Environment; the Fishmongers' Company; the Salmon and Trout Association; the Water Industry Training Association; the Water Authorities Association; the Fish Farming Section of the National Farmers' Union; the Institute of Fisheries Management; the National Anglers' Council; the International Society for the Prevention of Water Pollution; the National Federation of Anglers; the Anglers' Co-operative Association; the Institute of Water Pollution Control; M.L. Parry of the Severn-Trent Water Authority; and John Corrie, MP.

Particular thanks are due to those bodies that have given permission to use quotations in this book. These include the Water Authorities Association for permission to reproduce the map of water authority areas from *Who's Who in the Water Industry* (1986); Her Majesty's Stationery Office for permission to use quotations from the Bledisloe Report (1961); the Department of the

Environment for permission to quote from *Water and Sewage Law* (1986); Collins for permission to quote from *Salmon and Sea Trout Fishing* (1979); Barry Rose/Kluwer Law Publishers for permission to quote from A. S. Wisdom's *Aspects of Water Law* (1981); the Welsh Water Authority for permission to quote from *Welsh Salmon and Sea Trout Fisheries* (1985); Edward Arnold and Co. for permission to quote from T. E. Pryce-Tannatt's *Fish Passes* (1938); and Faber and Faber Ltd for permission to quote from R.S. Fort and J.D. Brayshaw's *Fishery Management* (1961).

Closer to home, I must thank all my colleagues in the Department of Law in the University of Wales at Aberystwyth for their help, and in particular Professor John Andrews, John Williams, Richard Kidner, Christopher Harding, Michael Hirst, and Richard Ireland. Meirion Derrick and Bill Hines in the Hugh Owen Library at Aberystwyth along with the staff of the National Library of Wales and the British Lending Library, proved to be of invaluable assistance in helping me to get to grips with the extensive literature on freshwater fishery law. Paul Morgan of Coch-y-Bonddu Books, Machynlleth, went out of his way to help me obtain copies of leading texts. The initial inspiration for writing a book on this subject is owed to the members of the Aberystwyth Angling Association, where, whilst chairman, I came to realise the importance of legal matters in the administration of fisheries. The Association is fortunate to have as secretary Dr John Fish who has, by his administration of the Association, provided me with practical insights into the operation of fishery law which would have been available from no other source.

Last, but far from least, the preparation of the manuscript of this work has been helped immeasurably by comments on style and typography from Ann Cresswell and Henry Howarth who have been a constant source of helpful suggestions. The same appreciation must extend to Heather Saward and Alistair MacQueen of Financial Training Publications Limited without whom this project would never have been realised.

Despite all this help, for which I am unreservedly grateful, any faults that remain are my own. My hope is that they are small and few and do not prevent this book being a useful one for all involved with freshwater fisheries.

William Howarth
Department of Law,
University College of Wales,
Aberystwyth

TABLE OF CASES

xiv

TABLE OF STATUTES

Note: Page references in **bold** type are to the text of the legislation.

List of Statutes before Short Titles

Statutory Instruments

1
INTRODUCTION

1.01 *Some General Themes in Freshwater Fishery Law*

As the editor of *Oke's Fishery Laws* commented scathingly on a forerunner of the Salmon and Freshwater Fisheries Act 1975 (the Freshwater Fisheries Act 1878): 'This Act has made the Fishery Laws' confusion worse confounded and it is impossible to state with any certainty what is the effect, or even the object, of the Act in many cases' (Oke (1878) by Willis-Bund, preface). It would be gratifying to be able to say that the modern law on freshwater fisheries is clearer than in times past, but arguably this is not the case. The Salmon and Freshwater Fisheries Act 1975 is at least as complicated and obscure as its predecessors, and it would be a brave commentator who would express total confidence in any one interpretation of some of the less simple provisions that it contains. Nonetheless, this work seeks to provide as complete and clear an account of the Act as is apparent from the sources of interpretation which are available. Where difficulties arise the attention of the reader is drawn to them and to the potential solutions, but in the last resort the feelings of the editor of *Oke's Fishery Laws* are shared by the present writer.

Rather than fall directly into the detailed provisions of the Salmon and Freshwater Fisheries Act 1975, this chapter provides an introduction to some general themes that run throughout the topic of freshwater fishery law. In most respects matters of detail are deferred for consideration in later chapters to which the reader is referred.

1.02 *Methods of Fishing under the Salmon and Freshwater Fisheries Act 1975*

The Salmon and Freshwater Fisheries Act 1975 is the principal statute governing all methods of fishing for salmon, trout, freshwater fish and eels in England and Wales. 'Fishing', as the term is used in this book, means the use of lawful methods to take fish. Broadly, fishing can be subdivided into three general methods which are used to take fish in accordance with the provisions of the Act: angling, netting and trapping. The first of these is generally regarded as a sporting method of taking fish whilst the other two are primarily commercial fishing methods. Although each of the three methods is capable of being conducted lawfully according to the Act, each is made subject to legal restrictions which if not observed will make the method unlawful. It may be helpful at this point to outline the general constraints which are imposed on the three methods of fishing and to refer forward to the parts of the text in which they are discussed in detail.

(a) *Angling* 'Angling' is used here to group together all methods of fishing which involve catching, or attempting to catch, fish by means of rod and line; that is, fly fishing, float fishing, ledgering, spinning and variants of these. Compared with the other methods of fishing, angling is generously treated under the Salmon and Freshwater Fisheries Act 1975 for the reason that most angling is conducted primarily for sport, and consequently the activity does not threaten the overall conservation of fish stocks to the same extent as commercial methods are capable of doing if conducted without regulation. Nonetheless, a collection of legal requirements must be observed if an angler is not to fall foul of the provisions of the Act. First, he must not engage in any of the practices grouped together under the title of 'prohibited methods of taking fish', which arise under the first part of the Act. Similarly, he must observe prohibitions arising under the Theft Act 1968, which may serve to give legal effect to rules imposed by a fishery owner, or make it unlawful to fish without permission. These are dealt with in Chapter 3. Second, the angler must not fish in any way which involves creating an obstruction to the passage of certain fish, or the use of tackle which is secured in such a way as to constitute a 'fixed instrument', as described in Chapter 4. Third, the angler is bound to observe close seasons for fishing as they arise both under the Act and under water authority byelaws. These are discussed in Chapter 5. Fourth, the angler must adhere to any licensing requirements imposed by the Act or by a water authority, as discussed in Chapter 6. Finally, the angler must observe the fishery byelaws for the water authority area in which he fishes. Examples of byelaws have been given in various places in the text, but it is to be stressed that these are used as illustrations and are not a complete statement of the byelaws in any water authority area. The fishery byelaws for the particular water authority area in which an angler proposes to fish should be obtained and studied before starting to fish.

(b) *Netting* The expression 'netting' is used here to refer to any method of catching, or attempting to catch, fish which involves the use of a net, other than an angler's landing net used as an auxiliary to fishing with rod and line. Clearly the use of a net as a commercial method of fishing is capable of being a very effective method of taking fish, especially where it is used near the mouth of a river or in freshwater through which migratory fish must pass to spawn. With not too much difficulty nets could be used to depopulate a river without regard to the interests of others or the future conservation of stocks. For this reason netting restrictions are stricter than those imposed upon anglers. The main restrictions are, first, that the net must not be of a prohibited size or used in a manner contrary to the Act, as described in Chapter 3. Second, the net must not be made stationary, or otherwise used in such a way so as to become a 'fixed engine'. The meaning of this term is explained in Chapter 4. Third, netting must not be conducted either during close seasons or weekly close times. These requirements are examined in Chapter 5. Fourth, netting is subject to a system of licensing, which is discussed in Chapter 6. In addition to these requirements the net must be used in accordance with the water authority byelaws and net limitation orders for the area in which it is used. Examples of such byelaws are given where they relate to issues discussed in the text, though each area has different byelaws and those given should not be taken to be a complete statement of the regulations governing any particular area.

(c) *Trapping* Potentially the most destructive method of fishing is by means of a fish trap. Although these devices were used in ancient times as a means of taking large quantities of fish for food, their capacity to render a watercourse completely devoid of migratory fish has long been recognised, and the law has made strenuous attempts to diminish the numbers and destructiveness of fish traps. Nowadays only a very limited amount of trapping of fish is permitted other than that conducted for fishery management or scientific purposes, often by means of electrical devices, and the trapping of eels. The few persons who are legally entitled to operate fish traps on a commercial basis are bound, first, to avoid creating obstructions to the passage of migratory fish under the second part of the Act, discussed in Chapter 4. Second, those trapping fish must observe the close seasons and weekly close times which apply to their method and are described in Chapter 5. Third, the trapping of fish is subject to the system of licensing discussed in Chapter 6. Finally, as with other methods of fishing, trapping is subject to the water authority fishery byelaws for the area in which it takes place.

Along with these three methods of fishing the Act is also concerned with the prohibition of certain methods of taking fish which would not be described as 'fishing' in any ordinary or colloquial sense, but rather as 'poaching' or 'theft'. These are considered in Chapter 3.

1.03 Categories of Fish under the Salmon and Freshwater Fisheries Act 1975

The species of fish governed by the Salmon and Freshwater Fisheries Act 1975 and other provisions relating to fishery law may be grouped in eight categories: salmon; trout; freshwater fish; eels; lampreys; sea fish; shellfish; and royal fish.

(a) *Salmon* The salmon has traditionally been the most highly valued sporting and commercial fish amongst those that inhabit the waters of England and Wales. For this reason it receives the greatest amount of protection from overexploitation under the Salmon and Freshwater Fisheries Act 1975. The Act defines salmon to mean all fish of the salmon species and states that the definition includes a part of a salmon (under s.41(1) of the Act). This brief definition avoids the problem of identifying the salmon by the numerous local names by which it is known. By contrast, the Salmon Fishery Act of 1861 had attempted to define salmon (in a broad sense including migratory trout) in an explicit way by stating an extensive list of the local names by which the fish was known. The 1861 definition was:

'Salmon' shall include all migratory fish of the genus salmon, whether known by the names herein-after mentioned, that is to say, salmon, cock or kipper, kelt, laurel, girling, grilse, botcher, blue cock, blue pole, fork tail, peal, herring peal, May peal, pugg peal, harvest cock, sea trout, white trout, sewin, buntling, guiniad, tubs, yellow fin, sprod, herling, whiting, bull trout, whitling, scurf, burn tail, fry, samlet, smoult, smelt, skirling or scarling, parr, spawn, pink, last spring, hepper, last brood, gravelling, shed, scad, blue fin, black tip, fingerling, brandling, brondling, or by any other local name:

'Young of salmon' shall include all young of the salmon species, whether known by the names of fry, samlet, smolt, smelt, skirling or skarling, par, spawn, pink, last spring, hepper, last brood, graveling, shed, scad, blue fin, black tip, fingerling, brandling, brondling, or by any other name, local or otherwise (s.4 of the Salmon Fishery Act 1861).

It is remarkable that even this lengthy and colourful collection of names for salmon and migratory trout, at various stages of development in different localities, is not presented as a comprehensive statement of all the names by which these fish are known. The task of identifying the fish by all its assumed names is an impossible one, and the definition in the 1975 Act declines any attempt to do so. Nonetheless, the present definition of salmon, along with that of migratory trout discussed below, would encompass all the fish noted on the 1861 list.

(b) *Trout* After the salmon the next most prized sporting and table fish is the trout. 'Trout' is defined in the Salmon and Freshwater Fisheries Act 1975 to mean any fish of the salmon family commonly known as a trout, including migratory trout and char, and also includes part of a trout. 'Migratory trout' in turn is defined to mean trout which migrate to and from the sea (s.41(1) of the Act). The definition of trout encompasses the non-migratory common brown trout, *Salmo trutta*, and its seaward-migrating variants such as sea trout and estuary or slob trout (see Houghton (1879) for other varieties of trout which would also come within the definition). The definition of trout also includes the non-migratory rainbow trout, *S. gairdneri*, though this species is separately provided for in respect of close seasons (see Chapter 5). In addition, the definition of trout includes species of fish which are not trout in the strict zoological sense, but rather members of the distinct genus of char, *Salvelinus*. The species of char which are found in England and Wales are the native Arctic char, *S. alpinus*, and the North American brook char, or brook 'trout', *S. fontinalis* (see Sedgwick (1982) Chapter 3). Although there are some behavioural differences between trout and char, such as the tendency for char to spawn earlier than trout (see Templeton (1984) p.59), in law the two species are not distinguished.

(c) *Freshwater fish* The Salmon and Freshwater Fisheries Act 1975 groups together a wide variety of fish that are sought for sporting purposes but have little culinary or commercial value under the title of 'freshwater fish'. This means any fish living in fresh water exclusive of salmon and trout and of any other kinds of fish which migrate to and from tidal waters and of eels (s.41(1) of the Act). Apart from the exclusion of eels (discussed below), this definition refers to the fish usually known to anglers as 'coarse fish', a term which contrasts with the collective description of salmon, trout and char as 'game fish'. It is clear that the definition of 'freshwater fish' takes in all the fish that are commonly sought by coarse anglers such as: carp, roach, chub, dace, tench, grayling, bream, pike and perch; along with smaller species such as stickleback, minnow, loach, ruffe and miller's thumb. The significance of the exclusion of 'fish which migrate to and from tidal waters' in the definition is to rule out, first, species such as the shad and sea lamprey (see below on lampreys) which spawn in freshwater but migrate seaward to feed, and, second, sea fish such as flounders and mullet which migrate from the sea into freshwater to feed (see below on sea fish).

(d) *Eels* A number of provisions in the Salmon and Freshwater Fisheries

Act 1975 apply specifically to eels, *Anguilla anguilla*, which are defined to include elvers and the fry of eels (s.41(1) of the Act). Because of their peculiar life history, involving spawning at sea and migration into freshwater for the main part of their lives, this species falls into a different legal category from other types of fish. For this reason, as will be seen, separate provision is made for the methods of fishing which can be used to catch eels and the times at which this can be done.

(e) *Lampreys or lamperns* Lampreys, *Petromyzonidae*, are jawless eel-like creatures with a cartilaginous skeleton and suctorial disc-like mouths which can feed parasitically by attaching themselves to other fish. Although there may be zoological doubts as to whether lampreys are properly classified as 'fish' because of their lack of a bony skeleton, Wheeler (1969 pp. 28–32) observes that at least they are usually thought of as fish. He contrasts three different species of lamprey: the sea lamprey (*Petromyzon marinus*); the river lamprey (*Lampetra fluviatilis*); and the brook lamprey (*L. planeri*). Of these the first two breed in freshwater and migrate to sea, but the third, a non-parasitic variety, remains in freshwater and therefore is classified as a 'freshwater fish' according to the definition of freshwater fish given in the Salmon and Freshwater Fisheries Act 1975. The Act makes one specific reference to lampreys (referred to as 'lamperns') concerning their capture using basket traps (s.21 of the Act; see para. 5.08).

(f) *Sea fish* 'Sea fish' is defined under s.20(1) of the Sea Fisheries Regulation Act 1966 to mean fish of any kind found in the sea, and includes shellfish (defined as crustaceans and molluscs of any kind) but does not include fish of the salmon species or migratory trout. From this definition it is apparent that the categories of freshwater fish and sea fish are mutually exclusive. The effect of this is that the Salmon and Freshwater Fisheries Act 1975 does not apply to sea fish. An exception to this is that certain sections of the Act refer to 'fish' or 'any fish'. For example, s.2 of the Act outlaws the use of 'fish' roe for bait; s.4 is concerned with polluting waters containing 'fish'; and s.5 creates offences in relation to the use of explosives and electrical devices to destroy 'fish' (see Ch.3 for a discussion of these offences). It is likely that where the general word 'fish' is used it must be understood to encompass all kinds of fish, *including* sea fish. Apart from the exceptional use of the word 'fish' in contexts such as these, however, the Act is primarily concerned with salmon, trout, freshwater fish and eels, in the senses in which these have been defined above.

(For the regulation of fishing for sea fish, see the Sea Fisheries Regulation Act 1966, the Sea Fish (Conservation) Act 1967, the Sea Fisheries Act 1968, the Sea Fish Industry Acts 1970 and 1973, and the Fisheries Act 1981.)

(g) *Shellfish* The application of most provisions of the Act to salmon, trout, freshwater fish and eels excludes freshwater shellfish by implication. As with sea fish though, it is arguable that those provisions of the Act which apply in respect of 'fish', apply in relation to freshwater shellfish such as mussels or crayfish, or any other kind of crustacea or mollusca. In *Caygill* v *Thwaite* (1885) it was held by the court that crayfish were 'fish' in the absence of any indication to the contrary, and a statute which made it unlawful to take 'fish' applied to crayfish equally as it applied to ordinary kinds of floating fish. By similar reasoning it follows that those provisions of the Salmon and Freshwater

Fisheries Act 1975 which are concerned with 'fish' are capable of being applied equally to shellfish as to finfish. As a matter of practice the application of the Act to shellfish is uncommon and there appear to be no reported cases where this question has been decided conclusively by a court.

(h)   *Royal fish*   Although not mentioned in the Act, a number of ancient legal provisions are concerned with 'royal fish' (Hall (1875) p.80). The royal fish are the sturgeon, porpoise and whale, though technically the last two are mammals rather than fish. According to an old statute, *De Prerogativa Regis* (1324), these are the property of the Crown, and the King or Queen is entitled to any such fish caught or found in territorial waters. Outside territorial waters, on the high seas, any royal fish which are taken belong to the taker (Hale (1787) Ch.VII). Similarly the right of the Crown to royal fish will cease to exist if for any reason it has been relinquished (*Cinque Ports (Lord Warden of)* v *R* (1831)). Though this royal privilege was of importance in times gone by, it is of little importance in the present day.

(For general reading on ichthyology see: Houghton (1879); Maxwell (1904); and Wheeler (1969)).

1.04   *Fishing in Freshwater and Saltwater under the Salmon and Freshwater Fisheries Act 1975*

The title of the Salmon and Freshwater Fisheries Act 1975 is a misnomer in suggesting that it is a statute governing only *freshwater* fishing. It is broader in its effects than that, and is capable of applying to brackish and salt waters as well as to freshwater. As has been seen, the concern of the Act is to regulate fishing for certain kinds of fish, whether they are found in freshwater or saltwater. Coarse fish, other than eels, though sometimes found in brackish water, tend not to venture into the sea, and for this reason the Act is unlikely to be relevant to coarse fishing in the sea. In the case of eels and game fish, however, a good deal of migration to and from the sea takes place, and these species travel many miles from freshwater. An inevitable question is that of the extent to which the Act applies to these species when they are present in saltwater. The simple answer to this question is that the Act applies to seagoing species of fish equally in saltwater as in freshwater. A more precise answer depends on the zone of the sea in which the fish are sought.

The general duty of implementation of the Salmon and Freshwater Fisheries Act 1975 is given to the regional water authorities (though see Ch.10 on prosecution and procedure generally). Each water authority possesses fishery functions under the Water Act 1973 (see Ch.7). On the geographical extent of these functions para.4(1) of Sch.2 to the Water Act 1973 (as amended by the Fishery Limits Act 1976, Sch.2, para.19) states that:

for the purposes of the functions of a water authority relating to fisheries, the area of the authority shall include those tidal waters and parts of the sea adjoining the coast of the water authority area to a distance of six nautical miles measured from the baselines from which the breadth of the territorial sea is measured.

One nautical mile is equal to 1,852 metres. As a result of this provision, the Salmon and Freshwater Fisheries Act 1975 regulates fishing for certain kinds of fish in both freshwater and the sea to a distance of six nautical miles measured, roughly, from the coast at normal low tide in water authority areas. Naturally, the greatest impact of the Act is upon coarse and game fisheries in freshwater, but its application to brackish and salt water should not be overlooked.

1.05 The Ownership of Fisheries

Another theme which runs throughout freshwater fishery law is that of the categorisation and ownership of fisheries. From the outset the ownership of a fishery must be distinguished from the ownership of water (see para. 1.09), or the ownership of soil either abutting the water or beneath it. Fishery ownership need not entail the ownership of any waterside or underwater land. The ownership of a fishery involves the possession of an abstract interest in the form of a legal right, which is distinct in character from any other interests in land or water which may be held along with the fishery. This will become clearer after consideration of the different kinds of legal interests which can subsist in fisheries.

The major legal distinction between different kinds of fisheries is that drawn between public fisheries and private fisheries. Although particular fisheries may be placed into various subcategories, the basic distinction concerns those fisheries where a public right of fishery exists and those where it does not.

1.06 Public Fisheries

A public fishery exists where the right of fishing is vested in the public at large. In the strict legal sense the only example of a public right of fishery is the public right of fishing in the sea in territorial tidal waters. As a matter of common law the public has the right to fish in the tidal parts of rivers and the sea except where the Crown or an individual has acquired a private right of fishery to the exclusion of the public, or where an enactment has restricted the general right of public fishery. Prior to Magna Carta (1225) it was open to the Crown to exclude the public right of fishery in tidal waters by granting the exclusive right of fishery to a private individual. Where this was done the public right of fishery came to an end and the fishery became a private fishery (*Neill* v *Duke of Devonshire* (1882)). Since Magna Carta, however, the Crown has had no right to grant public fisheries to private individuals, and today the public right of fishing can only be excluded or modified by Act of Parliament. Nonetheless, a small number of private fisheries remain in existence in tidal waters where private rights of fishery were granted before 1225.

The right of public fishery in tidal waters normally includes the right to fish upon the seashore between the high and low water marks of ordinary tides (*Lowe* v *Govett* (1832), and *Ingram* v *Percival* (1968) discussed in para. 4.09). The ownership of the foreshore is ordinarily vested in the Crown but is subject to the public right of fishery and activities incidental thereto (*Fitzhardinge* v *Purcell* (1908)). The public right to fish extends as far up arms of the sea and rivers as the tide ordinarily flows and reflows. In practice, however, the right to fish in tidal waters in river estuaries may be difficult to exercise because the right to fish tidal waters does not permit persons to enter upon land which is above the high water mark (*Ilchester (Earl of)* v *Raishleigh* (1889)). Consequently, a common difficulty is that of gaining access to tidal waters in river estuaries, and when angling associations 'lease' fisheries of this kind it is usually the case that what is being acquired is not a lease of a fishery as such, but rather a right of access over land to a fishery where a public right of fishery exists. As a matter of legal theory there is no reason why access could not be gained by boat, since a public right of navigation exists in tidal waters (*Blundell* v *Catterall* (1821)), and the use of a boat would not involve crossing private land. In practice, though, it may not always be feasible to exercise this option.

Where a public right of fishery exists in tidal waters, the right must nonetheless be exercised in a reasonable manner and in conformity with the general law (*Whelan* v *Hewson* (1871)). Although the public are entitled to fish using rods and lines or any other customary mode of fishing (*Bevins* v *Bird* (1865)) they must not do so in any way that contravenes the general statutory regulations relating to fishing. In particular, the existence of a public right of fishery does not carry with it the right to fish in a manner which is in breach of the Salmon and Freshwater Fisheries Act 1975.

No public fishery can exist in waters that are not tidal (*Reece* v *Miller* (1882)). Even where a public right of navigation exists, this does not imply any public right to fish (*Pearce* v *Scotcher* (1882)). Nor may such a right be acquired by custom or long use or otherwise (*Smith* v *Andrews* (1891)). In many situations the owners of fisheries, for a variety of reasons, take no action against persons fishing in their waters, to the extent that the waters are commonly termed 'public water', but nevertheless they remain the property of their owner, and as such are private fisheries. As Bowen LJ made the point:

> . . . although the public have been in the habit as long as we can recollect, and as long as our fathers can recollect, of fishing in the Thames, the public have no right to fish there—I mean they have no right as members of the public to fish there. That is certain law. Of course they may fish by the licence of the lord or the owner of a particular part of the bed of the river, or they may fish by the indulgence or owing to the carelessness or good-nature of the person who is entitled to the soil, but right to fish themselves as the public they have none (*Blount* v *Layard* (1891)).

Hence all fisheries in inland waters are the object of private ownership and this is so in law regardless of any common practice of fishing by members of the public. In the precise legal sense, public fisheries exist only in the sea and tidal waters.

1.07 *Private Fisheries*

As has already been noted, all fisheries in non-tidal waters are private, as are a small number of fisheries in tidal waters where fisheries were granted to a private individual by the Crown before Magna Carta. A private fishery may be classified in law as either a 'several fishery' or a 'common of fishery'.

(a) *Several fisheries* A several fishery is the exclusive right of fishing in a particular water. 'Exclusive' in this context means that the owner has the right of fishing independently of all others and that no other person has a co-extensive right to the fishery (*Seymour* v *Courtenay* (1771)). Although this definition conjures up a picture of a solitary person entitled to fish a particular water, the reality is capable of being quite different. A several fishery does not cease to be a several fishery where different owners own the several fisheries for different kinds of fish. For example, one several owner might own the several fishery in a water for game fish whilst another several owner owns the several fishery in the same water for coarse fish. Similarly, a several fishery is capable of existing where different owners fish at different times of the year (*Fitzhardinge* v *Purcell* (1908)). A several fishery does not cease to exist if the owner authorises others to fish the water.

(b) *Common of fishery* A common of fishery is a right of fishing which exists where two or more persons share the same right of fishing in a particular water. This may arise where the right to fish in common with others arises through the occupation of land, in which case it is referred to as a 'common appurtenant to the land'. Alternatively it may arise independently of the occupation of any land, where it is said to be held 'in gross'.

In the case of either a several fishery or a common of fishery the ownership of the fishery is capable of existing independently of the ownership of any waterside or underwater land. In the case where the owner of the fishery is also the owner of the soil over which the right of fishery may be exercised then the fishery is termed a 'corporeal fishery'. Conversely, where the owner of the fishery is not the owner of the soil the fishery is termed an 'incorporeal fishery'.

1.08 Presumptions in Relation to the Ownership of Fisheries

In the case of private fisheries in non-tidal waters three legal presumptions apply as to the ownership of fisheries, underwater and waterside land, in the absence of evidence to the contrary. That is to say, the presumptions will not apply where a lease or conveyance of a fishery or land determines the question of ownership which is at issue. The first presumption is that the owner of land which abuts a river or lake, known as the 'riparian owner', is the owner of the soil in the river bed up to the middle of the river (*Micklethwait* v *Newlay Bridge Co.* (1886)). So that in the absence of any contrary stipulation in a lease or conveyance, bankside, or riparian, owners own the bed of a river or lake up to the middle point.

The second presumption is that the owner of the soil is also the owner of the right of fishery over it (*Carlisle Corp.* v *Graham* (1869)). Clearly this presumption will be rebutted where it can be shown that ownership of the fishery has been severed from ownership of the land by a lease or conveyance of the fishery to someone other than the landowner, but in the absence of such evidence, the law assumes that the fishery is corporeal and so owned by the owner of the soil beneath it.

The third presumption is the converse of the second. The law presumes that the owner of the right of fishery is the owner of the soil beneath it (*Hanbury* v *Jenkins* (1901)). Where this leads into conflict with the first presumption, the soil is held to belong to the owner of the fishery rather than the riparian owner. That is, once again, in the absence of contrary evidence, the presumption that the soil is owned by the fishery owner prevails (*Hindson* v *Ashby* (1896)).

1.09   The Ownership of Water

In its natural state, flowing water in a watercourse is not owned by anyone. It may be said to be in public ownership in the sense that it may be taken and used by anyone who has a lawful right of access to it, and takes it without otherwise contravening the law (see Ch.12 on water abstraction). Hence each riparian owner is permitted to make ordinary use of the water flowing past his land and commits no crime according to common law by taking that which is not owned by anyone else (*Williams* v *Morland* (1824), though see Ch.12 on water abstraction). In contrast, however, once water has been taken from a flowing channel into the possession of a person then that person gains a property right in it and becomes the owner to the exclusion of others. Hence by abstraction or appropriation water may pass from public ownership into private ownership, and is then capable of being stolen from the person who has appropriated it (*Ferens* v *O'Brien* (1883)). If the owner then abandons the water by returning it to its natural watercourse then his right of ownership is lost and the water returns to public ownership (*Liggins* v *Inge* (1831)). It follows that water is owned by someone for so long as it is contained in some receptacle such as a pipe, tank, pond or lake, but as soon as it is permitted to flow in a watercourse it is publicly owned.

(See paras 3.20 to 3.22 on the ownership of fish.)

1.10   The Legal Distinction between Common Law and Statute Law in Freshwater Fishery Law

It may be helpful at this stage to provide a brief explanation of two legal distinctions which arise throughout freshwater fishery law. The first of these is the distinction between common law and statutory law, and the second is the distinction between civil law and criminal law (considered in the next paragraph).

The distinction between common law and statutory law concerns the origin of a particular legal rule. Statutory law consists of Acts of Parliament, otherwise termed 'statutes' or 'legislation', and statutory instruments or orders made under Acts of Parliament by persons or bodies authorised to make them. A large part of the law relating to freshwater fisheries is of this character. For example, the principal Act, the Salmon and Freshwater Fisheries Act 1975, orders made by the Minister by statutory instrument under s.28 of the Act (see Ch.7), and byelaws made by water authorities under para.14 of Sch.3 to the Act (see Ch.7), are all sources of law which are of statutory origin. It is the duty of the courts to apply these enactments according to the natural meaning of the words which are used. Hence, if a situation which has arisen is provided for under the Act, or another statutory provision, a court is bound to give effect to it.

By contrast, the other main source of freshwater fishery law is known as 'common law'. Although the term 'common law' is capable of being used in more than one sense, in this work it is used as a term of contrast to indicate legal rules that are not of statutory origin (see Williams (1982) Ch.2 for a discussion of other senses of 'common law'). Most importantly this means those legal rules which have been devised by judges in deciding past cases. With the exception of the House of Lords, any court in the hierarchy of courts that exists in England and Wales is bound by a 'doctrine of precedent' to follow an authoritative decision in a past case where the facts are materially similar to a present case before it. Clearly no two cases have identical facts, and a court may be able to find some reason to distinguish a present case from an earlier decision. Likewise, a change in legislation may mean that an earlier case need no longer be followed. As a matter of general practice, however, courts are bound to follow the law as it has been established in past cases. It is this body of law which is termed the 'common law'.

Common law has played a particularly important part in the development of modern freshwater fishery law. Partially this is because of the large number of cases which have been decided by courts over the years (see Ch.2). Also the nature of the subject is such that it is impossible for Parliament to draft Acts in such a way as to make provision in advance for every contingency that might arise. Because of this it falls to the courts to apply Acts of Parliament to situations which Parliament could never have foreseen, and so to interpret, or elaborate upon, the meaning of the words used. Over the years, the 1975 Act and other statutes which preceded it have accumulated a large amount of 'case law', in which judges have interpreted the words of these Acts and explained how provisions are to be applied to particular situations.

1.11   The Legal Distinction between Civil Wrongs and Criminal Offences in Freshwater Fishery Law

The second legal distinction which it may be helpful to outline at this stage is the distinction between civil wrongs and criminal offences. It is a common misapprehension to suppose that the law is invariably concerned with crime and punishment. This is certainly far from the truth in respect of freshwater fishery law, as will become apparent. Although a sizeable part of the subject is concerned with prohibited practices in relation to fish and their environment, another important part of the subject concerns the rights and duties that exist between individuals where no question of criminal activity is at issue. Parties may wrangle over the right to fish a water, or dispute the liability to pay compensation for causing pollution or interfering with a fishery, or contest the validity of a byelaw which purports to remove the right of a commercial fisherman to earn his livelihood. In none of these situations is any person accused of a crime: the legal actions which follow from such disputes are purely civil in character, and are pursued to determine the rights and duties of the parties towards one another. On other occasions matters of civil and criminal law are closely interwoven. An incident of pollution may result in both a criminal prosecution of the polluter and also a civil action for compensation by the owner of a fishery who has suffered detriment as a result of the pollution (see Ch.11). Even where particular facts give rise to both civil and criminal legal consequences, however, the questions of civil liability and criminal guilt must be kept separate.

Crimes are sometimes distinguished from civil wrongs on the basis that a crime results in proceedings being brought on behalf of the Crown with the primary objective of punishing the offender, whereas a civil action is brought between two ordinary persons to ascertain their rights with respect to one another. Ultimately, however, the distinction is drawn most precisely not in terms of the offending behaviour, or the status of the parties who are in dispute, but in terms of the legal proceedings which ensue, and in particular the courts which are able to hear the case. In England and Wales the courts having criminal and civil 'jurisdiction', that is, the capacity to hear cases, are largely separate. Criminal proceedings are said to be heard 'summarily' when the case is tried by magistrates, or justices of the peace, as is the practice in less serious cases. More serious charges are heard 'on indictment' by a Crown Court usually presided over by a circuit judge, assisted in finding matters of fact by a jury. Appeals from the Crown Court are heard by the Criminal Division of the Court of Appeal, and, in the rare event of a further appeal, by the House of Lords. In contrast, civil cases are heard by either a county court or the High Court, depending on the financial gravity of the issue, and appeals pass to the Civil Division of the Court of Appeal and ultimately to the House of Lords. It is these distinct systems of courts, and the remedies and penalties that they administer, which are the clearest indication of the civil or criminal character of a particular case.

(For more discussion of the distinction between civil and criminal proceedings see Williams (1982) Ch.1.)

1.12   Penalties under the Salmon and Freshwater Fisheries Act 1975

The detailed provisions relating to the prosecution and procedure in respect of criminal offences under the Salmon and Freshwater Fisheries Act 1975 are considered in Chapter 10. It is convenient at this point though, to explain the general system of fines which applies in respect of criminal offences, since this is referred to in the text at a number of places in relation to criminal offences arising both under the Act and under other statutory provisions.

Maximum penalties for criminal offences under the 1975 Act depend upon the procedure which leads up to conviction of the offender. In particular the penalties for most offences depend on whether the offence is heard before magistrates, in summary proceedings, or before a Crown Court, in proceedings on indictment. Usually less serious offences will be considered by magistrates whilst more serious offences will be heard in the Crown Court because of its greater sentencing powers. As a matter of general criminal law the upper limit upon a period of imprisonment which may be imposed by a magistrates' court for any criminal offence is six months in respect of a single offence. The maximum fine which may be imposed by a magistrates' court is £2,000 (under ss.31 and 32 of the Magistrates' Courts Act 1980). The maximum penalty which a magistrates' court may impose for any particular offence is set out in the Act under which the offence arises. Magistrates are not normally empowered to impose custodial sentences for fishery offences. By contrast, a Crown Court is not usually subject to general limits unless a maximum penalty is prescribed by statute for a particular offence.

The actual punishment imposed in any particular case will always depend upon a range of factors including the gravity of the offence, the previous conduct of the offender, and, in a case where a fine is imposed, on the means of the offender to pay. Consequently, criminal statutes usually specify only maximum penalties and leave the actual penalty in a particular case to be decided by the magistrates, or the judge, taking into account all the circumstances (see para. 6.11 for some examples of this). This is the position under the Salmon and Freshwater Fisheries Act 1975, which states only the maximum penalties which may be imposed for contravention of the different sections (Sch.4).

When the Salmon and Freshwater Fisheries Act 1975 first came into force, on 1 August 1975 (s.43(4)), the maximum fines which could be imposed were specified as amounts of money. For example, a £50 fine was stated to be the maximum punishment which could be imposed upon a person using a prohibited instrument contrary to s.1 of the Act where that person was acting alone, and the conviction was before magistrates on summary proceedings (para.1, Sch.4). With the decline in money values due to inflation, however, the real amount of fines diminished from their 1975 values. This was an aspect of the general problem of the effect of inflation on maximum fines of specified money amounts in criminal legislation. To remedy this the specified money amounts of fines were replaced by a 'standard scale' of fines for summary offences and a 'prescribed sum' for the general maximum amount for fines which can be imposed by magistrates (s.37, Criminal Justice Act 1982). This standard scale of fines replaced the original money values of fines specified under Sch.4 to the 1975 Act by 'levels' of fines on the scale which can be raised in money terms to allow for inflation (s.37, Criminal Justice Act 1982; s.143, Magistrates' Courts Act 1980).

The present standard scale of maximum fines is set at the following levels.

Level on the scale	Amount of fine
1	£50
2	£100
3	£400
4	£1,000
5	£2,000

The 'statutory maximum' fine which can be imposed by magistrates in normal circumstances is set at £2,000. (These penalties were fixed most recently under the Criminal Penalties Increase Order (1984) SI 1984 No.447.)

Applying the standard scale of fines to offences under the Salmon and Freshwater Fisheries Act 1975, the offence of using a prohibited instrument contrary to s.1 of the Act (discussed in Ch. 3), for example, is now stated to carry a fine of 'level 4 on the standard scale'. Translated into money terms, according to the present levels at which the scale is set, this means that the maximum fine which can now be imposed for the offence on summary conviction is £1,000. Other offences under the Act are now stated to be subject to 'the statutory maximum', for example, using explosives to take fish contrary to s.5(1) of the Act, discussed in Chapter 3, where the conviction follows summary proceedings. 'The statutory maximum' is another term which can be equated with differing amounts of money to take account of changes in the value of money. The present level at which it is set is £2,000 and thus the maximum fine that can be imposed by magistrates for an offence under s.5(1) of the Act corresponds with that amount.

The upper limits for fines imposed on summary proceedings for specific offences under the Salmon and Freshwater Fisheries Act 1975 are set out in a table in para.1 of Sch.4 to the Act. In respect of all offences under the Act which are not specified in this table, para.2 of Sch.4 states that a person found guilty shall be liable on summary conviction to a fine not exceeding level 4 on the standard scale, presently £1,000. This general maximum penalty for offences under the Act extends also to byelaws made by water authorities under their powers under the Act (s.28(7) of the Act).

2

A BRIEF HISTORY OF SALMON AND FRESHWATER FISHERY LAW

2.01   Ancient and Modern Freshwater Fishery Law

A glance back through the history of freshwater fishery law makes it immediately apparent that few of the problems that beset the fisheries of today are entirely new. Parliaments and courts, from the earliest times for which legal records exist, sought to control similar malpractices to those outlawed under the present law. Obstructions to the passage of fish, destructive and unseasonable fishing and, not least important, problems of administration and enforcement, run like threads through time linking together ancient and modern fishery legislation. This chapter provides a brief commentary on some of the more important developments in the history of fishery law, in order to impress the continuity of legal thought underlying the present law. It is through no quirk of antiquarianism that many of the illustrations provided in subsequent chapters, to show the operation of the Salmon and Freshwater Fisheries Act 1975, come from cases decided long before that date. Equally, a case which comes before a court tomorrow may share many features with those which have confronted courts since medieval times.

2.02   Early Laws on Obstructions to Migratory Fish

Of central importance amongst the matters governed by modern fishery law is the regulation of obstructions to the passage of migratory fish (see Ch.4). This also appears to be the first recorded issue of fishery law to be confronted by the legislature. The earliest enactment recognising the harmful effects of weirs was Chapter 23 of Magna Carta (1225), which stated that: 'All weirs from henceforth shall be utterly put down through Thames and Medway, and through all England, except by the sea coast.' Were such an enactment to have been passed in recent times, it might be taken to be a conservational measure designed to allow free passage to migratory fish, calculated to ensure that artificial obstructions would not bar their access to spawning grounds. The actual intention behind the decree, however, is not clear. Since no mention of fish is made in the sparsely worded edict, it may be that it was originally intended to bring about the protection of navigation rather than the conservation of fish (see Hale (1787) Ch.3 and Wrangles (1979) p.6). Subsequent enactments make it explicit that the protection of fish *was* an intended, if incidental, consequence of the enactment. A statute of 1472, 12 Edw.IV c.7 (that is, the seventh statute passed in the twelfth reignal year of Edward IV) provides the elaboration:

> Whereas, by the laudable Statute of Magna Carta, among other things, it is contained that all keddels [weirs] by Thames and Medway and throughout the

realm of England should be taken away saving by the sea banks, which Statute was made for the great wealth of all this land, in avoiding the straitness of all rivers so that ships and boats might have in them their large and free passage, *and also in safeguard of all the fry of fish spawned within the same.*

This interpretation of the provision from Magna Carta, though many years later, indicates that conservation of fish stocks was at least one purpose behind the removal of weirs. Despite this, the law requiring their removal was not, it appears, adhered to. The continuation of the problem is indicated by a series of later statutes outlawing weirs (25 Edw.III st.4 c.4 (1350), 45 Edw.III c.2 (1369) and 1 Hen.IV c.12 (1399)). These enactments gave justices powers to pull down offending weirs constructed in navigable waters before 1272 (see *Rolle* v *Whyte* (1868)). The destructiveness of weirs is expressly noted in the statute 4 Hen.IV c.11 (1402) which laments the damage done to fish stocks, whereby: '. . . the young fry of fish [are] destroyed, and against reason wasted and given to swine to eat, contrary to the pleasure of God, and to the great damage of the King and his people'. A curious local statute governing weirs in Cumberland (Cumberland Pacita 6 Edw.1 (1278)) sought to eradicate this misfortune and achieve free passage for migratory fish by stipulating that, in accordance with ancient custom, weirs on the Eden, Esk and Derwent should have a gap of such a size that 'a sow with her five little pigs can enter'.

The existence of these early statutes constitutes clear evidence that the law has long recognised the need for removal of obstructions to migratory fish passing upstream to their spawning grounds, and to their offspring passing downstream to the sea. This crucial conservational measure, today provided for under the second part of the Salmon and Freshwater Fisheries Act 1975 (see Ch.4), is well documented amongst the earliest fishery legislation. It has been an established principle of law, even if not always adhered to, for at least 500 years.

2.03 Early Statutes on Close Seasons

Statutory regulation of close seasons for fishing is also of early origin. In 1285 the Statute of Westminster (13 Edw.I st.1 c.47) declared that: 'It is provided that the waters of Humber, Ourse, Trent, Done, Arre, Derewent, Wherfe, Nid, Yore, Swale, Tese, and all other waters wherein salmon be taken, shall be in defence for taking salmon from the Nativity of Our Lady (8 September) unto St Martin's Day (11 November).' The Statute continued to prohibit fishing for young salmon between the middle of April and the Nativity of St John the Baptist (24 June). Remarkably, the Statute stipulated a mechanism for enforcement of these seasons in that: '. . . there shall be assigned overseers of this Statute, which being sworn shall oftentimes see and inquire of the offenders'. Although little is known about the implementation of this provision, it is thought to be the first mention of persons being charged with duties which are today undertaken by water bailiffs.

Later regulations governing close seasons are to be found in a statute of 1538 (25 Hen.VIII c.7) entitled, 'An Act against Killing of young Spawn or Fry of Eels and Salmon'. This Act noted

. . . [the] great hurt and daily inconvenience [which] do ensure unto all the King's subjects of the realm, by the greedy appetites and insatiable desire which sundry of them occupying fishings have used by taking, killing, and destroying the young spawn, fry or brood of eels and salmon . . . in many parts of this realm, to the no little hindrance and derogation of the common weal of the same, as also in killing of salmons when they be unseasonable and not wholesome for man's body, commonly called kipper salmons.

The solution provided to this complaint was the enactment of close seasons from 1 February to 31 July for the fry of eels, from 1 May to 1 September for young salmon, and from 14 September to 11 November for spawning ('kipper') salmon. A further Act of 1558, (1 Eliz. c.17) extended the protection of immature fish to all kinds of fish, and specified size limits for pike (10 in.), salmon (16 in.), trout (8 in.) and barbel (12 in.). Hence, close seasons and size limits, contrary to what may be thought by many present-day anglers, are not modern inventions. As will become apparent in Chapters 3 and 5, their continuing existence remains justified by the same considerations of conservation that brought about their inception.

2.04 Early Restrictions on Improper Netting

Improper netting seems also to have been a cause of concern to medieval parliaments. A Parliament roll of 51 Edw.III in 1376 registers the complaint that:

Where in creeks and havens of the sea there used to be plenteous fishing to the profit of the kingdom, certain fishermen for seven years past have subtily contrived an instrument which they called 'wondyrchoun', made in the manner of an oyster dredge, but which is considerably longer, upon which instrument is attached a net so close meshed that no kind of fish, be it ever so small, which enters therein can escape, but must stay and be taken . . . By which instrument in many places the fishermen take such quantity of small fish that they do not know what to do with them; and that they feed and fat their pigs with them, to the great damage of the Commons of the realm and the destruction of the fisheries . . . .

This early reference to trawling provides the substance of a complaint against excessively destructive use of nets which can be followed through a line of later statutes. The Act of 13 Ric.II c.12 in 1389 forbade the use of certain nets called 'stalkers', and another, 2 Hen.VI c.15 in 1423, whilst permitting the use of nets drawn by hand, prohibited those fastened and hanged continually by day and night in the Thames. With refinements of definition, and modification of language, the same distinction between permissible and impermissible uses of nets is to be found underlying much of our modern law (see *Holford* v *George* (1868) and Ch.4).

2.05 Early Enactments on the Theft of Fish

Prohibitions on improper taking of fish also have a considerable ancestry. The first recorded Act dealing with theft of fish was passed in 1539 (31 Hen.VIII c.2) and created a felony where fish were taken from ponds, stews and motes without the owner's consent. Another Act of 1562 (5 Eliz. c.12) punished the crime with three months' imprisonment and payment of treble damages. The problem persisted it would appear, since the legislature passed another Act concerning the crime in 1670 (22 Car.II c.25) and a more stringent measure in 1692 (4 Will & Mary c.23). The latter forbade anyone, who was not the owner or occupier of a fishery, to keep nets, rods or other fishing implements unless they had lawful authority to fish. Even this seems to have proved inadequate to suppress or deter the crime of unauthorised taking of fish, since an Act of 1765 (5 Geo.III c.14) increased the penalty for the offence to transportation for seven years. Although the punishment has been reduced somewhat, essentially the same offence exists today under the Theft Act 1968 (see Ch.3).

2.06 Early Administrative Provisions

Even the administrative aspects of fishery law, which many of today's anglers may be fond of dismissing as modern 'bureaucracy', have a lengthy ancestry. The indications are that the 'overseers' appointed under the Statute of Westminster 1285 (13 Edw.I st 1 c.47) to enforce the provisions of the Statute regarding close seasons, mentioned above, did not accomplish their task effectively. A statute of 1393 (17 Ric.II c.9) expressed dissatisfaction about the ineffectiveness of the earlier statute and another to the same effect, in saying:

> Which Statutes have not been hitherto duly executed, for default of good conservators, as our said lord the King hath perceived by complaint to him made in this present parliament; wherefore it is accorded and asserted that the Justices of the Peace of all the counties of England shall be conservators of the said Statutes in the counties where they be Justices, and that they and every of them at all times when they may attend shall survey the offences and defaults attempted against the Statutes aforesaid.

The job of enforcement of freshwater fisheries law was passed to the local justices of the peace, an office then only recently established during the reign of Edward III (1327–1377). The justices of the peace in turn were authorised to employ under-conservators, but essentially the enforcement of the fishery laws became one of the duties of the justices of the peace. With only minor modification, administration of fishery laws by the magistracy, with the assistance of appointed conservators, survived into the nineteenth century. An Act of 1818 (58 Geo.III c.43) forbidding the destruction of salmon using hot lime, or filth, or a drug pernicious to fish (now see Ch.3) reaffirmed that conservators appointed by the justices of the peace should be entrusted with the local implementation of the law. Whatever shortcomings may have overtaken this system of local administration of the law in the later part of the nineteenth century (see below), its survival for almost five hundred years is self-evident testimony of its administrative expedience. By comparison, the modern trend for frequent 'reorganisation' of administrative bodies makes it highly unlikely that the present-day water authorities can look forward to a similar life expectancy (see Command Paper 9734 (1986) on the Privatisation of the Water Authorities in England and Wales).

2.07 The Report of the Commissioners Appointed to Inquire into Salmon Fisheries (1861)

Despite the early legislation protecting fisheries, the decline in stocks of salmon had reached such a state by 1860 that Commissioners were appointed to investigate and report on the matter. In particular they were to consider whether allegations that the supply of salmon was dwindling were founded on fact. In a painstaking survey of the major salmon rivers of England and Wales, in which a vast amount of evidence was collected from all involved with salmon fishing, the emphatic message was that of a clear diminution of salmon stocks. The evidence gathered provided cogent proof that the price of salmon had increased, rents for fisheries had decreased, the number of persons employed in fisheries had declined, and that both the number and weight of fish taken in former times were very much greater than at the time of the report (1861). The Commissioners noted that the tradition whereby an apprentice should not be obliged to dine on salmon more than three times a week had long since fallen into dereliction through the shortage of supply. Their opinion was unequivocal:

> The conclusion as to the decline of the salmon fisheries, to which the evidence and records above referred to have led us, was irresistibly confirmed by what we ourselves witnessed in the course of our inspection. We had opportunities of seeing those causes in full operation to which the destruction of the fish was generally ascribed, and we have no hesitation in declaring that, in the face of the impediments and barriers, and other destructive agencies, which exist on all the rivers, it is impossible that any other result than a great deterioration of the fisheries could have taken place; indeed it is in some cases a matter of surprise, not that the supply should have greatly fallen off, but that the breed should not have been totally extinguished.

The Commissioners identified eight distinct causes to which this result was attributed: obstructions to the passage of fish; fixed engines; close times; illegal methods of fishing; poisoning of water by mining; pollution of water by factories and gasworks; absence of proper management; and confusion in the law. These in turn provided the foci for ensuing legislative attention.

(a) *Obstructions to the passage of fish* Of all the problems affecting salmon fisheries, obstruction to the passage of migratory fish was regarded as the most pernicious. Excluding fish from their spawning grounds was seen as a sure means of securing their destruction. Impossible barriers had been constructed across the whole breadth of rivers, often contrary to the law, for the purpose of milling and other industrial requirements. Their presence alone was a self-evident display that earlier laws prohibiting the construction of weirs had proved ineffective. The Commissioners emphasised:

> We could scarcely express in too strong terms our conviction that the existence of these obstructions in the rivers, unprovided with any means for enabling the fish to get up to spawn, is a cause fully adequate, even if no other existed, to account for the gradual disappearance of the fish, and that, if effectual means be not taken to obviate this evil, the gradual extinction of the breed of salmon in the rivers thus circumscribed must in no long time be anticipated.

With such strong words of deprecation, it was inevitable that, as will be seen, the majority of offences enacted under the subsequent legislation were concerned to remove or restrict obstructions to the free passage of salmon.

(b) *Fixed engines*   The various forms of fixed nets known as 'stake' nets, 'stop' nets, 'halve' nets, and basket traps, such as 'putts' and 'putchers', operating in freshwaters (described in Ch.4), exacerbated the problems for salmon ascending rivers to their spawning grounds. Although the policy of the law had been, and should continue to be, opposed to excessive or destructive use of these methods of taking salmon, the Commissioners conceded that in many instances such methods were exercised by virtue of ancient rights. Nevertheless, they proposed that, subject to respect for long-established privileges, these practices should be extensively curtailed.

(c) *Close times*   Second only to the removal of obstructions was the necessity to fix and enforce adequate close times for the taking of fish. The practice which had prevailed since 1818 (under 58 Geo.III c.43) of permitting magistrates to fix close seasons for their locality had proved unsatisfactory because of the diversity of close times which they had authorised. The times at which rivers closed in different parts of the country varied from 31 August to 15 January, and the times at which they opened varied from 31 December to 30 April. As rivers passed through different counties, the close season would change, often many times in the length of the river. In the opinion of the Commissioners, the incongruous assortment of seasons which existed could not be justified, and the determination of close seasons should be removed from the discretion of the justices of the peace.

(d) *Illegal methods of fishing*   Unlawful methods of taking fish, such as the use of spears, gaffs and nets, were found to be prevalent in some areas. Moreover, they were conducted '. . . with a high hand by large parties of men setting the law at defiance, and acting in such a manner as to strike terror and overawe resistance.' Such 'poachers and marauders' were often responsible for the taking of unseasonable and unwholesome spawning fish, or else large numbers of fry. Some of these illegally taken fish were, 'hawked about and sold with little disguise in the towns', and others were exported to a ready market in France, where: 'The ingenuity of French cookery succeeds, we may presume, in making palatable that which in its natural state would be both distasteful and injurious.' The Commissioners were insistent that the practice of unlawful fishing, and the encouragement of the trafficking in fish therefrom, should be checked by all practical means.

(e) *Poisoning of water by mining*   The Commissioners noted striking evidence of the effects of pollution on the rivers Rheidol and Ystwyth in mid-Wales, where a total extinction of animal life had taken place as a result of lead mining contamination. Whilst recognising the need to reconcile the interests of mines with those of fisheries in relation to the extent of industry and capital invested in the different undertakings, the Commissioners thought it possible that the effects of mineral waste could be mitigated or neutralised. They proposed that, without imposing an unfair burden upon mine owners, the law should adopt measures to compel them to reduce such discharges to the minimum that was reasonable in all the circumstances.

(f) *Pollution by factories and gasworks*　The same difficulty of balancing the needs of industry against those of fisheries was illustrated in respect of the pollution of rivers with the growth of manufacturing operations in heavily populated areas. The view of the Commissioners was once again that industrial pollution, whenever possible, should be minimised:

> The interests of manufacturers, nationally considered, must be deemed paramount to those of fisheries, but . . . we consider that a watchful eye should be kept over the introduction of new causes of pollution; that all such nuisances as may without undue sacrifice be preventable should be prohibited, and, if they arise, checked in the outset. For this purpose, it is necessary . . . that power and discretion should be vested in some constituted authority qualified to act both vigorously and impartially in the defence of the public rights, and to restrain the encroachment of interested parties.

(g) *Absence of proper management*　In many respects all the problems that have fallen under the previous headings were united by the common difficulty of giving effect to the existent law. Despite the antiquity of the system of conservators appointed by justices of the peace (instituted in 1285), the Commissioners regarded it as a totally inadequate means of managing fisheries of the mid-nineteenth century. The Commissioners viewed the reasons for this failure as obvious:

> The duties of the conservators are undefined, and their powers of inspection and of checking abuses are very limited. They are also unpaid officers, and a service of this kind, unless properly remunerated, is not likely to be well performed. Nor have the conservators power to employ and pay watchers and keepers, of whom a certain staff is absolutely necessary in order to protect the rivers. Again, the mode in which the magistrates exercise this power is not calculated to produce a vigorous execution of the laws. In many instances indeed the law in this respect is a dead letter.

The Commissioners' view was that the whole system of administration through magistrates and conservators, organised on a county basis, should be scrapped. In its place should be instituted a system which unified the fishery administration of whole rivers according to their common interest, and gave effect to the law through appropriate officials.

(h) *Confusion in the law*　Finally, but not of least significance, the Commissioners expressed criticism of the disorderly state in which the haphazard enactment of statutes, such as those described in earlier paragraphs of this chapter, had left the law. It was often far from clear which of the early statutes had been repealed and which remained in force. In some cases, the law itself was clear but lacked any means of enforcement, in which case magistrates were loathe to convict because of uncertainty as to their jurisdiction to do so. What was needed was a single clear statute which swept away all the earlier enactments, and provided precise definitions of the terms used, the offences created, and the procedures to be followed. In short, the approach that was required should be comprehensive, precise and systematic.

2.08   The Salmon Fishery Act 1861

The translation of the Commissioners' Report into law did not meet with unreserved support, and vigorous opposition was expressed towards the Bill implementing its major provisions in debate in the House of Commons. One Member of Parliament 'protested against damaging the commercial interests of the country for the sake of preserving a few fish'; another questioned 'whether the people of the country were to live by their industry, or whether their industry was to be suppressed that salmon might flourish' (House of Commons Debates Vol.164, col.769–72). Nevertheless, the Bill was passed into law giving effect to a large number of the Commissioners' recommendations. It is this legislative response to the Report of the Commissioners which marks the start of modern freshwater fishery law. By means of the Salmon Fishery Act 1861 the chaos of some 33 pre-existing statutes relating to salmon was swept away and replaced by an extensive, if not quite comprehensive, code of regulation. Although Parliament may have stopped short of implementing all that had been recommended, the Act of 1861 has provided the basis for all fishery legislation since that date. The wording of the Salmon and Freshwater Fisheries Act 1975 can in many places be traced directly back to its primogenitor of 1861. The case law which arose under the earlier statute still provides an invaluable guide to the present state of the law. Perhaps this may show something about the conservatism of the law, but equally it demonstrates the durability of the 1861 reforms.

The Salmon Fishery Act of 1861 set out a clear list of prohibited methods of taking fish, outlawing poison, gaffs, spears, roe, and nets with below minimum mesh dimensions. All the major problems of obstruction that the Commissioners had deprecated were made the subject of distinct offences. Greater uniformity of close seasons was introduced, and specific offences directed towards the taking of unclean (spawning) and immature fish. All these much-needed measures answered the criticisms of uncertainty that had been levied by the Commissioners. The parts of the statute which proved unsatisfactory were, as will be seen, largely those parts governing administration, which failed to follow the direction indicated by the Commissioners. Although the Act placed the general superintendence of salmon fisheries under the central control of the Home Office, it still left the appointment of conservators to justices of the peace, and failed to relate their jurisdiction to complete river systems. The Act also denied conservators the funding required to carry out their duties effectively.

Fortunately, many of the immediate shortcomings of the Salmon Fishery Act

1861 were patched up by subsequent legislation. The Salmon Fishery Act 1865 made provision for Boards of Conservators with jurisdiction of rivers or river systems determined by the Secretary of State. The Act of 1865 also introduced the imposition of licence duties and provided for local Boards to represent fishery interests. These measures were directly in keeping with the intention of the Commissioners' Report, though omitted from the principal Act of 1861. Further modifications to the constitution of the local fishery Boards, effecting an increase in their powers, were brought about in the Salmon Fishery Act 1873. By means of these addenda, and subsequent enactments passed at regular intervals up to the end of the nineteenth century, the major part of the Commissioners' plan was implemented.

2.09   The Regulation of Fishing for Freshwater Fish

The Salmon Fishery Act of 1861 did not only provide the legal basis for salmon fishing—directly in its wake, and following the same plan, came the first major provision governing coarse fishing, the Freshwater Fisheries Act 1878. This Act made possible the appointment of local Boards of Conservators in districts containing trout and char, but not salmon, and permitted charges to be levied on licences for these fish though not for other species of freshwater fish. Also the Act provided the first uniform close season for freshwater fish, the period between 15 March and 15 June including those dates (s.11(2) of the 1878 Act). This remains the standard freshwater fishing close season to the present day (see Ch.5). The Act of 1878 was followed by the Freshwater Fisheries Act of 1884, which permitted the appointment of local Boards of Conservators in fishery districts which contained only freshwater fish, and permitted them to make byelaws governing the size limits and methods by which freshwater fish could be legitimately taken. By these enactments, the legal and administrative structure governing coarse fishing was gradually brought into alignment with that which existed in respect of salmon fishing. The final stage in this progression was the enabling of the fishery boards to charge licence fees in respect of coarse fishing. This was eventually facilitated by the Salmon and Freshwater Fisheries Act 1907.

2.10   Twentieth Century Reforms in Freshwater Fishery Law

The incomplete way in which Parliament gave effect to the report of the Commissioners on Salmon Fisheries of 1861 had necessitated a series of Acts amending the Salmon Fishery Act of 1861. By 1923 the codification of the law into a single statute had been obscured by a diverse and uncoordinated collection of amending legislation. The major objective of the Salmon and Freshwater Fisheries Act of 1923 was to restore order by consolidating the original Act and some 18 amending Acts into a single statute. (See Oke (1924) p.188 for a table relating the provisions of the 1923 Act to the sections of earlier statutes which it repealed.) Along with this tidying-up exercise, the 1923 Act made provision for representation of county councils and for rod licence-holders, other than salmon anglers, to hold seats on fishery boards along with those fishery interests already represented. In addition, the Act sought to extend the coverage of the law to coarse fish, and remove anomalies by giving fishery boards powers to make provisions relating to freshwater fish by ministerial order. In presenting the Bill which became the 1923 Act to Parliament, Sir Robert Sanders, the Minister of Agriculture, described in a colourful passage the progression in the law which had taken place:

> One more difference this Bill makes in the law. It is a step in the direction of democracy among fish. Formerly, law gave precedence to the aristocratic fish like the salmon and the trout. Now, also it takes care of the *bourgeois* carp or the plebian roach or any other humble citizen of the river, even a member of the criminal classes like the pike, and it does not insult them by calling them 'coarse fish', a name by which they are often known; it speaks of them here as 'freshwater fish', and for the first time their rights are recognised. They get some of the protection that was formerly lavished only on their smart and fashionable compatriots.

2.11   Reforms in Fishery Administration

The structure of local fishery administration underwent extensive reform in 1948. The number of fishery boards had fallen from 53 in 1894 to 45 by 1948. This reduction was due to smaller boards encountering financial difficulties as a result of inadequate income, and being obliged to amalgamate with larger boards who were capable of operating more efficiently. This process of rationalisation was advanced by the River Boards Act of 1948, which replaced the 45 local fishery boards by 32 bodies now termed 'river boards'. The river boards operated within areas defined by ministers to consist of drainage areas for rivers or groups of rivers with such adjoining land as was considered expedient. The 32 such boards covered the whole of England and Wales, with the exception of the Thames and Lee catchment areas and the environs of London. To some extent the new river boards took over the duties of the fishery boards along with their assets and liabilities. In addition to assuming these functions in respect of the enforcement of the Salmon and Freshwater Fishery Acts, the river boards also took on responsibility for land drainage and the prevention of pollution. The funding of the river boards was from a combination of sources. They were permitted to charge fees for all kinds of fishing licence, and to levy contributions from the owners or occupiers of private fisheries. In addition to these, an important source of income came from a precept upon the councils of counties and county boroughs within their area.

Further rationalisations of administrative structure took place in 1963 and 1973, resulting in a reduction in the number of bodies concerned. In 1963 the Water Resources Act replaced the River Boards Act of 1948, and set up a central authority known as the Water Resources Board, along with area 'river authorities' who took on all the functions of the river boards and also new functions relating to the conservation of water resources. In turn the Water Act of 1973 established a National Water Council to promote a national policy for water use in England and Wales, and replaced the area river authorities with nine regional water authorities and the Welsh National Water Development

Authority (see Okun (1977)). The new regional water authorities covered all of England and Wales including the Thames and Lee catchment areas and parts of the London region that had previously been excluded from the control of the river boards. The regional water authorities, which came into being on 1 April 1974, took on all the functions exercised by the river authorities for the area. Their areas extended to the catchment limits for the rivers in their region and to tidal waters and any parts of the sea adjoining the coast in their area where there was a public right of fishing. (The present functioning of water authorities in respect of fishery administration is discussed in Ch.7.)

In the same way in which the Salmon Fishery Act of 1861 had been amended and extended by a string of subsequent statutes, the Salmon and Freshwater Fisheries Act of 1923 was supplemented by a series of minor reforms. An Act of 1929 amended it in relation to the sale of trout, and another Act of 1935 extended the powers of the Minister to regulate eel and elver fisheries. The major force behind the later amendment of the Salmon and Freshwater Fisheries Act 1923, however, was the report of the Bledisloe Committee on Salmon and Freshwater Fisheries in 1961. The Committee was appointed 'to review the Salmon and Freshwater Fishery Acts 1923–35 and their operation, taking into account the provisions of the River Boards Act 1948, and to make recommendations'. The ensuing report is an extensive and incisive discussion of the state of freshwater fishery law at the time it was published. The closely reasoned justification which it provided for numerous changes in the law made it a major force behind much subsequent legislation. An Act of 1964 modified the prohibition on the use of seine or draft nets. Another Act of 1965 imposed prohibitions on the use of explosives, poisons or electrical devices and the destruction of dams. The main attempt to give effect to the Bledisloe Report was the Salmon and Freshwater Fisheries Act of 1972, which gave effect to about 30 of the 150 recommendations which had been made in the Report.

2.12 The Salmon and Freshwater Fisheries Act 1975 and other Freshwater Fisheries Legislation

To bring the history of fishery law up to the present, another major consolidation of fishery law took place in 1975 resulting in the repeal and re-enactment of the previous Acts into the Salmon and Freshwater Fisheries Act 1975 (see 1976 supplement to Gregory (1974)). The 1975 Act provides the framework for the following chapters though this Act has been amended by the Salmon Act 1986. The Salmon Act 1986 is discussed in Ch. 13.

Finally, it must be noted that, contrary to the hopes of the Commissioners of 1861, fishery law still does not fall under any single comprehensive statute, and in addition to the matters governed by the Salmon and Freshwater Fisheries Act 1975, there are a number of other areas of law which have developed under separate statutory provision, and yet remain of central importance to the subject. Most important amongst these are: the unlawful taking of fish under the Larceny Act 1861 and now the Theft Act 1968 (see Ch. 3); the powers and duties of water authorities and the Minister under the Water Act 1973; the diseases of fish, under the Diseases of Fish Acts 1937 and 1983, and the import of fish, under the Import of Live Fish (England and Wales) Act 1980 (see Ch.8); the powers of water bailiffs under the Water Resources Act 1963 and the Police and Criminal Evidence Act 1984 (see Ch.9); the pollution of water under the Control of Pollution Act 1974 (see Ch.11); and provisions relating to water resources and abstraction under the Water Resources Act 1963 (see Ch.12). Although this body of law appears to venture some way from the topic of freshwater fishery law, its effects are fundamental, as will be seen in the chapters which follow.

(For general reading on the history of fishery law, see: *Report of the Commissioners Appointed to Inquire into Salmon Fisheries in England and Wales* (1861); *Leconfield* v *Lonsdale* (1870); Moore (1903) part II Ch.1; and the Bledisloe Report (1961) Ch.II.)

3
PROHIBITED METHODS OF TAKING FISH

3.01   Three Levels of Restriction on Improper Methods of Taking Fish

The central issues to be considered in this chapter concern the legal restrictions upon legitimate methods of fishing, such as angling, netting and trapping, and the legal prohibitions upon taking fish by the intrinsically improper methods that are commonly termed 'poaching'. In law the word 'poaching' has no precise definition, in that no distinction is drawn between the improper use of an otherwise lawful method of taking fish on the one hand, and the use of an intrinsically unlawful method on the other: both amount to criminal offences.

The rules governing proper and improper methods of taking fish arise at three levels. First, there are rules made by the fishery owner, that is, the individual or angling association who owns or leases the fishery. The owner is entitled to make rules stipulating which methods of fishing are permitted and stating what other activities are prohibited to persons who are allowed to fish. Disregard of such stipulations may entitle the owner to withdraw permission to fish, to evict the offender from the land, and in some circumstances may even amount to an offence under the Theft Act 1968 (see paras 3.20 to 3.22). At the second level of regulation, the water authority for the area in which the fishery is situated is empowered to make byelaws governing fishing methods which, if broken, will amount to criminal offences (see Ch.7 on the power of water authorities to create byelaws). Several examples of this kind of byelaw are given in this chapter. The third, and most important, level of legal restriction arises under Acts of Parliament having effect nationally and, in the event of inconsistency, overriding both rules imposed by the fishery owner and water authority byelaws. Acts of Parliament provide the most important source of law in respect of the prohibition of improper methods of taking fish. In particular the two statutes which are of special importance are the Salmon and Freshwater Fisheries Act 1975 and the Theft Act 1968. The pertinent provisions of these Acts are discussed in detail in this chapter.

3.02   Special Provision Relating to Fish Farms

A note of qualification to the following discussion must be issued with regard to fish farms. Many of the offences involving prohibited methods of taking fish which arise under the Salmon and Freshwater Fisheries Act 1975 are not committed by reason of anything done or omitted in the course of fish farming (s.33(1) of the Fisheries Act 1981). The effects of this exemption, and other legal provisions relating to fish farms are discussed in Chapter 8.

3.03   Part I of the Salmon and Freshwater Fisheries Act 1975

The most important legal prohibitions upon methods of taking fish arise under the first part (ss.1 to 5) of the Salmon and Freshwater Fisheries Act 1975. The first part of the Act, headed 'Prohibition of Certain Methods of Taking Fish', re-enacts a collection of restrictions upon methods of taking fish, many of which can be traced back to the original Salmon Fisheries Act of 1861. It is these rules which constitute the bedrock of fishery regulation in that, ordinarily, they are legally binding upon all to whom they apply: poachers, anglers and other fishermen, fishery owners and angling associations, and water authorities. Possession of a prohibited instrument with intent to use it to take salmon or trout is generally an offence (s.1(1)(b) of the 1975 Act). The use of these implements is rendered almost universally unlawful by the Act and will only be permitted where the user of such implements can prove to the satisfaction of the court that their use was for the purpose of preservation or development of a private fishery and previous written permission from the area water authority had been obtained (s.1(2)). Needless to say, the scope of this exception is narrow, both in theory and in practice, since the required permission will only be given in the rare cases where it is genuinely required for the preservation or development of a fishery.

Although the emphasis of some of the five sections in the first part of the Act is conservational rather than prohibitive, for the sake of methodical exposition all the offences which arise under the first part of the Act are considered in this chapter in the order in which they appear in the Act. Cross-references are included where prohibitions raise other issues which take the discussion outside the ambit of the first part of the Act.

3.04   Prohibited Methods of Taking Fish under s.1 of the Salmon and Freshwater Fisheries Act 1975

The first section of the Salmon and Freshwater Fisheries Act 1975 lists a number of prohibited implements which it is an offence to use to take or kill salmon, trout or freshwater fish, but surprisingly *not* eels. Given that a genuine intention to catch eels can be shown, no offence is committed by a person using a prohibited instrument unless the use of the instrument is made unlawful under a water authority byelaw. The exception with respect to eels is clearly capable of creating evidential difficulties where the excuse, 'I was only fishing for eels' is proffered. For this reason some water authorities make special provision with respect to the devices which may be used to take eels. North West Water Authority Fishery Byelaws include the rule:

> 25(a) The use of any instrument (other than rod and line) for taking eels is prohibited with the exception of the following . . . ' [there follows a list which does not include any of the instruments prohibited under s.1 of the Act].

The arsenal of devices made unlawful under s.1 of the Salmon and Freshwater Fisheries Act 1975 have been made proscribed because they are generally regarded as, 'neither *bona fide* commercial nor sporting; by them fish can be obtained with some ease but they are essentially methods used by poachers' (Bledisloe (1961) para. 49). For this reason the Salmon and Freshwater Fishery Acts since 1861 have contained an increasingly lengthy list of outlawed implements and methods for taking fish. The present list is discussed in paras 3.05 to 3.11. The penalties for the offences of using these are described in para. 3.18.

As an overrider to the following paragraphs it is important to point out that even if an implement is not prohibited under the first part of the Salmon and Freshwater Fisheries Act 1975 it may still require a licence to be used lawfully under the Act (see Ch.6). In addition, its use may be prohibited during a close season (see Ch.5), or in accordance with a water authority byelaw (see Ch.7).

3.05   Firearms

Section 1(1)(a)(i) of the Salmon and Freshwater Fisheries Act 1975 makes unlawful the use of firearms within the meaning of the Firearms Act 1968. This prohibition first appeared in the Salmon and Freshwater Fisheries Act 1972, before which it was not an offence to shoot fish within the general law relating to firearms. Under the present law, the meaning of 'firearm', taken from s.57(1) (the interpretation section) of the Firearms Act 1968, is: 'a lethal barrelled weapon of any description from which any shot, bullet or other missile can be discharged'. This definition also encompasses component parts of, and accessories to, firearms. In the past, courts have given a wide interpretation to the phrase 'lethal weapon', taking it to mean 'a weapon capable of causing injury' (*Read* v *Donovan* (1947)). Hence it has been held that an airgun is a lethal weapon, not because it is designed or intended to cause death or inflict injury, but because it is *capable* of doing so if misused (*Moore* v *Gooderham* (1960)). It has also been suggested that for this reason the definition will encompass underwater barrelled guns of the type used by skindivers (see House of Commons Parliamentary Debates 1972 Vol.835, col.1956). By contrast, however, the definition of 'firearm' as a '*barrelled* weapon' may serve to exclude weapons without a barrel. Into this category would come elastic powered spear guns without barrels, crossbows and catapults. Nonetheless, the overall effect of the broad definition of 'firearm', in conjunction with the provision in the Act dealing with the throwing or discharge of any stone or other missile (under s.1(1)(c) of the Act, considered in para.3.11 below) amounts to a comprehensive outlawing of the use of almost any type of projectile as a permitted method of taking fish.

3.06   'Otter Lath or Jack'

Subsection 1(1)(a)(ii) of the 1975 Act prohibits the use of an 'otter lath or jack'. The 'otter lath or jack' was first recognised as an improper method of taking fish under s.8 of the Salmon Fishery Act 1861, and was first defined under s.4 of the Salmon Fishery Act 1873. This definition has been substantially re-enacted into all subsequent Acts, so that under s.1(3) of the present Act the definition given states that: '"otter lath or jack" includes any small boat or vessel, board, stick or other instrument, whether used with a hand line, or as auxiliary to a rod and line, or otherwise for the purpose of running out lures, artificial or otherwise'. Essentially the device suggested by this definition involves the use of some kind of float to which the line is attached. This is used as a means of carrying a hook, or hooks, out beyond normal angling distances, or causing them to move in a manner in which they would not ordinarily do, through the action of wind, or water current, or some means of towing.

In the remarkable Irish case of *Alton v Parker* (1891) the accused was seen in a boat on Lough Derg with a line extending from the boat to a piece of wood about eighteen inches long, which served the purpose of a second boat to stretch and float the line. He was charged under an Irish statute which made it unlawful to use an 'otter' for taking fish (s.40, Fisheries (Ireland) Act 1842). In his defence it was claimed that *live* otters can be, and are, trained for the purpose of catching fish, and that the 'otter' referred to in the statute was the actual animal rather than the wooden device that he had used. This claim was unsuccessful. Because of the language of the statute, in which 'otter' was classed along with a number of inanimate and mechanical contrivances, the judge entertained no doubt that the live animal was not intended.

Having discounted live animals from the discussion, the precise definition given in s.1 of the Act is not altogether clear. The method of 'long trotting', by which some coarse anglers allow a bait to be taken downstream by the flow of water in a stream, using a float to keep the bait from becoming snagged on the bottom, appears to be 'using a stick for the purpose of running out lures' within the definition. Yet this would normally be thought of as a conventional method of angling without any taint of impropriety. Some water authorities make an effort to spell out more precisely the nature of the prohibition upon otters. Byelaw 16(ii) of the Northumbrian Water Authority Fishery Byelaws states that: 'No person shall use in connection with fishing with rod and line for salmon, trout or freshwater fish in any waters within the area [of the Authority] any bubble or like device which is fished with any kind of fly, lure or bait between it and the rod.' This looks to be an attempt to outlaw a particular kind of otter.

Although the definition of 'otter lath or jack' given in the Act suggests that a 'jack' is another name for an otter, it may be that this is a misunderstanding of the original prohibition of the 'jack' under s.8 of the Salmon Fishery Act 1861. It has been suggested by Fort and Brayshaw (1961 p.278) that a 'fire-basket suspended over the stern of a boat to attract fish, now replaced by a searchlight, used to be known as a "jack"', though those making this assertion concede that 'jack' has any number of meanings varying in different localities. Whatever the original meaning of the word 'jack', it is thought that, in law, the definition given in s.1 of the present Act equates the meaning of 'jack' with that of 'otter'.

3.07 *'Wire or Snare'*

Along with the prohibition of the otter, s.1(1)(a)(ii) prohibits the use of any 'wire or snare'. This prohibition refers to the use of a loop or noose of metal or other fibre which is placed usually around the tail or body of a fish, tightened, and the fish thereby pulled from the water. Although the use of such devices is made generally unlawful, an exception is provided for under s. 1(4) of the Act, which allows a similar instrument, known as a 'tailer', to be used as an auxiliary to angling with a rod and line. Thus it would not be an offence to use a tailer to lift a fish from the water where it had been previously hooked and brought to the bankside using legitimate angling methods. Similarly it would not be an offence for an angler to have in his possession a tailer intending to use it for this purpose (s.1(4)). A moot question is whether this exception permits one person to possess or use a tailer where another uses the rod and line, as where an attendant or fellow angler assists a rodholder to lift a fish on to the bank using a tailer. It is hoped that common sense would prevail here, and the phrase 'as auxiliary to angling with rod and line' would be interpreted to allow a person other than the rodholder to land a fish using a tailer without falling foul of the law.

The use of a wire or snare as a means of removing unwanted species from a water is not uncommon, and is traditionally used as a means of removing pike from waters preserved for game fish. If used in this way, however, to be within the law the user must show that the use was for the purpose of preservation or development of a private fishery, and that the use was with the previous written permission of the water authority for the area (s.1(2)).

3.08 'Crossline or Setline'

'Crosslines' and 'setlines' were first made unlawful under the Salmon and Freshwater Fisheries Act 1972, thereby implementing a recommendation of the Bledisloe Report (1961 pp.vii–viii). The Report defined 'crossline' and 'setline' in substantially the same way as they are now defined in s.1(3) of the Salmon and Freshwater Fisheries Act 1975: '"crossline" means a fishing line reaching from bank to bank across water and having attached to it one or more lures or baited hooks'; '"setline" means a fishing line left unattended in water and having attached to it one or more lures or baited hooks'. The Bledisloe Report had observed that a setline used at night is more commonly called a 'night line', though it is clear that the definition of setline given in the Act would include this. Some water authorities seek to avoid any uncertainty as to the breadth of the definitions of 'crossline' and 'setline' by stipulating that the use of *any* kind of line is unlawful unless used in conjunction with a rod. For example, rule 5(f) of the Severn-Trent Water Authority Fishery Byelaws states that: 'No person shall use any form of line otherwise than in connection with a rod.' This provision would make unlawful the use of a handline falling outside the definitions of either a crossline or a setline, though the use of a handline would also be unlawful in many water authority areas as an unlicensed instrument (see Ch.6 on unlicensed fishing).

The justification for banning the use of crosslines and setlines lies in the fact that they are neither sporting nor genuinely commercial methods, but merely methods of poaching. This is borne out by the reasoning in *Barnard* v *Roberts* (1907) where the accused had used implements, described as 'night lines', consisting of small pegs driven into the bank of a stream with lines and hooks attached, and with a stone weight attached to one of the lines to hold it in position. It was held that (for the purposes of s.25, Larceny Act 1861, the forerunner of the Theft Act 1968, see paras 3.20 to 3.22) this did not amount to 'angling'. As Philimore J commented: 'where the human element ceases when once the tackle has been set, I think that that is not angling'. It is for the same reason that crosslines and setlines are made unlawful under s. 1(1)(a)(iii) of the 1975 Act.

It is worth noting, however, that the terms 'crossline' and 'setline' are not incompatible with the use of a rod. Lines which traverse water, or are left unattended, fall within the definitions notwithstanding that they are used in conjunction with a rod. In effect the law places an obligation upon all anglers not to leave their tackle unattended at any time. This obligation is made explicit under some water authority regulations. The Thames Water Authority Fishery Byelaws state that:

> 10(ii) No person shall leave a rod and line with the bait or hook thereof in the water unattended or otherwise without having sufficient control thereof.

With the same purpose in mind rule 10(i) stipulates: 'No person shall fish with more than two rods and lines at the same time, and such rods when in use shall not be placed more than 2 metres distant the one from the other' (though the use of more than one rod may require the user to buy additional rod licences, see para. 6.03). In effect, this spells out, in terms of proximity, precisely what is meant by leaving a rod unattended when an angler fishes with two rods simultaneously. Another approach to essentially the same problem is the prohibition of methods of fishing with rod and line which involve the hooking of fish without skill or action by the angler. Hence rule 7(d) of the Anglian Water Authority Fishery Byelaws states that: 'Any person shall be guilty of an offence if without the previous consent in writing of the Authority he fishes with rod and line with any form of gorge bait.'

3.09 'Spear, Gaff, Stroke-haul, Snatch or other Like Instrument'

Subsection 1(1)(a)(iv) of the 1975 Act prohibits the use of 'a spear, gaff, stroke-haul, snatch or other like instrument'. These are traditional poaching instruments which were originally made unlawful under s.8(2) of the Salmon Fishery Act 1861. They all involve the capture of fish by impaling, other than by a hook being taken by the fish in the mouth. In the case of a spear the impaling is achieved by a downward motion on to the fish; with a gaff the fish is usually hooked with an upward stroke; whilst the stroke-haul and snatch involve the dragging of hooks across a fish with the intention that they will penetrate and secure a hold in any part of the fish's body. (For diagrams of these instruments, see Jenkins (1974) Ch.11, and Millichamp (1976) p.23.)

The prohibition upon the use of a gaff is subject to an analogous exception to that discussed above in respect of a tailer (in para. 3.07). That is, that a gaff (consisting of a plain metal hook without a barb) may be lawfully used as an auxiliary to angling with rod and line, and it is not an offence for an angler to have such an instrument in his possession intending to use it in this way. No other use of a gaff is permitted, however, not even where it is used as an auxiliary to licensed and legitimate netting (*Wedderburn* v *Duke of Atholl* (1900)).

Notwithstanding the general legitimacy of a gaff when used as an auxiliary to angling with rod and line, there are certain times of the year when anglers are most likely to hook unclean fish which must be returned to the water with the least possible injury (s.2(2)(a) and 2(3) of the 1975 Act, see para. 3.13). At these times it is undesirable to allow the use of a gaff which will inevitably cause injury to fish which must be returned. For this reason some water authorities prohibit the use of a gaff at these times of the year. For example, byelaw 19 of the Northumbrian Water Authority Fishery Byelaws states that: 'During the months of February, March, April and October in each year no person shall use a gaff in connection with fishing with rod and line in any waters within the Area [of the authority] other than landlocked lakes and ponds'. Some authorities go further than this by banning the use of a gaff altogether. Rule 7 of the Wessex Water Authority Fishery Byelaws stipulates that a gaff shall not be used in the Bristol Avon and Somerset divisions of the authority's area *at any time of the year*.

'Stroke-haul or snatch' is defined in s.1(3) of the Act to include any instrument or device, whether used with a rod and line or otherwise, for the purpose of foul hooking any fish. This definition is open-ended in that it is concerned with a particular *method of use* rather than a particular sort of instrument. The Bledisloe Report (1961 p.viii) adopted a similarly instrumental definition of a 'snatch', which was taken to be a hook deliberately worked in such a way as to impale a fish in any part of its body other than the mouth. Clearly both definitions contemplate *any* method intended to secure the capture of a fish by impalement other than through a fish taking a hook by the mouth. It follows from the definitions of 'stroke-haul' and 'snatch' that any fly, spinner or other hook is capable of constituting a 'snatch' if it is drawn over a fish with the object of foul-hooking. The method of use was described in *Prescott* v *Hutin* (1966) where a large treble hook, moved in swift jerks, was used to take sea fish.

Because an otherwise legitimate hook or lure is capable of being used to take fish by 'snatching' it may sometimes be difficult to establish that a fish was taken in this way rather than by accidental foul-hooking. To meet this difficulty some water authorities create byelaws governing the return of foul-hooked fish, or prohibit the use of lures which are capable of being used to snatch fish, or both. Rule 10 of the Welsh Water Authority Fishery Byelaws provides that:

(a) No person shall use a bait or lure furnished with more than one hook unless the gape thereof measured from the shank to the point does not exceed 10 mm (0.375 of an inch) save and except that the gape of hooks attached to a plug bait may be as great as 13 mm (0.5 of an inch) provided the said plug bait is used without any weight and in no case shall any bait or lure be furnished with more than nine hooks and no weight or sinker shall be attached below the lure or bait.

(b) (1) No person shall use a rod and line except with a permitted lure or bait and only for the purpose of taking fish by hooking them in the mouth.

(2) All salmon and migratory trout hooked otherwise than in the mouth shall be returned to the water without delay and with as little injury as possible.

The effect of the last part of this rule is that it would be an offence for an angler to keep a fish that had been improperly hooked even if it had been hooked by accident.

The phrase 'other like instrument' in s.1(1)(a)(iv) would appear to apply only to other instruments that facilitate the taking of fish by impalement or foul-hooking. In *Jones* v *Davies* (1898) the question before the court was whether a net, with which the accused had been caught in a field abutting a salmon river, was a 'like instrument' to an 'otter lath or jack, wire or snare, spear, gaff, stroke-haul or snatch' (s.8, Salmon Fisheries Act 1861 as amended by s.18, Salmon Fishery Act 1873). The court held that the general words 'like instrument' had to be limited in their meaning to things of the same kind as those listed by the particular words, and a net was not a thing of the same kind as a snare or any other of the listed instruments (contrast *Allen* v *Thompson* (1870)). Similarly, the scope of s.1(1)(a)(iv) of the 1975 Act will be limited to impaling devices (though the use of nets is covered elsewhere in the Act, see para. 3.15).

3.10 'A Light'

Subsection 1(1)(a)(v) of the 1975 Act prohibits the use of 'a light' to take fish. It is unclear what manner of use of a light the subsection makes unlawful. It is well known that fish may be attracted to a source of light, or mesmerised if subjected to bright light. Despite this, a light, on its own, is simply not a means of taking fish: some additional instrument or method must be used to remove the fish from the water. A favourable construction of the provision is reached by supposing that the use of a 'light' is to be understood to mean the use of a light *in conjunction with another instrument or method of taking fish*. If this is the correct meaning of the provision, then the legality of the method would invariably depend upon the legality of the other instrument used. Using a light in conjunction with a spear or gaff (other than auxiliary to a rod and line) would clearly be unlawful by virtue of the offences discussed in preceding paragraphs notwithstanding the use of the light. Alternatively, it is doubtful whether a legitimate angler fishing with rod and line at night would step outside the law merely by making use of a light to prepare his tackle or to find his way around the bankside.

(For an account of the uses made of light in different methods of fishing, see Ben Yami (1976).)

3.11 Stones or other Missiles

Section 1(1)(c) of the Salmon and Freshwater Fisheries Act 1975 makes it unlawful to throw or discharge any stone or other missile for the purpose of taking or killing, or facilitating the taking or killing of any salmon, trout, or freshwater fish. Clearly this provision would cover the offender who, by skill or luck, manages to kill or stun a fish by throwing stones into water, or more likely, by throwing stones at fish leaping from the water. What is less certain is the meaning of the word 'facilitating'. Does an otherwise legitimate angler who throws stones into the water in order to move a fish from its lie thereby 'facilitate' the later taking of the fish? In an illuminating passage from the House of Lords debates (1972 Vol.330, col.1239–43) Lord Balfour of Inchrye described the circumstances in which this might happen:

If you have what is called 'heavy water', a strong stream, and you are fishing with very light tackle and you get into a big fish, it may 'sulk' at the bottom for an indefinite period of time. . . . There are two traditional ways of moving that salmon. One is to take a coin, any coin, and tap your rod several times. The vibration from that coin will go right down the line, down the trace to the fly; the fish will feel those vibrations and may well move. The second way is for either the fisherman or someone else to throw a rock into the pool and this disturbs or moves the fish.

Giving a piece of extemporary legal advice, Viscount Dilhorne, passed the following comment: 'I am sorry to have to say, on my noble friend's own confession, that for the purpose of facilitating the taking of his salmon he committed an offence under the [Salmon and Freshwater Fisheries Act] of 1923. . . . I do not think my noble friend should be encouraged in these practices, which have been illegal since 1923.'

'Facilitating', therefore, appears to be capable of broad interpretation, and makes unlawful the throwing of any stone or missile which aids the subsequent capture of a fish. 'Missile' does, however, connote that the thing thrown, or otherwise projected, is used as a weapon of some kind. This excludes food or fish-attracting substances thrown into a water to be fished as ground-bait, where this is permitted. Although such tactics are generally thought to 'facilitate' the taking of fish, it would be an extraordinary use of language to describe the fish-attracting substance as a 'missile'. It is suggested that the meaning of this word should be confined to things which facilitate the taking of fish either by impact or by repulsion. On this interpretation, throwing stones, or projecting them by catapult, or releasing arrows from a crossbow or spear-gun would come within the offence (see para.3.05 on 'firearms'). The use of ground-bait would not.

3.12   Roe

Section 2 of the Salmon and Freshwater Fisheries Act 1975 creates two offences in connection with the misuse of fish roe for the purpose of taking fish. Under s.2(1)(a) it is an offence to use any fish roe for the purpose of fishing for salmon, trout or freshwater fish. Anomalously, the offence is not committed where the roe is used to fish for eels. The intention behind the subsection is to outlaw the use of salmon roe, or 'paste', as it is commonly called. This bait is reputed to have devastating fish attracting properties, and was used in the past as a means to take excessive numbers of fish. The wording of the subsection is not restricted to the use of salmon roe alone though, and is wide enough to encompass the use of *any* fish roe, from salmon, trout, freshwater fish or even sea fish. Moreover, the subsection covers *any* use of roe for the purpose of catching fish, so that using roe as ground-bait to attract fish would be an offence as much as using roe as a hook bait.

With the same malpractice in mind, s.2(1)(b) makes it an offence for any person, for the purpose of fishing for salmon, trout or freshwater fish (again *not* eels), to buy, sell or expose for sale, or have in his possession any roe of salmon or trout. Here the offence is drawn more narrowly in that only salmon and trout roe are at issue. It follows that a fishmonger selling cod roe or caviar would not commit the offence even if the purchaser bought the roe with the intention of using it as bait. The proviso to both subsections ('for the purpose of fishing for salmon, trout or freshwater fish') indicates that the possession of the roe must be accompanied by the intention to put it to illicit use. Therefore the possession of roe within a fish, without more, would not contravene these subsections.

Section 2(5) of the Act makes it a defence to the offences relating to the use, purchase and possession of roe in respect of acts done for scientific or conservational purposes. No offence will be committed where the accused can show that the act in question was done for the purpose of artificial propagation of salmon, trout or freshwater fish, or for some scientific purpose, or for the purpose of the preservation or development of a private fishery, and that, in each case, permission has been previously obtained in writing from the water authority for the area.

3.13   Unclean and Immature Fish

Section 2(2) of the Salmon and Freshwater Fisheries Act 1975 provides for two offences in relation to unclean or immature salmon, trout and freshwater fish (once again eels are excluded). The first offence is that of knowingly taking, killing or injuring any salmon, trout or freshwater fish which is unclean or immature, or attempting to do so (s.2(2)(a)). The second offence is that of buying, selling, or exposing for sale, or having in possession any salmon, trout or freshwater fish (not eels) which is unclean or immature, or any part of such fish (s.2(2)(b)). The interpretation section of the Act (s.41(1)) defines 'unclean' to mean any fish that is about to spawn, or has recently spawned and has not recovered from spawning. 'About to spawn' appears to be capable of a wider interpretation than 'on the point of spawning' since in the Crown Court decision in *Pyle* v *Welsh Water Authority* (1986) the court held that a gravid fish, which an expert thought might be up to 10 days before spawning, was nonetheless 'about to spawn' for the purpose of s.2(2)(b). 'Immature' in respect of salmon is defined as salmon of a length of less than 12 inches, measured from the tip of the snout to the fork or cleft of the tail. In respect of other fish 'immature' is merely stated to mean fish of a lesser length than that prescribed by the byelaws applicable to the water in which the fish is taken. Paragraph 28 of Sch.3 to the 1975 Act permits water authorities to make byelaws specifying sizes of trout and freshwater fish below which the taking of fish is prohibited.

An important feature of the offence of taking, killing, or injuring unclean or immature fish, under s.2(2)(a) of the Act, is the requirement that the fish be taken '*knowingly*'. In practice this may often provide a defence to inexperienced anglers who are unaware of the difference between clean and unclean fish, or mature and immature fish, and mistakenly take such fish without any intention to do so. From the point of view of the prosecution it may be advantageous to pursue charges under s.2(2)(b) rather than s.2(2)(a) since the word 'knowingly' is omitted from s. 2(2)(b).

Although the word 'knowingly' is not used in s.2(2)(b) of the Act it is not clear what state of mind must be shown on the part of the accused for the offence of buying, selling, exposing for sale or possessing unclean or immature salmon, trout or freshwater fish to be committed. In the past the offence has been interpreted as requiring wilfulness on the part of the accused. Thus in *Hopton* v *Thirlwall* (1863) the accused, one Reverend Thirlwall, whilst angling for trout caught several samlets, or young salmon, which he placed in his basket along with trout that he had caught. He had no knowledge that any of the fish were young salmon, honestly believing all the fish to be trout. Nonetheless, he was charged, under a forerunner of s.2(2)(b) of the present Act (s.15(2) of the Salmon Fishery Act 1861), with the offence of having in his possession the young of salmon. The Court of Queen's Bench found him not guilty when he was able to prove that he did not know the difference between samlets and trout and had no intention of taking or having the samlets in his possession. As Cockburn CJ put the point, 'he is bound to know the law, but is not bound to know the fact'. That is, the offence of possessing the young of salmon can only be committed where there is a *wilful* act upon the part of the accused, in effect, where he knows the wrongfulness of his behaviour. In contrast to this, however, in the recent Crown Court case of *Pyle* v *Welsh Water Authority* (1986) the accused was charged with taking an unclean sea trout under s.2(2)(b) of the present Act and convicted on the basis that this subsection does not require that the accused person should be aware that a fish is unclean, since the intention of the Act is that all anglers should be able to discern a fish's condition. This interpretation of the law makes offences under s.2(2)(b) absolute in character, in contrast to the decision in *Hopton* v *Thirlwall* which requires the accused to have knowledge of the wrongfulness of his behaviour. The correct interpretation of the law remains to be resolved.

Whichever interpretation of the law is correct, it is unlikely that a person accused of taking or possessing unclean or immature fish will always be able to plead ignorance as a defence. The outcome in *Hopton* v *Thirlwall* (1863) may be contrasted with that in the case of *Jones* v *Owens* (1870) where the accused had attempted to conceal young salmon from a police constable. The fact that he had taken steps to conceal his possession of the fish was taken by the court as an indication that he appreciated the wrongfulness of possessing them, and so had acted wilfully. He was found guilty of possession of immature salmon. The practical import of this is that a person found in possession of unclean or immature fish may sometimes encounter difficulty in convincing a court that he did not possess them wilfully.

An explicit exception to the offences in relation to unclean and immature fish is given under s.2(3) of the Act, which states that they do not apply to any person who takes a fish by accident and returns it to the water with the least possible injury (see the discussion of *Wells* v *Hardy* (1964) in para.3.22, on the meaning of 'taking'). Another exception is provided for, under s.2(5), where (as with the misuse of roe) no offence is committed where the act is done either for the purposes of artificial propagation, or scientific purposes, or for the preservation or development of a private fishery, and with the written permission of the appropriate water authority.

(For exemptions from the offence under s.2(2)(a) of the Salmon and Freshwater Fisheries Act 1975, and a defence under s.2(2)(b), relating to fish farming, see para.8.04.)

3.14   Disturbing Spawn or Spawning Fish

The third offence created under s.2 of the Salmon and Freshwater Fisheries Act 1975 is that of wilfully disturbing any spawn or spawning fish, or any bed, bank or shallow on which any spawn or spawning fish may be, otherwise than in the exercise of a legal right to take material from any waters (s.2(4)). This provision applies to two different kinds of situation. The first is where a poacher attempts to take fish from spawning beds. Usually this situation will be covered by another section of the Act, such as that governing prohibited instruments (s.1), or that governing unlicensed fishing (s.27, see Ch.6). Equally though, the situation will involve disturbing spawning fish, and the activity of attempting to take spawning fish will be an offence under s.2(4) of the Act.

The second situation to which s.2(4) of the Act might apply is that of a person carrying out operations on the bank or bed of a watercourse which is used by spawning fish in disregard of the disturbance caused to the spawning fish or to their spawn. No intention to take fish is normally present in this situation. Any pre-existing legal rights to behave in a way which would otherwise be in breach of this subsection are explicitly preserved by s.42(8) of the Act. This states that nothing in the Act shall affect the legal right of persons to dredge, scour, cleanse or improve any navigable river, canal or other inland navigation. Hence in *Proctor* v *Avon and Dorset River Board* (1953) an injunction to restrain dredging operations was refused because the defendants acted within statutory powers conferred under s.34 of the Land Drainage Act 1930 to maintain and improve works and construct new ones, and they had done so with due regard to the fishery interest. On the same facts it is likely that criminal proceedings under s.2(4) of the Act would have been similarly unsuccessful for the same reasons (though see para.11.23 on pollution of water by disturbing deposits).

The offence of disturbing spawn or spawning fish is only committed where a person acts 'wilfully', though it appears that the wilfulness involved may be either a wilfulness to disturb any spawn or spawning fish, or a wilfulness to disturb any bed, bank or shallow on which any spawn or spawning fish may be. If the latter of these is shown then a person may be found guilty of the offence without having wilfully disturbed spawn or spawning fish, providing that he wilfully disturbed a bed, bank or shallow where they may have been. This will not require any knowledge on the part of the accused that he knew that spawn or spawning fish may have been present, nor will it require the prosecution to prove that spawn or spawning fish were actually present, merely that they *may* have been at the time of the offence. The general defence to offences under s.2 of the Act applies equally in respect of s.2(4), that is, that no offence will be committed where the act in question is done for the purpose of artificial propagation, scientific purposes, or the preservation or development of a private fishery, and the written permission of the water authority for the area has been obtained (s.2(5)).

3.15   Nets

Two initial points must be made concerning the use of nets to take fish. The first is to reiterate the statements made in Chapter 1 about the different kinds of legal regulation of netting (see para.1.02). Briefly, the central consideration is that where a net, used in a particular way, does not amount to a prohibited method of taking fish under s.3 of the Salmon and Freshwater Fisheries Act 1975, this is not a sufficient ground to conclude that the use of the net is therefore lawful. Even if a particular net does not constitute a prohibited instrument for taking fish, it may still be unlawful as a 'fixed engine' or obstruction to the passage of migratory fish (see Ch.4), or unlawful if used outside permitted seasons or times (see Ch.5), or unlawful if not properly licensed (see Ch.6). This paragraph must be read alongside a collection of legal restrictions upon the use of nets which are discussed in the following three chapters. It is not a complete statement of the law on netting.

The second initial point about nets concerns the definition of 'net'. In this context the term 'net' does not include a net used as a landing net when used as an auxiliary to angling with a rod and line. Landing nets, properly used for this purpose, are specifically excluded from general regulations applying to nets by s.3(3) of the Act. In some water authority areas, however, the design of landing nets may be the subject of water authority byelaws. Thus rule 11 of the Yorkshire Water Authority Fishery Byelaws provides that: 'Any landing net which is used for taking freshwater fish within the area [of the authority] shall be of knotless material'. Similarly, rule 6 of the Anglian Water Authority Fishery Byelaws stipulates that a person will be guilty of an offence if, without the previous consent of the water authority in writing, he uses a landing net with knotted meshes or meshes of metallic material. The purpose of these byelaws is to prevent the use of landing nets which may cause injury, or the removal of protective slime, where fish are to be returned to the water.

Section 3 of the Act imposes two main restrictions upon the use of nets to take salmon and migratory trout. Along with other restrictions upon netting, these are designed to ensure that the method is not too effective and that it cannot be conducted in such a way as to prevent an adequate number of fish passing up-river both for the benefit of anglers and for the maintenance of the stock of fish (Bledisloe (1961) para.59). The first restriction is concerned with the permitted length of a net, and the second with the dimensions of the net mesh. The first restriction makes it unlawful for a netsman to shoot or work any seine or draft net in any waters across more than three-fourths of those waters (s.3(1)). 'Any waters' amounts to an explicit statement that the offence may be committed in both tidal and fresh water (see para.1.04). 'Draft net' is another name for a seine net.

The design and use of the seine net is described in the Bledisloe Report (1961 pp.144–5) as follows:

It is a wall of plain netting 200 yards or more long and of a depth suitable to the water in which it will be used, for it is desirable that it should extend from the surface to the bottom. The headrope is fitted with corks and the footrope with leads or other weights so that the net will stand vertically in the water. In order further to assist this, one end is sometimes attached to a wooden iron-shod staff, but this is not general. The net is usually fished by a crew of four. The net is stowed properly folded on the flat transom of a rowing boat. One of the crew stands ashore holding a rope attached to the end of the net. The boat is then rowed out from the shore on a more or less semi-circular course by two men whilst the fourth pays out the net over the stern. When all the net has been shot, the boat returns, without pause or delay (that is the law) to the shore, whence it set out. The landing place is usually downstream of the man on the shore, but a net can be shot upstream though this makes hard work for the oarsmen. When the boat reaches the shore all the crew disembark, if necessary the boat is made fast, and the net is hauled in by two men at each end. The hauling is fairly rapid and is conducted evenly and smoothly until the net is all drawn upon the beach when the catch, if any, is removed.

(For a discussion of the different types of seine net, see Davis (1958), and Jenkins (1974) Ch.9.)

The second restriction imposed upon lawful netting places a limitation upon the size of the mesh of any net used. Section 3(2) of the Act provides that unless other dimensions are authorised by byelaw, (para.21 of Sch.3 to the Act), it is an offence to take or attempt to take salmon or migratory trout with any net which has a mesh smaller than 2 inches measured from knot to knot, or 8 inches round each mesh. These measurements apply to the size of the mesh when wet. (A possible exception to this arises in the case of nets used in the Solway Firth, under s.39(2) of the Act; see para.10.13.)

A number of cases have arisen concerning the words 'take or attempt to take' within s.3(2). It was held in *Jones* v *Davies* (1898) that mere possession of a net with an unlawful size of mesh (varying from half an inch to one and a half inches in diameter) was not an offence. Even though the accused were found in the neighbourhood of a salmon river intending to catch salmon by means of the net, that did not constitute an offence under s.10 of the Salmon Fisheries Act 1861 (the forerunner of s.3(2) of the present Act, though see para.6.04 on possession of an unlicensed instrument). Hence 'taking fish' by means of a net involves something more than mere possession of a net in the vicinity of a water with the intention to use it.

On the other hand, the courts have adopted a broad definition of what is meant by 'using' a net for the purpose of catching salmon. In *Moses* v *Raywood* (1911) the accused was seen in a boat on a river where salmon were usually caught. He subsequently left the boat and walked along the edge of the river looking for salmon. A click net, the size and shape of a landing net, was found in the boat for the purpose of being put into the water when a salmon was seen near the surface. When interrupted by a water bailiff the net was dry, not yet having been put in the water. Despite this, it was held that the accused had begun to search for salmon and the net was with him ready for use, and that he was *using* the net without having a licence contrary to s.34 of the Salmon Fisheries Act 1865 (now an offence under s.27(b) of the present Act). The reasoning in *Moses* v *Raywood* has been reapplied recently to the context of sea fishing in *Alexander* v *Tonkin* (1979) where by searching for fish within a prohibited zone the skipper of a fishing vessel was similarly found to be 'fishing', without the need for more to be shown.

It is to be observed, however, that 'taking or attempting to take' salmon or migratory trout must be accompanied by an intention to do so. In *Davies* v *Evans*

(1902) the accused owned and used a net which was of a smaller mesh than allowed by a byelaw, but was, he maintained, primarily intended to catch coarse fish. It was found as a point of fact that salmon were occasionally caught in the net. The Court of King's Bench found that the evidence was sufficient to justify a conviction if an intention to catch salmon was found (one judge taking the view that the facts themselves were sufficient evidence of intention) and remitted the case back to the magistrates with the direction that they reconsider whether the accused actually had an intention to catch salmon. In cases of this kind the manner in which a net is used may often provide a clear indication of the intention of the person using it. For example, it is well known amongst netsmen that salmon tend to swim near the surface of an estuary whilst bottom feeding fish such as flatfish are usually found near the bottom. It would be incongruous if an experienced netsman were to claim he was fishing for flatfish if using a net which floated on the surface. The manner in which he fished would provide evidence of his true intention.

The restriction upon mesh size provided for under s.3(2) of the Act cannot be evaded by systems of nets or other materials which facilitate the reduction of mesh size. Section 3(4) explicitly outlaws the placing of two or more nets one behind another, or covering the nets used with canvas, or using any other device which has the practical effect of diminishing the size of the net used. The operation of a forerunner of this subsection (s.10 of the Salmon Fisheries Act 1861) is well illustrated by *Dodd* v *Armor* (1867). In this case the accused fished a salmon river with a 'trammel net' which consisted of a net having mesh of lawful dimensions with two nets of larger mesh known as 'walls' or 'hammies' in front of and behind the lawful net, which hung loosely between the two outside nets (a modern trammel net is described below). The operation of the net was such that whenever a fish struck against the threefold net it pushed the middle net through the large-meshed net behind it, thereby making a bag or purse in which the fish was entangled and caught. The Court of Queen's Bench affirmed the decision of the magistrates that the two outer walls practically diminished the size of the centre mesh and contravened the subsection. Despite the fact that trammel nets, which had been well known before the enactment of the Salmon Fisheries Act 1861, had not been explicitly named in the statute as prohibited devices, it was held that this type of net fell within the subsection.

An overriding exception to the general minimum net-mesh dimension of 2 inches from knot to knot, provided for under s.3(2) of the Act, is where smaller sizes of mesh are authorised by water authority byelaws. Thus, for example, rule 9 of the Anglian Water Authority Fishery Byelaws permits fishing for salmon and trout in tidal waters or in the sea with: 'a net provided that the dimensions of the mesh are not less than 3 cm in extension from knot to knot (the measurement to be made on each side thereof) or 12 cm measured round each mesh, the measurements to be made when the net is wet'. This rule involves a reduction of minimum net-mesh size below that provided under the Act (3 cm = 1.2 in. approx.).

Similarly, water authority byelaws may authorise the use of trammel nets, involving the placing of two or more nets behind one another in such a manner as practically to diminish the mesh. These are otherwise prohibited under s.3(4) of the Act, as described above. The Welsh Water Authority Commercial Fishery Byelaws authorise the use of four trammel nets on certain parts of the River Dee (contrast the ruling in *Dodd* v *Armor* (1867), discussed above, where the use of a trammel net was held to be unlawful). Rule (5)(c)(vi) of the Byelaws states that trammel nets:

> . . . shall be nets without bags or pockets consisting of a single sheet or wall of netting measuring when wet not more than 91 metres in length and having (in every part thereof) a mesh of not less than 5.75 centimetres from knot to knot or 23 centimetres round the four sides, and having attached round its four edges on one or both sides an outer sheet or wall of armour or outholes measuring not more than 91 metres in length and not more than 1.82 metres in depth and having (in every part thereof) a mesh of not less than 28 centimetres from knot to knot or 1.12 metres round the four sides.

This specification permits the use of two nets, one behind the other, without permitting the mesh of either net to be less than the minimum under s.3(2) of the 1975 Act (5.75 cm = 2.3 in. approx.).

(For exemptions from the offences, under s.3 of the Salmon and Freshwater Fisheries Act 1975 relating to fish farming, see para.8.04.)

3.16 *Poisonous Matter and Polluting Effluent*

Section 4(1) of the Salmon and Freshwater Fisheries Act 1975 makes it a crime for any person to cause or knowingly to permit to flow, or put, into any waters containing fish, any liquid or solid matter to such an extent as to cause the waters to be poisonous or injurious to fish or the spawning grounds, spawn or food of fish. From the outset it must be noted that, although this provision raises the general issue of water quality and pollution control, it does so in a way which is within the general objectives of the first part of the Act, that is, the 'prohibition of certain modes of taking fish'. It is for this reason that s.4(1) makes no attempt to impose any general system of legal control upon water quality (contrast Part II of the Control of Pollution Act 1974, discussed in Ch.11). This is apparent from the wording of the section, which makes it clear that the offence can only be committed by introducing the noxious substances into 'waters containing fish'. A consequence of this choice of words is that if a watercourse is already so heavily polluted that it cannot support fish, then no offence is committed under this section by further polluting it. Section 4(1) is concerned with the direct effect of poison and pollution upon fish, rather than the problem of water pollution in general. The law on water pollution in general is considered in Chapter 11, whilst this paragraph is confined to a discussion of s.4 of the 1975 Act.

The offence created under s.4(1) is committed where the poison or pollution is introduced into any 'tributary' of the water containing fish. The meaning of the word 'tributary' has been the subject of much judicial consideration especially in cases concerned with ministerial definitions of fishery districts. Essentially the term takes in all watercourses which supply a water, so that 'tributary' can include a tributary of a tributary and so on (*Hall* v *Reid* (1882), *Evans* v *Owens*

(1895)). Similarly, any pond which is formed by damming a stream to enlarge it without changing its course will also become a tributary (*Cook* v *Clareborough* (1903)). Where a water supply reservoir has been formed by damming a stream and water is redirected to supply another area, however, then it has been held that the reservoir is not a tributary of the stream which formed its original outflow (*Harbottle* v *Terry* (1882), *George* v *Carpenter* (1893)).

A major difficulty with the interpretation of s.4(1) concerns the state of mind of a person who brings about the poisoning or pollution of a watercourse. The section is concerned with 'any person who causes or knowingly permits to flow, or puts or knowingly permits to be put' the offensive matter into a stream. From amongst these words the expression 'cause or knowingly permit' has been a question discussed by courts on several occasions. In *Moses* v *Midland Railway* (1915) a tank containing creosote was transported by railway. Although servants of the accused railway company had inspected the tank at the commencement of the journey and found no defect, it transpired that there was a latent fault in a tap on the tank from which creosote leaked into a salmon river killing fish. On a charge under s.5, Salmon Fisheries Act 1861 (the forerunner of s.4(1) of the present Act) it was held that, in view of the fact that the tank in question was not owned by the railway company, who had no knowledge of the defect or control over it, they did not 'cause or knowingly permit' the creosote to enter the river.

It has to be stressed that 'causing' pollution is a different matter to 'knowingly permitting' pollution. An illuminating decision illustrating this contrast is *Alphacell Ltd* v *Woodward* (1972). In this case the accused prepared a material used in paper manufacture at their works on the banks of a river. Water used in the process became polluted and was piped into settling tanks which were maintained below their overflow level by means of pumps. Due to clogging of the intakes of the pumps with leaves and other matter the pumps failed to operate effectively and polluted water entered the river. The accused were convicted of having caused the pollution to enter the river under s.2(1) of the Rivers (Prevention of Pollution) Act 1951 (now replaced by s.31, Control of Pollution Act 1974, discussed in Ch.11 below). On appeal to the House of Lords, it was held that by operating the works without an effective safeguard against overflow of pollution into the river they had 'caused' the incident. In passing, the Lords noted that although the crime would be committed where it could be shown that a person had 'knowingly permitted' the pollution to occur, if it was alleged that the accused had 'caused' the pollution then it did not need to be established that the accused had knowingly, intentionally or recklessly done so. In effect 'cause' did not mean 'knowingly cause'. Short of the pollution resulting from an act of God such as the pumps being struck by lightning, or being caused by a trespasser (as in *Impress (Worcester) Ltd* v *Rees* (1971)) neither of which were argued, the accused were guilty of causing the pollution, however accidentally it might have occurred.

The same interpretation of 'cause' was applied in the recent case of *Wrothwell Ltd* v *Yorkshire Water Authority* (1984). Here a company deliberately poured into its drains 12 gallons of a concentrated herbicide, known to be toxic to fish. Unknown to the director of the company the system of drainage ultimately entered a stream and not, as had been assumed, the public sewerage system. The company were found guilty of having *caused* poisonous or injurious matter to fish to enter the stream notwithstanding that they did not know that their actions would have that effect.

The apparent breadth of the House of Lords' ruling in *Alphacell Ltd* v *Woodward* (1972) has been limited somewhat by the later case of *Price* v *Cromack* (1975). Here the accused accumulated industrial effluent in two lagoons on his land built especially for the purpose of containing the effluent. A river authority pollution officer discovered that cracks had formed in the walls of the lagoons allowing polluting matter to escape into a nearby river. On appeal to the Queen's Bench Divisional Court the accused's conviction was quashed on the ground that 'causing' polluting matter to enter the river required some positive act on his part, and not merely a passive looking on. Although the accused may have been guilty of 'knowingly permitting' polluting matter to enter the river (an offence with which he was not charged) passive inactivity, without more, was not sufficient to amount to 'causing' for the purpose of s.2(1) of the Rivers (Prevention of Pollution) Act 1951. The same conclusion would have been reached in respect of s.4(1) of the Salmon and Freshwater Fisheries Act 1975. *Price* v *Cromack* provides a neat illustration of the contrast between 'causing' and 'knowingly permitting' injurious matter to enter a water, and the potentially wider scope of the latter offence.

The scope of s.4(1) of the 1975 Act is limited by five exceptions: legal right; continuation of an existing method; radioactive matter; scientific purpose or fishery protection or improvement; institution of proceedings.

(a) *Legal right* The first exception to the offence under s.4(1) concerns the existence of a legal right to poison or pollute a water. Under s.4(2) of the Act a person shall not be guilty of an offence by exercising a right which he is legally entitled to exercise. This refers to persons who are excused where they have been granted consent to pollute water under s.34 of the Control of Pollution Act 1974. The effect of consent to pollute being granted in this way is considered in Chapter 11.

(b) *Continuation of an existing method* The second exception to s.4(1) is also provided for under s.4(2) and is to the effect that pollution may be excused where it comes about by the continuation of a method which was in use in connection with the same premises before 18 July 1923 (the date of the passing of the Salmon and Freshwater Fisheries Act 1923). This exception is available subject to the proviso that the person causing pollution in this way proves to the satisfaction of the court that he has used the best practical means, at a reasonable cost, to prevent such matter from doing injury to fish, or to spawning grounds, spawn or food of fish.

(c) *Radioactive matter* A third exception to s.4(1) arises where the pollution in question is of a radioactive nature. Section 9(1) of the Radioactive Substances Act 1960 (and para.2, Sch.1 to that Act) states that for the purposes of the operation of this provision, no account is to be taken of any radioactivity possessed by any substance or article or by any part of any premises. Radioactive pollution is to be judged according to its pollutant effects other than those attributable to the effects of the radioactive properties of the pollutant. (The topic of radioactive pollution is discussed in Chapter 11.)

(d) *Scientific purpose of fishery protection or improvement* A fourth exception is provided for under s.5(5) of the 1975 Act which states that no offence is committed under s.4(1) where the polluting substance is used for a scientific purpose, or for the purpose of protecting, improving or replacing stocks of fish, and permission has been given in writing by the area water authority. A safeguard against the possible overreadiness of water authorities to provide the necessary written permission is that where any noxious substance is concerned, permission will not be given by the water authority except with the approval of the Minister. The effect of this is to place a high burden of justification upon the person who seeks to use poison for scientific purposes or to maintain or develop a fishery.

(e) *Institution of proceedings* A final limitation upon the operation of s.4(1) is the constraint that proceedings under this subsection are not to be instituted except by the water authority for the area, or by a person who has first obtained a certificate from the Minister that he has a material interest in the waters alleged to be affected. This is provided for under s.4(3) of the 1975 Act. In practice, therefore, where a water authority declines to exercise its discretion to prosecute, a person wishing to institute proceedings will need to show that he has a 'material interest' in the waters. It is not clear what will amount to a 'material interest' for this purpose. Leasehold or freehold interest in the fishery would almost certainly be sufficient, but a mere licence to enjoy the use of the fishery might not be.

Along with the offence under s.4(1) of the Act of causing or knowingly permitting matter to enter waters to such an extent as to cause the waters to be poisonous or injurious to fish, water authorities are also given an explicit power to make byelaws relating to pollution. This power arises under para.31 of Sch.3 to the Act and permits water authorities to make byelaws regulating the deposit or discharge in any water containing fish of any liquid or solid matter specified by the byelaw which is detrimental to salmon, trout, or freshwater fish, or to the spawn or food of fish. This power is circumscribed by the proviso that such byelaws must not prejudice any powers of a local authority to discharge sewage in pursuance of any power given by a public general Act, a local Act or a provisional order confirmed by Parliament. It would appear that in practice there is little to be gained by a water authority creating a byelaw under this power, since in almost every case the activities that might be regulated already come within the existing provisions of the Salmon and Freshwater Fisheries Act 1975 or the Control of Pollution Act 1974 (discussed in Ch.11).

3.17 Explosives, Poisons, Electrical Devices and Malicious Injury

The final prohibition upon methods of taking fish under Part I of the Salmon and Freshwater Fisheries Act 1975 is contained in s.5 and covers a range of illegitimate methods brought together with the common element that they are intentionally used to take or destroy fish. Section 5(1) prohibits the use in or near any waters, including waters adjoining the coast of England or Wales to a distance of six nautical miles (see para.1.04), of any explosive device, any explosive substance, poison or other noxious substance, or any electrical device, with intent to take or destroy fish. The use of the word 'fish' makes it apparent that the offence can be committed in relation to any kind of fish, including sea fish.

'Explosive substance' must be taken to include the range of things encompassed by s.9 of the Explosive Substances Act 1883 where the expression is deemed to include 'any materials for making any explosive substance; also any apparatus, machine, implement, or materials used, or intended to be used, or adapted for causing, or aiding in causing, any explosion in or with any explosive substance; also any part of any such apparatus, machine, or implement'. The general impression is of a definition couched in the broadest possible terms anticipating every conceivable possibility.

'Poison or other noxious substance' creates an overlap between s.5(1) and s.4(1) of the Act in that a single act of poisoning is capable of constituting an offence under either section. The crucial differences between the two sections are, first, that s.5(1) requires an intention to take or destroy fish to be shown, whereas the offence under s.4(1) can be committed by a person who, amongst other things, 'causes or permits' pollution without any intention to take fish (see para.3.16). A second difference is that s.4(1) applies to 'waters containing fish', whilst s.5(1) concerns 'any waters'. These differences make s.5(1) the more appropriate section under which to charge a person who introduces poison, or an asphyxiant, into a river in the hope of removing any fish which are killed or incapacitated by the substance, whilst s.4(1) will be more appropriate to an industrial or agricultural polluter of a watercourse who may be oblivious as to the effects of his acts upon fishlife. Notwithstanding the apparent appropriateness of the two offences to different types of polluter, it may be easier for the prosecution to establish that the accused 'caused' or 'knowingly permitted' pollution for the purposes of s.4(1) than that he 'used' a noxious substance for the purpose of s.5(1). For this reason the prosecution may prefer to pursue the offence under s.4(1).

An exception to the offence of using a noxious substance to take or destroy fish under s.5(1) of the Act is created under s.5(2), which states that the offence will not apply to the use of a noxious substance which is for a scientific purpose or for the purpose of protecting, improving or replacing stocks of fish (see Mills (1978) s.7.4). This exception is only available where the permission of the water authority for the area has been given in writing, though this permission may not be given by the water authority otherwise than with the approval of the Minister. Thus in some exceptional cases it may be possible for a fishery owner to use a noxious substance to remove unwanted species of fish from a water in respect of which the required permission has been obtained.

'Electrical device' refers to the method of taking fish by passing an electrical current through water. This has the effect of stunning fish so making their capture more simple. This practice, though properly disapproved of in the Bledisloe Report (1961 para.50) as a method of illegally taking fish, is also widely used in scientific research as a means of sampling fish populations without causing permanent damage to a fishery. Similarly, it is put to legitimate use as a method of fishery management, and is also used occasionally to rescue fish from the effects of pollution or drought. To permit legitimate use of electrical devices, s.5(2) states that no offence will be committed where the method is used for a scientific purpose, or for the purpose of protecting, improving or replacing stocks of fish where permission has been obtained in writing from the area water authority. In contrast to the position regarding the use of noxious substances, discussed above, it is not necessary for the water authority to obtain the approval of the Minister before giving consent to the use of an electrical device. It is likely, however, that the use of the device will be made subject to conditions such as a licensing requirement (see Ch.6 on fishing licences) or stipulations as to the times and waters in which the device can be used (see Ch.5 on close seasons). Where consent to use an electrical device is made subject to such conditions it may amount to a breach of a water authority byelaw to operate the device otherwise than in accordance with the conditions (see Ch.7 on water authority byelaws).

(Useful reading on electrical fishing methods includes: Vibert (1967); Millichamp (1976) s.6; and Hickley (1985).)

Section 5(3) of the Act makes it an offence for a person to destroy or damage any dam, floodgate or sluice with the intent to take or destroy fish, subject to the proviso that this is done 'without lawful excuse'. Although the definition of 'lawful excuse' is open-ended, it would be satisfied where a person acted under a statutory power or where he acted with authorisation from a water authority. This might arise, for example, where the owner of water seeks to drain it in order to remove one species of fish to preserve the fishery for another and does so with the approval of the water authority. 'Dam' in this context carries the meaning given in the interpretation section of the 1975 Act (s.41(1)); that is, it includes any weir or other fixed obstruction used for the purpose of damming up water.

The enforcement of s.5 of the Act is greatly simplified by s.5(4), which makes it an offence for a person to have in his possession any explosive, noxious substance, or electrical device for the purpose of contravening the prohibition on the use of these devices under s.5(1). In contrast, as has been mentioned, the mere possession of other prohibited implements is not in itself an offence. This was illustrated in *Jones* v *Davies* (1898), discussed in para.3.09, where the possession of a net with an unlawful size of mesh in the proximity of a salmon river with the intention of catching salmon with it was not held to be an offence. Under s.5(4) possession of any of the devices mentioned, where it is possessed for the purpose of taking or destroying fish contrary to s.5(1), is an offence. (Possession of the device may also constitute the offence of possession of an unlicensed instrument, see para.6.04.)

(For exemptions from the offences under s.5(1) and (4) of the Salmon and Freshwater Fisheries Act 1975 relating to fish farming see para.8.04.)

3.18   Penalties under Part I of the Salmon and Freshwater Fisheries Act 1975

The maximum penalties for some of the offences under the first part (ss.1 to 5), of the Salmon and Freshwater Fisheries Act 1975 are specifically listed in the table in para.1 of Sch.4 to the Act. This table provides that the use of a prohibited instrument contrary to s.1, where the offender is not acting with another, will on summary conviction make the offender liable to a fine not exceeding level 4 on the standard scale, which presently stands at £1,000 (see para.1.12 on the standard scale of fines). If acting with another, on summary conviction, the punishment is the statutory maximum, presently £2,000. If the proceedings are in a Crown Court, on indictment, the maximum punishment is a period of two years' imprisonment or an unlimited fine, or both. For the offence of discharging poisonous matter into waters contrary to s.4, on summary conviction, the punishment specified is the statutory maximum of £2,000 plus an additional daily fine of £40 for each day on which the offence continues after conviction. On indictment, the corresponding punishment is a two-year term of imprisonment or an unlimited fine or both. In respect of offences under s.5(1) and (3) of the Act, such as the use of explosives or the destruction of dams to take fish, the penalty on summary conviction is a fine not exceeding the statutory maximum, presently £2,000. If the conviction under either of these subsections is on indictment, then the corresponding punishment is a period of two years' imprisonment or an unlimited fine or both.

For offences under the first part of the Act where the maximum punishment is not specified in the table in para.1 of Sch.4, an offender will be liable to the general penalty of a fine not exceeding level 4 on the standard scale, presently £1,000 (para.2, Sch.4). That penalty would apply to offences such as the use of roe under s.2 of the Act, or the misuse of nets under s.3. The same penalty would be applicable to breaches of water authority byelaws concerning prohibited methods of taking fish.

(The differential penalties where persons act together to commit an offence under s.1 of the 1975 Act are abolished by s.35 of the Salmon Act 1986. See para.13.06.)

3.19 *Prohibited Methods of Taking Fish under Water Authority Fishery Byelaws*

Along with the prohibited methods of taking fish under the first part of the Salmon and Freshwater Fisheries Act 1975, each water authority is empowered to make byelaws governing permitted methods of fishing within its area. Paragraph 21 of Sch.3 to the Act gives water authorities an explicit power to make byelaws specifying the nets and other instruments which may be used for taking salmon, trout, freshwater fish and eels and imposing requirements as to their construction, use, design, material and dimensions. Similarly, para.25 of Sch.3 permits water authorities to make byelaws prohibiting the use for taking salmon, trout, or freshwater fish of any instrument in the waters of a water authority area at such times as may be specified. A number of examples of byelaws of this character have been presented in the preceding paragraphs where they related directly to prohibitions under the Act. In this paragraph additional examples are provided of other angling equipment and methods that are the subject of byelaw regulation in particular areas. It is stressed that a byelaw will only apply within the area of the authority by which it was created. Byelaws vary considerably from area to area, and the angler is strongly advised to obtain and study in advance the byelaws applicable to any area in which he proposes to fish.

(a) *Prohibited baits*　Paragraph 33 of Sch.3 permits water authorities to make byelaws regulating the use, in connection with fishing with rod and line, of any lure or bait specified in the byelaw. Making use of this power, a number of water authorities prohibit the use of certain baits as a means of catching game fish. The rationale for this seems to be that the use of coarse fishing methods and baits would be unsporting or excessively destructive to fish stocks. Hence, byelaw 16 of the Northumbrian Water Authority Fishery Byelaws states: 'No person shall use in connection with fishing with rod and line for salmon or trout in any waters within the northern part of the Area [of the authority] (excluding the rivers Wansbeck and Blyth and the tributaries thereof) any worm or maggot before the first day of June in any year.' Similarly, rule 11 of the Severn-Trent Fishery Byelaws stipulates that:

No person shall—
(a) in fishing with rod and line for salmon in the Severn area use any float in conjunction with any lure or bait;
(b) in fishing with rod and line during the annual close season for freshwater fish, use any float or bait (including ground bait) other than artificial or natural fly, spinners, minnows or worms.

(b) *Keep nets* Many anglers use a cylindrical net known as a 'keep net' in which to retain their catch until the end of a session of angling, after which the catch is usually returned to the water. A number of water authorities impose regulations as to the use of keep nets to prevent injury to fish whilst retained in such nets. A typical example of such a regulation is rule 10 of the Yorkshire Water Authority Fishery Byelaws which states:

(1) No person shall use any keep net in any waters in the area [of the authority] during the annual close season for freshwater fish. [See Ch.5 below on close seasons.]
(2) Any keep net which is used for retaining trout or freshwater fish in any water within the area shall comply with the following specification—
(a) The net shall be of knotless material.
(b) The minimum dimension of the net shall be 200 cm in length and 35 cm in diameter or in the case of a rectangular net 200 cm in length and 35 cm × 25 cm in cross-section.
(c) The net shall have a spacing between rings of not less than 6 mm and not more than 47 mm round its edge. The mesh shall form not less than three quarters of the total surface area of the net.

(c) *Trolling* A method of taking fish which is generally regarded as unsporting and overdestructive of fish stocks is the use of a bait or lure trailed behind a boat moving under motor power. This method, sometimes termed 'trailing', is banned in several water authority areas. For example, rule 5(iii) of the Thames Water Authority Fishery Byelaws: 'No person at any time shall troll or trail from a boat any bait or lure unless it is attached to a rod and line and provided that the boat is drifting or propelled only by oars or paddle.'
(d) *Bag limits* In order to conserve fish stocks, a number of water authorities impose limits upon the number of fish that an angler is permitted to

take from a water in any one day. One provision of his kind is rule 5 of the Anglian Water Authority Fishery Byelaws:

Any person who without the previous consent of the Authority takes or removes more than two fish in any one day shall be guilty of an offence provided nevertheless that this byelaw shall not prevent a person:

(a) taking more than that number of fish if the fish are immediately returned alive to the water, or if the fish are retained in a keep net and released to the water alive within 5 metres of the place at which they were taken as quickly as possible after the person taking them has ceased to fish, or after the fish have been weighed in accordance with any recognised practice;

(b) taking in any one day fish not exceeding ten in number (excluding minnows and bleak) of which no fish may exceed 20 cm in length (measured from the tip of the snout to the fork of the tail) or minnows and bleak for his own use for live or dead bait fishing in the water from which the fish were taken.

But this byelaw shall not apply to brown trout and rainbow trout in enclosed waters and to migratory fish and eels.

(On the technical meaning of the term 'taking' in respect of fish, see para.3.22.)

(e) *Lead shot* At the time of writing there is considerable pressure on water authorities by ornithological and wildlife groups to make byelaws prohibiting the use of lead shot and lead weights by anglers because of their toxic effect upon swans and other birds (see Spillett (1985)). The Ministry of Agriculture, Fisheries and Food has drafted a model byelaw to outlaw the harmful use of lead:

No person shall on or after 1 January 1987 use for taking salmon, trout, freshwater fish or eels in any waters within a water authority area fishing gear—

(a) which incorporates a lead weight of which the weight is between 0.06 grams (No. 8) and 56.7 grams, or

(b) in the manufacture of which such lead weights have been used.

Interpretation: For the purpose of this byelaw lead weight means any weight of which the principal component is lead.

At present, however, though water authorities are considering the matter, none has yet created a byelaw prohibiting the use of lead weights. If a water authority were to enact a byelaw of the form of the model byelaw it would need to act in accordance with its power to make byelaws for specific purposes under s.28(6) of and Sch.3 to the 1975 Act. In this case the specific purpose for which the water authority is empowered to make byelaws is that of: 'specifying the . . . instruments which may be used for taking salmon, trout, freshwater fish and eels and imposing requirements as to their construction, use, design, *material* and dimensions . . .' (para.21, Sch.3, author's emphasis).

(See Ch.7 on the power of water authorities to make byelaws.)

3.20   'Theft of Fish' and 'Taking or Destroying Fish'

A natural charge which a fishery owner or angling association might seek to bring against a person taking fish from waters improperly is that of theft. It often appears to a layman that the taking of fish without permission ought to be regarded by the law on the same footing as the taking of a book or a car, that is, as 'a simple case of theft'. Unfortunately, because of an ancient quirk of the law, the taking of fish may not always be assimilated to the taking of other kinds of personal property. For reasons which will become apparent in the following discussion, the question of the appropriate legal charge for the taking of fish depends on whether the fish in question were confined within a water where the right of fishery is severally owned (see para.1.07 on the meaning of 'several ownership'), or whether the fish were wild and had been free to move between waters where the rights of fishery are owned by different persons. The distinction is sometimes expressed as that between fish which have been 'reduced into possession' and fish which are wild (this distinction is explained below). Where the fish which have been taken have been reduced into the possession of the fishery owner, then the person taking them is appropriately charged with 'theft of fish' under s.1 of the Theft Act 1968. Where the fish in question are wild fish, then the appropriate charge is that of 'taking or destroying fish' under para.2 of Sch.1 of the Theft Act 1968. Although the difference between these two offences might appear semantic rather than substantial, its significance will become clear in the following paragraphs.

3.21   The Theft of Fish

Section 1 of the Theft Act 1968 states that: 'a person is guilty of theft if he dishonestly appropriates property belonging to another with the intention of permanently depriving the other of it.' Although this might appear a suitable provision with which to charge a person who has taken fish improperly, the section has to be read subject to an important qualification upon the meaning of 'property' contained in s.4(4) of the Theft Act 1968. This stipulates that:

> wild creatures, tamed or untamed, shall be regarded as property; but a person cannot steal a wild creature not tamed nor ordinarily kept in captivity, or the carcase of any such creature, unless either it has been reduced into possession by or on behalf of another person and possession of it has not since been lost or abandoned, or another person is in the course of reducing it into possession.

The effect of this is that wild fish, since they have not been 'reduced into possession' cannot be stolen. It is only after fish have been 'reduced into possession', or are in the process of being reduced into possession, that they are capable of being the subject of theft. A possible exception to this is the case of 'royal fish' which are the property of the crown whether reduced into possession or not (see para.1.03 on royal fish).

Reduction into possession can be brought about in a number of ways. First, if a fish is confined in a bowl, or placed in a pool in a fish farm from which it has no escape, then it is reduced into possession and becomes the property of the captor, and anyone taking it will commit theft (*R* v *Steer* (1704)). Similarly, if a person were to remove a fish from a net in which it had been confined (see Hale (1736) Vol.I p.511, and *Young* v *Hitchens* (1844)), or to remove it from the bag of an angler who had captured it, that would be theft since the fish had in each case been reduced into possession and so ceased to be a wild creature. In the same way it would be open to the owner of a stocked fishery, where fish are confined within the limits of the fishery, to prosecute persons taking fish from it with theft, or persons attempting to do so with attempted theft.

The maximum penalty which a court can impose for theft is 10 years' imprisonment, provided for under s.7 of The Theft Act 1968, though the sentencing powers of magistrates do not permit them to impose penalties of this severity (see para.1.12).

3.22   Taking or Destroying Fish

In the case of fish which have not been 'reduced into possession', such as those in a stream or river which are free to move up or downstream beyond the fishery owned by any particular owner, a person taking such unconfined fish will not be committing theft. The situation does, however, fall directly under the special offence of taking or destroying fish provided for under para.2 of Sch.1 to the Theft Act 1968. This offence is committed without the need for fish to be 'reduced into possession'. Paragraph 2(1) of Sch.1 states that an offence is committed where: 'a person . . . unlawfully takes or destroys, or attempts to take or destroy, any fish in water which is private property or in which there is any private right of fishery'. On summary conviction under para.2(1), a person will be liable to imprisonment for a term not exceeding three months or to a fine not exceeding level 3 on the standard scale, presently £400, or both.

Along with the main offence of taking or destroying fish under para.2(1), a lesser offence is provided for under para.2(2) which concerns taking or destroying fish *by angling*. Paragraph 2(2) of Sch.1 states:

> [Paragraph 2(1) of Sch.1] shall not apply to taking or destroying fish by angling in the daytime (that is to say the period beginning one hour before sunrise and ending one hour after sunset); but a person who by angling in the daytime unlawfully takes or destroys, or attempts to take or destroy, any fish in water which is private property or in which there is any private right of fishery shall on summary conviction be liable to a fine not exceeding level 1 on the standard scale [presently £50].

'Daytime' here is defined as the period beginning one hour before sunrise and ending one hour after sunset. It has been held, however, that 'sunrise' and 'sunset' mean the times at which these events occur locally rather than at Greenwich (*MacKinnon* v *Nicolson* (1916)).

Both the offences provided for under para.2 of Sch.1 to the Theft Act 1968 concern 'unlawful' practices on 'private' fisheries. This means that the offences are not applicable where a public right of fishery exists, as is usually the case in tidal waters (see para.1.04). Neither would the offences be appropriate where the person taking fish has permission to fish from the owner of the fishery, and does so within the terms of the permission, since in such a case the fishing would be lawful. The precise meaning of the term 'lawful' in this context is not clearly determined. According to earlier authorities, under a forerunner of the present provisions (s.24 of the Larceny Act 1861) it appeared that it would be a defence to raise a claim of legal right to fish waters, even if that right was not proved, providing the accused genuinely believed that he was exercising a legal right to fish (*R* v *Stimpson* (1863), *Halse* v *Alder* (1874)). It has since been held that it would not be a defence to a prosecution for 'unlawfully and wilfully attempting to take fish' (under s.24 Larceny Act 1861) to show a genuine belief in a claim of a legal right to fish where no such right existed in fact. In *Smith* v *Andrews* (1891) it was decided that the fact that the public had angled freely on a stretch of the River Thames for over 40 years did not mean that any public right of fishing existed (see para.10.04).

The provisions enacted under para.2 of Sch.1 to the Theft Act 1968 are not confined to game fish. The use of the words 'any fish' in relation to both offences of taking or destroying fish, indicates that they are to be construed to cover freshwater fish and eels, and even sea fish where they are present in a private fishery (though see para.1.06). In *Caygil* v *Thwaite* (1885) it was held, under a forerunner of the present provisions, that the offences were capable of being committed where crayfish were taken.

The meaning of the word 'take' in relation to the offences of taking or destroying fish under para.2 of Sch.1 to the Theft Act 1968 is not without difficulty. In *Wells* v *Hardy* (1964) the facts were that the accused 'was angling solely for sport and intended to place each and every fish which he might catch . . . (being fish of and above a certain minimum size) alive in a keep net . . . until the end of the day's sport and then to release all such fish . . . and that he intended to return to the said water each and every fish which he might catch (being fish below the said minimum size) immediately after catching the same'. The question for the court was whether this constituted a 'taking' of fish for the purposes of a forerunner of the present provisions. The court held that the word 'take' did not involve any element of asportation and that the accused had 'taken' the fish even though he intended to return them to the water directly or at the latest at the end of his session of angling. Thus a fish may be 'taken' even if it is ultimately to be returned to the water unharmed.

Although it is generally the case that the offences of taking or destroying fish provided for under para.2 of Sch.1 to the Theft Act 1968 envisage persons who are unlawfully present on private property fishing private waters without permission from the owner, this need not always be the case. If a person is given permission to be on land and fish waters in a particular manner, for example by buying an angling permit from the owner, by stepping outside of the scope of the permission which has been given to him he may still commit the offences. So that if an angler is permitted to fish a water using one method of fishing, for example, 'fly only', but proceeds to use another which is prohibited, such as fishing with bait, then in the absence of a lawful excuse, he will commit one of the offences provided for under para.2 of Sch.1. It is for this reason that these provisions might be especially useful to fishery managers and angling associations against permit-holding anglers who disobey fishery rules.

(For a discussion of the powers of arrest for both offences under the Theft Act 1968, see Ch.9; and for the forfeiture of equipment used in transgression of the Theft Act 1968, see Ch.10).

4
OBSTRUCTIONS TO THE PASSAGE OF FISH

4.01   The Problem of Obstructions

The second chapter drew attention to the antiquity of statutes prohibiting weirs. Whatever the original purpose of such enactments, by 1861, when the Commissioners on Salmon Fisheries reported, weirs and other obstructions were seen as the principal cause of the decline in salmon stocks. The problem they presented to salmon fisheries was stated concisely in the submissions of the Special Commissioners for English Fisheries in the case of *Leconfield* v *Lonsdale* (1870, p.664):

> Nearly all the great rivers of England are frequented by salmon, a species of migratory fish which can only exist by alternately living in salt and fresh water. The law of their nature is, that the fish are bred in the upper and shallow waters of the great rivers and their tributaries, and at the age of about eighteen months they pass down to the sea and the rest of their existence is spent in passing every year to and fro between the sea and the upper fresh streams. At all times of the year the fish are either passing up or passing down the river. . . To enable the fish to inhabit a river, that is to say, to be found not only in the fresh but the tidal parts of rivers, it is thus essential that the parent fish should have an open passage from the sea to the source, or at least to the upper shallows of the river. The old fish require to go up the river to breed, and the young fish require to come down the river to grow; and after they are grown they still require to alternate between the fresh waters and the sea. If at any point between the tidal limit and the upper breeding grounds a barrier is made which obstructs this passage, the stock of fish is necessarily diminished and gradually annihilated. It thus follows that at the place where the salt water meets the fresh the whole stock of fish of the river and estuary must pass at least once in their lives, either coming or going. This is so in a state of nature, irrespective of all laws. If all the fish must pass a particular spot, it equally follows that they may all with certainty be caught at that spot if certain obvious means for that end are used.

It was essentially this problem which had warranted the devotion of some 13 sections of the Salmon Fishery Act 1861 to the reduction of obstructions to the passage of fish. The practical effect of the 1861 Act was to bring about a considerable reduction in the number of obstructions to migratory fish in salmon rivers. Consequently the problem of obstructions is much less serious today than in times gone by, but nonetheless the legacy of legislation remains to prevent a return to the 'bad old days'. Part II of the Salmon and Freshwater Fisheries Act

1975 contains 13 sections appertaining, directly or indirectly, to obstructions. These sections govern fixed engines, fishing weirs, fishing mill dams, fish passes, sluices and gratings. Despite the relatively narrow sphere of operation of these provisions, they remain a necessity to secure freedom of movement of migratory fish through our rivers.

4.02   Fixed Engines

The term 'fixed engine' is a general expression indicating a method of trapping fish by means of an immovable structure of some kind. This may be contrasted with the use of unfixed devices such as a moving net used to encircle fish, or a rod and line used in the ordinary way. Section 6(1) of the Salmon and Freshwater Fisheries Act 1975 makes it an offence either to place a fixed engine in any inland or tidal waters, or to use an unauthorised fixed engine for taking or facilitating the taking of salmon or migratory trout or for detaining or obstructing the free passage of salmon or migratory trout (these offences are discussed below). The interpretation section of the Act (s.41(1)) states that the term 'fixed engine' includes:

(a)   a stake net, bag net, putt or putcher;

(b)   any fixed implement or engine for taking or facilitating the taking of fish;

(c)   any net secured by anchors and any net or other implement for taking fish fixed to the soil, or made stationary in any other way; and

(d)   any net placed or suspended in any inland or tidal waters unattended by the owner or a person duly authorised by the owner to use it for taking salmon or trout, and any engine, device, machine or contrivance, whether floating or otherwise, for placing or suspending such a net or maintaining it in working order or making it stationary.

The use of the word 'includes' as a prefix to this list of different types of fixed engine indicates that this is not intended as a comprehensive statement of all the things that can constitute 'fixed engines'. Nevertheless, it provides a clear indication of the sorts of things intended. The instruments described under headings (a) to (d) are discussed in the following paragraphs.

4.03   Part (a) of the Description of 'Fixed Engine'

The meaning of 'stake net' and 'bag net' under part (a) of the description of 'fixed engine' is to be found in the Report of the Commissioners of 1861, where it was said that:

Stake Nets, as their name implies, are formed of netting attached to long stakes, driven firmly into the shore. They act upon the principle of a leader, running from or near high-water mark seaward, against which the salmon in their course along the coast, strike, and in their endeavour to find a passage, are guided into a narrow opening, the entrance to a chamber or trap, from which there is no escape. In some cases, these nets are of great extent, and have many chambers, the last being placed so far into the sea or channel as the very lowest tides will permit; it is never entirely dry and is generally waded into and fished with a scoop net, and to this chamber what is called a bag or fly net has of late been attached, which reaches still further seaward.

(The legality of a stake net was considered in *Bevins* v *Bird* (1865), discussed below. For an account of the use of these nets in Wales, see Jenkins (1974) pp.41–3, and for diagrams of a bag net, see Fort and Brayshaw (1961) p.286 and Millichamp (1976) p.29.)

The terms 'putt' and 'putcher' under part (a) refer to conical or funnel basket filter traps traditionally made of hazel or willow, but more recently of wire. These traps are fixed in rows at right angles to the direction of the tide. Fish swim along the coastline into the mouth of the basket, become lodged in the point, and are soon asphyxiated by the flow of water through the gills (see Davis (1958) p.46).

The Commissioners of 1861 gave the following description of putts and putchers (at p.xi):

They are baskets of wickerwork, erected upon stages. The stake or framework is about 13 or 14 feet high, firmly fixed in the shore, in two parallel rows of various lengths from high-water mark seaward. These are bound together by cross bars, on which rest the putts and putchers, placed one above the other with the side mouth up or down stream, as they are intended to take fish on the ebb or flow of the tide. The putchers themselves are long conical baskets, with a mouth from three to five feet wide, and end in a narrow point that will prevent a fish of moderate size passing through. They are set upon the stake stages one above the other, some stages having as many as three, four, or even five hundred several putchers. Some fishermen possess above one thousand putchers. The putts, or putt-nets, as they are sometimes called, are more complicated and more carefully constructed. They are about 12 feet in length, and consist of three parts, which can be attached to each other as occasion requires. The diameter of the chief part, or *kipe*, is five feet at the mouth, and about fourteen inches at the narrow end. The next part which fits on to the *kipe* is about six inches wide at the narrow end, and takes large fish, by having cross bars placed in the opening, and to this again can be affixed at will another machine called the *fore-wheel*, which is capable of taking everything down to the size of a shrimp; nothing in short can escape.

(A similar description of the use of putchers was given in *Holford* v *George* (1868), and see Jenkins (1974) Ch.3 for a discussion of the use of putts and putchers in Wales.)

4.04 *Part (b) of the Description of 'Fixed Engine'*

Part (b) of the description refers to 'any fixed implement or engine for taking or facilitating the taking of fish'. These words are capable of wide interpretation. They include fishing weirs and fishing mill dams, considered below. Similarly, grids or racks placed to capture eels would fall within this part of the definition (see Fort and Brayshaw (1961) p.107), along with other fixed devices set to capture unwelcome species such as funnel-shaped fyke nets to capture pike (see Millichamp (1976) p.9). Eel and lamprey baskets (discussed in Ch.5) would also count as fixed engines under this criterion, as would a setline (discussed in Ch.3). It is even arguable that an ordinary rod and line, if set in a rod rest and left unattended, would qualify as a fixed engine in the same way. The list of fixed fishing implements under category (b) is open-ended.

4.05   Part (c) of the Description of 'Fixed Engine'

Part (c) of the description indicates that the term is to encompass 'any net secured by anchors and any net or other implement for taking fish fixed to the soil, or made stationary in any other way'. Originally s.ll of the Salmon Fishery Act 1861 had provided only that 'a net that is secured by anchors or otherwise temporarily fixed to the soil shall be deemed to be a "fixed engine"'. Under this provision it was decided in *Thomas* v *Jones* (1864), that no fixed engine was used where a net had one end secured by a large stone which gave way when a salmon hit the net and caused the net to entangle the fish. The judges reasoned that because the stone was dislodged by the weight of the fish, it was not fixed (also see *Birch* v *Turner* (1864)). The perversity of this reasoning was acknowledged by s.39 of the Salmon Fishery Act 1865 which extended the definition of fixed engine to include devices 'made stationary in any other way', and so overturned the effect of the ruling in *Thomas* v *Jones*. In the later case of *Olding* v *Wild* (1866) a net was secured at one end to a pole temporarily fixed into the soil and stretched across a river channel to a boat made fast to a buoy which was anchored. It was held that this was 'a very clear case' of a fixed engine. The words 'made stationary in any way', from the amending Act of 1865, placed the matter beyond doubt.

The use of anchors attached to a net was considered in *Percival* v *Stanton* (1954) where the accused operated a T-shaped net off the coast using cork floats at the top of the net, and three light metal anchors at the bottom, to keep it upright. The effect of the anchors was to act as a drag or brake upon the movement of the net and to prevent it getting into a 'shapeless tangle'. The anchors did not, and were not intended to, secure the net to the sea-bed as a stationary object. It was held that in these circumstances the net was not a fixed engine since it was neither fixed, nor secured by anchors, nor made stationary in any way. Although the anchors acted as a drag to reduce the movement and maintain the shape of the net, the fact remained that it did move, and so could not constitute a fixed engine.

4.06   Stop Nets

Another type of fishing which tested the extent of the meaning of 'fixed engine' was that using 'stop nets'. The Commissioners of 1861 (at p.xii) described the method of use of this type of net as follows:

At the ebb or flow of the tide a large boat is fixed or moored by anchor and long sharpened poles, in what is supposed to be the run of the fish; a large bag net upon a frame of from 25 to 35 feet beam, capable of being raised easily by the fisherman, is let out upon the side nearest the ebb or flow, and the bag flows underneath the boat. When a fish strikes the net is quickly raised, and the salmon secured in the bag.

(Further discussion of this type of fishing is to be found in Jenkins (1974) Ch.6.)

The legal status of stop net fishing was considered in *Gore* v *Special Commissioners for English Fisheries* (1871). In this case the accused fixed his boat by means of large poles tipped with iron. He then rested the top of a large triangular net on the gunwale of the boat facing the direction of the tide. Although the weight of the net and the two beams keeping the mouth of the net open, rested upon the edge of the boat, the fisherman kept his hand on the end of the beams in order to steady the net and to jerk it upwards to the horizontal should a fish enter. The question before the court was whether the net, used in this fashion, amounted to a fixed engine. On the one hand the boat itself was clearly fixed in place, on the other hand, the net and its frame could be raised, and so moved, in order to trap fish. It was held that despite the fact that the net was not attached immovably to the anchored boat, it was nonetheless a fixed engine, made stationary by being rested upon the side of the boat, and steadied by the hand of the accused.

4.07 Part (d) of the Description of 'Fixed Engine'

Part (d), the final part of the description of 'fixed engine', concerns a net placed in any inland or tidal water, and any engine, device, machine or contrivance, floating or otherwise, for placing or suspending or maintaining the net in working order or making it stationary, where the net is unattended by the owner or by any person authorised by the owner to use it. Fixed nets, unlike those which are moved or worked to encircle fish, are usually set and left unattended for a period of time until the user returns to collect his catch. Part (d) of the description of fixed engines makes it possible for nets which are 'placed or suspended' in land or tidal waters to become 'fixed', even if *not* stationary in the sense required for the earlier parts of the description. Thus the effect of part (d) is that a net, which ordinarily would be operated by manual movement, can become a fixed engine merely by being left unattended by the owner or an authorised user.

The phrase 'unattended by the owner' is problematic in that it may not always be apparent who is the owner of an unattended net, or a person duly authorised by him. The problem was considered in *Vance* v *Frost* (1894) where the accused were seen to tie one end of a net to a bank and the other to a boat and to leave it in place for 15 minutes. The justices held that the net was a fixed engine, but declined to convict in the absence of evidence to show who owned the net. On appeal it was held that the justices were wrong not to convict. On the evidence before them, the possession of the net by the accused was sufficient ground to infer that they owned it, and the justices should have convicted on that basis. Had this conclusion not been reached it would be difficult to secure convictions in practice since misusers of fixed engines would, in all likelihood, deny ownership and so make it impossibly difficult for the prosecution to prove ownership of a net.

4.08 *'Unauthorised' Fixed Engines*

Section 6 of the Salmon and Freshwater Fisheries Act 1975 places a prohibition on the use of an 'unauthorised' fixed engine. This is a means of allowing exceptions where it can be shown that the use involves the exercise of ancient right. Section ll of the Salmon Fishery Act l861 had stated that the prohibition on fixed engines should not affect any ancient right or mode of fishing lawfully exercised at the time of the passing of that Act, by virtue of any grant or charter or immemorial usage. In law 'immemorial usage' means usage from the commencement of the reign of Richard I (1189), but the continued use for many years in modern times is taken to be evidence of a right existing from time immemorial. The Salmon Fishery Act of l865 extended the exception to fixed engines used in the four years before 1861 (s.39 of the 1865 Act). The l865 Act also established Special Commissioners to inquire into the legality of all fixed engines used at that time (s.40 of the 1865 Act). If the Special Commissioners were not satisfied that a fixed engine was lawful they were empowered to remove it, but if satisfied of its lawfulness by ancient right they provided a certificate to the effect that the engine was a 'privileged engine' for the purposes of the Salmon Fishery Acts 1861–5 (ss.40 and 4l of the 1865 Act). These 'certificates of privilege', issued between 1865 and 1873, continue to be of importance in the present day. Section 6(3) of the 1975 Act makes it explicit that the prohibition on 'unauthorised' fixed engines does not extend to a fixed engine 'certified in pursuance of the Salmon Fishery Act 1865 to be a privileged fixed engine'. Today the production of a certificate of this kind remains the most important means by which a user of a fixed engine can show that his use is authorised.

The Special Commissioners carried out a thorough job of certifying privileged fixed engines between 1865 and 1873, but to allow for the possibility of their having overlooked lawful users and failed to certify privilege, all fisheries Acts since 1861 have left the option of the original criteria of authorised use. Hence in s.6(3)(b) of the present Act it is stated that 'unauthorised fixed engine' does not include 'a fixed engine which was in use for taking salmon or migratory trout during the open season of 1861, in pursuance of an ancient right or mode of fishing as lawfully exercised during that open season by virtue of any grant or charter or immemorial usage'. The use of this provision to establish authorised use is unlikely today, however, since all the major issues of privilege were determined in the decade following the 1861 Act. It is almost inconceivable that a fixed engine, not investigated by the Special Commissioners or otherwise challenged on grounds of legality, should now come to light.

Moreover, if a user of a fixed engine which was not certified by the Special Commissioners, were to seek to establish that its use was authorised by ancient right he would have the difficult task of showing that the engine was in use in l861 by virtue of a grant, charter or immemorial usage. Two points that would handicap such a claimant are apparent from the case law of the l860s. First, the engine in question must have been in *lawful* use in 1861. In *Holford* v *George*

(1868) the accused claimed the right to use putchers and stop nets for the purpose of catching salmon. It was found that proof of 45 years' usage prior to 1861 was not sufficient to establish immemorial usage of the putchers. In respect of the stop nets it was found that under a statute of 1423 (2 Hen.VI c.15, discussed in Ch.2) the nets were rendered unlawful. Consequently, although the nets may have been in use in 1861, it could not be shown that they were *lawfully* used. A second difficulty confronting a person claiming 'authorised use' would be that he must show that the engine in question was used as a matter of *private* rather than public right. Thus in *Bevins* v *Bird* (1865) the accused was unable to establish authorised use when he set a stake net in an area in which a public right of fishing existed. It was decided that the ancient rights which were protected under s.ll of the 1861 Act were private rights of individuals, and that the use of a fixed engine could not be justified where only a public right to fish using other methods existed. The practical effect of these rulings is that it is highly unlikely that a present-day user of a fixed engine could establish authorised use except by means of a certificate of privilege issued by the Special Commissioners.

(See para.13.04 for the future power of water authorities and local sea fisheries committees to authorise fixed engines under s.33 of the Salmon Act 1986.)

4.09   Offences in Relation to Fixed Engines

Subject to the exceptions that have been discussed above, the offences that exist in relation to fixed engines are, first, the placing of a fixed engine in any inland or tidal water, and second, the use of such an engine for taking or facilitating the taking of salmon or migratory trout or for detaining or obstructing their free passage (s.6(1) of the 1975 Act). It is important to appreciate the distinction between these two offences. Under the original prohibition (s.11 of the 1861 Salmon Fishery Act) the offence had been the placing or use of a fixed engine *for the purpose* of catching or facilitating the catching of salmon, or detaining or obstructing their free passage. The courts had interpreted this to mean that the offence was not committed unless the instrument used was either an instrument peculiarly adapted for catching salmon, such as the putts used in *Lyne* v *Leonard* (1868), or the instrument was capable of being used to catch salmon *and* used with the intention of doing so. Hence in *Watts* v *Lucas* (1871) the accused was found not guilty of using a fixed engine to catch salmon where the stake net which he had placed was found to be not an instrument peculiarly adapted for taking salmon nor used with the intention of catching salmon. This interpretation of the law prevailed up until the enactment of the present Act in 1975.

A peculiarity of s.6 of the present Act is that it brings about a change in the law which was probably not intended. The 1975 Act was brought into effect, as stated in the preamble, 'to *consolidate* the Salmon and Freshwater Fisheries Act 1923 and other enactments relating to freshwater fisheries'. Nevertheless, the wording of s.6 of the present Act goes beyond 'consolidation' of the former law, and creates a substantially new offence of *placing* a fixed engine in any inland or tidal water. By subdividing the former crime into two offences of (a) placing a fixed engine . . . (s.6(1)(a)), and (b) using an unauthorised fixed engine for taking salmon or migratory trout . . . (s.6(1)(b)), the requirement of the old law that the placing of the engine is *for the purpose* of taking salmon is no longer present. Under the new law s.6(1)(a) makes it an offence to place a fixed engine without any requirement that it is placed for the purpose of taking, facilitating the taking, detaining or obstructing the free passage of salmon or migratory trout. In short, the offence has become one of strict or absolute liability, for which no intention to catch any particular kind of fish need be shown.

The interpretation of s.6(1)(a) of the Act was considered recently in *Champion* v *Maughan* (1984). It was found that the accused had set a net in tidal waters at right angles to a beach, the net was made stationary and so constituted a fixed engine. The net was set with the intention of catching cod, though it was found that it would form an obstruction to salmon and migratory trout swimming close to the shore in their passage along the coastline. On these facts the only issue was whether the accused had placed a fixed engine in any inland or tidal water. It was held that the words were clear and unambiguous and created an absolute offence which was committed notwithstanding the lack of an intention to take, or facilitate the taking, or detain or obstruct, the free passage of salmon or migratory trout. Thus the offence under s.6(1)(a) requires no more than the placing of a fixed engine in inland or tidal waters and the intention to catch sea fish will not be a defence.

The absolute offence of placing a fixed engine created under s.6(1)(a) of the Salmon and Freshwater Fisheries Act 1975 is capable of operating harshly if strictly applied. For this reason many water authorities have made byelaws modifying the operation of the Act within their areas which permit the placing of instruments which would otherwise fall within the description of 'fixed engine'. Typical examples of dispensations of this sort are made in respect of fixed fyke nets or traps for taking eels, basket traps for taking lampreys, bottle traps for taking minnows for bait, and other instruments specifically authorised by a water authority. Since water authorities have no explicit power to authorise the placing of fixed engines amongst the purposes for which they are empowered to make byelaws under Sch.3 to the 1975 Act, it must be assumed that byelaws authorising fixed engines have been created under the catch-all byelaw-creating power under para.36 of Sch.3 to the Act. This provision permits water authorities to create byelaws for the purpose of the better execution of the Act and the better protection, preservation and improvement of any salmon fisheries, trout fisheries, freshwater fisheries and eel fisheries in a water authority area. In addition to the power of a water authority to authorise fixed engines, a Ministerial order under s.28(3) and para.1(b) of Sch.3 to the Act may permit a water authority to erect and work a fixed engine for catching salmon or migratory trout within the area for which the order is to apply (see para.7.13).

The meaning of 'tidal waters' in s.6(1)(a) of the Salmon and Freshwater Fisheries Act 1975 (as the words featured in s.11(1) of the Salmon and Freshwater Fisheries Act 1923) was considered in *Ingram* v *Percival* (1968). Here a net intended for taking salmon and migratory trout was fixed at a point 100 yards from the shore and beyond the low-water mark. On behalf of the accused it was argued that 'tidal waters' meant that part of a river or the sea between the limits of ebb and flow of a normal tide; that is, those waters where tides have a lateral but not a vertical effect. The Queen's Bench Divisional Court declined to accept this view, and held that 'tidal waters' meant *any* water where the tide flowed or reflowed regardless of whether the flow could be observed by lateral or vertical motion. It followed that there was an overlap between 'tidal waters' and the sea, and the accused was convicted notwithstanding that the fixed engine was placed beyond the limits of the foreshore.

The meaning of 'inland water', as it arises under s.6(1)(a) of the 1975 Act, is defined in s.135 of the Water Resources Act 1963, and is considered in para.12.03.

Originally s.11 of the Salmon Fishery Act 1861 had given the right to *any person* to seize and destroy fixed engines for catching salmon. Now that right is restricted by s.6(2) of the present Act to persons acting under direction from the water authority. Such persons may take possession of or destroy engines placed or used in contravention of s.6. This provision provides an interesting contrast to other parts of the Act which permit forfeiture of nets and other equipment where ordered by a court (see para.10.06). Under s.6(2) no court order is required to authorise the destruction of a fixed engine in contravention of s.6, and therefore a water authority official would be empowered to destroy a fixed engine under s.6(2) even where a court declined to make an order for its forfeiture. (For discussion of other powers of water authorities, see Ch.7.)

As a postscript to this discussion of fixed engines, it is pertinent to note that even if a fixed engine is lawful under s.6 of the 1975 Act, it may be subject to a licensing requirement (see Ch.6). A fixed engine will also be subject to a weekly close time or close season (see Ch.5).

(See para.13.04 on amendments to the law relating to the placing and use of fixed engines made by s.33 of the Salmon Act 1986.)

4.10   Fishing Weirs and Fishing Mill Dams

Although capable of coming within the definition of 'fixed engine', discussed above, specific provision is made under the Salmon and Freshwater Fisheries Act 1975 for 'fishing weirs' (s.7) and 'fishing mill dams' (s.8). A 'fishing weir' is defined as any erection, structure or obstruction fixed to the soil either temporarily or permanently, across a river or branch of a river, and used for the exclusive purpose of taking or facilitating the taking of fish (s.41(1)). A 'fishing mill dam' is defined as a dam used or intended to be used partly for the purpose of taking or facilitating the taking of fish, and partly for the purpose of supplying water for milling or other purposes (s.41(1)). The essence of these definitions is the fish-catching capability of the operations. A dam built solely for milling purposes, and without any device for catching fish has been held not to be a fishing mill dam (in *Garnett* v *Backhouse* (1867)).

The purpose behind the restrictions upon the use of fishing weirs and fishing mill dams again lies in the need to maximise access to spawning grounds for migratory fish. Although the upper reaches of some rivers are inaccessible to fish because of natural obstructions such as waterfalls, many more watercourses are obstructed by man-made constructions. In the past some of these obstructions were so effective as to present a total bar to access by migratory fish. In the opinion of the Salmon Fishery Commissioners of 1861, it was:

obvious that to exclude the fish from entering the rivers at all is a surer way of destroying the breed than even the most deadly mode of making war upon them when they are there. Moreover it is certain that these barriers to the passage of the fish, even if they do not absolutely shut them out, offer great facility and encouragement to the unfair means employed for destroying them. (1861 Report p.ix.)

In response to this the Salmon Fishery Act 1861 made extensive provision for the regulation of artificial obstacles to the migration of fish, and in many cases made the use of fishing weirs and fishing mill dams unlawful. Much of the legislation introduced in 1861 has been re-enacted in the present legislation. It is, however, a testimony to the effectiveness of the original provisions of the 1861 law and their effective enforcement that very few fishing weirs or fishing mill dams remain in operation today. Reporting in 1961, the Bledisloe Committee were aware of only one example of a fishing mill dam operating at that time (Bledisloe (1961) p.29). Nonetheless, the law remains in force as a means of preventing a revival of the problem inherent in these kinds of obstructions.

4.11   Fishing Weirs

In respect of fishing weirs, the initial requirement, under s.7(1) of the Salmon and Freshwater Fisheries Act 1975, is that only 'authorised' weirs may be used for taking or facilitating the taking of salmon or migratory trout. 'Authorised', in this context, means that the weir was lawfully in use on 6 August 1861 by virtue of a grant or charter or immemorial usage. This requirement is analogous to the requirement of proving ancient right in respect of a fixed engine (discussed above) and presents the same difficulties to a person seeking to establish authorised use in the present day (this was considered in *Rolle* v *Whyte* (1868), and *Leconfield* v *Lonsdale* (1870)).

Given that a weir is 'authorised' in the required sense, if it extends more than half way across a river at its lowest state of water, it is required to have a free gap or opening situated in the deepest part of the river to allow passage of salmon or migratory trout (s.7(2)). Detailed specification of the size and positioning of the gap is provided for. The sides of the gap must be in line with and parallel to the direction of the stream at the weir; the bottom of the gap must be level with the natural bed of the river above and below the gap; and the width of the gap at its narrowest part must be not less than one-tenth of the width of the river (s.7(2)). Overall, however, a free gap need not be more than 40 feet wide but must not be less than 3 feet wide (s.7(3)). To prevent circumvention of these requirements it is made an offence to alter the bed of a river so as to reduce the flow of water through the gap (s.7(4)). (On the legality of a weir and the nature of a 'free gap', see *Devonshire* v *Drohan* (1900).)

4.12   Fishing Mill Dams

In respect of fishing mill dams the legal requirements are analogous. The initial requirement, under s.8(1) of the Salmon and Freshwater Fisheries Act 1975, is that a fishing mill dam must be 'authorised' to be used for the taking, or facilitating the taking, of salmon or migratory trout. 'Authorised' means that the fishing mill dam was lawfully in use on 6 August 1861 by virtue of a grant or charter or immemorial usage. A fishing mill dam so authorised may not lawfully be used for taking salmon or migratory trout unless it has attached to it a fish pass which is approved by the Minister. The fish pass must be maintained so that it has a flow of water running through it which will enable salmon and migratory trout to pass up and down at all times (fish passes are considered below). Use of a fishing mill dam in contravention of these provisions is an offence under s.8(3) of the Act. The effect of these provisions is emphasised and enhanced by s.8(4) which stipulates that failure to provide a fish pass will result in the right to use the dam for fishing being deemed to have ceased and forfeited for ever.

Failure to provide a fish pass will entitle the water authority for the area to remove any cage, crib, trap, box, cruive or other obstruction to the free passage of fish (s.8(4)). That is to say, the water authority will be entitled to remove whatever device was used in conjunction with the dam for trapping fish. It is likely that this provision and its predecessors have contributed to the decline in numbers of fishing mill dams. It is clear that the provision prevents the restoration of fishing mill dams which were once authorised but have subsequently fallen into disrepair, so that where a fishing mill dam was used for fishing, but was subsequently abandoned and appliances for fishing removed, it was held that it ceased to be a fishing mill dam (*Rossiter* v *Pike* (1878)).

Both fishing weirs and fishing mill dams may be subject to a licensing requirement (see Ch.6). Similarly, they will be subject to the general law with respect to close seasons and weekly close times (see Ch.5).

4.13   Boxes and Cribs in Fishing Weirs and Fishing Mill Dams

In addition to the requirements under ss.7 and 8 of the Salmon and Freshwater Fisheries Act 1975, a number of other restrictions govern the lawful use of either a fishing weir or a fishing mill dam to take salmon or migratory trout. These restrictions concern the use of a box or crib to take fish under s.16 of the Act. The mechanism by which fish are taken using such devices was considered in *Hodgson* v *Little* (1864) (discussed in para.5.05). If a box or crib is to be used lawfully, three requirements are imposed: (a) the upper surface of the sill must be level with the bed of the river; (b) the bars or inscales of the heck or upstream side must not be nearer to each other than 2 inches, and must be capable of being removed, and must be placed perpendicularly; (c) there must not be attached to any such box or crib any spur or tail wall, leader or outrigger of a greater length than 20 feet from the upper or lower side of the box or crib (s.16(2)). The restriction on bar separation and the requirement that bars be placed perpendicularly are intended to prevent a trap being used to take undersized fish. The limitations upon spurs, tail walls, leaders or outriggers are imposed in order to prevent the free gap being rendered less effective by funnelling fish into the trap.

4.14   Fish Passes

Notwithstanding the strict restrictions which the Salmon and Freshwater

Fisheries Act 1975 places upon fishing weirs and fishing mill dams, the law stops short of placing a total prohibition on artificial obstructions to the passage of migratory fish. Nevertheless, where an artificial·obstruction is not unlawful, the Act may still make it subject to a number of measures calculated to minimise the effect of the obstruction. The main solution provided to the problem of artificial obstructions that are not unlawful is that a fish pass, or ladder, should be provided, wherever possible, to allow salmon and migratory trout to bypass the obstruction on the way to their spawning grounds.

Reliable records exist of salmon jumping heights of up to ll feet 4 inches, from head-water level to tail-water level (Calderwood (1931) p.94), but in practice very much lesser heights serve to bar access to the higher reaches of a river. Pryce-Tannatt takes the view that a realistic maximum height for most salmon is only about half the record height:

A sheer fall of 6 ft. is probably, to all intents and purposes, about the maximum practicable for the great majority of salmon, even under the most favourable conditions, among the latter of which must be included plenty of room and' depth below to enable the fish to develop the necessary velocity. It would be safe to assume that a 6 ft. jump is not possible for any fish less than 2 lb. in weight, and accordingly for the majority of sea trout, for it needs no elaboration to appreciate that the lighter and weaker the fish the less chance will it have of successfully opposing its body against a mass of water moving against it with considerable velocity. (Pryce-Tannatt (1938) p.34.)

Heights of greater than six feet can be surmounted by migrating fish, however, where a channel of water is directed from the main flow over the obstruction, along a less steeply inclined route. This is the idea behind the fish pass. The designs and modes of operation of different types of fish pass are diverse, but the general idea is that the rate of water flow through the bypass channel is reduced to a much lesser rate than that in the main stream where the obstruction is situated. At most the flow through the fish pass should not exceed five feet per second, which in practice is thought to be the greatest water velocity that fish will be able to swim against (Fort and Brayshaw (1961) p.204). The diminution in water flow is brought about through a reduction in the gradient of the bypass channel, or a system of baffles to reduce flow, or a combination of both of these. Providing that the rate of flow is reduced sufficiently, and that the design of the pass is otherwise satisfactory, migratory fish are capable of surmounting obstacles of considerable height. The theory of fish passes is relatively simple. In practice, though, 'the construction of a fish pass is not an exact science' (Bledisloe (1961) p.30), and the fundamental and universal problem has never been conclusively solved 'namely [how] to induce fish to forsake the main obstructed flow for a smaller, easier channel, and implicit in this problem is the assumption that the discrepancy in the two flows is considerable (otherwise one is no longer discussing a fish pass but a diversion of the river)' (Fort and Brayshaw (1961) p.202).

Despite the scientific and practical reservations about the construction of effective fish passes, the Salmon and Freshwater Fisheries Act 1975 places faith in fish passes as a means of bypassing obstructions and securing the free passage of salmon and migratory trout to their spawning grounds. Sections 9 to 12 of the Act are devoted to the regulation of fish passes.

(The literature on fish pass construction and operation includes: Pryce-Tannatt (1938); Fort and Brayshaw (1961) pp.202–20; and Wrangles (1979) Ch.3.)

4.15 The Owner or Occupier's Duty to Construct a Fish Pass

Section 9 of the Salmon and Freshwater Fisheries Act 1975 imposes a general duty to construct a fish pass where an obstruction to the passage of salmon or migratory trout is created or restored. The first situation envisaged is where an innovation takes place: a new dam is constructed, or an existing dam is altered to create an increased obstruction, or any other obstruction is created, increased or caused (s.9(1)(a)). The second situation envisaged is where restoration takes place: a dam which by any cause has been destroyed or taken down to the extent of one half of its length is rebuilt or reinstated (s.9(1)(b)). In either of these circumstances, the owner or occupier of the dam or obstruction is required to construct a fish pass, of such a form and dimensions as the Minister may approve, if notice of the requirement is given by the water authority for the area. The owner or occupier is bound to construct the fish pass within such a reasonable time as may be specified in the notice, and after construction he must maintain it in an efficient state (s.9(1)). Should he fail to construct or maintain the fish pass, as required, he will be guilty of an offence (s.9(2)).

The Act does not stop at the creation of a criminal offence of failing to construct or maintain a fish pass. It goes further by providing that the water authority for the area may cause required work to be done (s.9(3)). Read literally, this appears to mean that the water authority may do the work themselves as soon as they have given notice that it is required. It is more likely, though, that it must be interpreted to mean construction or maintenance work *after* the expiry of the reasonable time given to the owner or occupier by the water authority's notice. Any other interpretation could lead to highly capricious results. Should the water authority cause the work to be done they are empowered to enter on the dam or obstruction or any land adjoining it, and recover the expense of doing the work from the person in default (s.9(3)).

A supplementary provision enacted under s.18(1) of the 1975 Act makes it an offence to obstruct any lawfully authorised person doing work authorised by s.9. This would make it an offence either for the owner or occupier to obstruct or interfere with water authority officials where he failed to perform the work himself, or for any other person to obstruct fish pass construction work performed either by the owner, occupier or the water authority.

To clarify and delimit the extent of s.9, s.9(4) imposes three qualifications. First, nothing in the section authorises the doing of anything that may injuriously affect any public waterworks or navigable river, canal, or inland navigation, or any dock, the supply of water to which is authorised under any Act of Parliament (s.9(4)(a)). The effect of this is to exclude the operation of s.9 from navigable and artificial watercourses where water supply has been specifically provided for by

Parliament. Second, nothing in s.9 prevents a person from removing a fish pass in order to repair or alter a dam or other obstruction provided that the fish pass is restored to its former state of efficiency within a reasonable time (s.9(4)(b)). Third, s.9(4)(c) provides that nothing in the section applies to an alteration of a dam or other obstruction unless the alteration consists of a rebuilding or reinstatement of a dam or other obstruction destroyed or taken down to the extent of one-half its length. Alternatively nothing in s.9 applies unless the altered dam or obstruction causes more obstruction to the passage of salmon or migratory trout than was caused by it as lawfully constructed or maintained at any previous date. Both of these things are implicit in the initial statement of the offence under s.9.

4.16   The Power of a Water Authority to Construct a Fish Pass

Section 9 of the Salmon and Freshwater Fisheries Act 1975, as has been seen, permits a water authority to compel an owner or occupier of a dam or obstruction to install a fish pass, either he may perform the work himself or the water authority will perform it on his behalf. The counterpart of this is s.10 of the Act, which empowers the water authority to construct or alter fish passes at their own initiative without assistance from the owner or occupier. With the written consent of the Minister, a water authority may construct and maintain, in connection with any dam, a fish pass of such form and dimensions as the Minister may approve so long as no injury is done to either milling power or the supply of water to any navigable river, canal or other inland navigation (s.10(1)).

The inherent difficulty with the power of the water authority to construct a fish pass under s.9 of the Act was noted in the Bledisloe Report: 'A fish pass without a supply of water is, of course, useless and the difficulty arises from the fact that any diversion of water from a pass must cause some degree of injury, however slight, to milling power or to the needs of navigation. If strictly construed, therefore, the requirement that no injury shall be done to these interests can render this provision of the Act . . . unworkable.' (Bledisloe (1961) p.32.) The Report suggested that the proviso should be reworded to require fish passes to be constructed with 'as little injury as is compatible with the presentation and passage of fish'. Regrettably this never became enacted into law. It is arguable that, given the unreasonableness of a literal reading of the requirement not to reduce milling power or the water required for navigation, something other than the literal meaning was originally intended by Parliament, and a judge should interpret 'no injury' to mean 'no significant injury', or 'no injury beyond that which would inevitably arise due to the reduction of water required for the fish pass to function properly'. The question remains to be determined by the courts (though it was raised incidentally in *Hodgson* v *Little* (1864), discussed in para.5.05).

Section 10(2) of the Act empowers a water authority, with the written consent of the Minister, to abolish, alter or restore to a former state of efficiency, any existing fish pass or free gap, or substitute another fish pass or free gap. ('Free gaps' were considered in relation to fishing weirs, in para.4.11.) Demolition, alteration and reconstruction of fish passes under this provision is also subject to the requirement that milling power, or the supply of water to any navigable river, canal or other inland navigation is not diminished. Within the sphere of s.10, any person who injures a new or existing fish pass will become liable to pay the expenses incurred by the water authority in repairing the damage (s.10(3)).

A consequence of fish pass construction not being an exact science is that a pass constructed in all respects in accordance with expert recommendations may still fail to operate effectively. With the present state of knowledge, the reaction of a population of migratory fish to a new or newly modified fish pass is impossible to predict. Sometimes a fish pass will be ineffective unless minor adjustments are carried out (see Bledisloe (1961) p.30). In order to give a legal power to bring about such alterations, s.11(1) of the 1975 Act makes it possible for ministerial approval or consent to be provisional until the Minister notifies the applicant, who is obliged to perform construction or restoration work on a fish pass, that the pass is functioning to the Minister's satisfaction. During a period of provisional approval or consent, the Minister may revoke his provisional approval after giving the applicant not less than 90 days' notice of his intention to do so (s.11(2)). In the event of revocation of the provisional approval, the Minister may extend the time period within which the fish pass is to be constructed (s.11(3)). Otherwise, the Minister may approve and certify the fish pass if he is of the opinion it is efficient in all respects, whether it was constructed under the provisions of the Act or not (s.11(4)). Where a pass has received the final approval from the Minister then it is deemed to conform with the requirements of the Act, whether or not it has been constructed by a person or in the manner specified by the Act (s.11(5)).

4.17 Supplementary Provisions on the Power of a Water Authority to Construct a Fish Pass

Section 18 of the Salmon and Freshwater Fisheries Act 1975 enacts a number of supplementary provisions in relation to the construction of a fish pass by a water authority under s.10. In the first place it is made an offence to obstruct a legally authorised person doing any act authorised under s.10 (s.18(1)). Second, a procedural constraint is imposed in so far as the Minister is not permitted to give his consent to the construction, abolition or alteration of a fish pass or abolition of a free gap under s.10, unless certain formalities are observed. They are that reasonable notice of the water authority's application under the section has been served on the owner or occupier of the dam, fish pass or free gap, and this notice includes a plan and specification of the work proposed. If the owner or occupier makes any objections to the work the Minister is bound to take these into account (s.18(2)). Third, if injury is caused to a dam by reason of construction, abolition or alteration of a fish pass or alteration of a free gap under s.10, the person suffering loss as a consequence is entitled to recover compensation from the water authority for the loss (s.18(3)). The compensation payable is subject to the reservation that proceedings for recovery are commenced within two years from the completion of the work. This is in contrast to the general limitation period of six years in respect of claims for tortious injury (s.2, Limitation Act 1980, see Winfield and Jolowicz (1984) p.734). In the event of a dispute as to the amount payable, the matter is to be settled by a single arbitrator appointed by the Minister (s.18(4) and (5)).

4.18 Offences in Relation to Fish Passes

The effectiveness of ss.9 to 11 of the Salmon and Freshwater Fisheries Act 1975, governing fish passes, is buttressed by s.12, which creates a range of criminal offences in relation to them. Section 12(1) concerns acts done by 'any person', and therefore extends beyond the owner or occupier of a dam or obstruction referred to in s.9. Offences are committed where a person: (a) wilfully alters or injures a fish pass; or (b) does any act whereby salmon or trout are obstructed or liable to be obstructed in using a fish pass or whereby a fish pass is rendered less efficient; or (c) alters a dam on the bed or banks of a river so as to render a fish pass less efficient; or (d) uses any contrivance or does any act whereby salmon or trout are in any way liable to be scared, hindered or prevented from passing through a fish pass. In each of these cases the offender will be liable to pay any expenses incurred in restoring the fish pass to its former state of efficiency (s.12(1)).

Two observations are in order here. First, it is to be noted that under s.12(1)(b) and (d) reference is made to 'trout' rather than 'migratory trout' as are referred to in the previous sections. The effect of this is that these offences are capable of being committed where no migratory trout are present if non-migratory trout such as brown trout or rainbow trout are present (see para.1.03 on categories of fish). A second observation is that only s.12(1)(a) is preceded by the word 'wilfully'. This means that the other offences are capable of being committed without a specific intention to obstruct fish. For example, doing an act whereby salmon actually *are* obstructed in using a fish pass, without *intending* to cause any such obstruction, would still be an offence under s.12(1)(b).

Section 12(2) of the Act provides an elaboration on the offence of altering a dam so as to render a fish pass less efficient, by extending the meaning of the word 'alter'. It states that an owner or occupier of a dam shall be deemed to have 'altered' the dam if it is damaged, destroyed or allowed to fall into a state of disrepair, and after notice is served upon him by the water authority for the area he fails to render the fish pass as efficient as before the damage or destruction. Hence it may be possible for an owner to 'alter' a dam not only by his acts but also by his omissions to act.

Additional offences created under s.12(3) are: (a) where *any person* does an act for the purpose of preventing salmon or trout from passing through a fish pass, or takes, or attempts to take, any salmon or trout in its passage through a fish pass; or (b) places any obstruction, uses any contrivance or does any act whereby salmon or trout may be scared, deterred or in any way prevented from freely entering and passing up and down a free gap at all periods of the year. In respect of the first offence of preventing fish passing through a fish pass, the wording makes it clear that the act must be for that purpose. That is, the act must be performed with the *intention* of preventing fish entering the pass: accidental or negligent acts which happen to have that effect will not be sufficient to constitute the offence. Taking a salmon in its passage through a fish pass may also amount to an offence under sections of the Act relating to prohibited methods (see Ch.3) or an offence of unlicensed fishing (see Ch.6). The offence under s.12(3)(b) of placing an obstruction whereby fish may be deterred from passing between a free gap is also an offence where no intention needs to be shown. The placing of the obstruction is all that is needed for the offence to be committed. As an exception to the offence of obstructing a free gap under s.12(3)(b), s.12(4) states that the provision is not to apply to a temporary bridge or board used for crossing a free gap, where it is taken away immediately after use.

4.19   Sluices

There was a great expansion in the use of water power for milling from the seventeenth century onwards. As a result of this many rivers became 'terraced' by weirs designed to provide milling heights of at least five feet to run undershot wheels. This was an ominous development for stocks of migratory fish for the reason pointed out by Hartley:

> A salmon can, in good conditions, swim under a sluice when the head is not greater than 2 feet, corresponding to a water velocity of 6 feet per second for a short distance. A mill working at a 5 feet head would thus represent an obstruction incapable of passage. Should the mill run down the level of the head pond, passage would be possible, but no miller would leave a sluice open when he was losing head, and his natural instinct would be to leave them shut overnight to ensure maximum power in the morning. (Wrangles (1979) p.7.)

Worse still, this accumulation of water for milling purposes was capable of depriving fish passes of the flow of water required for effective operation.

These threats were countered by a series of measures, the latest of which is s.13 of the Salmon and Freshwater Fisheries Act 1975. This section requires that in waters frequented by salmon or migratory trout, any sluices for drawing off water which would otherwise flow over a dam, must be kept shut on Sundays and at all times when the water is not required for milling purposes. This is to be done in such a manner as to cause water to flow through any fish pass connected with the dam, or if there is no fish pass, then over the dam (s.13(1)). Failure to close sluices as required by this section is an offence, subject to certain exceptions. First, there is a proviso to s.13(1) to the effect that the offence is not committed where permission in writing is granted by the water authority for the area. Second, sluices may be opened to let off water in a flood. At such a time there would not be any shortage of water passing through the fish pass or over the dam. Third, sluices may be opened where it is necessary for purposes of navigation. Fourth, sluices may be opened for the purpose of cleaning or repairing the dam or mill or its appurtenances, where previous notice in writing has been given to the water authority. Finally, s.13(3) allows sluices to be opened for 'milling purposes'. This is somewhat odd in view of the overall objective of the restriction, and appears capable of rendering the general prohibition on the misuse of sluices ineffectual should a miller wish to operate his mill at all times. Although the early mills had tended not to operate at night or on Sundays:

. . . by 1923 the impact of weirs and milling had assumed an altogether more dangerous dimension owing to the use of turbines for electrical generation, and this activity was accepted as milling for the purpose of the [1923 Salmon and Freshwater Fisheries] Act. It was possible therefore to justify the perpetual denial of water to a fish pass on the grounds that work was continuing day and night through the week, and in one case that the turbine provided power to blow the organ in the local church on Sunday as well. (Wrangles (1979) pp.7–8.)

This difficulty was considered in the Bledisloe Report (1961) where it was suggested that, to avoid damage to fisheries, there should be a power to prevent diversion of water for milling purposes unless a significant quantity is allowed to pass at all times of the year. Regrettably this recommendation never became enacted into law, and the problem remains. Fortunately the number of instances of misuse under this exception is likely to be small in view of the small number of dams or mills which are presently in operation.

4.20   Gratings

'Grating' is defined under s.41(1) of the Salmon and Freshwater Fisheries Act 1975 to mean 'a device approved by the Minister for preventing the passage of salmon or trout through a conduit or channel in which it is placed'. Although the word 'trout', rather than 'migratory trout', is used in this definition, the sections governing gratings make it clear that their main purpose is to safeguard stocks of *migratory* salmonids (ss.14 and 15 of the 1975 Act). The reason for seeking to prevent these fish from passing through diverted channels is that, unless grated, such channels would draw fish into mill turbines and so bring about extensive destruction of stocks.

Although salmon and migratory trout may be destroyed by mill turbines at any time of the year, there are three stages of migration at which they are especially vulnerable to this hazard. First, an ascending fish seeking access to spawning grounds may be attracted into the outflow, or tail race, of a mill, particularly if the channel is carrying a strong flow of water. Second, salmon which have spawned, known as 'kelts', migrate seaward and may drop down into the head race of the mill. Third, in the spring there are likely to be downstream migrations of shoals of young salmon, known as 'smolts', making their first journey to sea which, because of their size, require fine meshed gratings to prevent them passing down to be mutilated by mill turbines.

To prevent large-scale losses of fish at the three main stages of migration, the Act requires gratings to be placed at the inlets and outlets to diversions of water where a hazard exists. Usually this means the installation of a metal grid of a mesh size appropriate to the type of fish which it is intended to stop, though the definition of 'grating', given above, makes it clear that a 'grating' may be *any* device which prevents the passage of fish through a channel. Thus on a mill tail race, if approved by the Minister, it would be lawful for a miller to install a paddle wheel, sometimes known as an 'idle wheel', to prevent upstream migration. This would count as a 'grating' for the purposes of the Act. Similarly the use of an electric current, or 'electric screen', would constitute a grating if used with ministerial approval. (Contrast the view implicit in the Bledisloe Report (1961 p.35) that the present definition of 'grating' does not, but *should*, extend to idle wheels and electric screens.)

(For an account of the operation of idle wheels, see Fort and Brayshaw (1961) pp.290-2. On controlling fish by means of electrical screening, see Vibert (1967) and Wrangles (1979) pp.107-12.)

4.21   The Owner or Occupier's Duty to Install Gratings

The Salmon and Freshwater Fisheries Act 1975 provides for two sorts of obligation with respect to gratings. Section 14 is concerned with gratings installed by the owner or occupier of an undertaking which constitutes a hazard to fish, whilst s.15 deals with gratings placed by water authorities. The power of a water authority to install gratings is considered in the next paragraph. In respect of the owner or occupier's duty to install gratings, s.14(1) requires that where water is diverted from waters frequented by salmon and migratory trout by any conduit or artificial channel, to be used for a water or canal undertaking, or for the purposes of any mill, then the owner of the undertaking or the occupier of the mill must place a grating or gratings across the conduit or channel to prevent the descent of salmon or migratory trout. Similarly, the owner of the undertaking, or the occupier of the mill, is bound to place a grating or gratings across any out-fall of the conduit or channel for the purpose of preventing such fish entering the out-fall (s.14(2)). Having installed such gratings, the owner or occupier is then bound to maintain them at his own cost. In each case the grating in question must be constructed and placed in such a manner and position as may be approved by the Minister (s.14(3)).

The general obligation upon the owner or occupier to place gratings is made subject to a number of exceptions. First, both s.14(1) and s.14(2) allow an exemption to be granted by the water authority for the area. The second exception is that no such grating is to be placed in such a way as to interfere with the passage of boats on any navigable canal (s.14(5)). Third, a specific exception is made for the grating requirements to be held in abeyance during any period of the year prescribed by byelaw. In conjunction with this, para.27 of Sch.3 to the Act gives water authorities the power to make byelaws determining the period of the year during which gratings need not be maintained. A number of water authorities make explicit provision for the maintenance of gratings. For example, rule 16 of the Yorkshire Water Authority Fishery Byelaws states:

(a) The obligations imposed by section 14(1) of the Salmon and Freshwater Fisheries Act 1975 to place and maintain a grating or gratings across any conduit or artificial channel for the purpose of preventing the descent of salmon or migratory trout shall not be in force during the period from 1st June to the following 31st January.

(b) The obligations imposed by section 14(2) of the Salmon and Freshwater Fisheries Act 1975 to place and maintain a grating or gratings across the outfall of any conduit or artificial channel for the purpose of preventing salmon or migratory trout entering such outfall shall not be in force during the period from 1st February to the following 1st July.

The reasoning behind this exception is that the danger to fish stocks through water diversion hazards only exists at the times of the year when fish migration takes place. At least in respect of downstream migration, this is predominantly during the spring, and therefore the justification for requiring gratings to be placed and maintained may not hold at other times of the year.

The fourth exception is that under s.14(7) obligations upon the occupier of a mill to place gratings arise only where the conduit or channel was constructed on or after 18 July 1923, that is, the date of passing of the Salmon and Freshwater Fisheries Act 1923. Curiously this exception is limited to 'the occupier of a mill', which intimates that the owner of a water or canal undertaking cannot claim the benefit of the exception, and is bound to install gratings whatever the antiquity of the water diversion. The only conceivable justification for this difference of treatment is that water or canal undertakings generally operate under the ownership of large concerns which are better able to absorb the costs of grating installation and maintenance than a miller operating a much smaller enterprise.

4.22 The Power of a Water Authority to Install Gratings

As the previous paragraph indicated, the owner or occupier of an artificial diversion of water will not always be obliged to place gratings by s.14 of the Salmon and Freshwater Fisheries Act 1975. Where he is not obliged, a water authority may at its own initiative place and maintain a grating, and bear the cost of doing so. Water authorities, with written ministerial consent, are given wide powers to place gratings in waters frequented by salmon and migratory trout (s.15(1)). They may place gratings, of such form and dimensions as they may determine, at suitable places in any 'watercourse, mill race, cut, leat, conduit or other channel' for conveying water, for any purpose, from any water frequented by migratory salmonids. When so placed, the installation and maintenance will be at the expense of the water authority (s.15(1)(a)). The language of s.15 indicates that the general powers given to water authorities are more extensive than the duties placed upon other individuals and bodies under s.14. It is to be noted, though, that the power under s.15(1)(a) only arises where water flows *from* waters frequented by salmon and migratory trout (contrast s.15(3), discussed below).

Where a grating has been placed by a water authority, under s.15(1)(a), the water authority is also empowered to take measures to counteract any diminution of flow through the diversion which would otherwise be caused by the installation of the grating. In particular the water authority may cause the 'watercourse, mill race, cut, leat, conduit or other channel' where the grating is placed, to be widened or deepened so far as is necessary to compensate for the diminution of any flow of water caused by the placing of the grating. Alternatively, the water authority is empowered to take some other means to prevent the flow being prejudicially diminished or injured. In either case any measures taken are at the expense of the authority (s.15(1)(b)). The object behind this subsection is that the protection of fishery interests should not be pursued to the detriment of other water users. This is borne out by the express liability under which water authorities are placed to compensate persons who are injured by action taken under s.15, discussed below.

4.23   Offences in Relation to Gratings Installed by a Water Authority

Several offences are created in respect of gratings placed in accordance with s.l5(1) of the 1975 Act. It is an offence to: (a) injure a grating; or (b) remove a grating or any part of it, except during a period of the year when gratings need not be maintained under a byelaw; or (c) open a grating improperly; or (d) permit a grating to be injured, or removed (other than where permitted by byelaw under para.27 of Sch.3 to the Act) or improperly opened (s.15(2)). These offences apply only in respect of outflows of water from waters frequented by salmon and trout. In respect of inflows of water, water authorities may, with written ministerial consent, adopt any means approved by the Minister for preventing the ingress of salmon or trout into waters in which they or their spawning beds or ova are, because of the nature of the channel, liable to be destroyed (s.15(3)). This power exists in respect of 'trout' in general, and is not restricted to migratory trout. The power to place ingress-preventing devices is made subject to the constraint that the power may not be used to bring about prejudicial interference with water rights relating to manufacturing, milling, drainage or navigation (s.15(4)). Surprisingly, however, no explicit offences are created in respect of damaging ingress-preventing devices. This is in marked contrast to the offences that are created in respect of damaging outflow gratings under s.15(2), and looks to be a drafting oversight. As a matter of general criminal law though, damage to ingress-preventing devices would probably be covered by the law relating to criminal damage. Section 1(1) of the Criminal Damage Act 1971 creates an offence where a person destroys or damages property belonging to another without lawful excuse with the intention to cause such damage or being reckless as to whether such damage would be caused (see Smith and Hogan (1983) Ch.17).

For the sake of clarity s.15(4) makes it explicit that nothing in s.15 affects the liability of any person to place and maintain a grating. Hence it would be no defence for a person who is bound to place and maintain a grating under s.14 to claim that it was within the power of the water authority to take on his responsibility under s.15. Nothing under s.15 authorises the placing of a grating by a water authority during a period of the year when a byelaw stipulates that gratings need not be maintained. It follows therefore that by failing to remove a grating at the appropriate time it will become unauthorised. Although this is not stated to be an offence under s.15, it is capable of constituting an offence under other sections of the Act (see s.12(3)(b) and s.21(1)(a), discussed in Ch.5). Nothing in s.15 allows the placing or maintenance of a grating in such a way as to obstruct navigation or to interfere with the effective working of a mill.

An interesting illustration of the statutory duty to erect a grating is to be found in *R* v *Recorder and Justices for Londonderry* (1930). Although decided under the Irish Fisheries Act 1842, the provisions at issue were the same in all material respects as s.14(2) of the present Act in so far as they required the accused to install a grating across the outflow from the mill which he operated. On appeal to the King's Bench Divisional Court against a conviction for having failed to place the grating, the accused claimed he had been prevented from doing the required work because the tail race re-entered the river on land which he did not own. Although he had started the work, it had been abandoned before completion after the owner of adjacent land where the grating was to be positioned had objected to the trespass. The question for the court was whether the accused was absolved from his statutory obligation to place the grating where the objection to the trespass had been raised against him doing so. The court held in the first place that the occupier of the mill was bound to place the grating, and in the second place that his neighbour was not permitted to object to the work being done on grounds of trespass. Moore LCJ explained: '. . . if the erection of such a grating or lattice involved some slight interference with the banks of the tail race so far as they were in the possession of either party . . . it was not in the power of either party to object, for by virtue of the obligation in the statute such necessary portion of the banks became in effect part of the tail race in the occupation of [the mill occupier]'. The consequences of any other conclusion would be highly unreasonable: 'Were this not so, the occupier of any tail race which runs through the lands of an adjoining owner at the point of divergence from, or return to the river, by securing the collusive opposition of such adjoining owner, could frustrate the whole operation of the Act.'

Supplementary provisions relating to the powers given to water authorities to place gratings under s.15 of the Act, are set out in s.18. Section 18(1) provides that it is an offence to obstruct a legally authorised person doing work on the installation of a grating or an ingress-preventing device or the alteration of a water channel authorised under s.15. Before the Minister gives consent to the performance of work under s.15, reasonable notice of the water authority's application must have been served on the owner or occupier of the watercourse, mill race, cut, leat, conduit or other channel. Such notice requires the water authority to provide the owner or occupier with a plan and specification of the work proposed. Should the owner or occupier raise any objection the Minister is bound to consider it before giving consent (s.18(2)). In the event of injury being caused by anything done by the water authority under s.15, then the person suffering may recover compensation for his loss providing that he institutes proceedings for recovery within two years of the work being completed (s.18(3)). In the event of a dispute as to the amount of compensation to be paid, the dispute is to be settled by a single arbitrator appointed by the Minister (s.18(4)).

4.24 *Restrictions on Taking Fish in the Proximity of an Obstruction*

Even if all the legal requirements have been complied with in respect of fish passes, free gaps and gratings, the fact remains that fish are still likely to accumulate in waters near an obstruction. Fish will gather below natural or artificial obstruction in low or adverse water conditions, or above it for a period before continuing their migration. In these circumstances a concentration of fish may make commercial methods of taking fish excessively destructive, and for that reason such methods are outlawed in these circumstances under s.17 of the

Salmon and Freshwater Fisheries Act 1975.

Section 17(1) makes it an offence to take or kill, or attempt to take or kill, or scare or disturb any salmon or trout, except by rod and line, in three situations. The first situation is that of a place below or above a dam or natural or artificial obstruction which hinders or retards the passage of fish. This is an offence where the place is within 50 yards above, or 100 yards below, the dam or obstruction, or within such a distance as prescribed by byelaw. The second situation stated is any water under or adjacent to any mill, or the head or tail race of the mill, or any waste race or pool communicating with a mill. The third situation is any artificial channel connected with any dam or obstruction. In any of these three places the offences can be committed in respect of 'trout' without any need for migratory trout to be concerned (see para.1.03 on the categories of fish).

Two exceptions to the prohibition on commercial fishing near obstructions are, first, nothing in the prohibition under s.17(1) of the Act will apply to authorised and lawful methods of fishing at fishing weirs or fishing mill dams (ss.7, 8 and 16). This is made explicit by s.17(2) which provides that s.17 shall not apply to any legal fishing mill dam not having a crib, box or cruive, or to any fishing box, coop, apparatus, net or mode of fishing in connection with and forming part of such a dam or obstruction for the purposes of fishing. The second exception is that the offences under s.17 are not to be enforced where a fish pass, approved by the Minister, has been installed, if compensation has not yet been paid by the water authority to persons entitled to fish in the waters. This means that fishery rights are not to be expropriated without compensation being paid by the water authority. The amount of compensation payable, where a dispute arises, must be settled by a single arbitrator appointed by the Minister, providing that proceedings for recovery are commenced within two years of the completion of work on the fish pass in question (s.18(4) and (5)).

In *Moulton* v *Wilby* (1863) the accused was found guilty of placing a salmon cage within 50 yards below a mill dam, which had no fish pass attached, contrary to s.12 of the Salmon Fishery Act 1861 (the predecessor of s.17 of the present Act). Despite the fact that the accused possessed an ancient right of fishery empowering him to use the cage as a fixed engine (under a predecessor of s.6 of the present Act) the use contravened the prohibition on fishing within the specified distance below the obstruction, and the conviction was affirmed by the Court of Exchequer. The case illustrates that an authorised fixed engine which is otherwise lawful, and not a mode of fishing used in connection with a legal fishing mill dam, may still be rendered unlawful by a prohibition on fishing in the proximity of obstructions.

Although it is clear that a fishery owner's entitlement to compensation is provided for under s.17(3) and s.18(4) of the Act, the position under an analogous byelaw is not always clear. One question which arises is, will a fishery owner be entitled to compensation for loss of fishing rights where a byelaw prevents him fishing within a specified distance of an obstruction? A case which indicates a negative answer to this question is *Onions* v *Clarke* (1917). Here a local fishery board made a byelaw prohibiting fishing within 75 yards below a weir, under powers similar to those now provided under para.29 of Sch.3 to the Act. In contravention of the prohibition the accused fished from the window of his house which adjoined the river within the proscribed distance, in accordance with his previous right of fishery. No compensation had been paid by the fishery board for the loss of the accused's previous right of fishing. The accused claimed that the byelaw was invalid on the grounds that, either it was unreasonable in failing to provide for compensation to be paid, or it was excessive in that the proscribed distance was unnecessarily great for the protection of the fish which accumulated near the weir. On both of these counts the King's Bench Divisional Court held that the accused had failed to show that the byelaw was unreasonable, and the case was remitted to the justices with a direction to convict. It is implicit in this rather anomalous ruling that, where the offence in question originates under a byelaw it can be committed even where no compensation is paid. This is in marked contrast to the general position under s.17.

The wording of s.17 recognises the less destructive nature of angling by excepting it from the prohibition. Nonetheless, fishing with rod and line is capable of being unsporting where hazards or obstructions hinder free passage of fish, and many water authorities make regulations under para.29 of Sch.3 prohibiting or regulating the taking of fish *by any means* above or below a dam or other obstruction whether natural or artificial. An example is to be found in rule 19 of the North West Water Authority Fishery Byelaws:

No person shall, without the previous consent of the Authority, during the period between the 30th day of September and the first day of the salmon close season for rod and line in any year, take or attempt to take by any means, any fish within a distance of 20 metres above and 50 metres below the crest of any man-made construction which impounds water in the rivers and streams of the River Ribble catchment . . .

5

CLOSE SEASONS AND TIMES FOR FISHING, AND THE SALE AND EXPORT OF FISH

5.01   Close Seasons and Close Times

Part III of the Salmon and Freshwater Fisheries Act 1975, ss.19 to 24, is concerned with the close seasons and close times when fishing is not permitted, and prohibitions upon the sale, export and consignment of fish. In respect of close seasons and times, Sch.1 to the Act places a duty upon water authorities to make local byelaws fixing weekly close times and annual close seasons for fishing for salmon and trout (other than rainbow trout). Although not legally bound to do so, water authorities may also impose and specify annual close seasons for freshwater fish and rainbow trout (under paras 19 and 20 of Sch.3 to the Act). In the event of a water authority having failed to fix a close season or close time for salmon or trout (other than rainbow trout), before the commencement of the Act (1 August 1975), the Minister was empowered (under para.2 of Sch. 1 to the Act) to make such byelaws for the water authority area.

Under the Act byelaws governing close times and seasons are subject to periods of minimum but not maximum duration. These are set out in the table in Sch. 1. The periods shown in the table represent the lower limit upon the extent of the annual close seasons and weekly close times, but water authorities are permitted to vary the precise times of close periods according to considerations such as local climatic conditions and breeding times of fish. However, water authorities must impose close times of at least the minimum duration appropriate to the species sought and the method of fishing used, except in the case of freshwater fish, eels and rainbow trout, for which they are empowered to dispense with a close season altogether (para.20, Sch. 3).

Close seasons and times are essentially conservational measures. As the Bledisloe Report (1961) commented:

> In our view . . . the best method of conservation for salmon and sea trout in the sea, in estuaries and fresh waters is the imposition of a close season and close times when no fishing is allowed. It is effective, flexible and easy to enforce. We would like to emphasise that in our view a closed period—whether it be annual, weekly, or for some part of a day—acts by reducing proportionately to its length the fishing pressure on the stock. We think it is a fallacy that there is any over-riding merit, from the conservational point of view, in the close season coinciding with the breeding season; a salmon caught in April can no more contribute to the next generation than one caught (before it has spawned) in October or November. Nevertheless, we accept that it is generally

convenient that the annual close season should include the principal spawning period, for at that time the fish we are concerned with are in poor condition, their food value is low and their flavour is poor. We would call particular attention to the value of short periods of close time, like the present weekly close time, throughout the fishing season. We think that this arrangement tends to give an even spawning escapement throughout the season, it enables the upper river to receive stocks of all the different runs of salmon and sea trout that enter the river (a matter to which we must attach great importance unless it can be shown that the various runs are not genetically distinct), and it spreads the fishing pressure evenly throughout the season. (Para.64.)

Although these points are well made in relation to commercial methods of fishing for game fish, they are less relevant to angling, as a very much less efficient method of taking fish, and almost totally irrelevant to angling for coarse fish where the general practice is to return the catch to the water without injury. On conservational grounds alone it is difficult to construct an argument for close times and seasons for coarse angling. The reason for the legal restrictions upon fishing at certain times of the year by angling appears to be a recognition of the wishes of anglers rather than any conservational reason. The Bledisloe Report (1961 para.69) noted that: 'When we come to a close season for coarse fish we find it difficult to reconcile our aversion to the imposition of unnecessary restrictions with the almost unanimous demand for a close season of the present length.' Similarly, in respect of game angling, it was observed (para.67): 'It was, however, the unanimous view of all our angling witnesses that there ought to be statutory control of their sport, and we do not feel that we can oppose that weight of evidence. In general anglers wanted a close season, size limits below which fish must not be taken, power to regulate baits and methods of fishing and, in some cases, power to limit the number of fish which may be taken in any one day.' Hence, although the conservational argument might not be compelling, the reason for a close season for angling is that anglers want one, and the Act recognises this.

This chapter deals with: first, the provisions relating to weekly close times for commercial methods of fishing for salmon and trout; second, the close seasons for different categories of fish; and finally, the restrictions upon the sale, export and consignment of salmon and trout. Alongside the discussion of close times and seasons, the reader may find it helpful to look forward to the table in para.5.10 which sets out the times and durations for these periods as they are specified under the Act.

(For exemptions from offences under s.19 of the Salmon and Freshwater Fisheries Act 1975, relating to fishing during close seasons and times in respect of fish farming, see para.8.04.)

5.02 Weekly Close Times for Salmon and Trout

Three initial points of overriding importance concerning weekly close times are that, first, weekly close times only apply in relation to salmon and trout fishing. Second, weekly close times do not apply to fishing with rod and line, though water authorities are empowered to make byelaws prohibiting or regulating fishing with rod and line between the end of the first hour after sunset on any day and the beginning of the last hour before sunrise on the following morning (para.30, Sch.3 to the 1975 Act). Third, weekly close times do not apply to fishing for salmon with putts and putchers (described in para.4.03). In effect, weekly close times are only applicable to commercial methods of fishing, other than putt and putcher fishing, for game fish.

Section 19(2)(a) of the Salmon and Freshwater Fisheries Act 1975 makes it an offence for any person to fish for, take or kill or to attempt to take or kill any salmon during the weekly close time, except with a rod and line or putts and putchers. Section 19(4)(a) makes it an offence to fish for, take, kill or attempt to take or kill any trout, other than rainbow trout, during the weekly close time, except with a rod and line.

Section 19(1) states that Sch.1 is to have effect in relation to close times. Schedule 1 stipulates that it is the duty of every water authority to make byelaws fixing for its area, or respective parts of it, a weekly close time for fishing for salmon and trout (para.1, Sch.2). The close time that a water authority may fix is made subject to a requirement that it is not less than a period of 42 hours' duration for either salmon or trout, and in the absence of any contrary stipulation in byelaws the period is that between 6 a.m. on Saturday and 6 a.m. on the following Monday (paras 5.3 and 6, Sch.1). In practice, however, the close times which apply in different areas are often much longer than the statutory minimum. For example, rule 13 of the South West Water Authority Fishery Byelaws states: 'the weekly close time for salmon and trout for the Taw and Torridge District, excepting the River Lyn, for instruments other than rod and line, shall be the period between the hour of 6.00 on Friday evening and 6.00 on the following Monday evening.' Another variation is to be found in rule 6 of the Wessex Water Authority Fishery Byelaws, which provides that *in addition to the statutory weekly close period*: 'In the Avon and Dorset Division the weekly close season provided by schedule 1 clause 6 of the Act shall extend to include . . . the period between the hour of 9.00 p.m. on each of the evenings of Wednesday, Thursday and Friday and the hour of 5.00 a.m. on each of the respective following mornings.'

The offences of fishing for salmon or trout during the weekly close time using commercial methods, contrary to s.19(2) and (4) of the Act, are broadly worded to encompass any person who 'fishes for, takes, kills or attempts to take or kill' any salmon or trout. It has been held that the expression 'fishes for' salmon does not imply actually catching salmon. In *Ruther v Harris* (1876) the accused were found fishing for salmon with nets before 6.00 a.m. on Monday morning during the weekly close time, contrary to s.21 of the Salmon Fishery Act 1861 (which created substantially the same offence as s.19(2)(a) of the present Act in respect of fishing during the weekly close time). The accused claimed in their defence that it had not been proved that they had actually caught any fish. Despite this, the court held that they were still 'fishing for' salmon and that they were guilty of the offence. The same principle, that 'fishing for' fish need not entail the actual taking or killing of fish, runs throughout s.19 of the present Act, where all the offences of 'fishing for' fish during the close season or close weekly time are committed without the need for it to be shown that any fish have actually been captured.

(On the meaning of 'take', as it is used in s.19(2) and (4), see the discussion of *Wells* v *Hardy* (1964) in para.3.22 and *Lee* v *Evans* (1980) in para.6.05.)

A qualification to the offence of fishing during weekly close times for salmon is that the offence is not committed in respect of any act done for the purpose of artificial propagation of fish, or for a scientific purpose, where previous permission in writing has been obtained from the water authority for the area (s.19(3)). Where the offence of fishing for trout during the weekly close time is involved the same defence is available, along with the additional defence that the act was done for the purpose of stocking or restocking waters, and the written permission of the water authority for the area has been obtained (s.19(5)). It is not clear why a broader exception should be available in respect of trout at a time when the stocking of salmon into waters is becoming increasingly popular. Where fish are to be used for stocking or restocking written consent will also be required from the water authority for the area into which they are to be placed (s.30; see para.8.17).

5.03   Close Seasons for Salmon

Paragraph 1 of Sch.1 to the Salmon and Freshwater Fisheries Act 1975 places water authorities under a legal duty to make byelaws stipulating annual close seasons and weekly close times, between which, salmon fishing is permitted. The provisions under Sch.1 envisage three different salmon fishing seasons according to the method of fishing employed. First, there is the general annual close season, that is, the season for netting and commercial methods of fishing other than putts and putchers. This annual close season must be of a minimum duration of 153 days, and, unless otherwise specified in local byelaws, para.3 of Sch.1 stipulates that this is to be the period between 31 August and the following 1 February. The second annual close season envisaged under the Act is that governing the use of putts and putchers, for which the annual close season must be of a minimum duration of 242 days, and unless otherwise specified in local byelaws is the period between 31 August and 1 May. The third annual close season is that governing the use of rod and line, and is specified to be of a minimum duration of 92 days, and, subject to byelaws, is the period between 31 October and the following 1 February.

Since close periods for salmon fishing are determined both by provisions in the Act and by water authority byelaw, there is the inevitable possibility of inconsistencies arising between Act and byelaw. In such an event, an express provision in the statute, such as the minimum duration of close seasons, prevails over any inconsistent byelaw. This situation is illustrated by *Prosser* v *Cadogan* (1906), where a byelaw made by conservators of a fishery district (the predecessors of the present-day water authority) appeared to contradict an explicit statutory provision. Initially s.39(1) of the Salmon Fishery Act 1873 enabled the conservators to alter the commencement of the annual close season for putt and putcher fishing, providing that it should not commence later than 1 November in each year. The conservators enacted a byelaw fixing the commencement of the close season as 16 August. Subsequently s.2 of the Salmon Fishery Law Amendment Act 1879 said that, notwithstanding anything in the 1873 Act, the annual close season for putts and putcher should commence on 1 September each year. The accused fished for salmon with putchers on 22 August, that is, in breach of the local byelaw but not the later statutory provision. The King's Bench Divisional Court held that no offence had been committed. Despite the byelaw, it was the explicit statutory provision which prevailed, and of this there had been no contravention. Although the Salmon Fishery Law Amendment Act 1879 has been repealed, the principle of the case remains good law: that statutory provisions override byelaws in cases of direct conflict.

Section 19(1) of the 1975 Act creates certain offences in respect of fishing during the close seasons fixed by water authorities within the statutory limitations. First, it is an offence to fish for, take or kill, or to attempt to take or kill, a salmon during the annual close season, except with rod and line or putts and putchers (s.19(2)(a)). In effect, this is a convoluted way of saying that fishing by rod and line or putts and putchers is not subject to the same close season, or weekly close time, as applies to commercial methods of fishing for salmon. This is made explicit by the subsections which follow. Second, it is an offence to fish for, take or kill, or to attempt to take or kill salmon with a rod and line during the annual close season for rod and line (s.19(2)(b)). Third, it is an offence to fish for, take, kill or to attempt to take or kill salmon with putts and putchers during the annual close season for putts and putchers (s.19(2)(c)). The upshot of these three stipulations, stated simply, is that all who fish for salmon must observe the annual close season enacted by byelaw appropriate to their method of fishing.

The offences under s.19 regarding fishing for salmon during the close season are broadly worded so that they may be committed where a person 'fishes for' salmon. As has been noted, 'fishing for' a particular kind of fish does not entail actually catching that kind of fish, and consequently the offences of unseasonable salmon fishing can be committed by persons who have not succeeded in catching salmon (see the discussion of *Ruther v Harris* (1876) in the previous para.). To qualify this point, however, it must be stressed that the offence under s.19(2) and the other offences under s.19 are only committed where the accused fishes for *unseasonable* fish. This means that no offence will be committed where a person who is found to be fishing can show that it was his intention to catch seasonable fish. Thus in *Cain v Campbell* (1978) the accused staked out nets along the sea shore to catch sea fish. When his net was subsequently found to contain a salmon, he was charged under s.19 with having taken the salmon during the weekly close time other than with rod and line or putts and putchers. He was acquitted by the justices, and their decision affirmed by the Queen's Bench Divisional Court, on the ground that the salmon was taken when it was caught in the net, and at that time it had not been shown that he had any intention to catch salmon. (Contrast the decision in *Davies v Evans* (1902), discussed in para.3.15, on the question of intention.) As a principle of law the intention to catch an unseasonable species of fish is an essential ingredient in all the offences under s.19(2).

As with the offence of fishing during weekly close times, the operation of s.19(2) is made subject to the express proviso that no offence is committed in respect of acts done for the purpose of artificial propagation of fish, or for a scientific purpose, if permission has previously been obtained in writing from the water authority for the area in which the act is done (s.19(3)).

5.04   Close Seasons for Trout

Paragraph 1 of Sch.1 to the Salmon and Freshwater Fisheries Act 1975 imposes a duty upon water authorities to make byelaws fixing annual close seasons and weekly close times for fishing for trout other than rainbow trout (close seasons for rainbow trout are discussed separately in para.5.07). 'Trout' includes migratory trout and char (see para.1.03 on categories of fish), but rainbow trout are specifically excluded from the definition of 'trout' in this context. The provisions under Sch.1 relating to close seasons for trout are analogous to those for salmon discussed in the previous paragraph. The general annual close season for trout is of a minimum duration of 181 days, and, subject to local byelaws, is the period between 31 August and the following 1 March (paras 5.3 and 6, Sch.1). The annual close season for fishing with rod and line is stated to be a period of minimum duration of 153 days (para.3, Sch.1), and, in the absence of a contrary byelaw, is stated to be the period between 30 September and the following 1 March (para.6, Sch.1). This appears to be a mistake, however, since the period between 30 September and 1 March is less than 153 days. In respect of fishing with putts and putchers the position is obscure since, although para.6 of Sch.1 states that the minimum duration of the close season for fishing for trout with putts and putchers is to be 242 days, no dates are given to determine the start and finish of this period in the absence of byelaws.

Section 19(4) of the Act creates offences of fishing for, taking or killing, or attempting to take or kill, trout (other than rainbow trout) during the annual close season or weekly close time other than by rod and line, and with rod and line during the annual close season for rod and line fishing. Mysteriously, these provisions do not envisage the lawful taking of trout by putts and putchers at any time. Although water authorities are under a duty to make byelaws fixing the annual close season for any method of fishing for trout including the use of putts and putchers (para.1, Sch.1), nevertheless s.19(4)(a) makes it an offence to take trout other than by rod and line during the annual close season. On a literal reading of these provisions, it must be concluded that to avoid any offence being committed under s.19(4), the putts and putchers annual open season must always fall wholly within the general annual open season. The only apparent explanation for this is that of oversight on the part of the parliamentary draftsman who failed to make explicit provision legitimating putt and putcher fishing under s.19(4) of the Act whilst compelling water authorities to make provision for it under para.1 of Sch.1 to the Act.

As with salmon, it is an exception to the offences of fishing for trout during close seasons (s.19(4)) to show that the act was done for the purpose of artificial propagation of fish, or for a scientific purpose, and that previous permission, in writing, had been obtained from the area water authority (s.19(5)). Additionally, this exception extends in the case of trout to the stocking or restocking of waters where written permission has been obtained (s.19(5)). Where fish are to be used for stocking or restocking, written permission from the water authority for the area into which they are to be placed must be obtained (s.30; and see para.8.17).

5.05 The Removal of Fixed Engines and Obstructions during Close Periods

Section 20(1) of the Salmon and Freshwater Fisheries Act 1975 provides that, immediately after the commencement of the annual close season and the weekly close time, the occupier of any fixed engine for taking salmon or migratory trout shall cause it to be removed or rendered incapable of taking them or obstructing their passage. The terminology used in this section calls for explanation. It must be observed that the provision is concerned with the close season and weekly close time with respect to fishing methods other than rod and line or putts and putchers. The 'occupier' as defined under s.41(1) includes any person for the time being in actual possession of the fishery or premises. 'Fixed engine' includes a variety of different types of trap and net made stationary (see the discussion in Ch.4). 'Migratory trout' is more restrictive than 'trout' in that it encompasses only those trout that migrate to and from the sea (s.41(1)), and does not include rainbow trout (s.20(6)). Additionally, an offence will be committed if a fixed engine is not removed or rendered incapable of taking salmon or migratory trout or obstructing their passage (s.20(1)). Alternatively, the offence will be committed where the fixed engine has been removed but subsequently replaced or rendered capable of taking fish or obstructing their passage before the end of the close season or close time (s.20(2)). With the same objective of making close periods a genuine period for the conservation of migratory fish stocks, s.20(3) creates a similar offence where, during such periods, a person places any obstruction, uses any contrivance or does any act for the purpose of deterring salmon or migratory trout from passing up a river.

Two general exceptions exist to the offences relating to the removal of obstructions during close periods under s.20. The first of these is that the provisions relating to 'fixed engines' do not apply to putts and putchers during the weekly close times, but do apply during the annual close season (s.20(4)). The rationale for this is that these devices are relatively permanent and would be difficult to remove and replace over the short duration of a weekly close time. The second general exception is that for the purpose of offences relating to deterring salmon and migratory trout from passing up a river, it will be a defence to show that the act was done lawfully in the course of fishing for fish other than salmon or migratory trout (s. 20(5)).

An illustration of a forerunner of s.20 of the present Act, s.20 of the Salmon Fishery Act 1861, operating in the context of a fishing mill dam is to be seen in *Hodgson* v *Little* (1864). A 'fishing mill dam' means a dam used or intended to be used partly for the purpose of taking or facilitating the taking of fish, and partly for the purpose of supplying water for milling or other purposes (s.41(1) of the present Act, and see para.4.12). In this case the accused was charged with presenting an impassable obstruction to salmon for a period of days after the commencement of the close season. The mechanism of the fishery was described by Willes J as follows:

The appellant had a fishing mill-dam with a fish-lock through it. At the head of the lock was a sliding-door or hatch which moved as usual in grooves. When this door was down, no salmon could pass. Within three feet of these, down stream, was a frame in which the up-stream hecks of the fish-lock were placed when the lock was used for taking salmon. [A 'heck' is a grating or frame of parallel bars in a river to obstruct the passage of fish without obstructing the flow of water.] When this was down, the sliding-door or hatch was raised. This was of course done to cause a rush of water through the lock, against which the fish, following his natural instinct to ascend the river, would make what way he could, and so, swimming up the lock, and being stopped by the up-stream hecks, and prevented from returning by the down stream hecks or inscales, would be caught in a trap. The final capture might perhaps be aided by letting down the sliding-door or hatch, so as to leave the fish high and dry . . .

The hatch in question not only assisted in the capture of salmon, but, when left down, it increased the water flow and so increased the milling power of the mill. Despite the fact that removal of the hatch would injuriously affect the power of the mill, the court held that the close season use of the hatch was an obstruction to the free passage of salmon and the occupier of the mill was convicted of the offence.

An analogous example of a conviction for failure to allow free passage of fish through a trap during the weekly close time is *Bell* v *Wyndham* (1865). Here the use of a method of taking fish similar to that in *Hodgson* v *Little* during the weekly close time, was found to contravene s.22 of the Salmon Fisheries Act 1861. The same facts arising today would fall under s.20 of the present Act.

5.06 Close Seasons for Freshwater Fish

'Freshwater fish' means any fish living in fresh water exclusive of salmon, trout, eels and any other kinds of fish which migrate to and from tidal waters (see para.1.03 on categories of fish). Paragraph 6 of Sch.1 to the Salmon and Freshwater Fisheries Act 1975 provides that the minimum duration for the close season for freshwater fish shall be 93 days, and, if other dates are not specified by byelaw, the annual close season is the period between 14 March and 16 June. Paragraph 20 of Sch. 3 permits water authorities to make byelaws dispensing with a close season for freshwater fish altogether. The combined effect of these two provisions is that, although a water authority may dispense with a close season completely, if it does decide to have a close season, then it must be at least 93 days: no lesser period is permitted.

Any person who fishes for, takes, kills, or attempts to take or kill, any freshwater fish in any inland water during the close season for freshwater fish, or fishes for eels by means of a rod and line, is guilty of an offence (s.19(6)). The phrase 'inland water' is defined in s.41(1) as having the same meaning as under s.135(1) of the Water Resources Act 1963 (see para.12.03). The reference to fishing for eels with rod and line is not to be understood as a conservation measure designed to protect eels during their spawning season. Since eels do not spawn in freshwater such a provision would be unnecessary. It is a means of making the close season for freshwater fish more effective by preventing persons using eel fishing as an excuse for fishing for freshwater fish out of season. (The close seasons for eels are considered in para.5.08).

The annual close season for freshwater fish is subject to five general exceptions provided for under s.19(8): removal of fish by the owner of a several fishery; fishing with the permission of the owner of a several fishery; fishing for eels; scientific purposes; and taking fish for bait. These five exceptions are considered under the following subheadings.

(a)   *Removal of fish by the owner of a several fishery*   The first exception is that the prohibition of fishing during the annual close season for freshwater fish does not apply to the removal of any eels, freshwater fish or rainbow trout, by the owner or occupier of a several fishery where salmon or trout are specially preserved (s.19(8)(a)). 'Owner' here is defined to include any person who is entitled to receive rents from a fishery or premises, and 'occupier' is defined as the person who is in actual possession of the fishery or premises (s.41(1)). A 'several fishery' is the name given to 'the right of fishing independently of all others, as that no person should have a co-extensive right with him in the subject claimed' (*Seymour* v *Courtenay* (1771)), meaning that a person has the exclusive right to fish a particular water to the exclusion of others (see para.1.07). The exception permits the owner or occupier of a several fishery, where salmon or trout are preserved, to remove unwanted species during their close season where he can show that such species are not specially preserved. Where the removed fish are to be placed into another water, the written permission of the water authority for the area into which the fish are to be introduced must be obtained (s.30, and see para.8.17).

(b)   *Persons fishing with the permission of the owner of a several fishery*   The second exception to the annual close season for freshwater fish permitted under s.19(8) allows a person to fish with rod and line, with the written permission of the several owner or occupier of a specially preserved salmon or trout fishery, where the owner or occupier seeks to remove non-preserved fish such as eels, freshwater fish or rainbow trout (s.19(8)(b)). This is directly analogous to the previous exception, but extends the permission to persons other than the owner or occupier where they fish with rod and line with the written permission of the owner or occupier. This exception, like the first, applies only to specially preserved game fisheries, and yet, surprisingly, the Act makes no stipulation that persons fishing such fisheries during the annual close season for freshwater fish are required to remove any non-preserved fish which are caught in the water. The fact that they are not requested to do so by the owner might indicate that salmon or trout are not genuinely preserved.

'Specially preserved', as the words are used in the first two exceptions, is an obscure or ambiguous expression which is likely to cause difficulties in interpretation. The editor of *Oke's Fishery Laws* (1884, ed. Willis Bund), commented scathingly upon the expression as it arose in a forerunner of s.19(8) of the present Act (s.11(3)(a) of the Freshwater Fisheries Act 1878). He observed:

It is difficult to see what is meant by the word specially. A landowner preserves his fishery, and keeps down pike and coarse fish, does he specially preserve trout . . .? What constitutes special preservation? The prosecutor in any case will have to prove that trout . . . are not specially preserved. If a landowner calls his keeper, who swears that he is instructed to look after the trout . . . will this be a good defence? Again, if a stream belongs to two riparian owners, the one preserves his trout and the other does not, the one who preserves his trout, or says he does, can . . . fish during the close season; the one who does not cannot'. (Quoted by Ormrod LJ in *Thames Water Authority* v *Homewood* (1981), discussed below.)

More recently, it has been stressed that for the 'special preservation' of salmon or trout to be genuine under the exceptions under s.19(8)(a) and (b) of the present Act, justices considering whether the exception applied:

should take into account the numbers of trout introduced in relation to the area of the water, look at all the activities taking place in the water throughout the year, and come to a conclusion as to whether what had happened had been done with a view to preserving trout or if it had just been an attempt to create that impression whereas in fact the primary intention had been the conducting of freshwater fishing during the close season'. (From the judgment of Woolf J in *Thames Water Authority* v *Homewood* (1981), discussed below.)

Hence, both the preservation of salmon or trout and the desire to remove an unwanted species must be shown to be genuine before the benefit of the exception can be claimed.

The operation of this second exception under s.19(8)(b) is illustrated by *Swanwick* v *Varney* (1881), a case decided under a forerunner of the present provision (s.11(3)(b) of the Freshwater Fisheries Act 1878). In this case, the accused was found fishing with rod and line during the close season for freshwater fish. Although he initially denied that he had caught any fish, when searched by a police constable, he was found to have coarse fish on his person. He was charged with having caught fish during the close season contrary to s.11 of the 1878 Act. In his defence two points were argued. Firstly, although he had fish in his possession, there was no evidence that he had *caught* them within the meaning of the section. It was held that being found by the river fishing with rod and line and in possession of fish was, in the absence of other explanation, evidence that he had committed the offence. Secondly, he argued that before fishing he had obtained leave from the tenant of the land where he was fishing and that brought him within the exception, as it then was, of a 'person angling in a several fishery with the leave of the owner'. On this count it was held that, if the tenant was merely the occupier and not the owner, then he was not the proper person to give leave so as to confer exemption, and so the second argument failed. Were the same facts to arise today, the permission of the occupier would be sufficient since the modern exception is wider in this respect than under the 1878 Act. Today, however, the permission from the occupier would need to be given *in writing* to be effective as a defence and, if the 'leave' of the occupier was only given by word of mouth, then that would not be sufficient.

Recently the second exception to close season fishing for freshwater fish under s.19(8)(b) was considered in *Thames Water Authority* v *Homewood* (1981). The facts were that the owner of an enclosed water of about 13 acres, ran it on a commercial basis as a mixed fishery for trout and coarse fish. The lake was stocked annually with approximately 200 rainbow trout. During the close season for freshwater fish, persons were allowed to fish for pike and perch, on payment, with the written permission of the owner. Despite the relatively small number of trout introduced in relation to the size of the lake, the magistrates accepted that the close season fishing for pike and perch, which are predators of trout, was for the purpose of removing from the lake such predators as were caught. On appeal, the view was expressed that the conclusion of the magistrates was 'somewhat surprising' and the facts constituted 'a borderline case' in what was ultimately a matter 'of degree'. Nonetheless, the magistrates had asked themselves the correct questions in law and their finding of fact could not be overturned. The owner was found not guilty by virtue of the exception under s.19(8)(b).

(c) *Fishing for eels*   The third exception to the annual close season for freshwater fish permits persons to fish with rod and line for eels during the close season, where such fishing is authorised by byelaw (s.19(8)(c)). As was stated above, s.19(6) makes it an offence to fish for eels by means of rod and line during the close season for freshwater fish. As an exception to this, however, para.35 of Sch.3 to the Act states that water authorities are permitted to make byelaws authorising fishing with rod and line for eels during the annual close season for freshwater fish. The outcome of this is that, where such a byelaw exists, fishing for eels by rod and line during the close season for freshwater fish is not an offence under s.19(6). It is to be stressed, though, that this provision does not legitimate fishing for any fish other than eels and, where an intention to catch unseasonable fish can be shown, then an offence is committed notwithstanding the provision permitting eel fishing. (See the discussion of 'intention' in para.6.05.)

(d) *Scientific purposes*   A fourth exception to the close season for freshwater fish permits the taking of freshwater fish for scientific purposes under s.19(8)(d). This exception differs from those provided in respect of the unseasonable taking of salmon or trout, where in both cases artificial propagation was a permitted ground, and in the case of trout alone, stocking and restocking. The exception is wider than that in respect of salmon and trout in that permission in writing is not required from the water authority for the area. The Act provides no definition of 'scientific purposes' and it is possible that artificial propagation and stocking might be justified on scientific grounds in some circumstances.

(e) *Taking freshwater fish for bait*   The final exception to the close season for freshwater fish permits the taking of freshwater fish for use as bait, where the fishery is a several fishery, with permission in writing from the owner or occupier, or in any other kind of fishery, unless the taking would contravene a byelaw (under s.19(8)(e)). The types of byelaw which might be contravened by taking fish for bait are, for example, byelaws prohibiting the taking or removal of any fish, whether dead or alive, from any water without lawful authority (see para.6.04), or byelaws governing the taking of any freshwater fish less than a certain size prescribed by the byelaws (see para.3.13). If the fish to be used as bait are to be introduced into another water then permission of the water authority for the area into which the fish are to be introduced must be obtained (s.30; and see para.8.17).

The meaning of permitted taking of fish for use as 'bait' under this exception is not wholly clear, and as Oke (1878 p.61) commented: 'There are no restrictions as to what is meant by bait. A large pike will take a roach of a pound, and it will afford a great door to fraud if a person allege that he is taking fish for bait when he is angling against the provisions of the Act.'

5.07   *Close Seasons for Rainbow Trout*

The minimum annual close season for rainbow trout under para.3 of Sch.1 to the Salmon and Freshwater Fisheries Act 1975 is 93 days, the same period as for freshwater fish. No dates are given for the annual close season for rainbow trout but the period is specified as 'that fixed for those waters by byelaws'. The reason for this reluctance to offer guidance on a close season for rainbow trout stems from the difficulty which this introduced species of fish encounters in spawning in this country. The fact that rainbow trout rarely spawn successfully outside fish hatcheries makes it unnecessary to impose a close season in order to protect stocks. One exceptional place where rainbow trout have managed to breed in the wild is in the area of the Severn-Trent Water Authority who have made the following provisions in rule 3(d) of their fishery byelaws dealing with the close season for rainbow trout:

(1) The annual close season for fishing for rainbow trout with rod and line in those waters of the Rivers Derwent and Amber, including their tributaries, which are upstream of their confluence at Ambergate, Derbyshire excluding the stretch of the River Wye from Blackwell Mill to Cressbrook Mill above or upstream of Ashford-in-the-Water and excluding any reservoir formed by the construction of a dam across the valley of those rivers, or across one of their tributaries, shall be the period between the fifteenth day of November and the sixteenth day of May following.
(2) The annual close season for fishing for rainbow trout with rod and line in all other waters in the Water Authority area shall be dispensed with.

Where a water authority does set a close season for rainbow trout, it must be of minimum duration of at least 93 days. Otherwise, the provisions relating to close seasons for rainbow trout are the same as for freshwater fish. The wording of s.19(6), considered above, making it an offence to fish for freshwater fish during the close season is exactly paralleled by s.19(7), making it an offence to fish for rainbow trout during the close season. Similarly s.19(8) which creates the five exceptions to s.19(6), discussed in the previous paragraph, applies equally to s.19(7) in respect of rainbow trout.

5.08 Eels and Lamperns (Lampreys)

Because of its unique life cycle, the eel is set apart from other fish both zoologically and legally (see para.1.03 on categories of fish). The Salmon and Freshwater Fisheries Act 1975 places eels in a distinct legal category and incorporates a number of principles governing their lawful capture. The purpose of most of these regulations is to protect stocks of more highly valued fish, which might be adversely affected by eel fishing, rather than to protect eels themselves.

Although regulations governing fishing for eels have been mentioned in passing in the preceding paragraphs, it may be helpful to consolidate the key points here. Initially, there is no close season for fishing for eels provided for under the Act. Section 19(6) and (7) makes it an offence, however, to fish for eels in an inland water during the close season for freshwater fish or rainbow trout. Notwithstanding this, water authorities are empowered under para.35 of Sch.3 to make byelaws authorising fishing with rod and line for eels during the annual close season for freshwater fish. Where this is done, the effect is that eels may lawfully be fished for by rod and line all the year round.

Section 21 of the 1975 Act is concerned with the unseasonable use of implements for catching eels. It states that, before 25 June in any year (that is between 31 December and the 25 June following), it is an offence to hang, fix or use any baskets, nets, traps or devices for catching eels in any water frequented by salmon or migratory trout, or to place in any inland water any device whatsoever to catch or obstruct any fish descending a river (s.21(1)(a)). The purpose of the subsection is to prevent the traps from obstructing salmon and migratory trout in their passage to the sea, and other fish in their movements up and down stream in a watercourse. It is notable that the offence is committed in waters frequented by salmon or migratory trout during the part of the year when salmon that have spawned, known as 'kelts', are likely to be returning to the sea, and young salmon, known as 'smolts', descending to the sea for the first time. The offence is then committed where a device is placed in waters with the object of catching or obstructing descending fish. Section 21 continues to make it explicit that the prohibition does not extend to the use of eel baskets not exceeding 10 inches in diameter which are constructed so as to be fished with bait and not used at any dam or other obstruction or in any conduit or artificial channel by which water is deviated from a river. Neither does the prohibition extend to devices for taking eels which are authorised by the area water authority with the consent of the Minister (s.21(2)). Once again, the underlying purpose of these provisions is that more highly valued species of fish should not be harmed by eel fishing. For that reason the prohibition does not extend to devices having no catching or obstructing effect upon salmon or migratory trout.

The prohibition of unseasonable use of eel traps as a device to catch or obstruct other fish is illustrated by *Briggs* v *Swanwick* (1883), a case decided under a precursor of s.21 of the present Act (s.15 of the Salmon Fishery Act 1873). The case concerned the legality of out-of-season use of a permanent eel trap constructed as a feature of a mill weir. By directing water through the bars of a grating, the tenant of the mill caught eels and coarse fish during the period before the 24 June. The Queen's Bench Divisional Court clarified a number of points concerning the use of eel traps in deciding the case. They held that the section was not confined in its application to temporary features such as baskets or nets but extended to cover the permanent structure that was at issue, and that, by opening the shuttle that controlled the flow of water through the grating, the user had 'placed' the device to catch fish. Moreover, the court held that, although the primary intention of the enactment was the protection of salmon and migratory trout, the words used were of a general character and so must be interpreted generally. That is to say, the words 'inland water' and 'any fish' meant the provision should not be confined to salmon, and the presence or absence of salmon in the particular river was not material. The sole question was whether the device was one to catch or obstruct descending fish. The court held that it was and that the offence had been committed.

Another prohibition imposed under s.21 is on the placing of any basket, trap, or other device for taking fish on the apron of a weir (s.21(1)(b)). This prohibition, which encompasses a range of devices other than those for catching eels, is nonetheless subject to the same qualifications as the prohibition under s.21(2) of the Act. It is not, however, restricted to rivers frequented by salmon and migratory trout and may apply to devices placed upon the apron of 'any weir', regardless of whether the water contains migratory salmonids. An exception peculiar to the prohibition of devices placed upon the apron of a weir, is the exception of placing wheels or leaps for taking lamperns between 1 August and the following 1 March (s.21(1)(b); see para.1.03 on lampreys). This provision concerns the use of basket traps to catch lampreys, a fish otherwise left unmentioned and unconsidered by the provisions of the Act.

(A discussion of the methods used to capture eels and lampreys is to be found in: Jenkins (1974) Ch.10; Millichamp (1976); Forrest (1976); and Harrison (1984).)

5.09   *Penalties for Offences Relating to Unseasonable Fishing*

Although some of the offences relating to unseasonable fishing are specifically listed in the table in para.1 of Sch.4 to the Salmon and Freshwater Fisheries Act 1975, as having specified punishments, in each case the maximum is the same as provided for unspecified offences under the Act (para.2, Sch.4). That is to say, all the offences relating to unseasonable fishing carry, on summary conviction, a fine not exceeding level 4 on the standard scale, presently £1,000 (see para.1.12 on the standard scale).

5.10   *Table of Close Seasons and Weekly Close Times*

See table on p.93.

5.11   *The Sale, Export and Consignment of Salmon and Trout*

The remainder of Part III of the Salmon and Freshwater Fisheries Act 1975, ss.22 to 24, imposes restrictions upon the sale, export and consignment of salmon and trout. Ultimately these sections are another means of achieving the same object of conservation of fish stocks that underlie the provisions dealt with in the

Table of close seasons and weekly close times (under Sch.1 to the Salmon and Freshwater Fisheries Act 1975)
(To be read subject to byelaws and the qualifications discussed in the text.)

Species		*General season*	*Rod and line*	*Putt and putcher*
SALMON				
Annual close season	Duration (min.)	153 days	92 days	242 days
	Dates (between)	31 Aug–1 Feb	31 Oct–1 Feb	31 Aug–1 May
Weekly close time	Duration (min.)	42 hours	None	None
	Times (between)	6 a.m. Sat–6 a.m. Mon	None	None
TROUT				
Annual close season	Duration (min.)	181 days	153 days	242 days
	Dates (between)	31 Aug–1 Mar	30 Sep–1 Mar	Not stated
Weekly close time	Duration (min.)	42 hours	None	None
	Times (between)	6 a.m. Sat–6 a.m. Mon	None	None
RAINBOW TROUT				
Annual close season	Duration (min.)	None	93 days	None
	Dates (between)	None	Not stated	None
FRESHWATER FISH				
Annual close season	Duration (min.)	None	93 days	None
	Dates (between)	None	14 Mar–16 Jun	None
EELS				
Annual close season	Duration (min.)	None	93 days	None
	Dates (between)	None	14 Mar–16 Jun	None

preceding paragraphs of this chapter. By restricting the distribution of unseasonable fish an incentive to take such fish by improper methods is removed and stocks of fish are less vulnerable to unlawful fishing. As the Commissioners on Salmon Fisheries had observed in 1861, the incentive for much unlawful fishing was that of profit (see Ch.2). Immature and unseasonable fish, taken in contravention of the law, were sold locally or exported to foreign parts for considerable financial gain. Exporters found a ready market for fish in poor condition which might not have been saleable in this country. More recently the Bledisloe Report (1961 Ch.XX) commented upon the ready and profitable saleability of salmon and sea trout at any time of the year. The financial inducement for commercial dealing in unseasonable fish remains, and similarly the need for prohibitions on such dealing remains as a bolster to the effectiveness of close seasons.

Illegitimate trade in unseasonable fish is greatly reduced by the supervisory role exercised by the Fishmongers' Company (see Bledisloe (1961) para.302). This body regulates the sale of salmon and trout within the City of London during close times by demanding the production of a certificate of origin for fish exposed for sale. The requirement of such certification, in conjunction with the Company's practice of sealing or labelling salmon and trout kept in cold store during the close season, provides a reliable guide that a responsible person has satisfied himself that any fish so marked is of lawful origin. This in turn assists traders to discharge legal burdens of proving origin placed upon them by the sections discussed below.

The major difficulty with the restrictions upon dealing in unseasonable fish is that of establishing whether any particular fish was lawfully caught; that is, whether it was caught during the open season applicable to the method of capture in the locality of capture. To some extent this evidential problem has been reduced by the imposition of greater uniformity amongst commercial fishing seasons. Nevertheless, rod and line seasons generally extend into the close season for commercial fishing and so provide the dealer or possessor of fish during the close period for commercial fishing with the plausible excuse that they were seasonably caught by rod and line and are not within the restrictions. Moreover, the widespread availability of facilities for cold storage of fish, permitting them to be kept for long periods without deterioration, makes it unproblematic for fish captured during the close season to be retained until the open season, and then offered for sale.

In future the provisions discussed in the following paragraphs of this chapter must be considered alongside the new offences concerned with dealer licensing and handling salmon in suspicious circumstances, which arise under ss.31 and 32 of the Salmon Act 1986 and are discussed in paras 13.02 and 13.03.

5.12   The Sale of Salmon and Trout

Section 22 of the Salmon and Freshwater Fisheries Act 1975 commences by stating that it is an offence to buy, sell, expose for sale or have in possession for sale any salmon between 31 August and the following 1 February, or any trout, other than rainbow trout, between 31 August and the following 1 March. Under the interpretation section of the Act, s.41(1), 'salmon' and 'trout' are defined in such a way as to include parts of these fish. As a consequence of this, there may be an overlap between this offence and the offence of buying, selling or exposing for sale or possessing, any roe of salmon or trout, for the purpose of fishing for salmon, trout or freshwater fish (s.2; see para.3.12). The offence under s.22 is made subject to a string of geographical and temporal qualifications and refinements which make it clear that it is trade in unseasonably *caught* fish that is to constitute the main substance of the offence. Hence the offence is not committed where the fish in question falls under any one of the five exceptions under s.22(2):

(a)   any salmon or trout which has been canned, frozen, cured, salted, pickled, dried or otherwise preserved outside the United Kingdom (that is, England, Wales, Scotland and Northern Ireland, but not the Channel Islands or the Isle of Man);

(b)   any salmon similarly conserved within the United Kingdom between 1 February and 31 August;

(c)   any trout similarly conserved within the United Kingdom between 1 March and 31 August;

(d)   any salmon or trout (other than an unclean salmon or trout) caught outside the United Kingdom;

(e)   any salmon or trout, other than an unclean or immature salmon or trout (on the meanings of 'unclean' and 'immature' see para.3.13) caught within the United Kingdom, if its capture was lawful at the time and in the place where it was caught.

A further exception is created under s.22(3) which states that the offence is not committed where the act in question is done for the purpose of artificial propagation, stocking or restocking of waters, or a scientific purpose. It may well be asked whether one exception would serve the purposes of comprehensiveness and clarity better than the six. That exception would be that the offence would not be committed where the fish in question was not captured in breach of any provision of the Act relating to unseasonable, unclean or immature fish. Such an exception would obviate the mischief which the section is designed to outlaw. Regrettably the state of the law appears to be more complex than it need be.

In addition to the exceptions provided for under s.22, another exception arises in respect of fish that have been seized by water bailiffs. Where a fish has been seized by a water bailiff as liable to forfeiture, para.8 of Sch.4 to the Act provides that he is entitled to sell it and the net proceeds of sale are liable to forfeiture in the same way as the fish was. (On the power of water bailiffs generally see Ch.9, and on proceedings see Ch.10.)

The enforcement of s.22 is made less onerous by a reversal of the burden of proving that the section has not been contravened, brought about by s.22(4). This subsection provides that the burden of proving that there has been no infringement of the provisons of s.22 lies upon the person buying, selling or exposing a salmon or trout for sale, or having it in his possession for sale. That is to say, it is for the prosecution in a particular case to prove that a salmon has been bought, sold, exposed for sale or is in possession for sale, between the specified dates. Given that this has been shown by the prosecution, it falls to the defence to show that the transaction or possession comes within one of the exceptions.

Two points from the case law on this topic are worthy of note. The first point concerns the meaning of 'possession' for the purposes of s.22. In the Scots case of *M'Attee* v *Hogg* (1903) it was held that actual physical possession need not be shown. In the case five men were accused of having possession of two salmon during the annual close season which was in force at the time for the district contrary to s.21 of the Salmon Fisheries (Scotland) Act 1868 (a similar provision to s.22 of the present Act). It was argued on appeal that, since there were only two fish and five men, it was physically impossible that all five could have been in possession of the fish. The court declined to accept this argument, finding that the five might rightly be held to be in possession of the salmon although only one of them was actually found carrying them, even if some of the men had never touched them. Although *M'Attee* v *Hogg* is a Scots decision it is likely that the same result would have been reached under the law of England and Wales (though as an alternative it may have been possible to charge the men who were not in physical possession of the fish with being accomplices to the offence of possession). Despite the apparent breadth of the ruling, the question of possession remains an issue of fact. The case illustrates that actions indicating control short of physical possession may nonetheless amount to 'possession' for the purposes of s.22.

A second point which becomes apparent from the case law is that possession of fish within the close season must be for the purpose of sale *within the close season* before the offence under s.22 will be committed. In *Birkett* v *McGlassons Ltd* (1957) a number of salmon which had been caught by rod and line during the open season for rod and line fishing, but before 1 February, were deposited with a fishmonger. The terms of the deposit were that the captors could require the return of the fish before 1 February but, if they did not do so, the fishmonger was at liberty to sell the fish as their agent. After normal business hours on 31 January, the fishmonger dispatched the fish for sale in London where they arrived on 1 February. The fishmonger was charged with having the fish in his possession for sale contrary to s.30 of the Salmon and Freshwater Fisheries Act 1923 (a forerunner of s.22 of the present Act). The Queen's Bench Divisional Court held that on these facts no offence had been committed. The fishmonger had no intention to sell the fish prior to 1 February and, although he had them in his possession prior to that time, he held them pending recall by the fishermen and not for the purpose of sale. Thus, notwithstanding the finding that the fishmonger had possession of the fish, he did not have possession for the *purpose of sale*, and hence no offence was committed. It is to be noted that the reversal of the burden of proof contained in s.22(4) does not extend to any presumption that fish are intended for sale. The prosecution must show both that the fish are possessed and that they are for sale *before* the burden of proving that the section has not been contravened is put upon the accused.

(For a defence to the offence under s.22(1) of the Salmon and Freshwater Fisheries Act 1975 relating to fish farming, see para.8.04.)

5.13 The Export of Salmon and Trout

Further restrictions upon the distribution of unlawfully caught fish are imposed by s.23 of the Salmon and Freshwater Fisheries Act 1975, which governs the export of salmon and trout. Section 23(1) prevents evasion of the prohibitions upon selling unseasonable fish under s.22 of the Act by selling abroad by making it an offence to export unclean or unseasonably caught salmon or trout. In order to enhance the effectiveness of this restriction, s.23(2) requires that salmon or trout intended for export between 31 August and the following 1 May (a period which is likely to exceed annual close seasons for salmon or trout) shall be entered for export with the proper officer of Customs and Excise at the port or place of intended export. 'Proper officer', under s.8(2) of the Customs and Excise Management Act 1979, means any person engaged by the orders or with the concurrence of the Commissioners of Customs and Excise in the performance of any act or duty which is by law authorised to be performed by or with an officer. Failure to conform with s. 23(1) or (2) of the Salmon and Freshwater Fisheries Act 1975 by entering for export, or exporting, or bringing to any wharf, quay or other place for export of an unclean or unseasonable salmon or trout, or not entering a salmon or trout for export, will render any package containing the fish liable to forfeiture under the Customs and Excise Management Act 1979. Moreover, any person seeking to bring about export contrary to these provisions of the Act will be guilty of an offence (s.23(3), Salmon and Freshwater Fisheries Act 1975). Further powers are given to customs and excise officers under s.23(4) of the 1975 Act to open parcels for export which they suspect may contain salmon or trout, and to detain any such fish found until proof is provided that they are being legally exported. In the event of a fish becoming unfit for human consumption before such proof is given, the officer may have it destroyed (s.23(4)).

Finally, s.23(5) of the 1975 Act simplifies the task of enforcement of the section by customs officials by placing the burden of proving that any salmon or trout entered for export between 31 August and 1 May is not so entered in contravention of the section, on the person entering it. Hence, it is the duty of the exporter to show compliance with the section rather than that of the customs officials to show non-compliance.

(For a defence to the offence under s.23(1) of the Salmon and Freshwater Fisheries Act 1975 relating to fish farming, see para.8.04.)

5.14 The Consignment of Salmon and Trout

Similar restrictions in respect of inland consignment of salmon and trout are imposed under s.24 of the Act. The main offence involves the failure of a person consigning salmon or trout by common or other carrier to place a conspicuous mark on the outside of the package indicating the type of fish contained (s.24(1)). 'Common carrier' means a person or business concern that holds itself out as carrying goods for the general public, such as British Rail. 'Other carrier' extends the category to encompass any person or body that accepts goods for consignment from the consignor whether the goods are to be transported for payment or gratuitously. A number of powers are given to 'authorised officers' to assist in the enforcement of the prohibition on unmarked consignments of salmon and trout. 'Authorised officer' is defined under s.41(1) of the Act to mean:

(a)   any officer of a water authority acting within the water authority area;
(b)   any officer of a market authority acting within the area of the jurisdiction of that authority;
(c)   any officer appointed by the Minister;
(d)   any officer appointed in writing by the Fishmongers' Company;
(e)   any police officer.

Such authorised officers are empowered to open any package suspected to contain salmon or trout (s.24(2)). If the package is found to contain a salmon or trout without being conspicuously marked to that effect, or, alternatively, if it is reasonably suspected that salmon or trout in a marked package are being dealt with contrary to law, then the officer may detain the package and its contents until proof is provided that the fish is not being so dealt with (s.24(3)). The power to detain is similarly exercisable in respect of any salmon or trout not packed in a package (s.24(4)). In the event of any fish detained becoming unfit for human food, the authorised officer may have it destroyed (s.24(5)). Finally, the refusal to allow any authorised officer to exercise the powers conferred under s.24, or the obstruction of the officer in the exercise of the powers, is an offence (s.24(6)).

6

FISHING LICENCES

6.01   The Purpose of Licensing

The declining state of fisheries described by the Commissioners Inquiry into Salmon Fisheries in 1861 had been attributed largely to the absence of any satisfactory system of administration or efficient body of officials to give practical effect to the law. This in turn was a symptom of an acute lack of funding, which was itself a problem of fishery administration to which the Commissioners gave a good deal of consideration. It was clear that no solution which placed an additional charge on the public purse would be acceptable: 'those who benefit by protection should pay for protection'. It was natural therefore that the Commissioners should opt for a system of funding whereby all those who derived a benefit from a fishery were made to contribute to the cost of superintendence according to a regular scale. They suggested that the ordinary expenditure necessary for the protection of salmon fisheries, the employment of watchers and other paid officials, should be raised by a combination of a rate on private fisheries and a duty upon all methods of fishing. The continuance of essentially this same scheme of licensing to the present day is a self-evident demonstration of its suitability.

In the accounting year 1984–5 the ten regional water authorities received almost £4 million in income from the sale of licences of all categories, which for many authorities covered the greater part of their fisheries expenditure. In the calendar year of 1984 the water authorities issued 1,093,134 licences to fish with rod and line, producing an income of £3,620,592 (Water Authorities Association (1985) Ch.12). It is clear that the income from fishing licences remains a major source of funding for the legal and administrative work of water authorities in respect of their duty to 'maintain, improve and develop' fisheries in their area (s.28(1), Salmon and Freshwater Fisheries Act 1975; and see Ch.7 on water authorities generally).

It would be a misconception, though, to suppose that the only purpose served by the licensing system is that of obtaining funds. In addition to the fiscal effect, a number of other purposes are served by the licensing system. First, licences provide an important means by which water authorities can take action against persons taking fish by improper means where no prohibited method is involved (see Ch.3 on prohibited instruments). Thus a person taking a fish using no instrument other than his hands would nonetheless fall foul of licensing requirements, even though not using a prohibited method (see para.6.04). Licences therefore provide a useful means of prohibiting illicit fishing methods other than those dealt with explicitly under the Act. Second, limitations upon numbers of licences issued can be used as a conservational measure (s.26 of the Act, discussed below) in circumstances where it would be difficult to envisage any other means of reducing fishing pressure on a water. Third, the power to refuse to issue a licence to a person who has been disqualified from holding a licence by a court for offences under the Act, as well as being a deterrent, is an expedient means of preventing multiple offenders from causing further damage to a fishery (discussed in para.6.09 below). Fourth, the issue of licences is often the only accurate indication of involvement in fishing or fishing pressure on a water. Finally, the requirement that licence holders provide returns of fish taken (para.32 of Sch.3 to the Act) is a convenient means of monitoring the state of a fishery which would be difficult to achieve by other means. Taking these advantages together, the licensing system has a good deal to commend it.

On the other side of things, however, there are two main criticisms of the present licensing system that are frequently voiced by anglers. The first concerns the disproportionate contribution which anglers make, compared with net fishermen, by way of payment for licences. The anglers' argument is that the net fishermen take a greater proportion of the fish in many areas and should consequently pay a correspondingly higher licence fee. The net fishermen's reply is that to do so would make the exercise of commercial fishing financially unviable.

The second criticism of the present licensing system which is commonly raised by anglers concerns its regional subdivision. A licence to fish with rod and line is only valid within the area of the issuing water authority. This means that if an angler wishes to fish waters in different water authority areas he must purchase additional licences to cover each area in which he fishes. With the mobility of present-day anglers, the scheme is seen to discriminate financially against those who travel to fish in different regions and so are required to make multiple licence purchases. The problem was considered briefly in the Bledisloe Report (1961 para.277), but it was concluded that the introduction of a national licence would be '. . . a serious interference with the autonomy of river boards, and a restriction of their power to raise local revenue to meet essentially local expenditure', and that it would not be possible to make a 'radical' change in the licensing structure. The pressure for a national angling licence remains, however, and continues to be fuelled by the dissatisfaction of peripatetic anglers.

6.02   *General Provisions Concerning Fishing Licences*

Under Part IV of the Salmon and Freshwater Fisheries Act 1975, ss.25 to 27, water authorities are bound to operate a system of licensing within their area which covers all fishing for salmon and trout and, unless excused by the Minister, this system must also regulate fishing for freshwater fish and eels within the area (s.25(1)). The basis of the licensing system is that the issue of a fishing licence permits the licensee to fish, with the instrument, for the type of fish, and in the area specified by the licence during the period for which it is valid (s.25(2)). The terms on which particular types of fishing licence are issued in a locality will vary and be subject to different local byelaws. Unless granted an exemption as a 'special case', each licensee pays a duty on his licence which is fixed by the water authority according to the nature of the licence (paras.1 and 2, Sch.2 to the Act). Before fixing or altering such duties, water authorities are obliged to publish in one or more of the newspapers, circulating in the area for which the licence will be granted, notice of their intention to impose or change the licence duty, except where the licence is only temporary (para.3, Sch.2). A 'temporary licence' is a licence for a period not exceeding 14 days, the charge for which may be less than the duty ordinarily fixed for the instrument in question (para.7, Sch.2). If within one month after publication of the water authority's intention, a written objection to the proposed duty is made to the Minister by any interested party, then the water authority is not permitted to introduce or change the duty without the Minister's approval (para.4, Sch.2). The Minister in turn may refuse to approve the duty, or approve it with or without modifications, and direct the water authority to give notice of any modification (para.5, Sch.2). Ordinarily, new duties on licences take effect from the beginning of the year following that in which they are fixed but, if a duty has been the subject of ministerial approval, then it will take effect in the year in which it is approved by him (para.4, Sch.2).

Given these common principles governing the issue of all kinds of fishing licences by water authorities, the following paragraphs examine the features of the various kinds of licences that may be issued.

6.03   *Licences to Fish with Rod and Line and Unlicensed Fishing*

'Rod licences', as they are generally termed, permit the holder alone to fish with rod and line for the kind of fish specified in the licence within the area stated and for the duration stated, under s.25(2) of the Salmon and Freshwater Fisheries Act 1975. The term 'rod licence' is misleading in that it is not a particular rod which is authorised to be used, but rather that the named licensee is authorised to use *any* rod: it is the use of the rod rather than the ownership of it which is licensed. The main points concerning rod licences are discussed under the following subheadings.

(a)   *Single rod and line*   A rod licence is not transferable and so can only be used to authorise fishing by the person to whom it is issued. Contrary to the general rule of statutory interpretation that words in the singular include the plural (s.6, Interpretation Act 1978), 'rod and line' in this context is defined under s.41(1) of the Salmon and Freshwater Fisheries Act 1975 to mean *single* rod and line. In *Combridge* v *Harrison* (1895), the accused, who held a licence to fish for trout, fished with three rods and lines at the same time and was charged with fishing for trout without a licence under ss.34 and 35 of the Salmon Fishery Act 1865 as amended by s.7 of the Freshwater Fisheries Act 1878. It was held that the single rod licence which he possessed covered the use of one rod and line only and thus the offence was committed by using more than one. As Wright J put the point: 'It must not be assumed that the judgment of the court prevents a man taking with him more than one rod and line when he goes fishing, but he must use only one of them at a time.' Alternatively, it might be added that, should an angler wish to fish with two or more rods simultaneously, then to stay within the law he must obtain separate licences for the use of each rod. In some water authority areas the number of rods that may be used for particular kinds of fishing is limited. The Welsh Water Authority Fishery Byelaws provide, under rule 12, that: 'No person shall fish with more than one rod and line at a time for salmon and trout (including rainbow trout) or with more than two rods and lines at a time for freshwater fish and eels. PROVIDED that this byelaw shall not apply to any person fishing for char in the area of the former Gwynedd River Authority.' Other authorities appear to encourage the use of a second rod when fishing for freshwater fish. For example, the memorandum to the Wessex Water Authority Fishery Byelaws states that: 'If two rods are in use when fishing for freshwater fish, a licence is required for each rod. A reduced duty is available for a second annual licence, which must be taken out at the time of purchase of the original licence.'

A rod licence does not authorise fishing by any means other than that of rod and line. This principle is illustrated by *Williams* v *Long* (1893), where the accused took out a licence to fish for trout with rod and line but also used a night line. At this time, a night line was a lawful method of fishing for which a licence was required. (Contrast the general position today under s.1(1)(a)(iii) of the 1975 Act; see para.3.08.) It was found that rod and line, and night line, were two distinct methods of fishing, in respect of which separate duties were payable. Thus the rod licence did not cover the use of the night line, and the accused was guilty of unlicensed fishing.

(b)   *The use of a gaff or tailer*   Provided that an angler has first obtained a licence to use a rod and line, s.25(4) of the Act entitles him to use a gaff consisting of a plain metal hook without a barb, or a tailer or a landing net as an ancillary. The use of these accessories to rod fishing would otherwise constitute prohibited methods of taking fish under the first part of the Act (see para.3.09). Section 25(4), permitting the use of the ancillary equipment, has, however, to be read subject to para.34 of Sch.3, which empowers water authorities to make byelaws limiting the use of a gaff in connection with fishing for salmon or migratory trout. The purpose of this provision is to allow restrictions upon early and late season use of the gaff when its use might cause unnecessary injury to unclean fish which the angler is bound to return to the water with the least possible injury (s.2(3); and see para.3.09 for examples of water authority byelaws limiting the use of gaffs).

(c)   *Rod licences and permission to fish*   A rod licence, though conveying the permission of the water authority for the holder to participate in the activity of angling within the area of the authority on the terms on which it is issued, does not amount to permission for the holder to be on any particular piece of land for the purpose of pursuing the activity. Paragraph 16 of Sch.2 to the Act makes this point explicit in stating that a licence to fish does not confer any right to fish at a place or a time at which the licensee is not otherwise entitled to fish. In other words, an angler must normally obtain the permission of the owner of the fishery, and of the owner of any land over which access to the fishery is to be gained, *as well as* obtaining a rod licence. Unless the water to be fished is a public fishery, as is the case in most tidal waters, the angler should obtain permission to fish, for example, by buying a 'permit' from the owner of the fishing rights, or by becoming a member of the angling association that leases the fishery. Without such permission, the angler is a trespasser upon the land. Though not a crime, the civil wrong of trespass to land entitles the occupier to resort to self-help by removing a trespassing angler who declines to leave 'with the minimum of force that is reasonably necessary' to evict him from the occupier's land (see Winfield and Jolowicz (1984) Ch.13). Alternatively, the owner of the land might sue for damages where damage can be shown or, in a persistent case, gain a court order known as an injunction to compel the trespasser to desist (see, for example, the action brought against trespassing canoeists in *Rawson* v *Peters* (1972)). More seriously perhaps, an angler without permission of the owner of the fishery is likely to fall foul of the criminal provisions under the Theft Act 1968 concerning unlawful fishing (considered in Ch.3). In the event of any of these legal consequences, it would be no defence for the angler to rely upon his rod licence as providing any excuse.

(d)   *Categories of rod licences*   As indicated above, water authorities may issue distinct categories of rod licences for different types of fish. If this is the case, then the angler is required to have the category of licence which is appropriate to the species of fish he seeks. Having stated the basic principle, it is to be noted that it is qualified by s.25(5) of the Act, which states that a licence to use any instrument for fishing for salmon authorises that instrument to be used for fishing for trout, and by s.25(6) a licence to use any instrument for fishing for either salmon or trout authorises that instrument to be used for fishing for freshwater fish and eels. Hence, subject to contrary byelaws, a person licensed to fish for salmon using rod and line, is permitted to fish for all other species of fish. The converse of this is not authorised by these subsections, so that a person licensed to fish for freshwater fish will not be permitted to fish for trout or salmon unless he obtains a separate licence authorising him to fish for these species.

(e)   *Duration of rod licences*   Normally, the longest period over which a rod licence is issued is a calendar year, though many water authorities issue licences for lesser periods of a month, week or day. The issuing of licences on an annual rather than a seasonal basis means that, where a season spans two calendar years, as with the standard freshwater fishing season, then two rod licences must be purchased for the two calendar years in which the season falls. Such licences will authorise rod and line fishing from the time of issue, or a later time at which the licence states it is to commence, providing that such a time is during the open season for the type of fish for which the licence is issued.

A rod licence cannot be purchased to authorise previous unauthorised fishing, as was shown by *Wharton* v *Taylor* (1965). Here the accused was seen fishing with rod and line and found by a water bailiff not to have a River Board licence. Later the same day, the accused purchased a licence which stated that the holder was entitled to fish during the open season of the whole of that calendar year. He claimed that this licence legitimated any angling done during that year, including angling before the time when it was purchased. The Queen's Bench Divisional Court declined to accept this argument and sent the case back to the magistrates with a direction to convict.

There is no weekly close time for rod and line fishing, as was noted in Chapter 5. However, water authorities are empowered to make byelaws prohibiting or regulating fishing by rod and line between the first hour after sunset on any day and the beginning of the last hour before sunrise on the following morning (para.30 of Sch.3 to the Act; and see para.3.22 on the determination of this period). Thus, for example, rule 12 of the Yorkshire Water Authority Fishery Byelaws states that:

> No person shall fish for, take or kill any salmon, trout or freshwater fish with rod and line in the River Esk between the downstream side of Ruswarp Road Bridge and Whitby Harbour mouth between the expiration of the first hour after sunset on any day and the beginning of the last hour before sunrise on the following morning during the months of September and October in any year.

(f) *Unlicensed fishing* The principal offence with respect to fishing licences, either by rod and line or otherwise, is that of unlicensed fishing, provided for under s.27 of the Salmon and Freshwater Fisheries Act 1975 (though another major offence is that of failing to produce a licence under s.35 of the Act, discussed in para.9.08). A person is guilty of the offence of unlicensed fishing if he fishes for, or takes, a fish which is subject to a system of licensing otherwise than by means of an instrument which he is licensed to use to fish for, or take, that species of fish. Alternatively the offence is committed where a person fishes for, or takes, any fish otherwise than in accordance with the conditions of the licence. The offence extends to the possession, with intent to use for the purpose of fishing for, or taking fish, of any instrument other than one which the licensee is entitled to use for that purpose by virtue of a fishing licence (s.27(b)).

(For exceptions to the offences under s.27 of the Salmon and Freshwater Fisheries Act 1975, relating to unlicensed fishing, in respect of fish farming, see para.8.04.)

6.04 The Meaning of 'Instrument'

The word 'instrument' in s.27 of the Salmon and Freshwater Fisheries Act 1975 is somewhat obscure, but *Gibson* v *Ryan* (1967) provides some guidance as to the meaning of the word as it was used in the context of the Freshwater Fisheries (Protection) (Scotland) Act 1951. The accused in this case were found by the banks of a salmon river with a rubber dinghy and a fish basket which contained traces of salmon scales and blood indicating that they had recently been engaged in taking salmon. The question before the court was whether they were '. . . found in possession of any . . . instrument' under s.7 of the Scottish statute. It was held that a distinction should be drawn between an instrument used for the taking of salmon, and other things, such as the rubber dinghy in this case, which were used to assist in the commission of the offence but not in the actual taking of the fish. It follows from this distinction that 'instrument' under s.27 of the Salmon and Freshwater Fisheries Act 1975 is intended to cover things used directly to take fish such as a rod or a net, but not other items of equipment which assist indirectly in the taking of fish such as a boat or receptacle in which fish are placed after capture (though see para.10.06 for further discussion of the meaning of 'instrument').

The offence under s.27(a) of the 1975 Act of fishing for, or taking, a fish otherwise than by means of an 'instrument' which the user is licensed to use is worded in such a way that the offence is committed where a person takes fish using no instrument at all. Thus a person 'tickling' or 'groping' trout or other fish and so taking them using only bare hands, would be taking them otherwise than by means of a licensed instrument, and would therefore be guilty under s.27(a). In effect, s.27 makes unlawful *any* method of taking fish for which the area water authority does not issue a licence. The limitation to this underlying principle is that the section does not encompass the taking of *dead* fish. In *Gazard* v *Cook* (1890) the accused picked up a salmon of 27 lb that he had found on the sands of a river estuary left by the receding tide. Although it was not shown that the fish was dead, it had been attacked by gulls and when brought ashore had one of its eyes pecked out. The accused was charged with taking a salmon by means other than a properly licensed instrument (under s.22 of the Salmon Fishery Act 1873, the precursor of s.27(a) of the present Act). On appeal, it was held that the prosecution had failed to prove that the fish was alive, and that 'taking a fish' meant taking a *live* fish. The accused was found not guilty.

A neat contrast is illustrated between *Gazard* v *Cook* (1890) and *Stead* v *Tillotson* (1900). In the latter decision the accused were charged with taking trout other than by a properly licensed instrument under s.22 of the Salmon Fishery Act 1873, as amended by s.7 of the Freshwater Fisheries Act 1878. They were found to have taken the fish, which had apparently been poisoned and were dying, but not dead, using only their hands. No evidence was presented to connect the taking of the fish with the poisoning of the stream from which they were taken. On these facts, it was found that they should be convicted. Taking *dying* fish, though not dead fish, was within the wording of the section, and would be similarly within s.27(a) of the present Act.

The inapplicability of s.27(a) to the case of taking dead fish must make it difficult to show an offence where two persons work in collaboration, one killing fish by poison or other means, and another removing the dead fish from the water. It is for this reason that para.26 of Sch.3 to the Act empowers water authorities to prohibit the taking or removal from any water of *any* fish, whether alive or dead, without lawful authority. So, for example, rule 8 of the Welsh Water Authority Fishery Byelaws states that: 'No person (other than a Water Bailiff of the Authority acting in his official capacity) shall take or remove any live fish or dead fish from any waters within the Authority's area except in accordance with the written authority of the Authority or unless otherwise he is lawfully authorised so to do.' In an area where a byelaw to this effect is in force, a finder of a dead fish such as that in *Gazard* v *Cook* (1890) above, would be guilty of the offence under the byelaw.

6.05   The Problem of 'Intention'

A crucial problem concerning the application of s.27 and other sections of the Salmon and Freshwater Fisheries Act 1975, which has been considered by the courts on a number of occasions, lies in the interpretation of the phrase 'fishes for'. Is the offence of unlicensed fishing committed where a person, who is licensed to fish for one type of fish, fishes in such a manner that he might catch another type of fish for which he is not licensed to fish? For example, is the offence committed where a person, holding only a licence to fish for freshwater fish, fishes a river containing both freshwater fish and trout in such a way that he might catch trout? In these circumstances, can he be said to be 'fishing for' trout? In law the question concerns the *intention* of the angler, and the general conclusion which has been reached by the courts is that a person who 'fishes for' fish of a particular type must be shown to have an intention to catch that type of fish. Without the requisite intention, the offence under s.27 of the Act is not committed. This point is well illustrated by examples taken from the case law.

In *Marshall* v *Richardson* (1889), the accused was found fishing a trout stream with rod and line without having any licence, and was charged with fishing with a rod and line for trout without a proper licence under a forerunner of s.27 of the present Act (s.35 of the Salmon Fishery Act 1865, as amended by s.7 of the Freshwater Fisheries Act 1878). In his defence, he claimed that he was fishing for freshwater fish for bait and had no intention to catch trout. The justices decided that, even though no intention to catch trout had been shown, he was guilty of the offence in that he was fishing in a trout stream and *may have caught trout*. On appeal to the Queen's Bench Divisional Court, however, the decision was reversed when the judges found that, in 'about as clear a case as one can possibly have', the only question to be asked was whether the accused *was* fishing for trout. The justices having found, as a point of fact, that the accused had no intention of catching trout, the Appeal Court was bound to hold that no offence was committed. To 'fish for' a particular type of fish, one must fish with the intention of catching that type of fish and, without the requisite intention, the offence under s.27 of the present Act is not committed (see also *Watts* v *Lucas* (1871).

The presence of an intention to fish for a particular kind of fish may, however, be demonstrated by the method of fishing employed. In the past it has been held that persons have an intention to fish for a particular kind of fish where they adopt a method of fishing which is peculiarly adapted or reasonably calculated to catch that kind of fish. Thus in *Lyne* v *Leonard* (1868) the accused had placed putts which he alleged were placed for the purpose of catching shrimps and flat fish only, and not for the purpose of catching salmon (see paras.4.03 and 4.09). Blackburn J held that where the instrument used was a device 'reasonably calculated' to catch salmon a licence was required regardless of whether the instrument was actually used for that purpose. The accused was found guilty of unlicensed fishing. By the same reasoning it was held in *Short* v *Bastard* (1881) that a net which had been adapted to catch salmon and was fished in areas where salmon were usually caught was similarly an instrument calculated to catch salmon and so required a licence, notwithstanding the claims of the accused that he did not intend to catch salmon. Likewise, in *Hill* v *George* (1880) where the accused claimed that his intention was to catch eels, it was held that night lines were instruments which were reasonably calculated to catch trout and so required a licence to fish for trout (under s.36 of the Salmon Fishery Act 1865 as amended by s.7 of the Freshwater Fisheries Act 1878, though contrast the present-day position in respect of night lines, see para.3.08).

The intention which must be shown for the offence under s.27 of the 1975 Act to be committed is a matter of fact, which must be ascertained from all the circumstances of the case. It is to be noted, however, that there must come a point in practice where an angler will find great difficulty in convincing a court that it was his intention to fish only for authorised fish (see *Davies* v *Evans* (1902), para.3.15). The difficulty which may be encountered by a fisherman seeking to prove that he did not seek to fish for or take unauthorised fish, where the facts indicate the contrary, is well illustrated by *Lee* v *Evans* (1980). In this case the accused fished at night with a net in an estuary, claiming that he intended to catch sea fish. On lifting the net, which contained migratory trout, he placed the fish and the net in a sack and made his way home. Before reaching his home, he was stopped by water bailiffs who inspected the sack and found the fish. He claimed that he intended to return the migratory trout, for which he had no licence to fish, after he had examined the catch at his home. He was charged with taking the fish otherwise than by means of an instrument which he was entitled to use by virtue of a fishing licence, contrary to s.27. On appeal, Watkins J delivered an illuminating judgment which afforded little credence to the statement of intention given by the accused, commenting: 'I feel bound to say that the story told to the justices . . . was a tall one, measured even by the standards of fishing stories emanating from West Wales.' Having found that the accused knew that it was likely that he would catch migratory trout, the judge found it abundantly plain that he *intended* to take such fish and, despite the accused's conflicting statement of intention, the facts led to the unavoidable conclusion that the accused was guilty.

In addition to the instructive ruling on the question of intention, *Lee* v *Evans* (1980) also raises another important point concerning the interpretation of s.27—the meaning of 'taking' fish under that section. The accused claimed that he intended to return any unauthorised fish after he had identified them as such. Could he be said to have 'taken' the fish if he could show an intention to return them? It was found that 'taking' involves an intentional reduction into possession which need not be equated with 'keeping'. Reduction of the fish into possession for a short duration would be enough to constitute 'taking'. The court held that a *de minimis* rule should apply, to the effect that returning fish to the water at the first opportunity would render the 'taking' insignificant, and so this would not amount to a 'taking' of the fish for the purposes of s.27. This rule, though, is of narrow compass, and in circumstances such as those that arose in this case, the reduction into possession was significant and therefore there had been a taking of the fish.

The scope of the *de minimis* rule was narrowly construed in *Lee* v *Evans* (1980) but, nevertheless, would extend to cover the expeditious return of an unintentionally caught fish not covered by a licence. In all likelihood the extent of the rule is analogous to the exception to s.2(2)(a) of the Act (concerning the 'taking' of unclean or immature fish), where the offence 'does not apply to any person who takes a fish accidentally and returns it to the water with the least possible injury', in the least possible time (s.2(3)). By contrast, the keeping of fish in a keep net, even if for return to the water at a later time, is likely to amount to reducing the fish into possession, and so may similarly amount to a 'taking' of the fish for the purpose of s.27 (see *Wells* v *Hardy* (1964), discussed in para.3.22).

6.06 *Licences for Methods of Fishing other than Rod and Line*

Netting, and other authorised commercial methods of fishing, share many of the basic principles of licensing that have been discussed in the previous paragraphs. The licensing of types of fishing other than angling are, however, also subject to special regulations contained in ss.25 and 26 of and paras.9 to 14 of Sch. 2 to the Salmon and Freshwater Fisheries Act 1975. The effects of these provisions are discussed in this paragraph.

In contrast to the rule against transferability in respect of rod licences, licences for the use of other instruments will also authorise the use of such instruments by servants or agents (sometimes termed 'endorsees') of the principal-licence holder (s.25(3)). The names of the authorised servants, or agents, must be stated on the licence unless the person accompanies the principal licensee in using the instrument, or the water authority directs that a person be treated as an authorised servant owing to special circumstances, or unless the area is subject to a limitation order made under s.26 (under para.9 of Sch.2 to the Act, considered below). Changes can be made to lists of such authorised persons (under paras 11 to 12 of Sch.2) on payment of a nominal charge providing that the total number does not exceed twice the number of persons who, in the opinion of the water authority, are required to work the instrument at one time, or, if the licensee himself intends to be involved in the working of the instrument, one less than twice that number (para.13, Sch.2).

The situation of a person becoming an authorised servant or agent of the licensee by accompanying him in using the instrument raises the question of when a servant assisting the licensee becomes an independent user of the instrument. This difficulty was considered in *Lewis* v *Arthur* (1871). In this case, four men, A, B, C, and D, were coracle fishermen. A and B each had a licence to use a net, whilst C and D did not. A coracle net, it was agreed, could only be used by or between two persons at the same time in coracles, and no offence would be committed where one of the pair held a licence. On the facts which were established, A and B fished one net together, and C and D (both unlicensed) fished another. The question before the court was whether the latter pair were guilty of unlicensed fishing. Since the justices had found that the four men were fishing at the same time and in the same place and were by implication assisting each other, the appeal court were prepared to affirm their decision and find that the four men were conducting what was essentially one transaction in which it happened by 'accident' that the two unlicensed men were holding the same net. The two were found not guilty. The case illustrates the difficulty which survives, under para.9(b) of Sch.2, in respect of determining when servants are authorised by accompanying the licensee in using an instrument.

A special offence is created by para.14 of Sch.2 where any person who, with intent to deceive, either enters more names than are permitted as double the number required to work the instrument (para.13, Sch.2) or states a false date at which a name has been entered as a servant or agent to the licensee (para.14, Sch.2).

Along with the requirement that commercial fishing methods are conducted by licence, a water authority is also empowered to qualify the scope of the licence by byelaw provisions. Of particular importance is the power of water authorities to make byelaws requiring and regulating the attachment to licensed nets and instruments of marks, labels or numbers, or the painting of marks or numbers or the affixing of labels or numbers to boats, coracles or other vessels used in fishing (para.22, Sch.3). Additionally, water authorities possess a power to make byelaws prohibiting or regulating the carrying in any boat or vessel whilst being used in fishing for salmon or trout of any net which is not licensed, or which is without the mark, label or number prescribed by the byelaws (para.23, Sch.3). A water authority may also make a byelaw prohibiting or regulating the carrying in a boat or vessel during the annual close season for salmon of a net capable of taking salmon, other than a net commonly used in the area to which the byelaw applies for sea fishing if carried in a boat or vessel commonly used for that purpose (para.34, Sch.3).

(See para.13.07 for future changes to the criteria for endorsement of commercial fishing licences made by s.36 of the Salmon Act 1986.)

6.07   Net Limitation Orders

A major difference between rod licences and other types of fishing licence is the possibility of an order being made to limit the number of fishing licences of the latter but not the former kind. A water authority may, by order confirmed by the Minister, place a limit for up to 10 years upon the number of fishing licences issued in a year for fishing in any part of their area for salmon or trout, other than rainbow trout, with any specified instrument other than rod and line. Pursuant to this, the water authority may make provision for the means of selection of licences where demand for such licences exceeds the limitation imposed upon supply (s.26, Salmon and Freshwater Fisheries Act 1975). The formalities for such a limitation order require the water authority to publish the proposed order, with notice of the Minister's intention to confirm it, in order to allow written objections to be made (s.26(2)). In the event of objections being received by the Minister within a specified period, the Minister must hold a local inquiry if the proposed limitation reduces the number of licences to a lesser number than have been issued in any of the three years preceding the commencement of the order, and the complainant has held a licence for two years preceding the commencement (s.26(3)).

Section 26(4) seeks to minimise the extent to which commercial fishermen may be deprived of their living by limitation orders by imposing safeguards. The Minister shall not confirm such orders unless he is satisfied that persons who have held licences to use an instrument during a period preceding the order, and are dependent on fishing for a livelihood, will continue to be able to obtain a licence for the instrument. Initially, the preceding period for which the licence must have been held is one year but, where allowing licences to persons who have held them for one year previously could be detrimental to the conservation of the fishery, the period may be extended to two or three years (s.26(5)). The practical effect of this is likely to be a reduction in the number of fishermen who will be able to obtain licences under the proposed order. Further powers are given to the Minister to vary an order submitted to him before confirming it, with the consent of the water authority, and to require publication of any variation in the order by the authority in such a manner as he may specify (s.26(6)). Revocation of an order is brought about by the Minister or, alternatively, by the water authority with the confirmation of the Minister (s.26(7)).

The effects of s.26, and in particular the meaning of the phrase 'dependent on fishing for his livelihood' in s.26(4), were considered recently in *R* v *South West Water Authority ex parte Cox* (1981). Here, a number of netsmen, who had been denied licences by the South West Water Authority because of a limitation order, sought a declaration that the Authority had adopted an unduly restrictive interpretation of the phrase 'dependent on fishing for his livelihood'. The issue was whether the words should be understood to include only persons who are wholly dependent upon fishing for their income, or whether it should encompass others who were dependent upon fishing to a lesser extent. It was held that what was contemplated by the provision was that it should extend to cover a person whose occupation is that of a fisherman and who relies upon fishing to a substantial extent for his and his family's ordinary living expenses. The test of 'substantial extent' does not rule out a person who spends a short period of time doing some job other than fishing, or a person who has a subsidiary source of income such as a pension, providing that such a person can be said to carry on the occupation of a fisherman and to rely upon it for his ordinary living expenses.

6.08 General Licences

It is permissible for a water authority to issue a general licence to a person or association which has the exclusive right to fish an inland water under s.25(7) of the Salmon and Freshwater Fisheries Act 1975. Where this is done, the general licence may be made subject to conditions agreed between the water authority and the licensee and will permit any person authorised in writing by the licensee, or by the secretary of an angling association, to fish. The general licence is a convenient means by which the owner of a water can authorise others to fish his water without the necessity for them to obtain individual licences to fish the water.

The uncertain terms on which general licences are issued, 'subject to any conditions agreed between the water authority and the licensee', was the subject of dispute in *Mills* v *Avon and Dorset River Board* (1955). The dispute arose because an application for a general licence was declined as a consequence of the River Board having changed its general policy with respect to the issue of such licences. The policy was justified by the Board as a consequence of private owners commercialising their fisheries by authorising large numbers of persons to fish them upon payment, and so depriving the Board of the revenue that would have been forthcoming on individual licence sales. The particular applicant who brought the case, however, had not commercialised his fishery in this way, but was still denied a general licence as a consequence of the Board's policy. The court held that the indiscriminate withholding of general licences was unjustified and that the fishery owner was entitled to a general licence unless the Board could adduce some good reason for withholding it which was referable to the applicant himself, or to the conditions under which his fishery was administered. Although decided under the forerunner of s.25(7) of the 1975 Act (s.61(g) of the Salmon and Freshwater Fisheries Act 1923), this decision shows that owners of fisheries who apply for a general licence should not be denied such a licence without good cause being shown by the water authority.

6.09   The Issue of Licences and Provision of Returns

A number of additional points concerning licences fall to be considered under Part IV of the Salmon and Freshwater Fisheries Act 1975. The first of these concerns the issue of licences. Apart from where the availability of a particular type of licence is subject to a limitation order under s.26 of the Act, a water authority is *bound* to grant a fishing licence to any applicant who is not disqualified from holding such a licence, on payment of the appropriate duty (para.15, Sch.2). Disqualification from obtaining a water authority area licence may be ordered by a court for a period not exceeding one year where a person has been convicted of more than one offence under the Act. Alternatively, if the person convicted of offences under the Act holds a fishing or general licence, the court may order that that licence shall be forfeited (para.9, Sch.4; and see para.10.09). Other than in these cases, water authorities, or more likely their permit selling agents, cannot pick and choose their customers in respect of individual fishing licences.

In order to assess the effect of fishing upon fish stocks it is necessary for water authorities to have some means of finding out what number of fish have been taken from waters in their area by licence-holders. The capacity of a water authority to gain this information is achieved by means of an explicit power to create byelaws to require persons fishing for salmon, trout, or freshwater fish to send to the water authority returns, in such form, giving such particulars and at such times as may be specified in the byelaws, of any such fish which they have taken, or a statement that they have taken no such fish (para.32, Sch.3). This power does not extend to allowing a water authority to require a return for eels which have been taken in its area, and where such information is sought by the water authority it is necessary for a ministerial order under s.28(3) of the Act to be made to permit returns of eels to be required (see Ch.7 on ministerial orders). An example of this is SI 1983 No.1350, which causes para.32 of Sch.3 to the Act to have effect as if the power to require persons to send the water authority returns applies to eels as well as salmon, trout, and freshwater fish within the area of the Yorkshire Water Authority.

6.10   Penalties for Offences Relating to Fishing Licences

The maximum penalties provided for unlicensed fishing under s.27 of the Salmon and Freshwater Fisheries Act 1975 are specifically stated in the table in para.1 of Sch.4. If a person is found guilty of an offence under s.27 of the Act whilst not acting with another, then, on summary conviction, he is liable to a fine at level 4 on the standard scale, which presently stands at £1,000. If the offence is committed whilst acting with another, the maximum punishment which may be imposed summarily is the statutory maximum, which is presently £2,000. Where the punishment is imposed by a Crown Court on indictment, the maximum is a term of two years' imprisonment or an unlimited fine or both (see para.1.12 on penalties under the Act generally and Ch.10 on prosecution and procedure).

Other offences under Part IV of the Act, such as the offence of endorsing more names on a licence than are permitted with intent to deceive, under para.14 of Sch.2 and s.25(8), or breaches of byelaws enacted under s.26, carry the general maximum penalty for offences not specified in the table (para.2, Sch.4). This now corresponds, on summary conviction, to a fine not exceeding level 4 on the standard scale, presently £1,000.

(The differential penalties where persons act together to commit an offence under s.27 of the 1975 Act are abolished by s.35 of the Salmon Act 1986, see para.13.06.)

6.11 Sentencing Issues in Licensing Offences

It must be stressed that penalties provided for unlicensed fishing set out in Sch.4 to the Salmon and Freshwater Fisheries Act 1975, and noted in the previous paragraph, represent *maximum* punishments. No minimum punishment is provided for under the Act (see the discussion of penalties under the Act in para.1.12). In practice, the actual penalty in a particular case is likely to be well below the statutory maximum penalty unless it is very serious. Some insight into actual sentencing practice is to be gained from looking at two cases which were considered recently by the Criminal Division of the Court of Appeal. Both of these cases concerned offenders who appealed against sentences imposed by lower courts for offences of unlicensed fishing under s.27 of the Act. In both cases the offenders had previous convictions for poaching offences. The only major question raised by the appeals was that of the appropriate sentence to be imposed.

In the first case, *R v Parker* (1982), the offender, who had been found guilty of unlicensed fishing under s.27 of the Act in the company of others, had a previous conviction for poaching but, nonetheless, the appeal court held that this did not provide a ground for the trial judge to conclude that he was an 'habitual poacher'. Given one previous conviction to be taken into account, and that the accused had served seven days' imprisonment prior to being granted bail, the appeal court imposed a fine of £50. The view was expressed that ordinarily the proper sentence for the offence would have been a fine of a moderate amount. The £50 imposed took account of the seven days that the offender had already spent in prison.

In the second case, *R v Smith* (1982), an offender had six or seven previous convictions for a range of offences including burglary, theft, assault, and poaching offences, and a sentence of nine months' imprisonment was affirmed by the Court of Appeal. His accomplice, who was also found guilty under s.27 of the Act, and also appealed against a nine months' prison sentence imposed by the Crown Court, had four previous convictions, three of which were for poaching. In his case, the nine month sentence was reduced to the equivalent of six months, taking account of remission. Donaldson LJ left no doubt about the seriousness of their offences in saying:

It is quite clear that the learned judge had no alternative but to impose immediate sentences of imprisonment, because both these men must appreciate that poaching is merely another form of theft and that society will not tolerate it. They seem to have imagined, prior to this occasion, that the worst that was likely to happen would be that they would be fined, thereby adding slightly to the costs of their activities. We hope that, whatever else they may have learnt from this particular experience, they will have learnt that, if they are ever caught poaching again, they will find themselves serving long sentences of imprisonment.

It is not easy to generalise from past cases about the penalties which will be imposed in the future. All the factors must be taken into account in deciding upon the appropriate punishment; the gravity of the offence, the previous conduct and circumstances of the accused. In some respect every case will be unique. Nevertheless, the contrast between *R* v *Parker* and *R* v *Smith* gives a general indication that conviction on indictment of an offence under s.27 of the Act is unlikely to attract imprisonment unless the offender has a substantial criminal record. The imposition of a fine alone is more likely on a first or even a second offence (on sentencing practice generally, see Thomas (1979)).

7

POWERS AND DUTIES OF WATER AUTHORITIES AND THE MINISTER

7.01   Introduction

Part V of the Salmon and Freshwater Fisheries Act 1975, ss.28 to 37, is presented under the title of 'Administration and Enforcement', and takes in a number of distinct topics which are only loosely related to one another. Section 28 is headed 'General powers and duties of water authorities and the Minister' and the present chapter is devoted to the topics it raises. Sections 29 and 30 are headed 'Fish rearing licences' and 'Introduction of fish into inland waters' respectively, and are considered in Chapter 8. Sections 31 to 36, headed 'Powers of water bailiffs', are dealt with in Chapter 9. The final section, s.37, headed 'Prosecution of offences', and the provisions that it refers to from Parts I and II of Schedule 4 to the Act, are discussed in Chapter 10.

Within the present chapter a division exists between the powers and duties of water authorities, which are considered in paras 7.02 to 7.11, and the powers and duties of the Minister which are discussed in the remainder of the chapter.

7.02   General Functions of Water Authorities

Water authorities have so far been presented purely in their capacity as bodies administering and enforcing the law relating to freshwater fisheries. It is in order to take a step back to look at the fishery role alongside other water activity operations to place water authorities in their proper legal and administrative perspective. Many of the legal powers possessed by water authorities, and used in the performance of their fishery duties, are aspects of more general legal powers which follow from the other functions that they are obliged to perform. A brief glimpse at the scale of water authority operations is sufficient to put fishery functions into context.

At the present time water authorities employ over 51,000 people and have an annual turnover of about £2,600 million. In both manpower and money terms their major concern is with water supply and sewage treatment and in particular with the 139,000 miles of water mains, 141,000 miles of sews, 6,500 sewage treatment works, and 800 water treatment works that they presently administer. To place fishery-related duties in financial perspective, the whole of the 'environmental services' provided by water authorities amounted to only 3 per cent of the operating expenditure for all water authorities in 1984/5. 'Environmental services' encompass pollution control and monitoring, navigation, recreational and amenity services, *and* fisheries: hence, on a global view of water authority activities, fishery duties constitute only a very small part of the total sphere of water authority operations (Command Paper (1986) No.9734, and Water Authorities Association (1985)).

Many of the legal powers which are available to water authorities in administering fishery law are of a general nature, and are given to them as a consequence of their general functions rather than because of anything uniquely to do with their obligations in respect of fisheries. Their general functions amount to securing the effective execution of the national policy for water. A number of aspects of this policy are outlined in s.1 of the Water Act 1973:

(a) the conservation, augmentation, distribution and proper use of water resources, and the provision of water supplies;

(b) sewage and the treatment and disposal of sewage and other effluents;

(c) the restoration and maintenance of the wholesomeness of rivers and other inland water;

(d) the use of inland water for recreation;

(e) the enhancement and preservation of amenity in connection with inland water; and

(f) the use of inland water for navigation.

In addition to the functions of water authorities in relation to these activities, they also have duties in respect of land drainage, and flood protection and warning under the Land Drainage Act 1976. Finally, along with all of these functions, there are the obligations in relation to fisheries which arise under the Salmon and Freshwater Fisheries Act 1975.

Although many of the functions of water authorities will be accompanied by particular legal powers which will assist a water authority in exercising those functions, other powers are general in nature. The most important power of this kind arises under para.2 of Sch.3 to the Water Act 1973 where it is stated that: 'A water authority shall have power to do anything (whether or not involving the expenditure, borrowing or lending of money or the acquisition or disposal of any property or rights) which in the opinion of the authority is calculated to facilitate, or is conducive or incidental to, the discharge of any of their functions.' The breadth with which this power is worded makes it of more general application than specific powers given in respect of the exercise of any particular function. For this reason, a water authority may often find it more convenient to justify its actions by reference to this more generally worded power, rather than resort to the use of more specific powers, even if the more specific power appears more pertinent to the situation. Where the water authority has to justify its every action by reference to a statutory power, breadth is often more important than specificity, so that in practice a water authority may resort to general powers when exercising fishery functions rather than make use of powers under the Salmon and Freshwater Fisheries Act 1975.

7.03 Water Authority Areas

As was described in Chapter 2, the history of regional fishery administration in England and Wales is a tale of consolidation, which during this century has seen fishery boards become river boards (under the River Boards Act 1948), and river boards become river authorities (under the Water Resources Act 1963), and most recently river authorities become water authorities (under the Water Act 1973). At each transition the number of bodies in existence has been reduced, so that now there are just 10 water authorities covering the whole of England and Wales. To be more precise, nine regional water authorities and the Welsh National Water Development Authority were established by statutory orders made pursuant to the Water Act 1973, but the Welsh Authority was separately dealt with, and later renamed the Welsh Water Authority. Hence, although the Welsh Water Authority is not a 'regional water authority' as defined under the Water Act 1973, it is nevertheless properly described as a 'water authority'. In practical terms this makes little difference in relation to fishery law, and references to 'regional water authority' in this work should be taken to refer to the Welsh Water Authority on the same footing as the other regional water authorities.

In ordinary circumstances a water authority's powers of action are geographically limited. Regional water authorities are bound to exercise their functions within their respective areas. These areas are based upon the natural catchment basins of rivers or groups of rivers and are stated in Sch.1 to the Water Act 1973. It is possible, however, for the boundaries of water authorities to be altered for any particular function by a statutory order under s.2(5) of the Water Act 1973, and so a water authority may have a different area in respect of fisheries from that which it has in respect of, say, water supply. With regard to fisheries, the areas defined under the Water Act 1973 extend to include tidal waters and the sea adjoining the coastline up to six nautical miles out (para.4(1), Sch.2, Water Act 1973, and s.9(1) and para.19, Sch.2, Fishery Limits Act 1976; see para.1.04). By contrast, a water authority's river pollution functions extend only to tidal waters and parts of the sea within 3 nautical miles of the coast (see para.11.13).

7.04   Water Authority Personnel

The ultimate responsibility for the exercise of a water authority's functions rests with its 'members', rather than the employees of the authority. The members of a water authority consist of a chairman who is appointed by the Secretary of State, two members appointed by the Minister of Agriculture, Fisheries and Food, and not less than six nor more than twelve other members appointed by the Secretary of State. In making these appointments the Minister and Secretary of State are obliged to appoint persons who have had experience of, and shown capacity in, matters relating to the functions of water authorities, and regard should also be had to the desirability of the members of the authority being familiar with the requirements and circumstances of the authority's area (s.3, Water Act 1973 as amended by s.1(1), Water Act 1983).

Pursuant to a water authority's general power to do anything to discharge its functions (discussed in para.7.02) it has an implied power to employ whatever persons may be necessary for that purpose. This brings with it all the legal duties and responsibilities of a large employer. Water authorities may employ officers and other staff, provide them with equipment, facilities and accommodation, and administer pension schemes and schemes of training and education (s.26, Water Act 1973). In short, a water authority is authorised to act as would any

Figure 1 Water authorities in England and Wales

large business concern providing that its actions are 'calculated to facilitate, or conducive or incidental to' the discharge of its lawful functions (para.2 of Sch.3, Water Act 1973).

In addition to the management and the officers and staff that it employs, a large number of persons occupy consultative positions in relation to the activities of water authorities. Water authorities are under a duty to establish advisory committees of persons who appear to be interested in fisheries in the water authority area. A water authority is to consult such committees as to the manner in which it is to discharge its duty to maintain, improve and develop fisheries. The duty imposed upon a water authority is in the first place to establish a regional advisory committee for the whole of the area in which it exercises fishery functions under the Act. In addition to this, the second part of the duty is to establish such local advisory committees as the water authority considers necessary to represent persons interested in fisheries in localities within the region (s.28(1)(b) and (2), Salmon and Freshwater Fisheries Act 1975). Although the duty created here is to establish and consult these advisory committees, there is no compulsion on a water authority to act in accordance with the views of an advisory committee; the ultimate managerial functions of the authority remain with its members. A new provision has recently been added to the 1975 Act by para.4(1) of Sch.4 to the Water Act 1983, which permits water authorities to pay members of advisory committees. The new subsection, s.28(2A), states that: 'A water authority may pay any member of an advisory committee established by it in accordance with [s.28(1)(b) of the Salmon and Freshwater Fisheries Act 1975] such allowances as may be determined by the Minister with the consent of the Treasury.' In the new subsection para.4(2) of Sch.4 to the Water Act 1983 stipulates that the reference to 'the Minister' shall be construed as the Secretary of State in relation to the Welsh Water Authority (this stipulation is itself incorporated into the Salmon and Freshwater Fisheries Act 1975 as a new subsection: s.41(2A)).

7.05   Maladministration by a Water Authority

Because water authorities are corporate bodies created by statute, their powers of action are limited to the powers given to them by Acts of Parliament. If a water authority takes an action which goes beyond the powers given to it by Parliament then that action is said to be unlawful and subject to the doctrine of *ultra vires* (meaning beyond the powers of the acting body, see De Smith (1985) Ch.28). The fact that an action is outside the powers of a water authority will not necessarily make it a criminal offence.

A procedure is provided for under s.25 and s.26 of the Local Government Act 1974 for the investigation of complaints of injustice as a result of maladministration by the water authority. Where this procedure is followed a 'Local Commissioner', known popularly as a 'local ombudsman', conducts an investigation and reports on complaints made by an aggrieved complainant. If the complaint is submitted in the prescribed manner within a specified time it will become the subject of investigation unless excepted. The provisions allow exceptions where the complaint affects most of the inhabitants of a water authority area, or where the complainant has another remedy or right of action before a court or tribunal or an appeal to a minister (s.26, Local Government Act 1974).

If as the result of such an investigation the Local Commissioner discovers maladministration on the part of the water authority, the Commissioner is not empowered to order a water authority to desist from a particular course of action nor to direct them to follow a particular course of action. The water authority is able, after considering the Commissioner's report, to make a financial payment or provide some other benefit to the person who has suffered injustice as a consequence of maladministration (s.31, Local Government Act 1974 and s.1, Local Government Act 1978). This procedure may provide a last resort to the victim of maladministration, but in practice he would be more likely to pursue remedies provided directly under the statute under which a water authority purports to act, or else to pursue some common law remedy such as an action for compensation for trespass against the water authority.

7.06   General Fishery Powers of Water Authorities

Powers and duties of water authorities which are peculiar to the exercise of their fishery function may be grouped together under the headings of 'general fishery powers' and 'specific fishery powers'. The latter consist of powers which are specifically mentioned in the body of the Salmon and Freshwater Fisheries Act 1975 (that is, ss.1 to 43) and are listed in paras 7.10 and 7.11 below. The former are discussed in this paragraph.

As was noted in para.7.02, water authorities possess a general power, originating under the Water Act 1973, to do anything which in the opinion of the authority is conducive or incidental to the discharge of their functions. Without prejudice to the generality of this power, paras.37 to 39 of Sch.3 to the Salmon and Freshwater Fisheries Act 1975 spell out further general powers in respect of fisheries. In particular these paragraphs state that Part VI of the Water Resources Act 1963 is to be understood to permit a water authority to acquire property either compulsorily or voluntarily in three situations. The three types of property involved are:

(a)   any dam, fishing weir, fishing mill dam, fixed engine or other artificial obstruction and any fishery attached to or worked in connection with any such obstruction (see Ch.4 for the definitions of these terms);

(b)   so much of the bank adjoining a dam as may be necessary for making or maintaining a fish pass for the purposes of s.10 of the 1975 Act (see Ch.4 on fish passes generally);

(c)   for the purpose of erecting and working a fixed engine (where this is provided for by ministerial order under s.28 of the Act) any fishery land or foreshore specified in the order together with any easement over any adjoining land necessary for securing access to the fishery land or foreshore so acquired.

These powers will permit a water authority to alter or remove any obstruction which it acquires, or permit the water authority or its lessees to work the obstruction in a lawful manner for fishing purposes as would the owner, or in the case of an obstruction acquired under a lease, subject to the terms of the lease. This power is subject to the proviso that it shall not authorise anything to be done which injuriously affects any navigable river, canal, or inland navigation (paras 38 and 39, Sch.3).

In addition to these powers to acquire land, a water authority is provided with three further general powers under para.39 of Sch.3. These are that:

(a)   the water authority may take legal proceedings in respect of any offence or for the enforcement of any provision under the Act (see Ch.10 on prosecution and procedure), or for the protection of the fisheries in their area from injury by pollution or otherwise (see Ch.11 on pollution);

(b)   the water authority may purchase or lease by agreement any fishery, fishing rights, or any establishment for the artificial propagation or rearing of salmon, trout or freshwater fish, and may use, work or exercise any of these themselves or have them worked on their behalf by lessees or any person duly authorised in writing (see Ch.8 on fish farms);

(c)   the water authority may obtain the services of additional constables under s.15 of the Police Act 1964 (see Ch.10 on the powers of water bailiffs).

7.07   *The Power of a Water Authority to Enter on to Land*

A general power authorising entry on to land was given to the former river authorities under s.111 of the Water Resources Act 1963 and now applies to the corresponding functions of water authorities. The section provides that a water authority has the power to authorise any person in writing to enter upon land at a reasonable time for the purpose of performing any of the authority's functions whether in relation to that land or not. The power extends to permitting such a person to enter upon any land to inspect or survey it to determine whether, or how, the authority's functions are to be performed, or whether any statutory provision relating to its functions is being or has been complied with. The power of entry is distinct from that authorised by a Minister (see para.7.17), or given to a water bailiff (see Ch.9), or a power of entry given by a justice of the peace (see Ch.9). Where the owner or occupier of the land declines to allow the authorised person to enter land for these purposes, the right of entry may be enforced by a justice's warrant authorising the person to enter the land, if need be, by force. The application for a warrant must be made to the justice by sworn information in writing which shows to the satisfaction of the justice:

(a)   that admission to the land has been refused to the applicant, or that refusal is apprehended, or that the land is unoccupied or the occupier is temporarily absent, or that the case is one of urgency, or that application for admission would defeat the object of entry; and

(b)   that there is reasonable ground for entry upon the land for the purpose for which entry is required (s.111, Water Resources Act 1963).

7.08 The Power of a Water Authority to Make Byelaws

Water authorities are given extensive powers to make byelaws under Sch.1 and Sch.3 to the Salmon and Freshwater Fisheries Act 1975, and it is an offence to contravene or fail to comply with a water authority byelaw (s.25(7) of the 1975 Act). These powers may only be exercised to make byelaws for purposes permitted under the Act. The purposes for which byelaws may be made are the imposition of close seasons and times, and purposes stated in paras.19 to 36 of Sch.3 to the Act. For the most part these have been discussed in relation to the sections of the Act under which they arise. The final purpose for which byelaws may be made by a water authority under Sch.3 is stated to be: 'The better execution of this Act and the better protection, preservation and improvement of any salmon fisheries, trout fisheries and eel fisheries in a water authority area.' (para.36, Sch.3). This catch-all provision is in marked contrast to the other 17 listed purposes in Sch.3, which are all intended to achieve restricted and closely defined objectives. By contrast, para.36 appears to give an extensive power to make byelaws of diverse and unspecified kinds. It appears that the reason for providing water authorities with this power was to permit them to take actions to destroy predators on the understanding that this power was not otherwise provided for under the 1923 Act (see Bledisloe Report (1961) para.224). The actual wording of the provision, however, makes it far more general in its effect than merely allowing the destruction of predators. It is difficult to draw clear bounds to the range of things that might constitute 'protection, preservation and improvement' of a fishery.

7.09 The Procedure for Making Water Authority Byelaws

Given that the object of a byelaw is within the range of purposes for which a water authority is entitled to make byelaws, a number of general considerations apply to the procedure for making byelaws. Byelaws may be made to apply to the whole or to any part or parts of a water authority area, or for the whole or for any part or parts of the year (para.16, Sch.3, Salmon and Freshwater Fisheries Act 1975). When a byelaw has been formulated by a water authority it will not have effect until confirmed by the Minister in accordance with the general procedure governing the creation of water authority byelaws set out in Part II of Sch.7 to the Water Act 1973. In brief, this procedure requires the water authority to publish notice of their intention to have the proposed byelaw confirmed at least one month before they apply to the Minister for confirmation. This means that the water authority must publish notice of their intention to make the application in the *London Gazette* and in such other manner as they think best adapted for informing the persons affected. The water authority must serve notices of the application upon public authorities concerned, and provide reasonable facilities for inspection of the proposed byelaw at their offices, and any person who applies will be entitled to a copy free of charge. The proposed byelaw will not have effect until confirmed by the Minister, and the Minister will fix the date on which it is to come into operation. If no date is fixed the confirmed byelaw will come into operation one month after the date of confirmation (Sch.7, Part II, Water Act 1973).

Notwithstanding that there has been compliance with the general procedure for creation of a water authority byelaw, there are provisions made under paras 17 and 18 of Sch.3 to the Salmon and Freshwater Fisheries Act 1975 allowing for compensation to be paid to persons adversely affected by certain types of byelaw. If the byelaw is of a kind which specifies a net or other instrument which may be used (para.21, Sch.3 to the 1975 Act), or prohibits the use of an instrument (para.25, Sch.3), the owner or occupier of any fishery which is injuriously affected by the byelaw may claim compensation for loss. The claim must be made to the water authority in writing within a year of the confirmation of the byelaw, and the amount of compensation payable will be determined by a single arbitrator where no agreement is reached between the claimant and the water authority (para.17, Sch.3). The compensation agreed or decided upon can be paid as a lump sum or an annual amount, but where it is paid annually the recipient may at any time after five years from the date of the determination require it to be reviewed by a single arbitrator appointed by the Minister (para.18, Sch.3). In this way provision is made for changes in money values to be taken into account in annual compensation awards.

7.10 Specific Water Authority Powers to Make Byelaws

In addition to the specific powers to make byelaws that have already been mentioned, a number of other specific powers in respect of byelaws arise or are mentioned under the body of the 1975 Act (that is, ss.1 to 43). These are examined elsewhere in the text, but for convenience they are listed below in the order of the sections under which they arise:

s.3(2): power to authorise net dimensions.

s.5(5)(b): power to authorise the use of explosives, poisons or electrical devices for a scientific purpose, or for the purpose of protecting, improving or replacing stocks of fish.

s.14(6): power to prescribe the period for placing gratings.

s.15(2)(b): power to authorise the removal of gratings.

s.17(1)(a): power to impose restrictions on taking fish within prescribed distance below obstructions.

s.19(8)(c): power to authorise fishing with rod and line for eels.

s.19(8)(e)(ii): power to prohibit the taking of freshwater fish for bait.

s.39(1)(b): power to amend the Tweed Fisheries (Amendment) Act 1859.

s.39(2): power to determine mesh size on Solway Firth.

In addition to these purposes for which byelaws can be made, a number of other purposes are set out in paras 19 to 36 of the Act. These have been discussed elsewhere in relation to the topics which they concern.

7.11 Other Specific Powers and Duties of Water Authorities under the 1975 Act

Additional powers and duties of water authorities, other than those relating to the making of byelaws, arise under the body of the Act and are considered elsewhere in this text, but for convenience they are listed below in the order of the sections under which they arise. This list does not include those powers of a water authority which are made subject to the Minister's consent, nor powers given to a water bailiff appointed by a water authority (see Ch. 9).

s.1(2): power to authorise a prohibited instrument.

s.2(5): power to authorise the use of roe and taking of unclean or immature fish.

s.4: power to take proceedings where poisonous matter is put into water.

s.5(2): power to authorise the use of explosives and electrical devices.

s.6(2): power to authorise the possession or destruction of a fixed engine.

s.8(4): power to remove obstructions to free passage of fish.

s.9(1): power to require construction of a fish pass by an owner.

s.9(3): power to construct a fish pass and to recover expenses from owner.

s.10(3): power to recover expenses for injury to a fish pass.

s.12(2): power to require repair of a fish pass.

s.13(1): power to authorise the use of sluices.

s.13(3): power to authorise the use of sluices where a dam is under repair.

s.14(1): power to grant exemption from placing gratings.

s.18(3): duty to pay compensation for injury sustained in the construction of a fish pass or free gap (under s.16) or in placing a grating (under s.15).

s.19(3): power to authorise close season fishing for salmon.

s.19(5): power to authorise close season fishing for trout.

s.24(2): power to permit an 'authorised officer' to open a package suspected to contain salmon or trout.

s.24(3): power to permit an 'authorised officer' to detain a package.

s.4(4): power to permit an 'authorised officer' to detain salmon or trout not packed in a package.

s.24(5): power to permit an 'authorised officer' to destroy salmon or trout.

s.25(1): duty to operate a system of licensing.

s.25(7): power to grant a general licence.

s.28(1)(a): duty to maintain, improve and develop fisheries.

s.28(1)(b): duty to establish advisory committees.

s.30: power to give consent to introduction of fish into an inland water.

(Additional specific powers and duties arise under the schedules to the Act.)

7.12 Powers and Duties of the Minister

It is the duty of the Minister of Agriculture, Fisheries and Food to secure the effective execution of so much of the national water policy for England and Wales as relates to fisheries in inland and coastal waters (s.1(3), Water Act 1973). Accordingly, 'the Minister' in most references under the Salmon and Freshwater

Fisheries Act 1975 must be taken to refer to the Minister of Agriculture, Fisheries and Food (s.41(1), Salmon and Freshwater Fisheries Act 1975).

The exception to this generality is that there are a number of places in the Act where references to 'the Minister' are to be understood to mean the Minister of Agriculture, Fisheries and Food *acting jointly with* the Secretary of State for Wales. These concern actions in relation to water authority areas which are wholly or partly in Wales, and arise under five portions of the Act: Part IV, relating to fishing licences; s.28(3), relating to the power of 'the Minister' to make general orders for the regulation of fisheries; para.2 of Sch.1, relating to the power of 'the Minister' to make byelaws for a water authority in respect of close seasons and close times; paras 5 to 11 and Part II of Sch.3, relating to procedure for making 'ministerial' orders and water authority byelaws; and Sch.2, relating to licences. Along with these five portions of the Act where the Minister of Agriculture, Fisheries and Food acts jointly with the Secretary of State for Wales, under the new s.28(2A) of the Act concerning payment of members of advisory committees, the reference to 'the Minister' is apparently to be understood as the Secretary of State for Wales *acting alone* in so far as the new subsection applies to the Welsh Water Authority (under the new s.41(2A) of the Salmon and Freshwater Fisheries Act 1975 inserted by para.4(2), Sch.4, Water Act 1983). Outside the Welsh or Anglo-Welsh sphere of operation of the Act, however, 'the Minister' means simply the Minister of Agriculture, Fisheries and Food. It is in this sense that 'the Minister' is to be understood in relation to the general operation of the Act, and references to 'the Minister' in this book are to be understood in the same way unless the context indicates otherwise.

7.13   *General Powers of the Minister*

As with the water authorities, the Minister is provided with a diverse collection of general and specific powers under the Salmon and Freshwater Fisheries Act 1975. His specific powers are listed in para.7.18. The general powers arise under s.28(3) and Sch.3 to the Act. Section 28(3) states that the Minister may by statutory instrument make an order for the general regulation of the salmon, trout, freshwater and eel fisheries within an area defined by the order. The detail is filled in by para.1 of Sch.3 which describes three purposes for which such orders may be made:

   (a)   for the imposition, collection and recovery by a water authority of contributions assessed on several fisheries regulated by the order or on the owners or occupiers of such fisheries;

   (b)   for enabling the water authority with the approval of the Minister . . . to erect and work by themselves or their lessees any fixed engine for catching salmon or migratory trout within the area within which the order is to apply;

   (c)   for modifying in relation to the fisheries within the area any of the provisions of the Act which relate to the regulation of fisheries, or of any local Act relating to any fishery within the area.

Purpose (a) is fiscal in nature and allows the water authority to raise income for the funding of fishery functions by a charge on several fishery owners or occupiers (on the meaning of 'several fishery' see para.1.07). As has been noted, the major sources of funding for water authorities discharging their fishery functions are the revenue brought in by fishing licence sales and charges for environmental services (s.30, Water Act 1973 as amended by s.2, Water Charges Act 1976). In addition to these, purpose (a) permits revenue to be raised directly from several fishery owners or occupiers. It appears that the proportion of funds raised in this way is small relative to the other sources (Water Authorities Association (1985) p.40).

Purpose (b) provides a major exception to the prohibitions on placing and use of fixed engines under s.6 of the 1975 Act (discussed in Ch.4). Typically this power might be used by a water authority to trap migratory salmon or sea trout in order to monitor the levels of fish stocks, but it is not stated to be limited to scientific purposes and could be used as a means of permitting a water authority to embark upon a commercial venture. As Fort and Brayshaw (1961 p.288) point out:

> By the intelligent use of a fish trap a [water authority] might be able to put fish on the market at a small cost as far as labour is concerned, and at the same time have sufficient control over the number of fish taken to ensure that the stocks in the river of whatever type of fish they catch were not over depleted . . . Apart from being a possible source of supply for the market, fish traps can be used for reducing overstocked waters and for revealing the movements of fish, about which not a great deal is known at present.

In whatever manner a fixed engine is to be used, the Minister's order permitting it is subject to two conditions. First, the order authorising the fixed engine to be worked is not to exceed five years unless the period is extended from time to time by a licence from the Minister, and even then the licence given is not to be for longer than five years (para.2, Sch.3 to the 1975 Act). Second, the Minister is bound to enquire into the effect of the working of the engine on salmon or 'trout' fisheries within the area before granting the licence (para.3, Sch.3). 'Trout' is wider in meaning than 'sea trout', which the fixed engine will be authorised to catch (see s.41(1) to the 1975 Act). An example of an order of this kind is SI 1982 No.1420 which, subject to the approval of the Minister, permits the Thames Water Authority to erect and work a fixed engine for catching salmon or migratory trout within the area of the Authority for the purpose of artificial propagation or for scientific purposes. This order has the effect of excluding ss.6, 21(1) and any other sections of the Act which limit or prohibit the placing, use or working of a fixed engine in so far as they apply to the Water Authority.

Purpose (c) for which an order may be made is very wide in its scope and empowers the Minister to make changes to the substance of the Salmon and Freshwater Fisheries Act 1975 or local Acts as they apply to a particular water authority area. No express constraints limit the actions of the Minister in so doing other than the requirement that all orders made under any of the three purposes, (a), (b) or (c), may contain provisions for payment of compensation to persons injuriously affected by the order, where it appears necessary or proper for the purposes of the order.

7.14 Procedure in Relation to Ministerial Orders

Application for a ministerial order to be made under s.28(3) of the Salmon and Freshwater Fisheries Act 1975 can be made by four categories of applicant:

(a)   a water authority;

(b)   a county council;

(c)   persons who in the opinion of the Minister are the owners of one-fourth at least of the value of the several fisheries proposed to be regulated or constitute a majority of the persons holding licences to fish in public waters within the area of the proposed order;

(d)   any association of persons which in the opinion of the Minister is sufficiently representative of fishing interests within that area (para.5 of Sch.3 to the 1975 Act).

The applicant may be required to give security for the Minister's expenses if requested to do so (para.6, Sch.3).

In a similar way to that described in para.7.09 in relation to water authority byelaws, a ministerial order must be made in accordance with detailed procedural requirements calculated to ensure publicity of a proposed order and opportunity for objections to be raised and considered. The Minister must publicise his intention to make the draft order in the *London Gazette* and any other manner best adapted for informing persons affected, and indicate the place where copies of the order may be inspected and obtained and the manner in which objections should be made (para.7, Sch.3). The Minister must consider any objections which are made and hold a public local inquiry into objections (para.8, Sch.3). After the form of the order has been settled by the Minister, he is bound to publicise it with the indication that it will become final within a stated period of not less than 30 days unless a water authority, local authority or another person or association affected by it requests that it be made subject to special parliamentary procedure regulated by the Statutory Orders (Special Procedure) Acts 1945 and 1965 (para.9, Sch.3 to the 1975 Act). Unless such a request is made and not withdrawn, the Minister may confirm the order on the expiry of the period of notice, and that confirmation is taken to be evidence that the procedural requirements of the Act have been met (paras.10 and 11, Sch.3).

Special provisions apply where a ministerial order seeks to acquire property rights in a fishery or land owned by the Crown or a government department. Where this is sought the Minister must obtain consent from the Crown Estate Commissioners, the Chancellor of the Duchy of Lancaster, the Duke of Cornwall or the government department concerned (para.13, Sch.3).

7.15 The Minister's Powers on Default of a Water Authority

If it appears to the Minister that an inquiry should be held to ascertain whether a water authority has failed to perform any of its functions (see para.7.02 on the general functions of water authorities) in circumstances where it ought to have done, he may cause a local inquiry to be held (s.108(1), Water Resources Act 1963). In the event of the inquiry finding that there has been default on the part of the water authority, the Minister may make an order declaring the authority to be in default and direct the authority to perform its functions in a manner and at a time specified by the order. In the unlikely event of a water authority continuing to fail to perform its functions in accordance with the order, the Minister may, as a last resort, make a further order transferring the function of the defaulting authority either to himself or to an adjoining water authority. In such improbable circumstances the expenses incurred by the Minister or the adjoining water authority would be recoverable from the authority in default (s.108, Water Resources Act 1963).

7.16   The Minister's Power to Give General Directions to Water Authorities

The most general power possessed by the Minister with respect to water authorities is the power to give a general direction to a water authority. The Minister may give directions of a general character to water authorities as to the exercise of their functions in respect of fisheries so far as the exercise of those functions appears to the Minister to affect the execution of the national policy for water or otherwise to affect the national interest. Such a direction may be given to a particular water authority or to water authorities generally (s.5, Water Act 1973). The open-endedness of this power makes it difficult to comment upon. It appears to be a catch-all power to be used as a last resort if all lesser powers given to the Minister are inadequate. The scope of the lesser powers is in itself so broad that it is difficult to imagine a situation where the general power would be needed to achieve a purpose that could not be otherwise accomplished by the Minister. Nonetheless, it remains in reserve for the rare situation where the Minister would otherwise be lacking a lawful power to act in the national interest.

7.17   The Minister's Power to Authorise Entry

The Minister is empowered to authorise any person to enter land at a reasonable time for the purpose of exercising any water authority functions. This power entitles the person authorised to enter on to any land to inspect or survey the land or any article there, in order to determine whether or in what manner ministerial or water authority functions ought to be performed, or alternatively to determine whether or in what manner they are being, or have been, properly performed (s.111(2) and (3), Water Resources Act 1963). This authority is qualified in respect of land used for residential purposes, or admission with heavy equipment, by the proviso that admission to the land cannot be demanded as of right unless seven days' written notice of the proposed entry has been given to the occupier (s.111(3), Water Resources Act 1973). It is an offence to obstruct an authorised person exercising this power (s.112, Water Resources Act 1963).

7.18 Specific Powers and Duties of the Minister under the Salmon and Freshwater Fisheries Act 1975

In addition to the extensive general powers possessed by the Minister, a number of specific powers concerning fisheries are given to the Minister under the Act. Specific fishery powers given to the Minister under the Salmon and Freshwater Fisheries Act 1923 were subject to comment and criticism in the Bledisloe Report (1961 Ch.X). The basis of opposition to the continuation of many ministerial powers in respect of fisheries was that the river boards, who preceded today's water authorities, should be as free as possible to formulate their policies and to carry them out, and consequently ministerial control over executive functions should be relaxed. Regrettably this argument was not followed to any great extent in the enactment of the Salmon and Freshwater Fisheries Act 1975, and innumerable ministerial powers to regulate fisheries remain. In many cases it is hard to justify the need for a minister to give consent for actions which appear to be matters of day to day fishery management, properly left to be settled by the water authority concerned. On the other hand, specific powers conferred upon the Minister do sometimes involve property rights and the power to create criminal offences. Justifiably these matters should be subject to consideration by an outside body which is independent of the water authority concerned. The problem is that of finding a proper balance between water authority and ministerial powers which allows the water authorities to get on with their job of 'maintaining, improving and developing' fisheries without the need to be making constant reference to the Minister, whilst ensuring that individuals aggrieved by the actions of a water authority have the means to appeal to the Minister for redress.

The specific powers and duties of the Minister under the body of the Salmon and Freshwater Fisheries Act 1975 (ss.1 to 43) are considered elsewhere in the text, but for convenience they are listed below in order of the sections under which they arise. The list does not include the powers of a person appointed by the Minister which are analogous to those of a water bailiff (see Ch.9).

s.4(3): power to certify that an individual has a material interest in waters alleged to be affected by poisonous matter.

s.5(2)(b): power to approve the use of a noxious substance for a scientific purpose or to protect, improve or replace stocks of fish.

s.8(2): power to approve the form and dimensions of a fish pass at fishing dam.

s.9(1)(b): power to approve the form and dimensions of a fish pass where a new dam is constructed or an existing dam restored.

s.10(1): power to permit a water authority to construct a fish pass.

s.10(2): power to permit a water authority to modify a fish pass.

s.11(1): power to make approval of a fish pass provisional.

s.11(2): power to revoke a provisional approval of a fish pass.

s.11(3): power to extend a provisional approval of a fish pass.

s.11(4): power to certify that a fish pass is effective.

s.14(3): power to approve the construction and placing of a grating.

s.15(1): power to permit a water authority to place a grating and widen or deepen a channel.

s.18(2): duty not to give consent to water authority work unless reasonable notice has been served on occupier and objections considered.

s.18(4): duty to appoint an arbitrator to determine compensation.

s.21(2): power to authorise devices for taking eels.

s.25(1): power to excuse a water authority from operating licensing system for freshwater fish.

s.26(1): power to confirm a water authority licence limitation order.

s.26(2): duty to require a water authority to publish a limitation order.

s.26(3): duty to consider objections to a limitation order and to hold a local inquiry.

s.26(4): duty not to confirm a limitation order unless satisfied that persons dependent on fishing for a livelihood will be able to obtain a licence.

s.26(5): power to extend the period over which applicants have previously held licences.

s.26(6): power to vary a water authority's limitation order.

s.26(7): power to revoke or authorise the revocation of a limitation order.

s.28(3): power to make orders for the general regulation of fisheries.

s.29(1): power to license the artificial propagation of salmon or trout.

s.39(3): duty to determine the limits of the Solway Firth for the purposes of s.39.

8

FISH FARMING AND FISHERY PROTECTION

8.01   Introduction

This chapter takes as a basis two sections from Part V of the Salmon and Freshwater Fisheries Act 1975, ss.29 and 30, concerned with licences to rear fish and the introduction of fish into inland waters respectively. The issues raised by these sections are considered in the broader context of a number of legal provisions outside the Act. The topic of licences to rear fish leads the way into a discussion of the law relating to fish farming and the provisions of the Fisheries Act 1981, and the Diseases of Fish Acts 1937 and 1983. The introduction of fish into inland waters leads into a discussion of the Import of Live Fish (England and Wales) Act 1980. Although outside the strict provisions of the Salmon and Freshwater Fisheries Act 1975, these topics are of central importance to the law on freshwater fisheries.

8.02   Fish Farming Generally

Over recent years fish farming, or aquaculture, has developed from a small-scale means adopted by some progressive fisheries to enhance stocks, into a major branch of agriculture producing a vast tonnage of fish of various species both for the table and for restocking purposes. A survey conducted by Lewis (1984) found a total of 335 fish farms of all kinds in operation in England and Wales. Of these, 258 produced trout, either for the table or for restocking of fisheries, and the others produced a range of fish including carp, coarse fish, ornamental fish, salmon, eels, and shellfish. For the whole of the United Kingdom the output of farmed fish for the year 1982 was valued at over £25 million. Moreover, in response to a presently increasing demand for the produce of fish farms, all the indications are that fish farming is undergoing a dramatic expansion both in the number of farms in operation and in their scale and productivity (Corrie (1979)). In parallel with this growth and change in the nature of the industry, there have been a number of recent changes in the law relating to fish farms brought about under the Fisheries Act 1981 and the Diseases of Fish Act 1983.

A difficulty to note at this stage is that there is no universal legal definition of the meaning of the term 'fish farm'. The meaning of the phrase differs as it is used in different legal contexts. Hence the various definitions of 'fish farm' which exist are considered below in relation to the different statutes in which they arise. What is a fish farm for one purpose, it must be stressed, may not be for another. This will become apparent in the discussion which follows.

(On fish farming generally, see Sedgwick (1982); Ministry of Agriculture, Fisheries and Food (1983); and Sedgwick (1985).)

8.03   *The Licensing of Fish Farms*

Section 29 of the Salmon and Freshwater Fisheries Act 1975 provides that the Minister may grant a licence to carry on the business of artificially propagating or rearing salmon or trout in any waters. Licences may be granted subject to such conditions (if any) as the Minister thinks fit, and be revoked if he is of the opinion that any condition has not been observed. Two points may be noted concerning the wording of this power. First, it only applies to 'salmon and trout', so that the rearing of other types of fish commonly farmed, such as eels, carp and other freshwater fish, will not require a licence under this section. Second, the phrase 'in any waters' indicates that the section is not confined to freshwater, and so the rearing of salmon or other fish in sea cages set off the coast would fall within the section.

Mysteriously, s.29 of the 1975 Act gives no further details of the significance of the status of the licence that it provides for. Nothing is said on the question of whether the holding of a licence is a legal prerequisite to carrying on the business of fish farming, or whether any offence is committed by failing to obtain a licence. Moreover, it is understood that at the time of writing the Minister has granted no licences under s.29 of the Act and has no plans to do so. It is likely that the powers given by this section will be of no greater importance in the future in view of the requirement of registration of fish farms, and provision of information about fish farming activities, which arise under ss.7 to 9 of the Diseases of Fish Act 1983. These sections are discussed in para.8.15 below.

8.04   *The Fisheries Act 1981*

The Fisheries Act 1981 amounts to a legal recognition of the importance of fish farming as a branch of agriculture and a means of food production. The Act empowers the Minister, with the approval of the Treasury, to devise a scheme to make payable such grants as appear desirable for the purpose of reorganising, developing or promoting fish farming in Great Britain (s.31(1), Fisheries Act 1981). 'Fish farming' in this context means the breeding, rearing or cultivating of fish for the purpose of producing food for human consumption. In connection with this scheme, the Minister may carry out research and development for the purpose of promoting the breeding, rearing or cultivation of fish for consumption, and may provide advice on these matters whether or not the purpose of the enterprise is to produce fish for human consumption. Fees may be charged for advice given on these matters (s.32, Fisheries Act 1981). The ambiguity inherent in these provisions is whether fish which are reared artificially and then released into the wild, with the intention that they will subsequently be caught by anglers, will be reared 'for the purpose of producing food for human consumption'. It is hoped that the provisions would extend to encompass that situation, though it is doubtful that they would cover fish released into the wild purely for sporting purposes in a fishery where fish have to be returned to the water and do not provide food for human consumption at any stage.

(Further details of the scheme to provide financial assistance to fish farms are to be found in SI 1984 No.341.)

In acknowledgement of the gulf which exists between fish farming and the types of fishing regulated by the Salmon and Freshwater Fisheries Act 1975, s.33 of the Fisheries Act 1981 allows for a number of exceptions to the general law, in the special circumstances of a fish farm. In particular the Minister may make exemptions, depending on the method of fish farming and the circumstances, which exempt persons engaged in fish farming from committing what would otherwise be offences under the 1975 Act. The exceptions which may be made concern, first, any offence under s.2(2)(a) of the 1975 Act, relating to taking, killing or attempting to take, kill or injure unclean or immature fish (see para.3.13); second, any offence under s.3 of the 1975 Act, relating to restrictions on shooting or working seine or draft nets in certain waters and the prohibition on the use of certain nets (see para.3.15); third, any offence under s.5(1) of the 1975 Act, relating to the prohibition on the use of a noxious substance or electrical device to take or destroy fish, or under s.5(4), relating to the possession of such a substance or device (see para.3.17); fourth, any offence under s.19 of the 1975 Act, relating to fishing for, taking or killing or attempting to take or kill fish during close seasons or close times (see Ch.5); fifth, any offence under s.27 of the 1975 Act, relating to fishing for or taking fish without a licence or possession of equipment with intent to use it for an unlicensed purpose (see Ch.6). Finally, exemptions are provided for in respect of any offence under s.28(7) of the 1975 Act, which consists of contravention of a water authority byelaw concerning the description of nets and other instruments which may be used for taking fish and restrictions on their use (para.21 or 23 of Sch.3 to the 1975 Act); restrictions on carrying certain nets (para.23 or 24, Sch.3); restrictions on taking or removing fish from water without lawful authority (para.26, Sch.3); and the taking of fish of less than the prescribed size (para.28, Sch.3).

In addition to these exemptions s.33(5) of the Fisheries Act 1981 provides a defence to other offences where a person is able to show, on reasonable grounds, that the fish with respect to which the offence is alleged to have been committed was produced by fish farming, and has not subsequently been released into the wild. The offences in respect of which this defence is available include offences under a number of local and Scottish Acts, and also sections of the Salmon and Freshwater Fisheries Act 1975. These are, first, any offence under s.2(2)(b) of the 1975 Act, relating to buying, selling, exposure for sale or possession of unclean or immature fish or parts of such fish (see para.3.13); second, any offence under s.22(1) of the 1975 Act, relating to the buying, selling, exposure for sale or possession for sale of fish at prohibited times of the year (see para.5.12); third, any offence under s.23(3) of the 1975 Act, relating to the entry for export or exporting of fish which were unclean or caught at a time when their sale is prohibited (see para.5.13).

For the purposes of all these exemptions and defences, 'fish farming' is taken to mean the breeding, rearing or cultivation of fish whether or not this is for the purpose of producing food for human consumption (s.33(6), Fisheries Act 1981). Hence the defences would be available to persons rearing ornamental fish or coarse fish, even if the fish in question were not intended to provide food for human consumption.

8.05   The Rating of Fish Farms

As a consequence of the rearing of fish coming to be regarded in law as a branch of agriculture, it became subject to certain fiscal advantages shared with other forms of agricultural enterprise. The most important amongst these is that land or buildings used solely for or in connection with fish farming are not liable to rates, provided that the buildings in question are not occupied as a dwelling. 'Fish farm' in this context means the breeding or rearing of fish for the purpose of producing food for human consumption or for transfer to other waters, but does not include the breeding, rearing or cultivation of any fish which are purely ornamental, or which are bred, reared or cultivated for exhibition (s.26A(1), General Rate Act 1967 as amended by s.31, Local Government, Planning and Land Act 1980).

8.06   The Protection of Fisheries from Disease under the Diseases of Fish Acts 1937 and 1983

The increase in fish farming has made a considerable difference to the supply of fish both for the table and for the angler, and yet it brings with it the problems of any form of intensive agriculture. The containing of large numbers of fish in an unnaturally confined space inevitably makes them vulnerable to the spread of disease to an extent which would be unlikely to occur in the wild. Despite advances in the understanding of methods of treating these diseases, the hazard of an outbreak of an infection, which could result in the loss of thousands of pounds worth of stock, is a substantial one for the fish farmer or the owner of a stocked fishery.

The major legal provisions to protect fish farms and fisheries from the spread of disease were originally enacted under the Diseases of Fish Act 1937. Recently, however, this statute has been subject to extensive amendment under the Diseases of Fish Act 1983. In the discussion which follows reference to the 'Diseases of Fish Acts' is to be understood to refer to the 1937 Act *as amended by* the 1983 Act unless otherwise indicated. The combination of these two Acts provides the Minister and the water authorities with important powers in respect of fishery protection and the control of fish disease.

8.07   The Importation of Live Fish under the Diseases of Fish Acts

Section 1 of the Diseases of Fish Acts makes it unlawful to import or bring into Great Britain any live fish of the salmon family unless permitted to do so by ministerial order. The ministerial order may specify fish by reference to the particular species concerned, the place of origin, or any other factor. Where such an order exists, the fish in question are to be regarded as if they were freshwater fish, and be subject to a licensing procedure.

The general prohibition on importation of live fish of the salmon family extends to the importation of any live freshwater fish, or live eggs of fish of the salmon family or eggs of freshwater fish, unless they are consigned to a person who is licensed to receive them and who produces a licence to receive them. It is for the Minister to issue this type of licence subject to three provisions. First, he may grant the licence subject to requirements as to the quantity and kind of fish or eggs which may be imported and the conditions under which they are to be imported. In particular the Minister may specify measures to be taken as to the disposal, transport, inspection, cleaning and disinfection of fish or eggs and of the containers or other vessels in which they are to be transported or kept, or specify other precautions which are to be taken to avoid the spread of disease amongst salmon and freshwater fish. Second, the licence may be granted for any period not exceeding 12 months but may be suspended or revoked at any time before then. Third, a licence fee of a nominal amount is payable on the issue of a licence. (The precise form which licences of this kind must take is specified by SI 1984 No.455.)

The importation of live fish or eggs without a licence, or in contravention of the terms on which a licence is issued, is an offence. In such circumstances, a police officer, or a customs and excise official, or a person appointed by the Minister as an inspector under the Diseases of Fish Acts, may seize the fish or eggs concerned if he has reason to believe that an offence has been committed, pending legal proceedings, or until the Minister is satisfied that no proceedings are likely to be instituted. An exception to these provisions is that they may be waived by the Commissioners of Customs and Excise if they are satisfied that the fish or eggs in question are being imported solely for the purpose of re-export (s.1, Diseases of Fish Acts).

(For further restrictions upon the import of fish, see para. 8.18 below.)

8.08   Infected Areas

A key element amongst the legal powers which exist to control fish disease is the power of the Minister, under s.2 of the Diseases of Fish Acts, to designate areas which are infected by fish diseases. This section states that if the Minister has reasonable grounds to suspect that any inland or marine waters are, or may become, infected waters, he may designate those waters or land adjacent to them as a 'designated area'. In that event the Minister may prevent or regulate the movement of live fish, or the live eggs of fish, or foodstuff for fish, for the purpose of preventing the spread of infection amongst fish. Persons who are the occupiers of inland waters within the designated area, or are fish farmers in marine waters within the area, are entitled to a report of the evidence on which the designation of the area was made free of charge. Intentional contravention of the order is a criminal offence (s.2(6), Diseases of Fish Acts).

The key terms used in connection with the Minister's power to designate infected areas under s.2 of the Diseases of Fish Acts, and to define the terms used in the Acts generally, are specified under s.10 as follows.

'Fish farm' means any pond, stew, fish hatchery or other place used for keeping, with a view to their sale or to their transfer to other waters (including any other fish farm), live fish, live eggs of fish, foodstuff for fish, and includes any buildings used in connection therewith, and the banks and margins of any water therein.

'Foodstuff for fish' means any substance used, or intended or likely to be used, as food for fish, including natural food.

'Infected' means, in relation to fish, infected with any of the diseases respectively known as bacterial kidney disease (BKD), furunculosis of salmon, infectious haematopoietic necrosis (IHN), infectious pancreatic necrosis (IPN), spring viraemia of carp (SVC), viral haemorrhagic septicaemia (VHS), and whirling disease (Myxosoma cerebralis). (This definition was amended under SI 1984 No.301.)

'Waters' means any waters (including any fish farm) which are frequented by, or used for keeping, live fish of the salmon family or live freshwater fish, live eggs of fish, or foodstuff for fish, and includes the banks and margins of any such waters and any buildings used in connection therewith.

(Accounts of the symptoms and treatment of diseases which constitute infection for the purposes of the Diseases of Fish Acts are to be found in Roberts and Shepherd (1986); Sedgwick (1982) Ch.11; and Sedgwick (1985) Ch.4.)

8.09   Removal of Fish from a Designated Area

In addition to the power of the Minister to prohibit or regulate the movement of fish in a designated area, he has powers to serve a notice on the occupier of a fish farm in an inland water within a designated area (s.2A, Diseases of Fish Acts). A notice of this kind may direct the fish farmer to remove dead or dying fish, and may regulate the way in which any parts of such fish are disposed of. Similarly, where a fish farmer carries on his business in marine waters within a designated area, a notice may require him to remove and dispose of dead or dying fish in a specified manner. In the event of the recipient of the notice failing to comply with the directions, the Minister may authorise an inspector to carry out the directions, and any expenses incurred by the inspector will be recoverable from the person on whom the notice was served. Any person who intentionally does an act which is prohibited by a notice of this kind is guilty of an offence unless he is able to show that he did not know that the act was prohibited (s.2A, Diseases of Fish Acts).

Notwithstanding the existence of a ministerial order designating an area under s.2 of the Diseases of Fish Acts, authority may be given to the occupier of a fish farm in inland waters to remove fish, where the Minister is satisfied that it is necessary to do so for the protection of stock against disease. Where this is permitted the removal of the fish may be authorised by whatever means the Minister considers to be expedient, even if the method used would otherwise be unlawful. Similarly, where the fish farming takes place in marine waters, an order may be made by the Minister to permit the removal of fish from sea cages. In either case, however, the person who is authorised to remove fish must comply with any directions given by the Minister as to the manner in which the fish must be disposed of and intentional failure to do so will amount to a criminal offence (s.2B, Diseases of Fish Acts).

8.10   The Duties of a Water Authority

Section 3 of the Diseases of Fish Acts requires any water authority which has reasonable ground to suspect that any inland waters, other than a fish farm, are infected, is bound to report the matter to the Minister. The section also empowers the water authority to take any practicable steps to secure the removal of dead or dying fish from the waters. When the Minister receives a report to this effect from a water authority he must cause an investigation to be conducted to ascertain whether the waters are actually infected. Where an order under s.2 of the Diseases of Fish Acts is in force, the Minister may authorise a water authority to remove fish from any inland waters other than a fish farm by such methods as he considers to be most expedient, even if the authorised methods would otherwise be illegal. The water authority is then bound to destroy or properly dispose of the fish removed and send the Minister a return of the fish removed at such time as he may direct (s.3, Diseases of Fish Acts).

8.11 Preliminary Precautions

A number of measures are required under s.4 of the Diseases of Fish Acts where waters are suspected to have become infected. In the case of a fish farm in inland waters, if an inspector, appointed under the Diseases of Fish Acts, has reasonable grounds to suspect that the waters are infected waters, he is empowered to serve notice on the occupier and report the matter to the Minister. The effect of such notice is to place the fish farm under quarantine so that no live fish, eggs of fish, or foodstuff of fish may be transported into or out of the farm, without the permission of the Minister, until the expiry of a period of 30 days from the service of the notice. The period can be extended to 60 days where the Minister authorises an inspector to serve a further notice on the occupier. It is an offence for a person intentionally to take any fish, eggs or foodstuff of fish into or out of a fish farm whilst prohibited in this way unless he shows that he did not know that the taking was prohibited (s.4(4), Diseases of Fish Acts). Depending on developments during the period of quarantine, it is open to the Minister to give written intimation to the occupier that permission for the removal of the restricted items is no longer required. On the other hand, if the Minister is satisfied that the waters constitute an infected area he may make an order to that effect, under s.2 of the Diseases of Fish Acts, and so bring about an indefinite extension of the period during which movement of the fish, eggs or foodstuff will be prohibited.

The Diseases of Fish Acts place extensive duties upon persons other than appointed inspectors to report fish diseases. Section 4(5) of the Acts requires suspected infection to be reported by 'any person entitled to take fish from any inland waters or employed for the purpose of having the care of any inland waters'. This appears to refer to anglers, water keepers, water bailiffs and persons employed on fish farms. Such persons are obliged to report to the Minister, by letter or telegram, if they have reasonable grounds to suspect that a fish farm is infected. In the case of waters other than a fish farm, the report must be made to the water authority for the area. To fail to make a report in either of these circumstances, without reasonable excuse, will make a person guilty of an offence. Anglers are often urged to report fish disease where they encounter it: the effect of this provision is that it is capable of being a criminal offence to fail to report disease under certain circumstances.

Analogous provisions apply under s.4A of the Diseases of Fish Acts in respect of marine waters, where similar restrictions may be imposed in respect of the movement of fish, eggs or foodstuff into or out of sea cages. An offence of moving these things is committed unless the person so doing is able to show that he did not know the moving was prohibited. Persons owning sea cages and using them for fish farming or employed to have care of such cages are bound to report to the Minister if they have reasonable grounds to suppose that the cage is situated in infected waters. Failure to do so will amount to a criminal offence (s.4A(5), Diseases of Fish Acts).

8.12   The Duty of the Minister to Examine Waters

A water authority or the occupier of any inland waters is entitled to demand of the Minister an inspection of waters with a view to discovering whether they are infected (s.5, Diseases of Fish Acts). If such a demand is made, the Minister is bound to have the waters inspected and to issue a report to the water authority, or occupier, free of charge. As an exception to this duty, however, the Minister is not bound to bring about an examination where an examination of the same kind has been conducted previously and the period which has elapsed is so short that in his opinion a further examination is not necessary. This duty to inspect may be contrasted with the *power* to provide scientific, technical and other advice and instruction on matters relating to the breeding, rearing or cultivation of fish, and to charge for so doing, under s.32 of the Fisheries Act 1981 (discussed in para.8.04).

8.13   Powers of Entry

Extensive powers of entry are given under the Diseases of Fish Acts. Section 6 states that a justice of the peace may warrant a person to enter on to land where information is given on oath that there is reasonable cause to suspect that an offence under the Act has been committed. The warrant may allow entry on any land specified, at such time as is mentioned, to seize any fish, eggs of fish, foodstuff or article which is suspected to have been imported into Great Britain or otherwise dealt with in contravention of the Acts. Alternatively, the warrant may authorise the boarding of or entry into a cage situated in marine waters which is used for the purpose of fish farming. The warrant may not continue in force for more than one week from the date on which it is granted. These powers are in addition to those granted under other statutes (see, for example, the powers of entry given under the Salmon and Freshwater Fisheries Act 1975, discussed in Ch.9).

An inspector authorised by warrant, or a person authorised in writing by a water authority to exercise functions under the Diseases of Fish Acts, is empowered to conduct a range of investigations (under s.6 of the Acts). He may inspect inland waters where fish or the eggs of fish or foodstuff are likely to be found and take samples of fish, eggs of fish or the foodstuff of fish, or samples of mud, vegetation or other matter. Similarly, he may examine marine waters and cages used for fish farming situated therein and take samples of the same kind. For these purposes he may enter upon any land, or board and enter any cage situated in marine waters which is used for fish farming, upon production, upon demand, of his authority. Any person who refuses to admit, or intentionally obstructs, an inspector in the execution of these powers, or a person authorised in writing by a water authority to perform duties imposed upon the water authority under the Diseases of Fish Acts, will be guilty of an offence. In the event of a sample of fish being taken either from an inland water or from a cage in marine water, which subsequently proves not to be infected, the Minister is bound to pay to the occupier of the land or the owner or user of the cage a sum equal to the market value of the fish taken as a sample. The exercise of these powers is made subject to the proviso that a person exercising them on land used for a railway or canal undertaking is bound to conform to reasonable requirements imposed by the undertakers to prevent the obstruction of railway or canal traffic. In the event of the powers being exercised over railway or canal land, the undertakers will not be liable for any accident or injury caused to a person exercising such powers (s.6, Diseases of Fish Acts).

8.14   Penalties and Proceedings

A person found guilty of an offence under the Diseases of Fish Acts will be liable on summary conviction to a fine not exceeding level 4 on the standard scale, at present £1,000 (see para.1.12 on the standard scale of fines). In addition to the imposition of a fine, the court convicting a person under the Diseases of Fish Acts may order the forfeiture of any fish, eggs of fish, foodstuff or other article in respect of which the offence was committed (s.8, Diseases of Fish Acts).

Water authorities are empowered to take legal proceedings to enforce the provisions of the Diseases of Fish Acts in respect of waters in their area (under s.8 of the Acts). The Minister retains the power to make regulations prescribing: the form of licences granted under the Acts; the manner in which orders under the Acts are to be published; the form of the notice to be served on an occupier of waters suspected of being infected; and the manner in which anything forfeited or seized under the Acts is to be dealt with (s.9, Diseases of Fish Acts).

8.15   Registration of Fish Farms

Although the Diseases of Fish Act 1983 is for the most part an amending Act, updating the provisions of the 1937 Act, one important innovation that it introduced was the facility to require registration of fish farms. Although s.29 of the Salmon and Freshwater Fisheries Act 1975 permits the Minister to grant licences to carry on the business of artificially propagating or rearing salmon or trout, this provision is far from comprehensive in its scope (as was noted in para.8.03). Section 7 of the Diseases of Fish Act 1983 now provides the Minister with considerable powers to make orders for the purpose of obtaining information about fish farming operations for the purpose of preventing the spread of disease. A ministerial order may require a person occupying a fish farm in inland waters: first, to register the business; second, to furnish specified information in respect of the farm, fish, eggs of fish and foodstuff for fish; third, to compile records on these matters; and fourth, to retain such records for a period of up to three years. The same requirements are imposed upon persons carrying on the business of fish farming in marine waters. If an enterprise requires registration under an order of this kind the Minister may require the payment of a nominal sum not exceeding the administrative cost of the registration. A person authorised by the Minister, on producing evidence of his authority, if demanded, may require production of, and inspect and take copies of, any records which a person is required to retain under the ministerial order.

Section 8 of the Diseases of Fish Act 1983 creates a number of offences in relation to contravention of fish farm registration orders. It is an offence: first, to fail to comply with the requirements of a registration order without a reasonable excuse; second, knowingly to furnish information which is false in a material particular; third, knowingly to alter a record to make it false in a material particular; fourth, to fail to produce records for a person authorised by the Minister or to allow such a person to inspect or take copies of any records without reasonable excuse; and fifth, to obstruct a person authorised by the Minister in exercising his duties. In any of these instances a person found guilty of an offence on summary conviction will be liable to a fine not exceeding level 4, presently £1,000 (s.8(1), Diseases of Fish Act 1983). It will be no defence for an offender to claim that the unlawful act in question was committed by a company rather than the particular individual responsible since specific provision is made for individual liability in such circumstances. Section 8(2) states that if the offence in question is committed by a corporate body, such as a company, and the offence is committed with the consent or connivance of a director, manager, secretary or other similar official, or is attributable to neglect on the part of such a person, then he, as well as the corporate body, will be liable to be proceeded against and punished accordingly.

The information provided to the Minister under the fish farm registration provisions of the Diseases of Fish Act 1983 is inevitably of a confidential nature, since much of it will be of commercial significance and open to misuse if freely available to fish farming competitors. To preserve this confidentiality s.9 of the 1983 Act stipulates that information given for registration purposes shall not be disclosed except in three circumstances: first, with the written consent of the person by whom the information was provided; second, where it is presented in such a way as not to enable particulars relating to any one person or business to be ascertained from it; and third, for the purpose of any criminal proceedings or for a report on any such proceedings. The disclosure of information other than under one of these exceptions is a criminal offence, which on summary conviction will attract a fine not exceeding level 4 on the standard scale, presently equivalent to £1,000 (s.9, Diseases of Fish Act 1983).

(See para.13.09 on the disclosure to water authorities of confidential information given in accordance with the fish farm registration scheme under s.38 of the Salmon Act 1986.)

8.16 *The General Problem of Importation and Introduction of Fish*

The Diseases of Fish Acts, as has been seen, strive to protect fish farms from the threat of disease and the consequent losses that disease may involve. Disease, though, is not the only fishery hazard that is subject to legal control, and another general hazard to fisheries arises from the import or stocking of fish into waters without adequate safeguards. Along with the possibility that a stocked fish might carry an infection into a water into which it is introduced, the introduction of a foreign species is capable of having a devastating effect on the natural balance amongst the resident fish population in a water. A dramatic example of this effect has been seen over recent years in Africa where in 1960 the Nile perch was introduced into Lake Victoria in the hope that the species would provide a source of food for local people. As events transpired the carnivorous species has brought about an ecological catastrophe in devouring all the indigenous species of the lake to the point of extinction. Worse still, the interloper proved to be almost uncatchable using the traditional fishing methods of the locality! (see *New Scientist*, 6 March 1986, p.24). The clear moral of the tale is that the introduction of a new species to a water should only be brought about under expert supervision. Essentially the same caution is reflected in the legal provisions governing the importation of fish and the introduction of fish into inland waters.

8.17 The Introduction of Fish into Inland Waters

Section 30 of the Salmon and Freshwater Fisheries Act 1975 makes it an offence to introduce any fish or spawn into an inland water, or for a person to possess any spawn or fish with the intention of introducing it unless he first obtains the written consent of the water authority within whose area the water is situated. Inland water here has the same meaning as under s.135 of the Water Resources Act 1963 (discussed in para.12.03). The practical effect of this section is that the owner of a water, or the secretary of an angling association with the fishing rights to a water, who wishes to stock with fish must obtain the written permission of the water authority before doing so. Similarly it would be unwise for a fish farmer, or other supplier of fish, to introduce them into a water until satisfied that the appropriate permission had been obtained.

A considerable overlap exists between s.30 of the Salmon and Freshwater Fisheries Act 1975 and the provisions of the Wildlife and Countryside Act 1981 relating to the introduction of new species. Section 14(1) of the 1981 Act states that it is an offence to release, or to allow to escape into the wild, any animal which is not ordinarily resident or a regular visitor to Great Britain in a wild state or is specified in Part I of Sch.9 to the 1981 Act. 'Animal' in this context encompasses foreign species of fish and certain types of fish which have been introduced into Great Britain are listed in the schedule. These are: the large-mouthed black bass; the rock bass; the pumpkinseed (otherwise known as the sun fish or pond perch); the wels (otherwise known as the European catfish); and the zander. In the case of either a fish which is not ordinarily resident in the wild, or is a specified fish, introduction will require a licence issued by the 'appropriate authority' under the 1981 Act. In these cases this means the Minister of Agriculture, Fisheries and Food, who is bound from time to time to consult with the Nature Conservancy Council as to the exercise of his functions in this respect (s.16, Wildlife and Countryside Act 1981).

8.18   The Import of Live Fish (England and Wales) Act 1980

Along with the hazard of disease transmission, discussed in paras 8.06 and 8.07 above, the import of fish is equally to be regarded as a danger in that it is capable of leading to the introduction and establishment of potentially unwelcome species of fish in the waters of England and Wales. The hazards involved in the introduction of non-native species of fish is tackled at the stage of importation under the Import of Live Fish (England and Wales) Act 1980. Although overlapping to a large extent with s.1 of the Diseases of Fish Acts, the Import of Live Fish Act 1980 places emphasis upon the ecological rather than the infectious characteristics of the imported species. Section 1 of the 1980 Act allows the Minister to make an order to forbid the importation of non-native species of fish or their eggs absolutely if he is of the opinion that the non-native species might compete with, displace, prey upon or harm the habitat of any freshwater fish or salmon in England or Wales. Alternatively the Minister may make an order making the import, keeping or release of non-native species subject to a licence if he is of that opinion. Before granting a licence of this kind he is obliged to consult the Nature Conservancy Council and any other body with whom he considers consultation is appropriate. The licence, which may be issued subject to a charge, may impose upon the holder whatever conditions the Minister may think fit and may be varied or revoked by the Minister (s.1, Import of Live Fish Act 1980 as amended by s.37, Fisheries Act 1981).

Powers of entry and inspection are given under the Import of Live Fish Act 1980 to oversee that persons possessed of a licence to keep non-native species are adhering to the terms on which the licence permits the fish to be kept. An officer commissioned by the Commissioners of Customs and Excise, or a person duly appointed by the Minister may, at all reasonable times, enter on and inspect land occupied by a person holding a licence to keep the fish or eggs of fish, providing that authority is produced if it is required. In the same way such inspectors are entitled to enter on any other land if they have reason to believe that live fish or the live eggs of fish are present in contravention of the Act, and they produce authority if so required. In this context 'land' is defined to include land covered by water, but to exclude a dwelling house (s.2, Import of Live Fish Act 1980).

A number of specific offences are created in respect of contravention of the Import of Live Fish Act 1980. In the first place it is an offence to import or to attempt to import, or to keep or release, any live fish or live eggs of fish contrary to an order absolutely forbidding their import, keeping or release. Second, in the case of a person who is granted a licence to import, keep or release non-native species of fish, it is an offence to act in contravention of, or to fail to comply with, the terms of the licence. Third, it is an offence to obstruct any authorised person from entering or inspecting land, to ascertain whether an order or licence is being complied with. Additionally, it is an offence to obstruct an inspector where he has reasonable cause to believe that live fish or live eggs of fish are being kept in contravention of the Act. In any of these three situations a person will become liable on summary conviction to a fine not exceeding level 4 on the standard scale, presently equivalent to £1,000 (see the discussion of the standard scale in para.1.12). An exception is created where the act involved was done for some scientific or research purpose and authorised by the Minister (s.3, Import of Live Fish Act 1980).

In the event of a conviction under the Import of Live Fish Act 1980, the court may order that any fish or eggs in respect of which the offence was committed are to be forfeited and destroyed. Prior to the commencement of legal proceedings, a person authorised to enter as an inspector under the Act may seize any fish or eggs in respect of which he has reasonable cause to believe an offence has been committed, and may detain them pending the determination of any proceedings, or until the Minister is satisfied that no such proceedings are likely to be instituted (s.3, Import of Live Fish Act 1980).

9

POWERS OF WATER BAILIFFS AND WATER KEEPERS

9.01 *Water Bailiffs and Water Keepers*

The terms 'water bailiff' and 'water keeper' are often used interchangeably by anglers and others. In law, however, 'water bailiffs' and 'water keepers' possess different legal powers, and their status should be distinguished accordingly. A water bailiff is a person appointed by a water authority principally to enforce the Salmon and Freshwater Fisheries Act 1975 and byelaws under it. As a consequence of this duty, water bailiffs have a range of legal powers given by ss.31 to 36 of the 1975 Act. In addition, water bailiffs have a number of other powers originating from the diverse statutory and common law sources discussed below. By contrast, a water keeper, or warden as he may be called, is a person who is employed by the owner of a fishery to look after the fishery and carry out such duties as are specified by his employer. In law the water keeper is given no additional powers beyond those possessed by the owner of the fishery and the ordinary citizen. Whilst acting in his capacity as a water keeper alone he has no special powers given by the 1975 Act or other enactments.

The plan of this chapter is to consider in the first place the powers of water bailiffs that arise under the 1975 Act, and then to look at the range of other legal powers possessed by bailiffs. The powers of water keepers are discussed in passing, and summarised in para.9.21.

(General reading on the powers and duties of water bailiffs and water keepers includes: Fort and Brayshaw (1961); Seymour (1970); and Millichamp (1982).)

9.02 *Powers of Water Bailiffs under the Salmon and Freshwater Fisheries Act 1975: the Production of Evidence of Appointment*

Section 36(2) of the Salmon and Freshwater Fisheries Act 1975 provides that the production by a bailiff, or a person appointed by the Minister, of evidence of his appointment shall be a sufficient warrant for him exercising the powers conferred by the Act. This means that a prerequisite to a water bailiff exercising any of his statutory powers under the Act is the production of his warrant of authority. Evidence of authority must be produced whenever it is demanded if a water bailiff purports to be exercising statutory functions under the Act. It may also be prudent for a water bailiff to produce evidence of authority to establish his status without any demand to see it having been made. In the absence of evidence of authority a water bailiff's actions may take him outside the scope of his lawful authority and so make him civilly liable for trespass, or guilty of criminal offences. For this reason the requirement that a water bailiff must produce evidence of authority before exercising powers under the Act cannot be overstressed.

The effect of a water bailiff failing to produce evidence of his appointment is illustrated by *Barnacott* v *Passmore* (1887). In this case a water bailiff demanded to search a boat, which he suspected to contain salmon, as he was empowered to do under s.36(2) of the Salmon Fishery Act 1873 (now see s.31(1)(c) of the present Act, discussed in para.9.03). A fisherman in the boat resisted the search by holding an oar in his hand and saying 'if you attempt to come aboard I will knock your brains out'. At no point did the water bailiff produce his warrant of authority or state that he had it with him, although he had it in his pocket at the time. The fisherman made no request to see the warrant. The question for the court was whether the bailiff had been resisted in the execution of his duty. On appeal the court drew attention to s.36(5) of the Salmon Fishery Act 1873, to the effect that 'the production by a water bailiff of the instrument of his appointment . . . shall be a sufficient warrant for any water bailiff exercising the authorities given to him under the Salmon Fishery Acts 1861 to 1873' (now see s.36(2) of the present Act). In the opinion of the court it was necessary for the offence of resisting a water bailiff to be committed, for the person resisting to know that the person being resisted is a water bailiff. The way in which a water bailiff should make his status known is prescribed in the statute: by producing his instrument of appointment. Failure to do so in the circumstances of the case meant that the bailiff had no authority to search the boat. Consequently the fisherman was justified in resisting the search, and he was acquitted of the offence.

The requirement that a water bailiff should produce a warrant of authority is, however, subject to the proviso that it may not apply where production is impracticable. It is possible that circumstances may make it impossible or pointless for a water bailiff to produce his warrant. An instance of this is shown in *Cowler* v *Jones* (1890) where a water bailiff was, once again, resisted in searching a boat. On this occasion the bailiff took his warrant of authority from his pocket and held it up doubly-folded, with the writing pointing inwards. When requested by the accused to read the warrant, the water bailiff replied that it was too dark to do so. On these facts the issue was whether there had been sufficient production of authority to show that the water bailiff was authorised to act as he claimed to be empowered to do. The court held that the water bailiff had done sufficient to establish his authority, and the subsequent resistance of the accused to the search of the boat amounted to the offence of resisting a water bailiff in the execution of his duty. In the words of Lord Coleridge CJ: 'It is enough that the water bailiff carries the instrument with him and is able to produce it, and offers it for inspection, for that is sufficient to show that he is authorised to act as he professes; and from that moment the person resisting him is in the wrong.'

By way of elaboration upon Lord Coleridge's statement it may be observed that a water bailiff will not act unlawfully where he is unable to produce his warrant of authority because no occasion to produce the warrant has arisen. This point was graphically illustrated in *Edwards* v *Morgan* (1967) where two water bailiffs saw two men behaving suspiciously and called out 'water bailiffs'. The men ran off dropping a sack containing a salmon. A struggle ensued in which one of the men struck a bailiff in the stomach. Because a water bailiff when acting in the execution of his duty is deemed to be a police constable (see para.9.09), the man was convicted of assaulting a constable in the execution of his duty (contrary to s.51(1), Police Act 1964, discussed in para.9.19 below). The convicted man appealed on the ground that until the bailiff produced his instrument of appointment, which he had not done, he had no authority as a water bailiff and therefore was not acting in the execution of his duty. The Queen's Bench Divisional Court held the water bailiff was acting within the execution of his duties when on patrol, and so was deemed to be a constable. The conviction was therefore affirmed. Although a water bailiff must produce his authority when searching boats, examining nets, seizing fish and so on, he does not step outside the execution of his duty by not producing his authority where no occasion to produce the authority arises.

9.03 The Water Bailiff's Power to Search under the Salmon and Freshwater Fisheries Act 1975

The first of the powers given to water bailiffs, and also to any person appointed by the Minister, is the power to examine and search, arising under s.31(1) of the Salmon and Freshwater Fisheries Act 1975. The section permits three types of investigation to be made. The water bailiff:

(a)   may examine any dam, fishing weir, fishing mill dam, fixed engine or obstruction, or any artificial watercourse, and for that purpose enter any land;
(b)   may examine any instrument or bait which he has reasonable cause to suspect of having been or being used or likely to be used in taking fish in contravention of the Act, or any container which he has reasonable cause to suspect of having been or being used or likely to be used for holding any such instrument, bait or fish;
(c)   may stop and search any boat or other vessel or vehicle which he has reasonable cause to suspect of containing—
(1)   fish which had been caught in contravention of the Act;
(2)   any such instrument, bait or container as aforesaid.

The power under s.31(1)(a) to examine dams, etc., must be read alongside the various provisions under Part II of the Act relating to obstructions to the passage of fish (considered in Ch.4). Without some power to permit examination of such obstructions, it would be very difficult to enforce the law. (Further discussion of the power to enter land is to be found in paras 9.04, 9.05 and 9.17).

Subsection 31(1)(b) permits a water bailiff to inspect tackle used by anglers and, amongst other things, bags or baskets likely to be used for the storage of illegally caught fish or improper equipment. It is not clear whether this power will permit searches of the person, though water bailiffs do possess such a power (see para. 9.16).

Subsection 31(1)(c) provides water bailiffs with extensive powers to stop boats, cars and other vehicles suspected to contain fish taken in contravention of the Act, or instruments which have been used, or are likely to be used, to take fish in contravention of the Act. Cases concerning the exercise of this power to search boats were discussed in the previous paragraph. The water bailiff's power to search when an arrest has been made are discussed in para.9.17 below. By contrast, the powers given to police officers to stop and search boats and vehicles are contained in ss.1 and 2 of the Police and Criminal Evidence Act 1984. In some circumstances these powers are capable of being exercised by bailiffs, as is explained in para.9.09.

In the event of a water bailiff finding any fish, instrument, vessel, or vehicle liable to be forfeited under the 1975 Act he may seize that thing under s.31(1)(d) of the Act. The items which are subject to forfeiture under the Act are specified in para.5 of Sch.4 to the Act, and are discussed in para.10.06. The power of a water bailiff to seize items that are evidence of an offence when an arrest has been made are discussed in para.9.17.

It is an offence to resist or obstruct a water bailiff in entering land, or conducting a search or examination, or in seizing anything authorised to be seized under the Act, where the bailiff is acting within the sphere of his authority (s.31(2)). A prerequisite to the exercise of such authority is the production of the water bailiff's warrant of authority (see the previous paragraph). Similarly it is an offence to obstruct a person appointed by the Minister. Although the penalties for these offences are not specified under s.31, in accordance with para.1(2) of Sch.4 to the Act, the maximum penalty on summary conviction is a fine at level 4 on the standard scale, presently £1,000 (see para.1.12 on the standard scale of fines).

9.04 The Water Bailiff's Power to Enter Land under the Salmon and Freshwater Fisheries Act 1975

Section 32 of the Salmon and Freshwater Fisheries Act 1975 provides extensive powers of entry on to land to three categories of person: a water bailiff under a special order in writing from the water authority; any other officer of a water authority under a similar order; a person appointed by the Minister under an order in writing from him. In each case the orders in question may not remain in force for more than 12 months. These persons are permitted to enter, remain upon and traverse any lands adjoining or near waters within a water authority area, at all reasonable times, for the purpose of preventing any offence against the Act. This power is subject to two explicit exceptions in that it is stated not to be given in respect of: first, a dwelling house or the curtilage of a dwelling house (the meaning of 'curtilage' was discussed in *Pilbrow* v *St Leonard, Shoreditch, Vestry* (1895)); and second, decoys or lands used exclusively for the preservation of wild fowl.

Three points are worthy of note regarding s.32. First, it is likely that the categories of person permitted to enter land will be strictly construed. Thus *only* the three categories of person mentioned will be entitled to claim the benefit of the section. It follows that a water bailiff will not be able to take an unauthorised companion with him on to land, and even a police officer will not be able to enter land under this provision unless he is acting as a water bailiff (under s.36(3), discussed in para.9.09 below, though he may be able to claim other lawful authority to enter land). Notably the section confers no authority upon a water bailiff to take a dog with him on to land even where it is specially trained to assist him in his work.

A second point of observation concerning s.32 is the wording of the phrase, 'for the purpose of *preventing* any offence against this Act'. 'Preventing' here indicates a contrast between the power under s.32 and that under s.31(1)(a) to enter on to land in order to 'examine' dams, etc. If understood literally, 'preventing' indicates that the power of entry relates to future rather than past contraventions of the Act, since it would be physically impossible for the persons given the power of entry to prevent an offence which has already taken place. In most cases, it is likely that the offence will be of a continuing character as where persons remain in possession of fish or instruments prohibited under the Act. Where this is the case a bailiff can justifiably claim to be 'preventing' an offence.

A third observation concerning s.32 is that it is an offence to resist or obstruct an authorised person exercising his power to enter, remain upon or traverse land (s.31(2)). This point was illustrated in respect of a precursor to s.32 of the present Act (s.37 of the Salmon Fishery Act 1873) in *Heseltine* v *Myers* (1894). Here it was held that an occupier of land, who ordered a water bailiff to leave the land, was guilty of resisting the bailiff in the execution of his duty. The water bailiff left the land in order to prevent a breach of the peace, but it was decided that the offence had been committed notwithstanding this.

9.05 Orders and Warrants to Enter Premises under the Salmon and Freshwater Fisheries Act 1975

Along with the powers provided under s.32 of the Salmon and Freshwater Fisheries Act 1975, which are exercisable by a water bailiff on the authority of a warrant of appointment from a water authority, additional powers are provided under s.33 which may be exercised under the authority of a magistrate's order or warrant. These powers are of particular importance where entry into a dwelling place is sought since this power is specifically excluded under s.32.

Where a water bailiff, or other officer of the water authority, or a person appointed by the Minister, seeks to enter premises he must obtain a warrant from a justice of the peace to do so. The procedure provided for under s.33(1) requires the water bailiff, water authority officer, or appointee of the Minister, to make a statement on oath. This statement is to the effect that the person making the statement has good reason to suspect that an offence under the Act is being committed or is likely to be committed, on any land situated on or near to any waters. If satisfied by the sworn statement, a justice may authorise the applicant to enter upon and remain on the land, during the hours of day or night, for the purpose of detecting persons committing the offence. The maximum duration for which an order of this kind may be given is 24 hours. An order under s.33(1) is available only where an offence is 'being or likely to be committed', and so would not be available where an offence has already been committed.

Where there is probable cause to suspect that an offence *has been* committed a justice of the peace may make an order under s.33(2) of the Act. The procedure here is analogous to that under the previous subsection. Where an information is given on oath by any person that there is probable cause to suspect that an offence against the Act has been committed on any premises, or any salmon, trout, freshwater fish or eels have been illegally taken, or any illegal nets or other instruments are on any premises, a justice may make an order authorising entry into the premises. The order may permit a water bailiff, or an officer of the water authority, or a person appointed by the Minister, or a police constable, to enter the premises for the purpose of detecting the offence or the fish, nets or other instruments, at such times of the day or night as are mentioned in the warrant. Moreover, the warrant may permit the seizure of any illegal nets and other instruments, and any salmon, trout, freshwater fish or eels suspected to have been illegally taken and found on the premises. A warrant of this kind may not continue in force for more than a week (s.33(2) and (3)).

Three points of contrast may be noted between subsections 33(1) and 33(2) of the Act. First, s.33(1) only authorises the entry of the person making the statement under oath, whilst s.33(2) allows a justice to authorise the entry of *any* water bailiff, officer of the water authority, appointee of the Minister, or police constable. It is not clear why no mention of police constable is made in the earlier subsection. Second, there are no explicit powers of seizure given under s.33(1) as appear in s.33(2). Third, an order under s.33(1) may remain in force for up to 24 hours, whilst an order under s.33(2) may remain in force for up to a week.

The issue of search warrants to police constables is now subject to ss.15 and 16 of the Police and Criminal Evidence Act 1984. These provisions will apply to applications for authorisations to enter premises by police constables under s.33 of the Salmon and Freshwater Fisheries Act 1975, and may also apply to applications by water bailiffs under s.36(1) (discussed in para.9.09).

9.06 Powers of Water Bailiffs to Enter Land under the Water Resources Act 1963

In addition to the powers of entry and search which water bailiffs derive from ss.31 and 32 of the Salmon and Freshwater Fisheries Act 1975, considered in the previous paragraphs, they also possess powers of entry arising under the Water Resources Act 1963 (see para.7.07 above). At this juncture it is worth drawing out some points of comparison and contrast.

Section 111(1) of the Water Resources Act 1963 states that a person duly authorised in writing by a water authority may at any reasonable time:

(a)   enter upon any land for the purpose of performing any functions of the water authority, whether in relation to that land or not;
(b)   enter upon any land and carry out inspections or surveys for the purpose of determining whether, and if so how, any of the authority's functions are to be performed in relation to any land, or whether any statutory provision relating to its functions is being or has been complied with.

The generality of this power is to be noted. It is not limited to the exercise of fishery functions nor to the inspection of specified things as is s.31 of the Salmon and Freshwater Fisheries Act 1975. For this reason it may be more advantageous for a water bailiff to exercise the power under s.111 of the Water Resources Act 1963 rather than the power under s.31 of the 1975 Act.

Where a bailiff exercises a power to enter land under s.111 of the Water Resources Act 1963, s.112 of that Act states that he may take with him such other persons and equipment as may be necessary. Except in an emergency, however, admission to land used for residential purposes, or admission to other land with heavy equipment, may not be demanded as of right unless seven days' written notice of the intended entry has been given to the occupier. Again this illustrates some points of contrast with the provisions under the Salmon and Freshwater Fisheries Act 1975. First, the powers of entry under the 1975 Act are limited to water bailiffs, officers of the water authority, and appointees of the Minister, and are unlikely to extend to 'such other persons . . . as may be necessary'. Second, the powers under the 1975 Act say nothing about a bailiff taking with him 'such . . . equipment as may be necessary'. It is arguable that the provision under the 1963 Act might even permit a bailiff to take a dog on to land with him, if a dog can be counted as 'equipment'. Third, the combined effect of ss.32 and 33 of the 1975 Act is that a bailiff will not be permitted to enter the curtilage of a dwelling house unless he has obtained a warrant from a magistrate permitting him to do so. In contrast, s.112 of the 1963 Act permits entry to land used for dwelling purposes after the expiry of seven days' written notice to the occupier, without the need for an order from a magistrate. Even the seven days' notice may not be necessary if the circumstances amount to an 'emergency'.

Section 111 of the Water Resources Act 1963 provides that a right of entry on to occupied or unoccupied land may be enforced by a justice's warrant, if need be by force. Application for such a warrant must be made by a sworn information in writing which, amongst other things, may be granted where it is shown to the satisfaction of a justice that the case is one of urgency, or that application to the occupier for admission would defeat the object of the entry, and that there is reasonable ground for entry for the purpose for which entry is required. In contrast to warrants obtained under s.33 of the Salmon and Freshwater Fisheries Act 1975, which are of limited duration (see para.9.05), a warrant to enter land obtained under the 1963 Act continues in force until the purpose for which entry is required has been satisfied. This permits a bailiff to defer a search until the time is ripe (see Parry (1976 p.23)).

In summary, the contrast between the provisions of the Water Resources Act 1963 and the Salmon and Freshwater Fisheries Act 1975 indicates that there are a number of advantages, from the water bailiff's point of view, to be gained from exercising powers under the 1963 Act. In respect of the power to enter land at least, there appear to be few benefits to be gained by the exercise of powers under the 1975 Act.

9.07 The Water Bailiff's Power under the Salmon and Freshwater Fisheries Act 1975 to Apprehend Persons Fishing Illegally at Night

The only explicit power of arrest given to a water bailiff under the Salmon and Freshwater Fisheries Act 1975 arises under s.34. This provides that the water bailiff, or person appointed by the Minister, and any assistants, may apprehend a person at night in three situations: first, where the person illegally takes or kills salmon, trout, freshwater fish or eels; second, where the person is found on or near waters with intent illegally to take or kill salmon, trout, freshwater fish or eels; and third, where the person has in his possession, for the capture of salmon, trout, freshwater fish or eels, any instrument prohibited by the Act. This would include the instruments prohibited under Part I of the Act (see Ch.3) and might also include an instrument such as a rod and line where it is unlicensed (see s.27 and Ch.6). Where an arrest is made by the exercise of this power the person making the arrest must place the arrested person into the custody of a police officer as soon as possible (see para.9.14 on the procedure for making an arrest).

The power of arrest provided under s.34 is available only during the hours of night. 'Night' is defined as the period between the end of the first hour after sunset on any day and the beginning of the last hour before sunrise on the following morning. The ambiguity inherent in this specification is the question of whether sunset and sunrise are to be understood to mean local times of sunset and sunrise, or those according to Greenwich mean time. This question arose in the context of s.27 of the Salmon Fisheries (Scotland) Act 1862, making it an offence to fish for salmon 'at any time between the expiration of the first hour after sunset on any day and the beginning of the last hour before sunrise on the following morning'. In *MacKinnon* v *Nicolson* (1916) it was decided that the times of sunset and sunrise are the times at which the sun sets and rises at the locus of the alleged offence and not the times at which it rises and sets at Greenwich. Similarly, in the context of s.34 of the present Act, it is the local times of sunset and sunrise that determine when an arrest may be made under the section.

Although s.34 provides a bailiff with the power to make an arrest, the procedure by which the arrest is made must still comply with legal requirements. Failure to comply with the law when making an arrest will make the person making the arrest legally liable for assault or false imprisonment. These are both crimes and civil wrongs and may lead to either criminal proceedings or a claim for compensation against the person making the unlawful arrest. For the arrest to be lawful a strict procedure must be followed. This procedure is embodied in s.28 of the Police and Criminal Evidence Act and is discussed in para.9.14 below.

9.08 The Power to Require Production of Fishing Licences under the Salmon and Freshwater Fisheries Act 1975

The checking of fishing licences, issued in accordance with the licensing system discussed in Chapter 6 above, is one of the main duties of water bailiffs. Section 35(1) of the Salmon and Freshwater Fisheries Act 1975 permits a water bailiff or any constable to require the production of a valid fishing licence or other authority to fish in three situations: first, where the person is fishing; second, where the person is reasonably suspected to be about to fish; and third, where the person is reasonably suspected to have fished in the water authority area within the preceding half hour. In addition to the production of a licence or other authority the person may be required to state his name and address. The phrase 'or other authority' in this power is somewhat obscure. It may refer to the possibility that a person is fishing under a general licence pursuant to s.25(7) of the 1975 Act and is authorised in writing by the owner of the fishery to fish without the need for purchase of a licence from the water authority (see para.6.08

on general licences). If that is the position then the fisherman must produce his written authorisation from the general licence-holder. On the other hand, 'other authority to fish' appears capable of including an angling permit issued by the owner of the fishery allowing the angler to be on the land for the purpose of fishing and taking fish. If this is the case, then the power under s.35(1) allows the water bailiff or constable to check that the person is not committing an offence under the Theft Act 1968 (see Ch.3).

In addition to the power given to water bailiffs, a person who holds a licence for a water authority area may, on production of his licence, require the production of a licence, or other authority to fish, by any other person who is fishing in the area, and require him to state his name and address (s.35(2)). This power may be made use of by a water keeper who holds a water authority licence for the area, or any holder of a water authority licence for the area. It is to be noted, however, that in contrast to the previous subsection of the Act, this power to require the production of a licence or authority to fish is only available where the person required to produce his license is *actually fishing*, and is not available where he is reasonably suspected to be about to fish or to have been fishing in the preceding half hour.

It is an offence for a person who is required to produce his fishing licence or other authority to fail to do so, or to fail to state his name and address, but if within seven days after production was required the person produces the authority at the office of the water authority he will not be convicted of the offence of failing to produce it (s.35(3)). It is to be noted that the later production of a valid licence does not absolve a person who has failed to give his name and address. Naturally, the licence which is produced within the seven day period must have been valid at the time when production of it was originally requested. It follows that a person could not avoid conviction of the offence where the licence was purchased subsequently to his failure to produce it on request (see *Wharton* v *Taylor* (1965) discussed in para. 6.03).

The penalty for the offence of failing to produce a licence or other authority or failing to state name and address under s.35 of the 1975 Act is not specified. This means that it is punishable at most by the maximum penalty for offences on summary conviction where the penalty is unspecified (para.1(2), Sch.4 to the 1975 Act). This is stated to be a fine at level 4 on the standard scale, presently £1,000 (see para.1.12 on the standard scale of fines).

9.09 Supplementary Provisions on the Powers of Water Bailiffs under the Salmon and Freshwater Fisheries Act 1975

Section 36 of the Salmon and Freshwater Fisheries Act 1975 is headed 'provisions supplementary to sections 31 to 35', and contains three miscellaneous provisions relating to water bailiff's powers. Subsection 36(1) states that a water bailiff, and a person appointed by the Minister, shall be deemed to be a constable for the purpose of the enforcement of the Act or any order or byelaw under it. This is a very important provision. It provides a water bailiff with all the same powers and privileges, and makes him subject to the same duties and liabilities, as a constable by virtue of the common law or any statute. Since the powers of a police constable are in many respects more extensive that those ordinarily possessed by a water bailiff acting in his capacity as such, s.36(1) leads the way into an important range of police powers, most of which are now contained in the Police and Criminal Evidence Act 1984. A point to stress about the deeming of a water bailiff to be a police constable is that it is 'for the purpose of the enforcement of this Act', that is, the Salmon and Freshwater Fisheries Act 1975. It follows that where a water bailiff is acting to enforce another Act, such as the Theft Act 1968 (see para.9.20 below), he will not be deemed to be a constable. Water bailiffs are only empowered to exercise the powers of constables when acting under the Salmon and Freshwater Fisheries Act 1975 and should not do so in other circumstances. The powers of a water bailiff when acting in his capacity as a constable are discussed in following paragraphs.

Subsection 36(2) of the 1975 Act states that the production by a water bailiff, or a person appointed by the Minister, of evidence of his appointment shall be sufficient warrant for him exercising the powers conferred upon him by the Act. As was seen in para.9.02, the practical effect of this is that a water bailiff must produce his warrant of authority before exercising powers under the Act wherever an occasion to do so arises.

Subsection 36(3) is, in effect, the converse of s.36(1). It provides that where a water authority exercises its power under para.39(1)(c) of Sch.3 to the Act to obtain the services of additional constables under s.15 of the Police Act 1964, then any police constable whose services are provided shall have all the powers and privileges of a water bailiff. Hence if a police constable whilst engaged as a water bailiff were to find himself without sufficient power to act in his capacity as a constable, then he would be lawfully entitled to make use of powers given to water bailiffs under the Act. It is likely that this provision is only applicable where a constable is formally engaged to act by a water authority, and doubtful if he would be within the subsection where acting informally to assist a water bailiff.

9.10   The Power to Arrest for Breach of the Peace

Although most powers of arrest which exist today are of statutory origin, one power which is not is the power of a water bailiff to arrest for a breach of the peace. This power arises from the judge-made common law and permits a water bailiff to make an arrest where there has been a breach of the peace, or where a breach of the peace is reasonably apprehended (Hawkins (1716) Vol.2 Ch.13 s.8, and *Leigh* v *Cole* (1853)). This power does not obviate the need for the correct procedure for making an arrest to be observed (see para.9.14 below).

Unfortunately the expression 'breach of the peace' has no precise legal definition. It is established that it will include a situation where there is an assault or an affray, or any situation where a water bailiff reasonably anticipates violence to his person. On the other hand there will not be a breach of the peace where threatening, abusive or insulting language is used unless it leads to the reasonable apprehension that violence is likely to follow. Hence the power of arrest should be confined to circumstances where a person is either engaged in, or about to engage in, acts of violence (see Leigh (1985) Ch.IX). In practice a water bailiff should find little occasion to make use of the common law power to arrest for breach of the peace since in all situations where he might seek to arrest for breach of the peace he is now likely to have statutory powers to make an arrest under the Police and Criminal Evidence Act 1984. Nonetheless, the common law power survives the 1984 Act.

9.11   The Police and Criminal Evidence Act 1984 Generally

From 1 January 1986 the powers of water bailiffs were greatly extended by the Police and Criminal Evidence Act 1984. Since a water bailiff is deemed to be a police constable for the purposes of enforcement of the Salmon and Freshwater Fisheries Act 1975 (under s.36(1) of that Act) he acquires the range of new police powers under the 1984 Act in so far as they concern the enforcement of fishery law (on the 1984 Act generally see Leigh (1985) and Zander (1985)).

Amongst other objectives, the aim of the Police and Criminal Evidence Act 1984 is to rationalise the powers of arrest possessed by police constables and so, vicariously, by water bailiffs. Three powers of arrest possessed by water bailiffs survive the 1984 Act: first, the power to arrest under s.34 of the Salmon and Freshwater Fisheries Act 1975; second, the common law power to arrest for breach of the peace discussed in the previous paragraph; and third, the power to arrest under Sch.1 to the Theft Act 1968, discussed in para.9.20 below. Apart from these three powers of arrest, however, all other powers of arrest that a water bailiff possesses, by virtue of being deemed to be a police constable, are now subject to the 1984 Act. To this effect, s.26 of the 1984 Act provides that any part of any previous Act which enables a constable to arrest a person for an offence without a warrant shall cease to have effect. Whilst acting in the capacity of a police constable, a water bailiff's powers to arrest are now circumscribed by the power to arrest for 'arrestable offences' under s.24 of the 1984 Act, and 'non-arrestable offences' subject to the 'general arrest conditions' set out in s.25 of the 1984 Act. These powers, and others applicable to water bailiffs that arise under the 1984 Act, are discussed in the following paragraphs.

9.12   'Arrestable Offences' under the Police and Criminal Evidence Act 1984

The Police and Criminal Evidence Act 1984 places powers to arrest into two categories according to the seriousness of the offence involved. The first category concerns more serious offences, which are termed 'arrestable offences', and the second category concerns lesser offences, termed 'non-arrestable offences' where a power of arrest only arises when criteria known as the 'general arrest conditions' are met. This paragraph deals with arrestable offences, whilst non-arrestable offences are considered in the next paragraph.

The category of arrestable offences is defined in s.24 of the 1984 Act to include, amongst other things, offences for which a person of 21 years of age or over (not previously convicted) may be sentenced to imprisonment for a term of five years. The practical import of this is that none of the offences which arise directly under the Salmon and Freshwater Fisheries Act 1975 are arrestable offences, since none of them carry a maximum punishment of five years' imprisonment for a first offender. Nonetheless, other offences which a water bailiff might encounter do carry penalties which exceed five years for a first offence and so constitute arrestable offences. Arrestable offences which a bailiff might encounter include: the theft of fish under s.1 of the Theft Act 1968 (see Ch.3 and para.9.20), and serious assaults and wounding under ss.18, 20 and 47 of the Offences Against the Person Act 1861. In the case of these offences a water bailiff, and in some instances a water keeper or an ordinary citizen, will be empowered to arrest for an arrestable offence under s.24 of the 1984 Act.

Section 24 of the 1984 Act states that any person may arrest without warrant:

(a)   anyone who is in the act of committing an arrestable offence;
(b)   anyone whom he has reasonable grounds for suspecting to be committing such an offence (s.24(4)).

Where an arrestable offence has been committed, any person may arrest without a warrant:

(a)   anyone who is guilty of the offence;
(b)   anyone whom he has reasonable grounds for suspecting to be guilty of it (s.24(5)).

These powers of arrest are possessed by 'anyone'; that is, water bailiffs, water keepers and ordinary citizens.

The power to make an arrest has, however, to be exercised with caution. Under s.24(4) of the 1984 Act any person may arrest without warrant a person who is in the act of committing an arrestable offence. It is likely, however, that the power of arrest is only available where an arrestable offence is *being* committed. The power to arrest is not available where an arrestable offence *has been* committed. The power of arrest under s.24(5) is only available where an arrestable offence has *actually been* committed, and it will not be any excuse to the person making the arrest to maintain that he had good grounds for thinking that an offence had been committed if for any reason it turns out that no offence has actually been committed. Hence although an angler or a water keeper has the power to arrest a person whom he sees apparently stealing fish from a water, he must be absolutely sure that the provisions of either s.24(4) or s.24(5) are satisfied before making an arrest (on the theft of fish see Ch.3 and para.9.20). In a case of doubt the angler or keeper is well advised not to make an arrest but to report the matter to either a water bailiff or a police constable who have more extensive powers to make an arrest under the 1984 Act.

Subsections 24(6) and (7) of the 1984 Act set out the powers of arrest for an arrestable offence which are stated to be given to police constables. By virtue of s.36(1) of the Salmon and Freshwater Fisheries Act 1975 these same powers are also given to water bailiffs for the purpose of enforcement of that Act or any order or byelaw under it. Section 24(6) of the 1984 Act states that where a constable has reasonable grounds for suspecting that an arrestable offence has been committed, he may arrest without warrant anyone whom he has reasonable grounds for suspecting to be guilty of the offence. Section 24(7) states that a constable may arrest without warrant: (a) anyone who is about to commit an arrestable offence; (b) anyone whom he has reasonable grounds for suspecting to be about to commit an arrestable offence. These powers of arrest are wider than those discussed in the previous paragraph in that they will justify an arrest, even if no arrestable offence has actually been committed, if the water bailiff has *reasonable grounds* to suspect that an offence has been committed. Moreover, they empower a water bailiff to make an arrest even where no arrestable offence has been committed if the water bailiff has reasonable grounds to suspect that an offence is *about to be committed*. This means that there is no need for the bailiff to wait for a poacher to cause extensive damage to a fishery before making an arrest; he is empowered to make the arrest as soon as the arrestable offence is reasonably apprehended. The powers of arrest for arrestable offences given to water bailiffs are therefore of much greater extent than those of the water keeper or the ordinary citizen. For this reason, in practice, arrests are better left to water bailiffs in all but the most urgent circumstances.

9.13 *'Non-arrestable Offences' and 'General Arrest Conditions' under the Police and Criminal Evidence Act 1984*

Apart from theft and serious assault, all the other offences that a water bailiff is likely to encounter are classified as 'non-arrestable offences' for the purposes of the Police and Criminal Evidence Act 1984. In particular, all the offences under the Salmon and Freshwater Fisheries Act 1975 fall into this category. For non-arrestable offences the 1984 Act provides that a constable or water bailiff only has the power to arrest where the 'general arrest conditions' are satisfied. These conditions are set out in s.25 of the 1984 Act. In so far as they are capable of being relevant to the work of a water bailiff, they are as follows. Section 25(1) of the 1984 Act states that where a constable, which a water bailiff is deemed to be, has reasonable grounds for suspecting that any offence which is not an arrestable offence has been committed or attempted, he may arrest 'the relevant person' if it appears to him that the service of a summons is impracticable or inappropriate because any of the 'general arrest conditions' is satisfied. 'The relevant person' means any person whom the constable has reasonable grounds to suspect of having committed or having attempted to commit the offence or being in the course of committing or attempting to commit it. The 'general arrest conditions', in so far as they are likely to be applicable to fishery offences, are:

(a)   that the name of the relevant person is unknown to, and cannot be readily ascertained by, the constable;

(b)   that the constable has reasonable grounds for doubting whether a name furnished by the relevant person as his name is his real name;

(c)   that—

(i)   the relevant person has failed to furnish a satisfactory address for service; or

(ii)   the constable has reasonable grounds for doubting whether an address furnished by the relevant person is a satisfactory address for service.

For the purposes of the conditions an address is a satisfactory address for service if it appears to the constable: (a) that the relevant person will be at it for a sufficiently long period for it to be possible to serve him with a summons; or (b) that some other person specified by the relevant person will accept service of a summons for the relevant person at it.

In summary, the new powers of arrest given to water bailiffs for non-arrestable offences where the general arrest conditions are satisfied are a considerable extension of their previous powers of arrest. The difficulty of an offender under the Salmon and Freshwater Fisheries Act 1975 refusing to give his name and address, or giving a false one, is met with a power to arrest providing the general arrest conditions are satisfied.

9.14 The Procedure for Making an Arrest and Information to be Given on Arrest under the Police and Criminal Evidence Act 1984

The procedure which must be followed on making an arrest is provided for under s.28 of the Police and Criminal Evidence Act 1984. Even though a water bailiff or other person is empowered to make an arrest under s.24 or s.25 of the 1984 Act, the arrest will be unlawful unless the stipulated procedure is adhered to, as will an arrest for any offence made by any other person. An unlawful arrest may entitle the arrested person to resist the arrest. Additionally, an unlawful arrest may lead to legal proceedings being brought against the person making the arrest, either by way of civil proceedings for compensation, or as criminal proceedings for assault or wrongful arrest. The importance of following the correct procedure cannot be overstressed.

Section 28 of the Police and Criminal Evidence Act 1984 imposes two procedural requirements upon a person making an arrest. First, an arrest is not lawful unless the person arrested is informed that he is under arrest as soon as practicable after the arrest. Where the arrest is made by a water bailiff, acting in his capacity as a constable, this requirement applies even where the fact of the arrest is obvious. Where the arrest is made by a water keeper or an ordinary person it is not necessary to tell the arrested person that he is under arrest if it is obvious, but it may be prudent to do so. Second, an arrest is not lawful unless the person arrested is informed of the ground for the arrest at the time of the arrest or as soon as practicable after the arrest. Once again, where the arrest is made by a water bailiff, acting in his capacity as a constable, this requirement applies even where the ground for the arrest is obvious. In the case of an ordinary person making an arrest, it is not necessary to tell the arrested person of the ground for the arrest where it is obvious, as in the case of a person caught red-handed, but it is wise to do so. The exception to these requirements is that they do not apply where it is not reasonably practicable to inform the person arrested because of his having escaped from the arrest before the information could be given.

A point to be noted concerning the duty to inform a person of the ground for an arrest is that this does not necessitate the use of precise technical language. For example, it is not necessary for the person making the arrest to cite the exact section and subsection of the Act under which the offence arises. Colloquial language may be used so long as the arrested person is informed of the behaviour which is said to constitute a crime on his part (see *Christie* v *Leachinsky* (1947)).

9.15 *The Questioning and Cautioning of Arrested Persons under the Police and Criminal Evidence Act 1984*

The detention, treatment and questioning of suspects and arrested persons is now primarily governed by a Code of Practice issued by the Secretary of State under s.66 of the Police and Criminal Evidence Act 1984. The Code of Practice contains a set of rules concerning the detention and treatment of persons who are being questioned. Failure to comply with the Code on the part of a police officer will make him liable to disciplinary proceedings. Persons other than police officers, who are charged with the duty of investigating offences or charging offenders, are bound to discharge their duties with regard to any relevant provisions of the Code. Failure to have regard to the Code does not of itself render such a person liable to any criminal or civil proceedings (s.67 of the 1984 Act). Nonetheless, the likelihood is that water bailiffs will be under an obligation to follow the Code wherever it is applicable to their work.

Aspects of the Code which will be of central importance to water bailiffs are those concerning questioning and cautioning of persons. A basic principle is that although a water bailiff is entitled to ask questions of any person in order to obtain information relating to offences there is no legal duty to answer, and no lawful means by which the bailiff can compel a person to answer. If, however, a person does answer questions in a way which leads the bailiff to suspect him of an offence then the Code requires that the person is cautioned before further questions are asked. The caution must take the following terms: 'You do not have to say anything unless you wish to do so, but what you say may be given in evidence.' No caution of this kind need be given unless questions are put to the person for the purpose of obtaining evidence which may be given to a court in a prosecution. Hence no caution is required where a person is questioned to establish his identity, or the ownership of a vehicle (para.10 of the First Code of Practice under the 1984 Act).

A person must be cautioned when placed under arrest except under two exceptional circumstances. These are, first, where it is impracticable to do so by reason of his behaviour, and second, where he has already been cautioned immediately prior to the arrest. The caution must take the same form as described above, although minor deviations in the words used are of no consequence providing that the sense of caution is preserved. Indeed, if the person does not understand what the caution means the water bailiff should go on to explain it in his own words (para.10 of the First Code of Practice under the 1984 Act).

9.16 *The Power to Search an Arrested Person under the Police and Criminal Evidence Act 1984*

Having made a lawful arrest in conformity with the requirements discussed in the preceding paragraphs, s.32 of the Police and Criminal Evidence Act 1984 permits a water bailiff, acting in his capacity as a constable, to search the arrested person for certain items. In so far as this power is likely to be relevant to fishery offences, a water bailiff is empowered to search an arrested person if he has reasonable grounds for believing that the arrested person has on him anything which might be evidence relating to the offence for which he has been arrested, and that such a search is reasonably required. The power to make a search of this kind is limited to the extent that it does not authorise a water bailiff to require a person to remove any of his clothing in public other than an outer coat, jacket or gloves. Nevertheless, this power should be sufficient for most purposes for which a bailiff might wish to conduct a search of an arrested person. Common use is made of so-called 'poachers' pockets' for the storage of fish or illegitimate implements for taking fish (see *Taylor* v *Pritchard* (1910)). The search of such pockets by a water bailiff would now be permitted under s.32 of the 1984 Act.

9.17 The Power to Search Premises on Arrest under the Police and Criminal Evidence Act 1984

Where an arrest has been made, s.32(2)(b) of the Police and Criminal Evidence Act 1984 permits a water bailiff to enter and search any premises in which the arrested person was when arrested, or immediately before he was arrested. Such a search will be permitted where the water bailiff has reasonable grounds for believing that there is evidence on the premises, and the search is reasonably required for the purpose of discovering anything which might be evidence relating to the offence. This power would, for example, permit a water bailiff to search land or buildings which a person arrested for a fishery offence had recently left, if the bailiff had reasonable grounds for thinking that the arrested person had abandoned fish or poaching equipment on the premises before the arrest. The extensive power to make a search of this kind is, however, conditional on an arrest having been made. The power may be contrasted with powers to examine and search specified things which arise under s.31 of the Salmon and Freshwater Fisheries Act 1975. Although the powers to search under s.31 of the 1975 Act are less extensive, in that, for example, they do not permit searches of the person, they are not conditional upon any arrest having been made.

In the event of a water bailiff finding anything which he has reasonable grounds for believing is evidence of an offence he may seize and retain that thing, under s.32(9) of the 1984 Act. This power is not limited to the seizure of fish or prohibited instruments, but extends to *anything* which the water bailiff has reasonable grounds to believe is evidence. It may be contrasted with the power under s.31 of the Salmon and Freshwater Fisheries Act 1975, to seize anything which may be liable to forfeiture under that Act. A water bailiff may, for example, seize a vehicle under s.31 of the 1975 Act because it is liable to forfeiture under the Act, without the need for an arrest to have taken place. Under s.32 of the 1984 Act the seizure of a vehicle would only be permitted after an arrest has taken place providing the water bailiff has reasonable grounds for believing that it is evidence of an offence.

9.18 Disposition of Arrested Persons under the Police and Criminal Evidence Act 1984

Section 30 of the Police and Criminal Evidence Act 1984 imposes a duty upon a water bailiff who has made an arrest to ensure that the arrested person is conveyed into police custody as soon as practicable after the arrest. In exceptional circumstances, however, the water bailiff may delay in taking a person who has been arrested to a police station and take him elsewhere if this is necessary in order to carry out such investigations as it is reasonable to carry out immediately.

9.19   Powers of Water Bailiffs under the Police Act 1964

The effect of s.36(1) of the Salmon and Freshwater Fisheries Act 1975, to the effect that a water bailiff shall be deemed to be a constable for the purpose of the enforcement of the 1975 Act, is not confined within the scope of the Police and Criminal Evidence Act 1984. There are other statutory provisions which distinguish a police constable from an ordinary citizen, and these also apply to a water bailiff when acting as a constable. Important examples of legal provisions of this kind arise under s.51 of the Police Act 1964.

Section 51 of the Police Act 1964 creates two offences in relation to police constables which may also be of relevance to water bailiffs. Under s.51(1) of that Act any person who assaults a constable in the execution of his duty, or assaults a person assisting a constable in the execution of his duty, shall be guilty of an offence and liable on summary conviction to a fine not exceeding level 5 on the standard scale, presently £2,000 (see para.1.12 on the standard scale) or to imprisonment for a term not exceeding six months, or both. Section 51(3) states that any person who resists or wilfully obstructs a constable in the execution of his duty, or resists or wilfully obstructs a person assisting a constable in the execution of his duty, shall be guilty of an offence and liable on summary conviction to imprisonment for a term not exceeding one month or to a fine not exceeding level 3 on the standard scale, presently £400, or both. By s.36(2) of the Salmon and Freshwater Fisheries Act 1975 these offences extend to assaults upon, or obstruction of, water bailiffs (see, for example, *Edwards* v *Morgan* (1967) discussed in para.9.02).

Although s.51 of the Police Act 1964 creates offences in respect of assaults upon, and obstruction of, water bailiffs, no specific powers of arrest arise in respect of these offences. Moreover, since the maximum penalties do not exceed five years' imprisonment on first conviction, they do not amount to 'arrestable offences' for the purpose of s.24 of the Police and Criminal Evidence Act 1984, and arrest will only be permitted where the 'general arrest conditions', under s.25 of the 1984 Act, are satisfied (see paras 9.12 and 9.13). Hence, it is a specific offence to assault or obstruct a water bailiff, but there is no power of arrest peculiar to the offence.

9.20   Powers of Arrest under the Theft Act 1968

As was seen in Chapter 3, the Theft Act 1968 has application to fishery law in two main respects. The first is that where fish are confined in a pond they are capable of being owned and so may be the subject of theft under s.1 of the Theft Act 1968 where a person dishonestly appropriates them with the intention of permanently depriving the owner of them. In such a case the maximum punishment on conviction on indictment is a term of imprisonment not exceeding 10 years (s.7, Theft Act 1968). Because the punishment for theft exceeds five years' imprisonment, the offence is an arrestable offence under s.24 of the Police and Criminal Evidence Act 1984. In turn, this means that a water bailiff can arrest any person who is in the act of committing theft or who is guilty of theft (s.24(4) or (5) of the 1984 Act).

The second respect in which the Theft Act 1968 is relevant to fishery law concerns the taking of wild fish. If fish are not confined to a pond and are free to move between lands of different owners they cannot be the subject of theft (see s.4(4) of the Theft Act 1968 and para.3.21). Nonetheless, this situation is covered by para.2 of Sch.1 to the Theft Act 1968, which creates two offences relating to taking fish in private waters. The first offence concerns unlawfully taking or destroying or attempting to take fish in water which is private property or in which there is a private right of fishery. The maximum punishment for this offence, on summary conviction, is imprisonment for a term not exceeding 3 months or a fine not exceeding level 3 on the standard scale, presently £400, or both. The second offence is the less serious crime of angling during the daytime in private waters. The maximum punishment for this offence, on summary conviction, is a fine not exceeding level 1 on the standard scale, presently £50. In respect of the first offence, para.2(4) of Sch.1 to the Theft Act 1968 states that any person may arrest without warrant anyone who is, or whom he with reasonable cause suspects to be, committing the offence. Hence a water bailiff, water keeper or ordinary angler could arrest a person committing this offence. In respect of the second offence, no power of arrest is given. Consequently, an arrest could only be made by a constable, or a water bailiff acting in his capacity as constable, where the general arrest conditions under s.25 of the Police and Criminal Evidence Act 1984 are satisfied (see para.9.13).

In the case of an arrest for the more serious offence under para.2(1) of Sch.1 to the Theft Act 1968, the person making the arrest may seize anything which would be liable to be forfeited upon conviction for the offence. This amounts to anything which the arrested person has with him at the time of the offence for use for taking or destroying fish (para.2(3) and (4) of Sch.1 to the Theft Act 1968).

9.21   Powers of Water Keepers

A number of references have been made to the powers of water keepers in the preceding parts of this chapter. For convenience of reference it may be helpful to group together the legal powers of water keepers at this point.

An initial principle to note is that there are no legal powers explicitly given to water keepers by statute. Though water keepers perform an invaluable role in practice, their status is not recognised by legislation. As a consequence of this, the legal powers that are possessed by persons who act as water bailiffs derive from two sources: first, there are those powers which water keepers possess in common with ordinary citizens; and second, there are those powers which water keepers possess by the authority of their employer, that is, the person or association that owns the fishery.

A water keeper possesses four legal powers in common with ordinary citizens. First, under s.35(2) of the Salmon and Freshwater Fisheries Act 1975, where a water keeper holds a water authority fishing licence and produces it he may require any person who is fishing in the area to produce his licence or other authority to fish and to state his name and address (considered in para.9.08). Second, a water keeper possesses the power to arrest for an arrestable offence under s.24 of the Police and Criminal Evidence Act 1984, subject to the qualifications discussed in para.9.12, and the requirement that the arrest is lawfully made under s.28 of that Act (discussed in para.9.14). Third, a water keeper possesses the same common law power to arrest for breach of the peace as a water bailiff, providing that the formalities for a lawful arrest, discussed in para.9.10, are adhered to. Fourth, a water keeper possesses the power to arrest a person taking or destroying fish in private waters contrary to para.2 of Sch.1 to the Theft Act 1968, discussed in para.9.20.

In his capacity to act on behalf of his employer, the owner of the fishery, a water keeper has powers which are aspects of his duty to prevent the civil wrong of trespass (discussed in para.6.03). The owner of land is entitled, *if reasonably necessary* (see *Hughes* v *Buckland* (1846)), to use reasonable force to remove a trespasser from his land. The same power is given to a water keeper to act on behalf of the owner. Similarly, although the owner of a fishery may permit a person to be on his land for one purpose, that permit does not allow the visitor to be upon the land for other purposes. So, for example, permission to be on the land for the purpose of angling would not permit the licensee to pick mushrooms. Similarly, where a fishing permit allowed the holder to angle in a particular way, for example, 'fly fishing only', using any other method would take him outside the scope of his permit and make him a trespasser. The point at which this happens depends entirely upon the terms of the permit which is issued, and because of this, it is advisable for the owner of the fishery to pay careful attention to the wording of any angling permits that he issues. The wording of such permits will determine the powers of a water keeper to check anglers' permits, tackle, bags or baskets, and the circumstances in which a permit holder will become a trespasser.

10

PROSECUTION, PROCEDURE AND MISCELLANEOUS PROVISIONS

10.01 Punishments under the Salmon and Freshwater Fisheries Act 1975 Generally

Section 37 of the Salmon and Freshwater Fisheries Act 1975, headed 'Prosecution of Offences', is a briefly worded provision to the effect that: 'Parts I and II of Schedule 4 to this Act shall have effect with regard to the prosecution and punishment of offences against this Act and the procedure on such prosecutions.' Part I of Sch.4 to the Act sets out the maximum punishments for offences under the Act. In respect of some offences an explicit penalty is specified in the table in para.1(1) of Sch.4. In respect of those offences where the penalty is not specified in the table, para.1(2) of Sch.4 states that, on summary conviction, the maximum penalty is a fine not exceeding level 4 on the standard scale of fines, which at present is equivalent to £1,000 (see para.1.12 on the standard scale). This penalty also applies to summary convictions of offences under byelaws to the Act (s.28(7) of the 1975 Act).

Paragraph 1(3) of Sch.4 to the Act is of special relevance to offences arising under s.1 (dealing with the use of prohibited instruments; see Ch.3) and s.27 (dealing with unlicensed fishing; see Ch.6) where two persons act together. As a general principle of criminal law, accomplices, or 'secondary parties', to an offence are punishable to the same extent as the principal offender (see s.8 of the Accessories and Abettors Act 1861). In respect of the offences under ss.1 and 27 of the Salmon and Freshwater Fisheries Act 1975, however, greater penalties may be imposed where two or more persons act together to commit an offence. Because of this it becomes necessary to determine when two persons are to be considered to be 'acting together'. Paragraph 1(3) of Sch.4 states that in the case of an offence under s.1 or s.27, other than one committed by means of a rod and line or with no instrument at all, two persons are to be treated as acting together if one is 'aiding, abetting, counselling or procuring the commission of such offence by the other' (on the meaning of these words see *Attorney General's Reference (No. 1 of 1975)* and Smith and Hogan (1983) Ch.8). It is an anomaly that two persons are not to be regarded as acting together for these purposes when a rod and line is used since there are clear circumstances where a rod and line can be used in a collaborative way, as where one person uses the rod and line to snatch fish (see para.3.09), and the other assists in the landing of fish with a landing net. By contrast, the use of a line without a rod to snatch fish with another person landing the fish with a landing net would be considered as 'acting together' for the purposes of para.1(3) of Sch.4 to the Act.

(The differential penalties where persons act together to commit offences under s.1 or s.27 of the 1975 Act are abolished by s.35 of the Salmon Act 1986. See para.13.06).

10.02 Prosecution and Procedure Generally

Part II of Sch.4 to the Salmon and Freshwater Fisheries Act 1975, headed 'Procedure', covers matters relating to the prosecution of offences under the Act. The following paragraphs examine the issues raised in Part II of Sch.4 alongside other related matters of procedure.

It will be evident from what has been said in earlier chapters (especially Ch.7) that the main prosecuting authorities in fishery cases are the regional water authorities. The powers and duties of water authorities in respect of enforcement of fishery law in the courts do not prevent any other person taking legal proceedings to enforce the Act or byelaws under it. Although earlier statutes restricted the right to bring proceedings (see s.62 of the Salmon Fishery Act 1873 and *Anderson* v *Hamlin* (1890)), the present law does not impose any limitation of this kind. In *Pollock* v *Moses* (1894) a water bailiff appointed by a board of conservators brought a prosecution for unlawful use of a 'snatch' (see para.3.09) without any authority from the Board of Conservators. It was argued on behalf of the accused that the water bailiff had no power to bring the prosecution without the authority of the Board. In reply the attention of the court was drawn to s.13 of the Fisheries Act 1891 which states: 'The powers conferred . . . by any Act relating to salmon and freshwater fisheries, upon any authorities or officers to enforce such Act, shall not be construed as limiting or taking away the power of any other person to take legal proceedings for the enforcement of any such Act or of any byelaw made thereunder.' The court concluded that the water bailiff was entitled to bring proceedings without the authority of the Board of Conservators. The same conclusion would be reached today, under s.13 of the Fisheries Act 1891, even if a prosecution were to be brought by an ordinary member of the public (see s.21 and Sch.1 Part 1 of the Sea Fisheries Act 1966; and s.22(1) and (2) and Sch.1 Part II and Sch.2 Part II of the Sea Fisheries Act 1968).

Any offence under the 1975 Act may be prosecuted summarily, that is, before magistrates. Although there may be good reasons for more serious cases to be considered by a Crown Court, in practice, the great bulk of fishery offences come before magistrates in the first instance. Their general capacity to hear cases under the Salmon and Freshwater Fisheries Act 1975, termed 'jurisdiction', is subject to three main exceptions: first, territorial limitations upon the jurisdiction of magistrates; second, the ouster of magistrates' jurisdiction by a claim of right; and third, the disqualification of magistrates from hearing a case. These exceptions to the general capacity of magistrates to hear cases under the Act are considered in the next three paragraphs.

10.03 The Territorial Jurisdiction of Magistrates

As was seen in Chapter 7, water authorities are bound to exercise their fishery functions within an area which includes tidal waters and parts of the sea adjoining the coast of a water authority area extending to a distance of six nautical miles out. Ordinarily the territorial jurisdiction of magistrates extends only as far as the county boundary for their county (s.2(1), Magistrates' Courts Act 1980). County boundaries usually run along the coastline at the low-water mark (see *Embleton* v *Brown* (1861)). Consequently, magistrates would be without jurisdiction to try offences beyond the low-water mark unless special provision was made. In order to ensure that offences committed at sea are triable by magistrates, para.2 of Sch.4 to the Salmon and Freshwater Fisheries Act 1975 stipulates that any offence committed on the sea coast shall be deemed to have been committed in any place abutting on the sea coast or adjoining the sea and may be tried and punished accordingly. A qualification to this is that s.3(1) of the Magistrates' Courts Act 1980 provides that where an offence has been committed on the boundary between two or more counties, or within 500 yards of such a boundary, or any harbour, river, arm of the sea or other water lying between two or more counties, the offence may be treated as having been committed in any of those counties.

On another matter of territorial jurisdiction, para.3 of Sch.4 to the Salmon and Freshwater Fisheries Act 1975 states that offences against the Act committed in Scotland shall be proceeded against and punished in Scotland. This provision is likely to be of limited effect in view of the narrow application of the Act to Scotland. Subject to three exceptions the Act applies only to England and Wales (s.43(2) and (3)). The exceptions are: first, the Act applies to so much of the River Esk, with its banks and tributary streams up to their source, as is situated in Scotland (s.39(1)(b), and see para.10.13); second, s.28(1) and (2), concerning the general powers and duties of water authorities, applies in respect of any water authority whose fishery area extends into Scotland with the watershed of the River Esk; and third, s.42(1) extends the repeal of s.15 of the Salmon and Freshwater Fisheries Act 1972 and s.18 of the Water Act 1973 to Scotland.

10.04   *The Ouster of Magistrates' Jurisdiction*

The capacity of magistrates to hear a case will be exceeded where an alleged offence is something done by the accused in good faith in exercising a legal claim or asserting a legal right. Thus, for example, magistrates cannot convict a person of taking or destroying fish contrary to Sch.1 to the Theft Act 1968 where the accused person raises a bona fide (good faith) claim that he is actually the owner of a right of fishery in the waters from which the fish were taken (see para.3.22). Similarly, magistrates would be prevented from convicting for use of an unauthorised fixed engine contrary to s.6(1) of the Salmon and Freshwater Fisheries Act 1975, in a case where the accused presents a bona fide claim that he was legally entitled to use the fixed engine. The underlying dispute in cases such as these involves something more than a mistake on the part of a fisherman as to his right to fish. It concerns a dispute as to the ownership of a right of fishing, and this is a matter of property law upon which justices have no power to adjudicate. Consequently, where claims of this kind are made it is not open to the magistrates to determine the guilt of the accused person, nor is it for them to determine the validity of the claim of right which is raised; the magistrates' jurisdiction to hear the case is said to be 'ousted'.

A couple of examples may help to illustrate the type of claim which has the effect of ousting magistrates' jurisdiction. In *R* v *Stimpson* (1863) the accused was charged with attempting to take fish from a private water contrary to s.24 of the Larceny Act 1861 (the forerunner of Sch.1 to the Theft Act 1968). The accused gave evidence that the river where the alleged offence had taken place was a tidal navigable river which witnesses claimed to have fished for 40 years without interruption. Since the right of fishing in a tidal navigable river is ordinarily a public right, without evidence to the contrary, the accused had shown a bona fide claim of right to fish and therefore could not be convicted of the offence with which he was charged. In *Raby* v *Seed* (1864) the accused was charged with fishing for salmon with an unauthorised fixed engine. He produced a lease of the fishery and maintained that the use of the fixed engine was authorised by ancient use. On appeal, it was held that the evidence was sufficient to establish a bona fide claim of right to fish. The effect of this was that the jurisdiction of the justices was ousted so that they were not empowered to convict the accused of the offence.

Although, as these examples show, the jurisdiction of magistrates to hear a case may sometimes be ousted by a bona fide claim of right, it is clear that there must be limitations upon this principle. If there were not, then anyone contravening fishery law could always claim in his defence that he thought that he was legally entitled to do whatever constituted the alleged crime. The major limitation upon ouster of magistrates' jurisdiction is that the person claiming the existence of a legal right must show that his claim is genuinely made in good faith and that there is *some evidence*, even if only slight, of the right claimed. Hence in *Booth* v *Brough* (1869) there was held to have been no ouster of the magistrates' jurisdiction where the accused failed to produce any evidence of the existence of a public right of fishery on which he based his claim of right. In *Wells* v *Hardy* (1964) (discussed in para.3.22) it was held to be legally impossible to establish a claim of right to fish based upon a public right of fishery where a previous decision (*Blount* v *Layard* (1891), discussed in para.1.07) had established that no public right of fishery was capable of existing in the waters in question. On similar facts, it was held in *Hudson* v *MacRae* (1863) that an honestly held, though mistaken, notion that a claim of right existed would not be sufficient to oust the jurisdiction of the justices, only evidence of an *actual* legal claim will suffice.

To summarise these points, it is clear that a bona fide claim of right is capable of preventing magistrates deciding on a criminal charge against fishery law, where doing so involves them reaching a decision upon a disputed right of ownership of a fishery. Questions of this kind are a matter of civil law on which they have no power to reach a decision. On the other hand, the circumstances in which this issue is likely to arise are uncommon, and probably limited to situations where a dispute about the title to a fishery exists. In such circumstances it would be improper to allow the criminal law to be used to resolve a property dispute, and for that reason justices are without jurisdiction to reach any decision on the alleged offence.

10.05   *The Disqualification of Magistrates*

It is a fundamental principle of the law of England and Wales that any person who is charged with an offence is entitled to a fair trial. As Lord Hewart CJ made the point: '[it is] of fundamental importance that justice should not only be done, but should manifestly and undoubtedly be seen to be done' (*R* v *Sussex Justices ex parte McCarthy* (1924)). This principle is sometimes expressed as the rule against bias: no man may be a judge in his own case. It follows from this principle that a conviction will not be allowed to stand where there is any reasonable ground for suspicion of bias on the part of any member of an adjudicating body. It is to be noted that the rule is not concerned with *actual* bias on the part of a judge or magistrate, but only with *reasonable grounds for suspecting bias*. If this is shown, then the decision of a court will be quashed, without any need for actual bias to be established.

In the context of fishery offences the application of the rule against bias has arisen on a number of occasions where a magistrate involved in the hearing of a case in court has previously been involved in the decision to bring the prosecution. The question which this situation raises is whether the justice should have been disqualified from hearing the case because his earlier involvement gave the impression of bias. Paragraph 4 of Sch.4 to the Salmon and Freshwater Fisheries Act 1975 provides that a justice of the peace is not disqualified from hearing any case under the Act by reason only of being a subscriber to any society for the protection of fish, but a justice shall not be entitled to hear a case in respect of an offence committed on his own land or in relation to any fishery of which he is owner or occupier. This means that magistrates who happen to be members of angling associations are not, for that reason alone, barred from hearing poaching cases on grounds of bias, but may not hear cases which concern offences alleged to have been committed on their own land or in relation to a fishery which they own or occupy. A number of illustrations of this principle are to be found in decided cases.

In *R* v *Hodgson* (1860) the accused was convicted of an offence of failing to render a fish catching device in his dam inoperative during the close season. The justices before whom the prosecution was brought were members of a salmon fishery landowners' association, and one of them had attended a meeting at which the association had passed a resolution that the association should bring legal proceedings against the accused. It was held that those who are parties to a prosecution should not act as judges and convict in their own case, and the conviction was set aside because of the interest of the magistrate.

The decision in *R* v *Hodgson* (1860) may be contrasted with that in *R* v *Pwllheli Justices ex parte Soane* (1948) where the accused was convicted of an offence of polluting a river. He claimed that the decision of the magistrates should be set aside because the chairman was a member of a fishery board which had instituted the proceedings. Although the chairman of the justices admitted that he had been present at the meeting of the board at which the decision to prosecute had been taken, he had taken no part in deciding the question of whether the prosecution should be brought and had not voted on the resolution. The Court of King's Bench held that since the justice had taken no part in instituting the prosecution or the preliminary proceedings the conviction should stand. (Other cases illustrating similar reasoning are *R* v *Spedding Justices* (1885) and *R* v *Henley* (1892)).

The outcome of this line of cases is that a magistrate must avoid participation in any preliminary proceedings leading to a prosecution which might give the impression of bias. Hence it has been suggested that a justice who is a member of a prosecuting water authority, or even a member of a local authority which appoints representatives to a water authority, should regard himself as being disqualified from hearing any case brought by the water authority (see Stone (1986) s.4–9059). Membership of an angling association, however, does not, of itself, amount to bias. It is essentially this rule which is embodied in para.4 of Sch.4 to the 1975 Act.

10.06   The Forfeiture of Fish and other Items

As was described in para.9.03, under s.31(1)(d) of the Salmon and Freshwater Fisheries Act 1975, water bailiffs are empowered to seize any fish, instrument, vessel, vehicle or other thing liable to forfeiture under the Act. Paragraph 5 of Sch.4 to the 1975 Act sets out the range of things which are liable to forfeiture. In the event of a person being convicted of an offence under the Act the court may order the forfeiture of:

(a)   any fish illegally taken by him or in his possession at the time of the offence;

(b)   any instrument, bait or other thing used in the commission of the offence;

(c)   in the case of an offence of unlawful possession of any substance or device in contravention of s.5, that substance or device; and

(d)   on conviction on indictment, any vessel or vehicle used in or in connection with the commission of the offence or in which any substance or device unlawfully in his possession was contained at the time of the offence.

Any object so forfeited may be disposed of as the court thinks fit.

The wording of the provision under para.5(a) of Sch.4 relating to the forfeiture of fish is somewhat ambiguous. It is not clear whether fish 'in his possession at the time of the offence' is to be understood to mean fish *illegally* in his possession at the time of the offence or *any* fish which happen to be in his possession at that time. It is suggested that the provision should only extend to fish which are unlawfully obtained in contravention of the Act. If this is the correct interpretation, however, it means that fish which have been obtained unlawfully without any proven contravention of the Act would not be liable to forfeiture under this provision. Hence if a person was in possession of fish which have been stolen under s.1 of the Theft Act 1968, then a court would not be empowered to order their forfeiture under this provision (although s.28 of the Theft Act 1968 permits an order to be made for restitution of stolen goods to their owner).

The provision for forfeiture of any instrument, bait or other thing used in the commission of the offence under para.5(b) of Sch.4 raises the issue of what things can properly be said to be *used* in the commission of the offence. In *Gibson* v *Ryan* (1967) (discussed in para.6.04) the question arose as to whether an inflatable rubber dinghy or a basket was an 'instrument . . . used in the taking of salmon' within the meaning of s.7(1) of the Salmon and Freshwater Fisheries (Protection)

(Scotland) Act 1951. The court drew a distinction between instruments used for the taking of salmon, and other items such as the dinghy and the basket which were used to assist in the commission of the offence. If the same distinction is to be drawn under the Salmon and Freshwater Fisheries Act 1975, then para.5(b) of Sch.4 is limited in its extent to things *used* in the commission of the offence, as opposed to things which might *assist* in the commission of the offence. It is regrettable that the distinction was not more clearly explained by the court.

The provision, under para.5(c) of Sch.4, for the forfeiture of a substance or device in contravention of s.5(4), relates to the unlawful possession of explosives, poisons and electrical devices with intent to take or to destroy fish. This was considered in Chapter 3 above.

The final category of things which a court may order to be forfeited, under para.5(d) of Sch.4, is any vessel or vehicle used in connection with the commission of the offence or in which any substance or device unlawfully in a person's possession was contained at the time of the offence. The effect of this provision is that the forfeiture of a vessel or vehicle is capable of adding considerably to the effective punishment for an offence. This power of forfeiture arises only where the conviction is brought on indictment, that is, before a Crown Court. Because of this, it may be advisable for a water authority, seeking to secure the maximum punishment for an offence, to have a case heard before a Crown Court where there is any likelihood of the court ordering forfeiture of a vessel or vehicle. There is an argument, however, that certain uses of a boat to take fish improperly, as where a boat is used to trawl a net, or where a boat is used as an 'otter' contrary to s.1(1)(a)(iii) of the 1975 Act (see para.3.06), involve a boat being used as an 'instrument' used in the commission of an offence. If this is the case it might be possible for magistrates to order the forfeiture of a boat under para.5(b) of Sch.4 to the Act (discussed above).

In addition to the provisions relating to forfeiture under the Salmon and Freshwater Fisheries Act 1975, a court will be empowered to order the forfeiture of items which are seized where a person is arrested for taking or destroying fish under para.2(1) of Sch.1 to the Theft Act 1968. The categories of things which are liable to forfeiture under Sch.1 to the Theft Act 1968 are less extensive than those under the 1975 Act. Paragraph 2(3) of Sch.1 to the Theft Act 1968 states that: 'The court by which a person is convicted of an offence under this paragraph [para.2] may order the forfeiture of anything which at the time of the offence, he had with him for use for taking or destroying fish.' It is notable that this only encompasses poaching equipment, and would not permit a court to order the forfeiture of a vehicle or even fish which had been taken in committing the offence.

10.07 *Forfeiture of Items Seized by Customs and Excise Officers*

Officers of Customs and Excise are given powers to bring about the seizure of certain things pursuant to their powers to oversee the export of salmon and trout under s.23 of the 1975 Act (see Ch.5). Their powers relating to seizure of items which may be forfeited under a court order are set out in Sch.3 to the Customs and Excise Management Act 1979. Paragraph 6 of Sch.4 to the Salmon and

Freshwater Fisheries Act 1975 modifies those powers of seizure in respect of a vessel or vehicle to the extent that a court may not order forfeiture if the owner did not know, and could not reasonably have foreseen, that the vessel or vehicle was to be used in connection with the offence. For these purposes the 'owner' of the vessel or vehicle which is the subject of a hire-purchase agreement means the person in possession of it under the agreement.

10.08   The Seizure of and Disposal of Fish

Paragraph 7 of Sch.4 to the Salmon and Freshwater Fisheries Act 1975 empowers an authorised officer to seize any salmon, trout or freshwater fish bought, sold or exposed for sale by, or in the possession for sale of, any person in contravention of the Act. This power relates to the offences of possessing roe under s.2(1)(b) (discussed in para.3.12), selling unclean or immature fish under s.2(2) (discussed in para.3.13) and the sale of unseasonable salmon and trout under s.22 (discussed in para.5.12). The meaning of 'authorised officer' is defined in s.41(1) of the 1975 Act and was discussed in para.5.14. Fish that have been seized under this power are liable to forfeiture by order of the court where the person possessing them is convicted of an offence by virtue of para.5(a) of Sch.4 to the 1975 Act.

Where any fish or other thing of a perishable nature is seized under para.5 of Sch.4, the person by whom it is seized may sell it, and the net proceeds of sale are liable to forfeiture in the same manner as the fish or other thing sold. In so far as no order for forfeiture is made by the court, the money which constitutes the proceeds of sale is to be paid to the owner on demand. In the event of neglect or failure to exercise these powers no legal liability arises against any person (para.8, Sch.4). Hence the provision gives a *power* to sell perishable items which have been seized without imposing any legally enforceable *duty* to do so. In practice it may be preferable for a person seizing fish to place them in cold storage rather than to sell them, since this allows the fish to be produced in court as evidence of an offence (see Millichamp (1982) s.5.10 on the disposal of seized fish).

10.09   Disqualification from Holding a Fishing Licence

Along with the penalties and forfeiture provisions under the Salmon and Freshwater Fisheries Act 1975, another punitive measure which it permits is brought about through the system of fishing licences discussed in Chapter 6. Paragraph 9 of Sch.4 states that if a person is convicted of an offence against the Act and is subsequently convicted of any such offence, the court may order that any fishing or general licence held by him shall be forfeited, and that he shall be disqualified from holding and obtaining a fishing or general licence for such period not exceeding one year as the court thinks fit. The meaning and effects of this provision were considered in para.6.09.

In the event of a person who is the holder of a fishing or general licence being prosecuted for an offence under the Act he must either:

(a)   cause it to be delivered to the clerk of the court not later than the day before the date appointed for the hearing; or

(b)   post it, at such a time that in the ordinary course of post it would be delivered not later than that day, in a letter duly addressed to the clerk and either registered or sent by the recorded delivery service; or

(c)   have it with him at the hearing (para.10 of Sch.4).

If he is then convicted and the court makes an order under para.9 of Sch.4 (mentioned in the previous paragraph) the court shall order the licence to be surrendered to it. In the event of the convicted person failing to deliver the licence in accordance with the provisions for doing so, and not surrendering it as required then he will be guilty of an offence and the licence will be revoked from the time when its surrender was ordered. The penalty for this offence is not expressly stated, and so must be taken to be the general penalty for offences under the Act (para.1(2), Sch.2 to the Act). This is a fine not exceeding level 4 on the standard scale, presently equivalent to £1,000 (see para.1.12 on the standard scale).

Where a court orders a fishing or general licence to be surrendered or disqualifies a person from holding or obtaining a licence, the court shall:

(a)   send notice of the order to the water authority within whose area the offence was committed, unless the authority prosecuted in the case;

(b)   if the licence has been so surrendered, retain it and forward it to that authority, who may dispose of it as they think fit (para.11, Sch.4 to the Act).

10.10   Certification of Conviction

Where a person is convicted of an offence against the Act, the clerk of the court before whom he is convicted shall within one month of the date of the conviction, forward a certificate of the conviction to the water authority for the area in which the offence was committed (para.12, Sch.4). A certificate of this kind will be receivable in all subsequent legal proceedings (para.13, Sch.4). If a person who has previously been convicted of a fishery offence is subsequently convicted of another fishery offence the court may take the certificate of previous conviction into account in determining the sentence for the later offence. The general rule is that magistrates will not be told of previous convictions when deciding upon the guilt or innocence of a person, but if they decide that he is guilty of the offence, they may then, and only then, inquire into previous convictions (see *Hastings* v *Ostle* (1930)). At that stage a certificate of conviction may be presented to the court.

10.11   Miscellaneous Provisions

Part IV of the Salmon and Freshwater Fisheries Act 1975, ss.38 to 43, deals with a collection of miscellaneous matters. Many of these matters have already been considered, but in so far as they have not, they are discussed in the following paragraphs.

10.12   *Works below High-Water Mark*

Section 38 of the Salmon and Freshwater Fisheries Act 1975 is concerned with works constructed under the Act on, over, or under lands below the high-water mark of ordinary spring tides. This is capable of including works in respect of fish passes (under ss.9 and 10), gratings and watercourses (under ss.14 and 15), and water authority works on fixed engines and obstructions (under s.28 and Sch.3). The most important of these, though, is where a water authority seeks an order under s.28 and para.1(b) of Sch.3 to erect and work a fixed engine for catching salmon and migratory trout (see paras.7.06 and 7.13). Section 38(1) stipulates that the works shall be constructed in accordance with such plans and sections and subject to such regulations as the Secretary of State approves in writing before they are commenced. Any alteration or extension of such works shall be subject to the same approval (s.38(2)). The strictness of this requirement is further emphasised by s.38(3) which provides that if work is commenced or completed contrary to his written permission the Secretary of State may abate and remove it and restore the site to its former condition at the cost of the person who commenced or executed the work. In the case of work being executed by a person other than the owner of the work, the Secretary of State may recover the cost of restoring the site to its former state from the owner. Works of this kind must also conform with the provisions of any relevant local Act (s.38(4)).

10.13   *Border Rivers and the Solway Firth*

As has previously been stated (in para.10.03), the Salmon and Freshwater Fisheries Act 1975 is, apart from narrow exceptions, only applicable to England and Wales (s.43(2)). In order to place the matter beyond doubt, s.39(1)(a) states that it is not to apply to the River Tweed, which for part of its length constitutes the boundary between England and Scotland. The geographical extent of the River Tweed is determined by the Tweed Fisheries (Amendment) Act 1859 and any byelaw amending that definition. The applicability of the 1975 Act to the Esk was considered in para.10.03.

In respect of the Solway Firth, which is split by the boundary between England and Scotland, the basic rule applies, to the effect that only that part of the Firth which is in England is governed by the Act. By way of exception, this rule is modified to harmonise the law of England and Scotland in respect of the permitted net mesh which may be used in the Firth. Section 39(2) of the 1975 Act provides that if the minimum size of net mesh which may be used on the English side of the Firth is greater than that which may lawfully be used on the Scottish side, then the minimum net mesh permitted under Scots law will prevail on the English side of the Firth; that is, English netsmen in the Firth are to be permitted the same advantage as their Scots counterparts. (The minimum size of net mesh permitted under the Act was considered in para.3.15.) For these purposes the limits of the Solway Firth are to be determined by the Minister.

10.14   *The River Severn*

Section 40 of the Salmon and Freshwater Fisheries Act 1975 makes special reference to fish passes in dams constructed on the River Severn. This is because the general duty upon the owner or occupier of a dam or obstruction to make and maintain fish passes does not apply where the dam has been constructed under a special Act of Parliament (s.9(4)(a) of the 1975 Act; see para.4.15). Since dams on the Severn had been constructed by the Severn Commissioners under the Severn Navigation Acts of 1842 and 1853, the owners of them, the British Waterways Board, were empowered by statutory provision to stop up fish passes in the dams (s.28, Severn Navigation Act 1881). Contrary to this, however, s.40 of the present Act states that the British Waterways Board are not empowered to stop up these fish passes and must maintain them in an efficient state.

10.15   *Interpretation*

Section 41 is the interpretation section of the Salmon and Freshwater Fisheries Act 1975, providing definitions of many terms which are peculiar to the Act. The meanings of these definitions have been discussed in the text in connection with the areas of law to which they relate. Other words in the Act are to be interpreted in accordance with the Interpretation Act 1978.

10.16   *Repeals*

Section 42 of the Salmon and Freshwater Fisheries Act 1975 contains nine subsections concerned with repeals. Subsection 42(1) states that the enactments specified in Sch.5 to the Act are repealed to the extent specified by that schedule. Schedule 5 consists of a table listing the extent of repeal of certain statutes.

Subsection 42(2) of the Act amends s.18 of the Sea Fish (Conservation) Act 1967 to the extent that s.31(1)(d) of the 1975 Act, conferring powers of seizure and ancillary provisions, applies in relation to the 1967 Act.

Subsection 42(3) of the Act is a rather convoluted provision to the effect that repeals will be of no consequence in so far as the Act has the effect of restating the law since the restated provision will now govern the situation. Moreover, provisions under s.93(2) of the Salmon and Freshwater Fisheries Act 1923, which deemed orders made under previous fishery Acts to have effect as if made under the 1923 Act, are to be treated as done under the corresponding provision of the present Act so far as is necessary for preserving continuity in the law. Thus an order made before 1923 was capable of continuing in effect by virtue of s.93(2) of the 1923 Act, and may now continue in effect by virtue of s.43(3) of the present Act.

Subsection 42(4) of the Act again strives to preserve continuity by providing that any enactment or other document referring to an enactment repealed by either the 1975 or the 1923 Salmon and Freshwater Fisheries Acts shall be construed to refer to or to include a reference to the 1975 Act in so far as may be necessary in order to preserve its effect.

Subsection 42(5) stipulates that nothing in the 1975 Act is to affect the admissibility in evidence of any instrument made under the Salmon Fishery Act 1865. This stipulation will be of particular importance in respect of the certificates of privileged use issued by the Special Commissioners for Fisheries under the 1865 Act in respect of fixed engines and other obstructions (see para.4.08).

Subsection 42(6) of the Act states that s.254 of the Local Government Act 1972 (relating to the power of the Secretary of State to amend enactments by order) is to apply to the 1975 Act as if it had been passed before 1 April 1974. Section 254 of the Local Government Act 1972 empowers the Secretary of State to amend any Act or instrument under an Act made before 1 April 1974 in so far as appears to him to be necessary for the purposes of the Local Government Act 1972. The effect of deeming the Salmon and Freshwater Fisheries Act 1975 to have been passed before 1 April 1974, for these purposes, is that the Secretary of State is similarly empowered to amend the 1975 Act.

Subsection 42(7) of the Act stipulates that the Water Act 1973 is to have effect as if the functions conferred by s.28(1) and (2) of the 1975 Act were conferred under the 1973 Act. This means that the duties of water authorities to maintain, improve and develop fisheries and to establish liaison committees, discussed in Chapter 7, are to have effect as if conferred under the Water Act 1973.

Subsection 42(8) of the Act affirms that nothing in the Act is to affect the legal right of any conservators, directors, commissioners, undertakers or other persons to dredge, scour, cleanse or improve any navigable river, canal or other inland navigation. This provision is to be read alongside s.2(4), relating to disturbing the spawn of fish or spawning fish, discussed in para.3.14.

Finally, s.42(9) of the Act originally stated that nothing in the Act was to be taken to prejudice the operation of s.38 of the Interpretation Act 1889. The 1889 Act has now been replaced by the Interpretation Act 1978 (see s.25(1) of the 1978 Act). Subsection 42(9) of the present Act must be taken to refer to provisions of the Interpretation Act 1978 which relate to repeals of statutes (see ss.15, 16 and 17 of the 1978 Act). The effects of these are, amongst other things, to substitute 'the Salmon and Freshwater Fisheries Act 1975' for references to 'the Salmon and Freshwater Fisheries Act 1923' where the earlier Act has been repealed or re-enacted.

10.17   Citation

The final section of the Salmon and Freshwater Fisheries Act 1975, s.43, follows the general protocol for final sections of Acts of Parliament in stating the official title of the Act, the geographical extent of its applicability, and its date of commencement. The Act is to be cited as 'the Salmon and Freshwater Fisheries Act 1975', it is to extend only to England and Wales (subject to the qualifications which have been discussed in this chapter and Ch.7), and it came into force on 1 August 1975.

11

WATER POLLUTION

11.01   *The Problem of Water Pollution*

The existence of any fishery must necessarily depend upon the availability of water of a sufficiently high quality in a sufficient quantity to support fish life. Different species of fish are suited to different types of water and to an extent the type of fish that will be found in any particular water will tend to be determined by the overall natural environment of the water. Fast-flowing moorland streams, for example, will tend to suit trout to the exclusion of other types of fish, whilst lowland stillwaters tend to be populated with coarse fish such as roach and carp which have lower oxygen requirements (see Fort and Brayshaw (1961) Ch.1). The general preferences of particular species of fish for particular kinds of habitat is a consequence of the way that fish have evolved independently of the influence of man. Other factors, however, are a direct consequence of the effect of human activity on the water environment. Broadly these factors can be considered under the two headings of 'water pollution' and 'water abstraction'. The law relating to the former is considered in this chapter, whilst the law relating to the latter is considered in the next chapter.

Although the natural quality of water may not always be ideal to support fish life, all the major problems of pollution which beset waters of the present day are of human creation. It has been suggested by Templeton (1984 p.24) that pollution caused by man can be placed into three categories according to its effect upon the environment, fish and other aquatic life. In the first category is pollution by poison, which will kill fish by toxic action if present in sufficient concentration. Typically, the poisons which are likely to cause damage to fisheries will include acids and alkalis and other by-products of the chemical industry, metal waste produced by mines and industrial processing, and pesticides used in agriculture. In the second category of pollution is pollution by the introduction of suspended solids or colloidal matter which have the effect of making water cloudy or opaque. The consequences of this are that light is excluded from the water and plants and other organisms decline, suspended particles of matter cause fish to suffer respiratory difficulties, and those species that spawn in gravel are prevented from doing so by accumulations of silt. Normally this type of pollution is associated with washing processes such as those used in gravel extraction, mining and in the cleaning of root crops. The third category of pollution arises from the deoxygenation of water through the introduction of excessive amounts of organic material. Normally an amount of organic matter is generated naturally in any aquatic environment and is decomposed through bacterial action without any harmful effects. Where a large amount of organic matter is deposited in a water, however, the decomposition process utilises large amounts of oxygen from amongst that dissolved in the water and as a consequence fish die of oxygen starvation. Notable contributors of this kind of waste are dairies, breweries, slurry tanks, silage processors, and sewage treatment works.

Although most kinds of water pollution fall into one of these three categories, it is commonly the case that aspects of all three are present concurrently in badly polluted waters, often discharged by a number of different polluters (see *Pride of Derby and Derbyshire Angling Association Ltd* v *British Celanese Ltd* (1952) discussed in para.11.11). Other factors may also be present and exacerbate the problem. For example, a problem of oxygen deficiency will be worsened by the discharge of warm effluent, since an increase in water temperature will cause a reduction in the initial amount of oxygen dissolved in the water. Similarly, a film of surface oil will reduce the contact between water and air, through which oxygen is absorbed, and bring about additional deoxygenation.

In addition to the interactive effects of pollutants another dimension to the problem is that of the time-scale involved. Some cases of pollution are a consequence of a continuing discharge which causes damage to a fishery over a long period of time, even though the pollutant involved is not of a highly toxic nature. Other types of pollution are the result of a transitory cause such as an accidental discharge of highly toxic matter destroying a fishery in the relatively short period taken by the matter to flow through a watercourse. In each case the appropriate legal approach depends upon the circumstances. In some instances the legal objective may be to gain a court order to restrain future pollution, in other cases the objective is to obtain an award of damages to compensate for injury to a fishery, or else to punish the polluter by means of criminal proceedings, or a combination of these. The appropriate legal remedy is intimately related to the nature of the problem.

(For general reading on the problem of water pollution see: Turing (1952); Fort and Brayshaw (1961) Ch.VIII; and Templeton (1984) part 1.2.)

11.02   *Legal Approaches to the Problem of Pollution*

The topic of water pollution has already been touched upon in Chapter 3 in relation to the offence of causing or knowingly permitting matter which is poisonous or injurious to fish to enter waters containing fish contrary to s.4 of the Salmon and Freshwater Fisheries Act 1975. Although this provision makes certain kinds of pollution unlawful, it falls far short of a comprehensive legal attack upon the general problem of water pollution. Regrettably the law on water pollution is not to be found under any one Act, but is spread around the diverse collection of statutes and case law decisions which are discussed in this chapter. Consequently, no excuse is required for this eclectic treatment of the topic.

The plan of this chapter is to look firstly at the common law provisions relating to water pollution (paras 11.03 to 11.11). These provide the grounds on which a fishery owner or an angling association might be able to bring civil proceedings for redress where loss or damage to a fishery has been suffered as a consequence of pollution (see para.1.11 on the distinction between civil and criminal law). Secondly, the chapter turns to consider the criminal law under Part II of the Control of Pollution Act 1974 which creates a number of criminal offences in relation to the pollution of water (paras 11.12 to 11.23). These will be of importance to water authorities and other bodies that are primarily concerned with punishment, rather than compensation, for acts of pollution. Finally, the chapter concludes by looking at a number of miscellaneous offences relating to pollution which exist outside the Control of Pollution Act 1974 (paras.11.24 to 11.29).

(For general reading on the law relating to water pollution see: Wisdom (1966b)); McLoughlin (1972) Ch.2; Newsom and Sherratt (1972); and Hughes (1986) Part IV.)

11.03   The Legal Definition of Water Pollution

Despite the importance of the term, 'pollution' has never been precisely defined in any Act, and therefore its meaning must be ascertained from judicial interpretation in past cases. As a fundamental principle of common law, a riparian owner, owning land forming the bank of a river or stream is entitled to receive the river water in its natural state, and is bound to allow water in that same state to flow on to his downstream neighbours. Hence, it is said that every riparian proprietor is entitled to the water of his stream in its natural flow, without sensible alteration of its character or quality (see *John Young and Co.* v *Bankier Distillery Co.* (1893)). Consequently, at common law 'pollution' is anything which, when added to water, changes the quality of that water.

Clearly the common law definition of pollution will include trade waste discharged into a stream from a factory (see *Crossley & Sons* v *Lightowler* (1867)), or the discharge of domestic sewage (see *Jones* v *Llanrwst Urban District Council* (1911)). It has even been held that the discharge of hot, though clean, water into a stream is capable of being actionable because it has the effect of increasing the temperature and so changing a natural quality of the water in the stream (in *Tipping* v *Eckersley* (1855)). Similarly, the addition of hard water to a stream of soft water is capable of constituting pollution by changing the natural chemical quality of the water (*John Young and Co.* v *Bankier Distillery Co.* (1893)). Indeed, any change in the quality of a stream is capable of amounting to pollution in so far as it is substantial in its effect. There would not be pollution of a stream, for example, where a discharge of water merely has the effect of disturbing the mud on a river bed for a short time without changing the natural quality of the water (*Taylor* v *Bennett* (1836), though see s.49 of the Control of Pollution Act 1974 and para.11.23 below).

It would not be a defence to a common law action for pollution of a stream to claim that the stream was already polluted from another source, since, in ascertaining whether pollution has occurred the amount of pollution already in the water is not considered (*Staffordshire County Council* v *Seisdon Rural District Council* (1907)). The sole question is whether the person against whom a legal action is brought has contributed some significant part to the pollution of the water. So that if water is polluted from several separate sources it may be possible for separate actions to be brought against different polluters. In such a situation it would not be a defence for any individual polluter to claim that his contribution was only a small part of the whole (*Wood* v *Waud* (1849)). Providing that it can be shown that a particular individual or company has caused some substantial contribution to the pollution of a river, then he will be liable even if it cannot be shown that the fishery owner has suffered any loss as a result (*Crossley & Sons* v *Lightowler* (1867) and *Jones* v *Llanrwst Urban District Council* (1911)).

11.04 Common Law Actions against Pollution

In the event of a person polluting a stream by impairing the natural quality of the water, a range of common law actions are available as legal grounds on which to compensate others for the resultant loss, and to restrain future pollution. The four principal actions under which civil law claims may be brought are: Trespass, Nuisance, the Rule in *Rylands* v *Fletcher* (1868), and Negligence. The requirements for these claims are outlined in the following four paragraphs.

11.05 The Common Law Action for Trespass

Trespass has already been mentioned in paras.6.03 and 9.21. Essentially it is a civil wrong, which involves unjustified interference with the possession of land. A person commits trespass when he enters upon another's land without permission or lawful excuse. Similarly trespass will be committed by depositing anything upon another's land without permission, and in particular where refuse or polluting matter is dumped or discharged directly into a pond or stream (*Jones* v *Llanrwst Urban District Council* (1911)). In such a case the riparian owner or the owner of the fishery may bring an action without the need to prove actual damage to the fishery.

The availability of an action in trespass is limited, though, to those with a legal interest in land, and it will not be open to a person to sue for trespass unless he is the freehold or leasehold owner of land or a fishery which has deteriorated as the result of the pollution. Hence the members of an angling club who fish a water on an informal basis, without a lease of the fishery, may find themselves unable to bring an action of this kind if no leasehold ownership of the fishery is established. Another limitation is that it is not clear whether trespass will apply where pollution is carried by water without any direct or perceptible deposit upon the bed of the stream. In such a case a more appropriate action is that of nuisance (*Esso Petroleum Co. Ltd.* v *Southport Corp.* (1956) and *Pride of Derby and Derbyshire Angling Association Ltd* v *British Celanese Ltd* (1952) discussed in para.11.11).

11.06 The Common Law Action for Nuisance

'Nuisance', properly called private nuisance, is another form of common law action which arises as a result of impairment of enjoyment of an interest in land. As with trespass, it is only available to persons with a legal interest either in riparian land or in a fishery which suffers as a consequence of pollution. If noxious matter is discharged into a stream causing water to be polluted, then owners of downstream fisheries which suffer as a consequence of the pollution may bring an action in nuisance against the polluter (*Pride of Derby and Derbyshire Angling Association Ltd* v *British Celanese Ltd* (1952), discussed in para.11.11). Although it is sometimes maintained that, in contrast to trespass, damage must be proved before an action in nuisance will succeed, in the past the law has presumed that damage has occurred from the fact of the pollution itself (*Nicholls* v *Ely Beet Sugar Factory* (1936)). Private nuisance is probably the most important common law action available in a case of pollution.

A distinct kind of legal action may sometimes be brought on account of what is properly termed 'public nuisance'. Public nuisance arises where the effect of pollution is to cause offence to the public at large rather than to any particular property owner. If pollution has this effect then an action of a criminal character may be pursued on behalf of the general public by the Attorney General (*Attorney General* v *Luton Local Board of Health* (1856)). Public nuisance is also a common law criminal offence (*R* v *Medley* (1834)), and a ground for civil redress where a private individual or corporate body can show that particular damage has been suffered, over and above that suffered by the general public. If this can be shown it is not necessary for the person bringing the action to establish a legal interest in the land which is polluted, providing that he has suffered special loss as a result of the pollution. Although this type of action has been useful in the past as a means of punishing polluters (*R* v *Bradford Navigation Co.* (1865)), the likelihood of water becoming so badly polluted as to become a public nuisance today is small. In all probability a water would cease to support fish life long before that stage was reached.

11.07   The Rule in Rylands v Fletcher (1868)

Another form of common law action which might be available in the event of pollution of water originated in the case of *Rylands* v *Fletcher* (1868). In this case a mill owner had a reservoir constructed upon his land. When the reservoir was completed and filled with water, water burst through some old mine shafts and flooded his neighbour's mines. The issue before the court was whether the mill owner, who had employed reputable contractors to build the reservoir, should be liable for the damage caused to the mines. The House of Lords found that the mill owner was liable for the damage according to the principle which has since been referred to as 'the rule in *Rylands* v *Fletcher*': '. . . the person who for his own purposes brings on his lands and collects and keeps there anything likely to do mischief if it escapes, must keep it at his peril, and, if he does not do so, is *prima facie* answerable for all the damage which is the natural consequence of its escape'. Although *Rylands* v *Fletcher* was not a case of pollution, it is clear from the words used that pollution, as something 'likely to do mischief if it escapes', is capable of coming within the rule (*Smeaton* v *Ilford Corp.* (1954)). Moreover, in the event of pollution escaping from land in this way the polluter is strictly liable for the natural consequences of the escape. This means that liability will arise unless the polluter can establish one of a limited number of defences, namely: statutory authority, an act of God, an act of an unauthorised stranger, or that the escape was due to the fault of the person who claims as a consequence of it.

Despite the apparent breadth of the principle established by *Rylands* v *Fletcher*, it has undergone a number of restrictive interpretations in the courts over the years and is now generally thought to be of much narrower extent than was first indicated. In particular the courts have restricted its application to 'non-natural' uses of land, which amounts to a limitation of the principle to situations where persons use land in an unreasonable or exceptionally hazardous way. For instance, it was held in one case that the accumulation of industrial waste was not a non-natural use of land (*British Celanese Ltd* v *A.H. Hunt (Capacitors)Ltd* (1969)), and in another case that the manufacture of explosives in time of war was probably not a non-natural use of land (*Read* v *J. Lyons & Co. Ltd* (1947)). As a result of these decisions a person who accumulates pollution on his land may well be able to claim that the accumulation constitutes a natural use of the land and that the rule does not apply. Because of the liberal interpretations of 'natural' use of land, and other restrictions upon the operation of the rule, it has been said: 'The rule in *Rylands* v *Fletcher*, by reason of its many limitations and exceptions, today seldom forms the basis of a successful claim in the courts' (Law Commission Report (1965) No.32 at p.7). Nonetheless, the *possibility* remains that it might ground a claim against a person causing pollution in extreme circumstances.

11.08   *The Common Law Action for Negligence*

Another possibility is that pollution will serve as the basis for a common law action in negligence against the polluter (*Esso Petroleum Co. Ltd* v *Southport Corp.* (1956)). An action for negligence arises:

(a)   where a duty of care is owed by the person who causes the pollution to those who might reasonably be supposed to be affected by it;

(b)   where there has been a breach of the duty of care by causing pollution; and

(c)   where the result of the breach of duty is that the person bringing the action has suffered damage or loss.

Classically these principles were expressed by Lord Atkin in his speech in *Donoghue* v *Stevenson* (1932):

> The rule that you are to love your neighbour becomes, in law, you must not injure your neighbour; and the lawyer's question, Who is my neighbour? receives a restricted reply. You must take reasonable care to avoid acts or omissions which you can reasonably foresee would be likely to injure your neighbour. Who, then, in law is my neighbour? The answer seems to be— persons who are so closely and directly affected by my act that I ought reasonably to have them in contemplation as being so affected when I am directing my mind to the acts or omissions which are called in question.

Put into the context of the law on pollution, Lord Atkin's neighbour principle requires that a person who has control of a pollutant should take reasonable care to prevent it causing injury. In particular, this care should be exercised in relation to persons who might reasonably be expected to suffer loss as a result of the misbehaviour of the person with control of the pollutant. In the event of reasonable care not being taken to prevent injury, a person towards whom care should have been exercised will be entitled to compensation for negligence.

The common law action in negligence is rather open-ended in nature in that it is impossible to specify in advance the range of conduct which is capable of being held to be negligent by a court. Nonetheless, it is clear that it provides an important means by which compensation for the effects of pollution can be obtained. Moreover, it is a remedy which is not restricted to persons who possess a legal interest in land. The action for negligence is dependent, however, upon the ability to show loss, rather than merely the infringement of a legal right. For this reason any compensation which is payable on account of negligence would depend upon factors such as the provable damage to fish stocks or the devaluation of a fishery caused by pollution.

(For further discussion of liability for negligence and the other common law actions discussed here, see Winfield and Jolowicz (1984).)

11.09 Pollution which is not Actionable at Common Law

As has been seen, the common law gives extensive rights against those causing pollution. Despite these, there are many situations where the common law fails to provide a remedy against pollution. This is for two reasons: first, there may be no person who is both willing and legally entitled to pursue proceedings; and second, the person causing the pollution may have gained a legal right to pollute.

As a general rule, the legal right to pursue common law proceedings against a person polluting a stream is only available to persons who possess a legal interest in property which is affected by the pollution. Because of this no action can be brought against a person causing pollution where the polluted water is entirely upon his own land and leaves the land unpolluted and no other substantial injury is caused (*Elmhirst* v *Spencer* (1849)). Moreover, unless the complainant has a proprietary interest, such as the freehold or leasehold ownership of land or fishing rights which are affected by the pollution, in most cases he will not be allowed to bring any action. Thus in the case of *Stockport Waterworks Co.* v *Potter* (1864) a waterworks company was unable to succeed in an action for pollution of water which it was permitted to abstract because they had no riparian, fishery or other water rights apart from the right to abstract water. This was an insufficient legal interest for the action to succeed. Normally a fishery owner or an angling association with a lease of a fishery would possess a sufficient legal interest to pursue common law proceedings against a person causing pollution of the fishery.

The other reason why common law proceedings against a person causing pollution might not succeed is that the polluter may have acquired the legal right to pollute. There are four legal grounds on which a right to pollute might be based: grant, custom, prescription and statute.

(a) *Grant* A right to pollute based upon grant arises where an agreement in the form of a deed gives the express or implied right to pollute. Hence in *Hall* v *Lund* (1863) it was held that an implied condition of a lease of a bleaching works was that an adjacent stream could be fouled by the discharge of waste into it. It was held that it was not open to the landlord of the works to maintain an action for pollution of the stream since the right had impliedly been granted in the lease.

(b) *Custom*   A right to pollute based upon custom may be shown where the right is not indefinite, nor illegal or unreasonable and has existed since time immemorial. (On the meaning of 'time immemorial' see para.4.08.) On this ground, a right to pollute was established in *Carlyon* v *Lovering* (1857) where it was accepted by the court that it was an immemorial custom of miners in the Stannaries to use streams to wash away stones, rubble and other material dislodged in the course of working a mine. On this ground, the pollution caused by the practice was permissible so long as the customary use was not exceeded.

(c) *Prescription*   Prescription is the legal presumption whereby a person who has exercised a right over property of another for a long period of time in an open manner is assumed to have acquired the right by lawful means. So, for example, a person may establish the right to pollute a stream by showing that he has done so for a lengthy period of time (*Wood* v *Sutcliffe* (1851)). Under the Prescription Act 1832 the enjoyment of a right to pollute for 20 years without interruption raises the presumption that the right has existed since time immemorial, but this presumption can be defeated if it is shown that there was some previous time at which it did not exist. The enjoyment of a right for 40 years is sufficient for the right to be presumed to be absolute and not open to defeat unless it can be shown that the right was originally granted in a written agreement or deed (s.2, Prescription Act 1832).

For prescription to be claimed it is essential that the exercise of the right has been open and undisputed over the prescriptive period, otherwise prescriptive rights cannot be established. Thus in *Liverpool Corp.* v *Coghill* (1918) it was held that no prescriptive right to pollute was acquired where effluent was discharged during the night in such a manner that it was unknown to the body against whom the prescriptive right was claimed. Moreover, since prescriptive rights are assumed to be of lawful origin, no such rights will be accepted by a court where the exercise of the right would be contrary to statutory authority, or a public nuisance, or injurious to public health (see Wisdom (1966b) p.60). In short, the difficulties involved in establishing a prescriptive right to pollute are considerable.

(d) *Statute*   Finally, a common law right to pollute may be acquired under statute. Where pollution is authorised by statute then that authority overrides the common law, as in *Lea Conservancy Board* v *Hertford Corp.* (1884), where it was held that a public body could not be liable for pollution at common law since they had performed their duties as required by statute even though this resulted in effluent being discharged into a river (see also *Somerset Drainage Commissioners* v *Bridgwater Corp.* (1899) and the Radioactive Substances Act 1960 discussed in para.11.28).

11.10   *Common Law Remedies*

If it is established that a riparian or fishery owner suffers an actionable deterioration in water quality as a consequence of pollution, then the main common law remedies open to him are either an award of damages to provide redress for losses suffered as a consequence of pollution, or the granting of a court order known as an 'injunction' to prevent future pollution of the water. Another possible remedy is the abatement of pollution.

Damages   Where pollution causes injury to a fishery the fishery owner is entitled to an award of damages to compensate him for the loss suffered. Since the object of an award of damages is to compensate for loss, it follows that the amount of the award of damages is the amount which is necessary to make good the loss of fish and to restore the fishery to its former state, in so far as this can be done by an award of money. In a case of pollution causing fish mortality this would correspond with the cost of restocking (*Granby (Marquis of)* v *Bakewell Urban District Council* (1923)).

Injunction   Where an existing source of pollution is established, or the likelihood of future pollution is shown, a court may grant an injunction to prevent the continuation or recurrence of pollution. This remedy may be given in addition to damages compensating for losses which have already been suffered. An injunction has the effect of restraining a person from continuing to pollute a watercourse. Disobedience to such an order will amount to contempt of court, for which, ultimately, the court can commit a non-compliant polluter to prison.

The granting of an injunction to restrain pollution is regarded by the courts as the proper remedy for the infringement of a right to a flow of unpolluted water (*Attorney General* v *Birmingham Corp.* (1858)) and will be granted even though no actual loss is shown on the part of the complainant (*Clowes* v *Staffordshire Potteries Waterworks Co.* (1872)). It is a common practice of courts to suspend the operation of an injunction if, on the balance of convenience, it is impossible to stop the pollution immediately, or if it is thought that the polluter should be given time to rectify the situation (*Attorney General* v *Colney Hatch Lunatic Asylum* (1868)). An injunction will not be granted by a court where damages are adequate (*Wood* v *Sutcliffe* (1851)), or where the pollution has been abated since the commencement of the proceedings (*Lillywhite* v *Trimmer* (1867)), or where the injury complained of is too trivial (*Attorney General* v *Preston Corp.* (1896)), or where the pollution is unlikely to recur (*Chapman, Morsons and Co.* v *Aukland Union* (1889)).

Abatement   Apart from damages and the injunction another possible, though rather uncommon, remedy is that of self-help or abatement of pollution. This will only arise where the person who suffers as a result of pollution is in a position to abate or prevent the pollution and the need to do so is urgent. In such a case it is legally permissible to take reasonable steps to abate the pollution. Such a situation arose in *Cawkwell* v *Russell* (1856), where a person discharged foul water into a drain into which he was only permitted to discharge surface water. The court held that in these circumstances it was permissible to abate the nuisance by obstructing the whole drain. Care must be exercised in the rare situations where this remedy is possible since unreasonable actions intended to abate pollution may make the person liable to trespass or other civil actions if he exceeds his lawful right to abate the nuisance.

The common law power of abatement of pollution given to a private individual may be contrasted with the statutory powers possessed by a water authority to remedy or forestall the pollution of water and to remove polluting matter from inland waters. These arise under the Control of Pollution Act 1974. Where it appears to a water authority that any poisonous, noxious or polluting matter or any solid waste is likely to enter or is present in waters in its area, the authority may carry out such operations as it considers appropriate. In particular, two situations in which action may be taken by the water authority are made explicit:

(a) in a case where the matter appears likely to enter such waters, for the purpose of preventing it from doing so; and

(b) in a case where the matter appears to be or to have been present in such waters, for the purpose of removing or disposing of the matter or of remedying or mitigating any pollution caused by its presence in the waters or of restoring the waters (including the fauna and flora in them), so far as it is reasonably practicable to do so, to the state in which they were immediately before the matter became present in the waters (s.46(4), Control of Pollution Act 1974).

In a case where a water authority carries out operations of this kind it is entitled to recover the cost of doing so from any person who caused or knowingly permitted the matter in question to be present at the place from which, in the opinion of the authority, it was likely to enter or to be present in the waters. Where work of this kind is carried out by the water authority, the extent to which damage has been reduced as a result is taken into account in assessing any award of damages which might be claimed by a person who has suffered as a consequence of the pollution (s.46(5) and (7), Control of Pollution Act 1974). In effect, if work is done by the water authority to prevent loss, then a court must make a lesser award of damages to take account of the extent to which loss has been reduced because of the action taken by the water authority. This does not mean that the polluter will get off lightly if the water authority steps in to help since the water authority will be able to recover its costs from the polluter directly.

In practice the powers given to water authorities to act to remedy or forestall pollution are likely to be of greater importance than the common law right to abate pollution. Providing that water authorities are expeditious in acting in cases of pollution, there will be few occasions where any advantage will be gained by a private individual taking the matter into his own hands by exercising his common law right of abatement.

11.11 A Leading Case: Pride of Derby and Derbyshire Angling Association Ltd v British Celanese Ltd and others (1952)

The application of the principles of common law to the protection of fisheries is well illustrated in a leading case—*Pride of Derby and Derbyshire Angling Association Ltd* v *British Celanese Ltd and others* (1952). The facts were that the Pride of Derby and Derbyshire Angling Association was the owner of a fishery on the Rivers Derwent and Trent below Derby, which was polluted to the extent that the waters were foul and black and contained few, if any, fish. This pollution was attributed to at least three causes. First, heated effluent containing suspended organic matter was discharged into the river by British Celanese Ltd. Second, insufficiently treated sewage matter was discharged into the river from Derby Corporation's sewage works. Third, the damage to fish stocks was further aggravated by a rise in water temperature brought about by large quantities of heated effluent contributed from a power generating station operated by the British Electrical Authority. The combined effect of these sources of organic and thermal pollution was to deoxygenate the water and so to depopulate it of fish, and consequently to damage the Angling Association's fishery. On these facts the Association claimed an injunction to restrain each of the three bodies from continuing to allow their effluent to pollute the rivers. In addition the Association claimed damages in nuisance and trespass against the three polluters.

On behalf of Derby Corporation, a defence was raised on the ground that the Corporation was absolved from having caused a nuisance because it was under a statutory duty to do the thing which had caused the nuisance; that is, the Corporation was bound to operate the sewage works under powers conferred by the Derby Corporation Act 1901. Although the sewage works that they had constructed had been built strictly in accordance with the 1901 Act, the population of Derby had increased to such an extent that the works had become inadequate, and this was a matter which was beyond the control of the Corporation. In declining to accept this argument, the Court of Appeal found that the 1901 Act specifically stated that the Corporation were not to operate the sewage works in such a manner as to cause a nuisance or to allow any sewage matter to be carried into the rivers. Therefore the defence of acting under statutory authority failed.

The other bodies who had caused the pollution were also unable to justify their acts, and the court held that an injunction to restrain future pollution and an award of damages for nuisance were the appropriate remedies. In accordance with the usual practice in such circumstances, the court suspended the operation of the injunction for a period in order to allow work to be done to bring discharges of water into the rivers up to an acceptable standard.

In his judgment in the Court of Appeal, Denning LJ made a number of observations of general relevance to common law actions on account of pollution. Despite the lower court having made an award of damages in *both* trespass and nuisance against the three bodies who had caused the pollution, he thought that the only cause of action which was available to the Association was in nuisance. Negligence was never alleged, and Denning LJ doubted whether the rule in *Rylands* v *Fletcher* (1868) applied where a local authority operated a sewage works for the general benefit of the community, since this would not amount to non-natural use of the land (see para.11.07). Interestingly, he made no mention of the possibility of an action for trespass, perhaps because he thought trespass inappropriate to a situation where the pollution had been transported by the stream rather than being deposited directly on to land (see para.11.05). The indications given in Denning LJ's judgment are that nuisance, and perhaps negligence, are the more appropriate common law actions to follow in a case of river pollution, and that the scope for actions in trespass and under the rule in *Rylands* v *Fletcher* (1868) is strictly limited.

11.12   The Control of Pollution Act 1974

Apart from the common law actions which have been discussed, and a number of miscellaneous statutory provisions which are considered at the end of this chapter, the law concerning the control and prevention of pollution of water is now contained in Part II, ss.31 to 56, of the Control of Pollution Act 1974. This Act adopts an integrated approach to the problem of water pollution, and repeals and replaces a large part of the earlier legislation, in particular most of the Rivers (Prevention of Pollution) Acts 1951 and 1961, which until recently were the major statutory provisions governing water pollution. The 1974 Act does not affect the common law actions or other proceedings instituted otherwise than under the Act where they remain available (s.105, Control of Pollution Act 1974). In short, all the main criminal proceedings which may follow from pollution of water now arise under the Control of Pollution Act 1974, referred to as 'the 1974 Act' in the remainder of this chapter.

(For general reading on water pollution under the Control of Pollution Act 1974 see: Garner (1975); Walker (1979) Ch.2; Wisdom (1979) Ch.15; and Hughes (1986) Part IV.)

11.13   Causing Polluting Matter to Enter a Stream under the Control of Pollution Act 1974

The main criminal offence relating to pollution of waters arises under s.31(1) of the Control of Pollution Act 1974. This key provision is to the effect that:

a person shall be guilty of an offence if he causes or knowingly permits—

(a)   any poisonous, noxious or polluting matter to enter any stream or controlled waters or any specified underground water (hereafter referred to collectively as 'relevant waters'); or

(b)   any matter to enter a stream so as to tend (either directly or in combination with other matter which he or another person causes or permits to enter the stream) to impede the proper flow of the water of the stream in a manner leading or likely to lead to a substantial aggravation of pollution due to other causes or consequences of such pollution; or

(c)   any solid waste matter to enter a stream or restricted waters.

A number of definitions are pertinent both to the interpretation of this provision and to other sections of the 1974 Act. The phrase 'causes or knowingly permits' has already been discussed in para.3.16 in relation to s.4(1) of the Salmon and Freshwater Fisheries Act 1975. The meaning of 'stream' is given in s.56(1) of the Control of Pollution Act 1974, where it is stated that:

'stream' includes any river, watercourse or inland water, whether the river, watercourse or inland water is natural or artificial or above or below ground, except—

(a)   subject to [regulations to the contrary] any lake, loch or pond which does not discharge into a stream;

(b)   any sewer vested in a water authority;

(c)   any tidal waters;

and any reference to a stream includes a reference to the channel or bed of the stream which is for the time being dry; and 'tidal waters' includes the waters of any enclosed dock which adjoins tidal waters.

'Controlled waters' is defined in s.56(1) of the Control of Pollution Act 1974 as:

the sea within three nautical miles from any point on the coast measured from low-water mark of ordinary spring tides, such other parts of the territorial sea adjacent to Great Britain as are prescribed by regulations and other tidal waters in Great Britain.

'Restricted waters' is stated in the same subsection to mean:

controlled waters in—

(a) areas designated by regulations as tidal rivers for the purposes of this definition; and

(b)   other areas of a kind prescribed for the purposes of this definition as areas in which, in the opinion of the Secretary of State, vessels commonly lie at moorings in close proximity to one another.

The effect of these definitions is that virtually all inland and coastal waters are brought under the Control of Pollution Act 1974.

Attention must be drawn at this point to some contrasts which exist between s.31(1)(a) of the Control of Pollution Act 1974 and s.4(1) of the Salmon and Freshwater Fisheries Act 1975 (discussed in para.3.16). Section 31(1)(a) of the 1974 Act provides for the offence of causing or knowingly permitting poison, or noxious or polluting matter to enter any stream or controlled waters, whilst s.4(1) of the 1975 Act provides for the offence of causing or permitting to flow, or putting or permitting to be put into any waters containing fish, any liquid or solid matter to such an extent as to cause the waters to be poisonous or injurious to fish or the spawning grounds, spawn or food of fish. The two main differences between these offences are that, first, the offence under s.4(1) of the 1975 Act is only concerned with waters containing fish, whilst the offence under s.31(1)(a) of the 1974 Act is not restricted to waters containing fish. The second difference is that the offence under s.4(1) of the 1975 Act requires it to be shown that the polluting matter causes the waters to be injurious to fish or the spawning grounds, spawn or food of fish. In contrast the offence under s.31(1)(a) of the 1974 Act is committed by allowing the polluting matter to enter the water without any requirement that the matter causes injury to fishlife. Because of these differences, and the evidential difficulties involved in showing the presence of fish populations and injury to them, there are advantages to the prosecution in proceeding under s.31(1)(a) of the 1974 Act rather than under s.4(1) of the 1975 Act.

11.14 Defences and Exceptions to the Offence of Causing Polluting Matter to Enter a Stream Contrary to s.31(1) of the Control of Pollution Act 1974

The principal offence of causing pollution under s.31(1) of the Control of Pollution Act 1974 is made subject to seven defences and exceptions set out in s.31(2) and (3) of the Act. These are: consent; statutory authority; 'good agricultural practice'; emergency; trade or sewage effluent; abandoned mines; and refuse from mines and quarries. These are discussed under the following subheadings.

(a) *Consent*   It is stated in s.31(2)(a) of the Control of Pollution Act 1974 that a person shall not be guilty of an offence if the entry of the pollution in question is authorised by a disposal licence or a consent given by the Secretary of State or a water authority and the entry or act is in accordance with the conditions, if any, to which the licence or consent is subject. This relates to the provision for consent to be given to the discharge of pollution under s.34 of the Act. (The circumstances in which such consent will be given are considered in para.11.21.)

(b) *Statutory authority*   Subsection 31(2)(b) of the 1974 Act provides that a person shall not be guilty of the offence of causing pollution under s.31(1) if the entry of poisonous, noxious or polluting matter is authorised by certain statutory provisions. These are:

(i)   section 34 of the Water Act 1945 (which amongst other things relates to temporary discharges by water undertakers in connection with the construction of works) or any prescribed enactment, or

(ii)   any provision of a local Act or statutory order which expressly confers power to discharge effluent into water, or

(iii)   any licence granted under Part II of The Food and Environmental Protection Act 1985.

In effect, the right to pollute with immunity from s.31(1) of the Control of Pollution Act 1974 is preserved where it is granted by any of these provisions. In this context, 'local act' includes enactments in a public general Act which amends a local Act. 'Statutory order' means an order, byelaw, scheme or award made under an Act of Parliament, including an order or scheme confirmed by Parliament or brought into operation in accordance with special parliamentary procedure (s.31(9), Control of Pollution Act 1974). Part II of The Food and Environmental Protection Act 1985 prohibits the disposal of substances in United Kingdom waters from British ships except where this is authorised by licence from the Minister.

(c) *'Good agricultural practice'*   Subsection 31(2)(c) of the Control of Pollution Act 1974 states that no offence is committed under s.31(1) of the Act where the entry of any poisonous, noxious or polluting matter is attributable to an act or omission which is in accordance with 'good agricultural practice'. This is a reference to a code of agricultural practice approved by the Minister, which is deemed to be good agricultural practice (s.31(9) of the 1974 Act). Despite this general exception, a water authority may apply to the Secretary of State to have an order served on an occupier to request the occupier to prevent acts or omissions which are likely to cause pollution of waters (s.51 of the 1974 Act). Where such an order is made by the Secretary of State, and the act or omission in question continues after 28 days from the date when notice of the order was served, then the defence of conformity with good agricultural practice ceases to be available (s.31(2)(c)(i) and (ii) of the 1974 Act).

(d) *Emergency* Under s.31(2)(d) of the Control of Pollution Act 1974 an exception to the offence under s.31(1) of the Act is permitted in the event of an emergency. Subsection 31(2)(d) provides that a person shall not be guilty of the offence of causing pollution where the entry of the matter in question is caused or permitted in an emergency in order to avoid danger to the public. In such circumstances this defence is only available if, as soon as reasonably practicable after the entry occurs, particulars of the entry are furnished to the water authority for the area in which it occurs.

(e) *Trade or sewage effluent* Separate provision is made under s.32 of the Control of Pollution Act 1974 for the control of trade and sewage effluent, and for that reason this type of pollution is specifically excluded from the offence under s.31(1) of the Act (see para.11.18 on s.32 of the 1974 Act). This exception does not apply to the discharge of trade or sewage effluent from a vessel since legal provision for such effluent is also provided for elsewhere in the Act (see para.11.20 on s.33 of the 1974 Act).

(f) *Abandoned mines* No offence under s.31(1) of the Control of Pollution Act 1974 is committed by reason of a person permitting water from an abandoned mine to enter any stream or controlled waters (s.31(1)(e) of the 1974 Act). The meaning of 'mine' is given under s.180(1) of the Mines and Quarries Act 1954 as: 'an excavation or system of excavations made for the purpose of, or in connection with, the getting, wholly or substantially by means involving the employment of persons below ground, of minerals (whether in their natural state or in solution or in suspension) or products of minerals'.

(g) *Refuse from mines and quarries* The final exception to the offence under s.31(1) of the Control of Pollution Act 1974 concerns solid refuse of mines or quarries. The offence of causing pollution will not be committed where a person deposits solid refuse of a mine or quarry on any land so that it falls or is carried into a stream or restricted waters if:

(i)   he deposits the refuse on the land with the consent (which shall not be unreasonably withheld) of the water authority in whose area the land is situated; and

(ii)   no other site for the deposit is reasonably practicable; and

(iii)   he takes all reasonably practicable steps to prevent the refuse from entering the stream or restricted waters (s.31(3) of the 1974 Act).

In this context 'mine' is defined as for the previous exception. 'Quarry' is defined under s.180 of the Mines and Quarries Act 1954 as: 'an excavation or system of excavations made for the purpose of, or in connection with, the getting of minerals (whether in their natural state or in solution or in suspension) or products of minerals, being neither a mine nor merely a well or borehole or a well and borehole combined'.

11.15 Penalties under s.31 of the Control of Pollution Act 1974

The maximum penalties for causing or knowingly permitting pollution contrary to s.31(1)(a) and (b) of the Control of Pollution Act 1974 are, on summary conviction, a period of imprisonment for a term not exceeding three months or a fine not exceeding the prescribed sum, presently £2,000, or both. On conviction on indictment, the maximum penalties are a term of imprisonment not exceeding two years or a fine or both. In respect of the offence of causing or knowingly permitting solid waste matter to enter a stream contrary to s.31(1)(c) of the 1974 Act, the maximum penalty on summary conviction is a fine not exceeding level 4 on the standard scale, presently £1,000 (see para.1.12 on the standard scale of fines).

11.16 Regulations and Byelaws under s.31 of the Control of Pollution Act 1974

In addition to the offences created under s.31(1) of the Control of Pollution Act 1974, further offences may be created under the same section in respect of contravention of regulations and byelaws. Subsection 31(4) states that regulations may be made by statutory instrument as to the precautions to be taken, by any person having the custody or control of any poisonous, noxious or polluting matter, for the purpose of preventing the matter from entering any stream or controlled waters. Moreover, these regulations may provide that a contravention shall be an offence. For this offence the maximum penalty may be equivalent to the maximum under s.31(1), that is, on conviction on indictment imprisonment for a term not exceeding two years or a fine or both, and on summary conviction imprisonment for a term not exceeding three months or a fine not exceeding the prescribed sum, presently £2,000, or both. In the case of a summary conviction for an offence which continues after the conviction it is also possible for the court to impose a daily fine of £50 for each day on which the offence continues after conviction of the offence (s.31(8) of the 1974 Act).

Where it appears to the Secretary of State to be appropriate to prohibit or restrict the carrying on of activities which he considers are likely to result in pollution of a stream or controlled waters he may make regulations with a view to preventing poisonous, noxious or polluting matter from entering the waters. In particular these regulations may:

(a)   designate the area; and
(b)   provide that prescribed activities shall not be carried on at any place within the area except with the consent (which shall not be unreasonably withheld) of the water authority in whose area the place is situated and in accordance with any reasonable conditions to which the consent is subject; and
(c)   provide that a contravention of the regulations shall be an offence and prescribe the maximum penalty for the offence (s.31(5) of the 1974 Act).

Where such regulations are made by the Secretary of State the maximum penalties which can be given for contravention are the same as described in the previous paragraph.

A water authority is also permitted to make such byelaws as it considers appropriate to provide for the prohibition or regulation of washing or cleaning of things of a specified kind in a stream or controlled waters in its area. If such prohibition is made a person who contravenes a byelaw will commit an offence (s.31(6) of the 1974 Act). The maximum penalty which may be imposed for a breach of a regulation of this kind is, on summary conviction, a fine not exceeding level 4 on the standard scale, presently £1,000, or any smaller sum specified in the byelaw (see para.1.12 on the standard scale of fines).

11.17 Trade and Sewage Effluent Discharge under s.32 of the Control of Pollution Act 1974

The offence of causing pollution under s.31(1) of the Control of Pollution Act 1974 does not arise where the matter which is discharged is trade or sewage effluent (s.31(2)(e) of the 1974 Act). This is because separate provision is made for this kind of pollution under s.32 of the 1974 Act. There are three situations which are envisaged. These are considered under the following three subheadings.

(a) *Discharge into certain waters* The first situation envisaged under s.32 of the Control of Pollution Act 1974 concerns unlawful discharge into certain waters. This arises under s.32(1)(a) which provides that a person shall be guilty of an offence if he causes or knowingly permits any trade effluent or sewage effluent to be discharged:

(i) into any relevant waters, or

(ii) from land in Great Britain through a pipe into the sea outside controlled waters, or

(iii) from a building or from plant on to or into any land or into any lake, loch or pond which does not discharge into a stream.

The key terms used here are defined in the Act. 'Trade effluent' includes any liquid (either with or without particles of matter in suspension in it) which is discharged from premises used for carrying on any trade or industry, other than surface water and domestic sewage (s.105(1) of the 1974 Act). 'Sewage effluent' includes any effluent from the sewage disposal or sewage works of a local authority (s.56(1) of the 1974 Act). 'Relevant waters' is defined under s.31(1) of the Act to encompass any stream or controlled waters or any specified underground water. 'Controlled waters' are defined as, amongst other things, the sea within three nautical miles from the coast (see para.11.13). The application of the prohibition of discharges into certain waters to any 'lake, loch or pond which does not discharge into a stream' is a point of contrast with s.31 of the Act in that s.31 does not apply to these waters because 'stream' is specifically defined to exclude a lake, loch or pond which does not discharge into a stream (s.56(1) of the 1974 Act).

Specific provision is made under s.32(2) of the Control of Pollution Act 1974 for situations where a water authority is bound to receive sewage or effluent which is discharged into the waters stated under s.32(1)(a) of the Act. Subsection 32(2) provides that if sewage or effluent is of a kind which a water authority was bound to receive, either unconditionally or subject to conditions which were observed, then the authority will be deemed to have caused the discharge for the purposes of s.32(1)(a); that is, the water authority will be taken to have caused or knowingly permitted a discharge if the matter in question was matter which they were bound to treat even if they did not actually cause or permit the discharge. Thus a water authority's default in failing to provide adequate sewage treatment will not amount to a defence to a charge of causing or permitting the discharge of effluent under s.32(1).

(b) *Discharges from sewers and drains*   The second situation, covered by s.32(1)(b) of the Control of Pollution Act 1974, involves discharges from sewers and drains. It is stated that it is an offence to cause or knowingly permit 'any relevant matter other than trade or sewage effluent to be discharged into relevant waters from a sewer . . . or from a drain'. The term 'sewer', under s.343 of the Public Health Act 1936, is stated to include 'all sewers and drains used for drainage of buildings and yards appurtenant to buildings'. 'Drain' in turn is stated to mean 'a drain used for the drainage of one building or of any buildings or yards appurtenant to buildings within the same curtilage'. Garner (1975 p.62) takes these rather uninformative definitions to lead back to the ordinary dictionary definitions of the terms. He suggests that a sewer may be described as: 'a large drain, whether natural or artificial, and whether above or below ground, used for the carrying off from point A to point B of surface water, sewage, faecal or other waste matter'.

The prohibition of discharges from sewers will primarily affect water authorities in whom public sewerage works are vested (s.20, Public Health Act 1936, discussed in para.11.18). It is not confined to public sewers and drains, however, and would apply equally to private sewers and drains.

(c) *Highway drains*   The third situation, provided for under s.32(1)(c) of the Control of Pollution Act 1974 as amended by the Highways Act 1980, Sch.24, para.24(b), concerns highway drains. An offence is committed where a person causes or knowingly permits: 'any matter other than trade or sewage effluent to be discharged into relevant waters from a drain which a highway authority or other person is entitled to keep open by virtue of section 100 of the Highways Act 1980.' This offence is made subject to the proviso that the offence is not committed unless the water authority for the area has given at least three months' notice that this provision is to apply to the drain.

11.18   Defences and Exceptions to the Offence of Discharging Trade or Sewage Effluent Contrary to s.32 of the Control of Pollution Act 1974

The offence of discharging trade or sewage effluent contrary to s.32(1) of the Control of Pollution Act 1974 is made subject to the six defences and exceptions discussed under the following subheadings.

(a) *Consent*   It will not be an offence to discharge effluent if this is permitted by consent given by the water authority in whose area the discharge occurs or the

Secretary of State, under s.34 of the Control of Pollution Act 1974, and any conditions in the consent are observed. The granting of consent to effluent discharges is discussed in para.11.21.

(b) *By order of the Secretary of State* Subsection 32(3) provides that the Secretary of State may make an order to prevent s.32(1) of the Act applying where consent to discharge under earlier statutes would not have been required. The previous statutes, in so far as they apply to England and Wales, are the Rivers (Prevention of Pollution) Acts 1951 and 1961 and s.72 of the Water Resources Act 1963.

(c) *Discharges from vessels* Section 32(1) of the Act does not apply to discharges from vessels (s.32(4)(a) of the 1974 Act). These are dealt with under s.33 of the Act and considered at para.11.20.

(d) *Dumping at sea* No offence under s.32(1) of the Act arises in respect of depositions which are authorised by a licence granted under Part II of The Food and Environmental Protection Act 1985.

(e) *Emergency* A further exception to s.32(1) of the Act is provided for where a discharge is caused or permitted in an emergency in order to avoid danger to the public if, as soon as reasonably practicable after the discharge occurs, particulars of the discharge are furnished to the water authority in whose area it occurs (s.32(4)(c)of the 1974 Act).

(f) *Water authorities* As has been stated, the basic position is that where water authorities are bound to receive effluent which is discharged into their sewers then they are unable to claim not to have caused or permitted the discharge of effluent contrary to s.32(1) of the 1974 Act (s.32(2)). Where, however, a discharge made from a water authority sewer or sewerage works appears to contravene s.31(1), then the water authority will not be guilty of committing the offence of causing or permitting the discharge of effluent if three conditions are satisfied. The conditions are:

(i) the contravention is attributable to a discharge which another person caused or permitted to be made into the sewer or works; and

(ii) the authority either was not bound to receive the discharge into the sewer or works or was bound to receive it there subject to conditions but the conditions were not observed; and

(iii) the authority could not reasonably have been expected to prevent the discharge into the sewer or works (s.32(5)).

In the case of a person making a discharge into a sewer or works vested in the water authority, he will not be guilty of the offence under s.32(1) of the 1974 Act if the authority were bound to receive the discharge either unconditionally or subject to conditions which were observed (s.32(5)).

11.19 Penalties under s.32 of the Control of Pollution Act 1974

Subject to the exceptions discussed in the previous paragraph, the maximum penalty for a person who is found guilty of the offence of discharging trade or sewage effluent contrary to s.32(1) of the Control of Pollution Act 1974, is, on conviction on indictment, imprisonment for a term not exceeding two years, or a fine, or both. On summary conviction the maximum penalty is imprisonment for a term not exceeding three months or a fine not exceeding the prescribed sum, presently £2,000, or both (s.32(7) of the 1974 Act).

11.20 Sanitary Appliances on Vessels under s.33 of the Control of Pollution Act 1974

Although not yet fully in force at the time of writing, s.33 of the Control of Pollution Act 1974 regulates the use of sanitary appliances on vessels. 'Sanitary appliance' is stated to mean 'a water closet or other prescribed appliance (except a sink, a bath and a shower-bath) which is designed to permit polluting matter to pass into the water on which the vessel in question is for the time being situated' (s.33(10)). A water authority is empowered to make byelaws prohibiting or regulating the keeping or use on restricted waters of vessels of specified kinds which are provided with sanitary appliances (s.33(1)). Similarly, the Secretary of State may order that byelaws relating to sanitary appliances made under previous Acts will have effect as if made by the water authority for the area to which they apply (s.33(2) of the 1974 Act). Moreover, any person who keeps or uses any vessel provided with a sanitary appliance on a stream will be guilty of an offence, unless the appliance is sealed in such a manner that while the seal is affixed matter cannot pass from the appliance into the water on which the vessel is for the time being situated (s.33(3) and (8)). Additionally, a water authority may apply to the Minister and the Secretary of State for an order to be made to provide that a person who keeps or uses any vessel provided with a sanitary appliance which is not sealed, on specified restricted waters within the water authority's area, will be guilty of an offence (s.33(4)).

When implemented, the effect of these provisions will be that it is almost certainly an offence to keep or use a sanitary appliance on board a vessel on a stream or restricted waters unless it is sealed in such a way as to prevent material passing from the vessel into the water. The maximum penalty for this offence is, on summary conviction, a fine not exceeding level 3 on the standard scale, presently £400 (s.33(11) of the 1974 Act; and see para.1.12 on the standard scale).

11.21 Discharges Permitted by Consent under s.34 of the Control of Pollution Act 1974

Alongside the offences relating to water pollution created by the Control of Pollution Act 1974, the Act also provides for permitted discharges to be made under a system of consents. In effect the system allows water pollution to take place where it is of a kind which is licensed by a water authority.

In the first place an application for a consent to a discharge of trade or sewage effluent must be made to the water authority for the area in which the discharge is to take place. The application must state:

(a) the place at which it is proposed to make the discharges to which the application relates;

(b)   the nature and composition of the matter proposed to be discharged and the maximum temperature of it at the time when it is proposed to be discharged;

(c)   the maximum quantity of the matter which it is proposed to discharge on any one day and the highest rate at which it is proposed to discharge it (s.34(1) of the 1974 Act).

If an applicant for consent to discharge effluent giving this information makes any statement which he knows to be false in a material particular, or makes any statement recklessly and it is false in a material particular, then he is guilty of an offence (s.34(5)).

When an application has been made to a water authority for consent to discharge effluent the water authority must either give consent unconditionally, or subject to conditions, or refuse to give consent, but consent must not be withheld unreasonably (s.34(2)). The conditions, subject to which consent may be given, must be reasonable and may relate to any of the things noted under s.34(4) of the 1974 Act; that is, the water authority may stipulate:

(a)   as to the places at which the discharges to which the consent relates may be made and as to the design and construction of any outlets for the discharges;

(b)   as to the nature, composition, temperature, volume and rate of discharges and as to the periods during which the discharges may be made;

(c)   as to the provision of facilities for taking samples of the matter discharged and in particular as to the provision, maintenance and use of manholes, inspection chambers, observation wells and boreholes in connection with the discharges;

(d)   as to the provision, maintenance and testing of meters for measuring the volume and rate of the discharges and apparatus for determining the nature, composition and temperature of the discharges;

(e)   as to the keeping of records of the nature, composition, temperature, volume and rate of the discharges and in particular of records of readings of meters and other recording apparatus provided in accordance with any other condition of the consent;

(f)   as to the making of returns and the giving of other information to the water authority about the nature, composition, temperature, volume, and rate of discharges; and

(g)   as to the steps to be taken for preventing the discharges from coming into contact with any specified underground water.

Although applications for consent to discharges are ordinarily made to water authorities, s.35 of the Control of Pollution Act 1974 provides that the Secretary of State may direct the water authority to transmit the matter to him for determination. In such a situation the Secretary of State may in any case hold a public inquiry, or give the water authority and the applicant the opportunity to be heard. The Secretary of State must do this if requested by either the authority or the applicant. If the application is determined by the Secretary of State in this way then the water authority is bound to comply with whatever directions he gives (s.35(4)).

A number of measures are introduced under s.36 of the Control of Pollution Act 1974 regarding the publicity which must be given to an application for consent to a discharge. The water authority concerned are bound to publish particulars of the application on two successive weeks in newspapers circulating in the area in which the discharge is to be made and in areas which are likely to be affected by the discharge, and also publish a similar notice in the *London Gazette*. The water authority must send copies of the application to each local authority in the area in which the discharge is to be made, or to the Secretary of State and the Minister if the application relates to controlled waters or to the sea outside controlled waters. The water authority must also consider any written representations relating to the application made by any person within six weeks after the date on which notice of the application appeared in the *London Gazette* (s.36(1)).

The duty upon the water authority to publicise applications for consent to discharges under the Control of Pollution Act 1974 is made subject to a power given to the Secretary of State to exempt applications from publicity (s.42 of the 1974 Act). An applicant for consent may apply to the Secretary of State for a certificate of exemption from the provisions relating to publicity, described in the previous paragraph, and others relating to disclosure of conditions to be imposed by the consent or publicity of the analysis of samples of effluent. In such a case the Secretary of State may issue a certificate of exemption from publicity if he is satisfied either that disclosure of the information concerned would prejudice a private interest to an unreasonable degree by disclosing information about a trade secret, or that disclosure of the information would be contrary to the public interest.

11.22   *Appeals to the Secretary of State*

In the event of an applicant for consent to a discharge under the Control of Pollution Act 1974 being dissatisfied with the determination of the water authority, he may appeal to the Secretary of State against the determination. Section 39(1) of the 1974 Act provides that an appeal to the Secretary of State may be made where the claimant alleges any of the following:

(a)   that a water authority has unreasonably withheld consent to the deposit of solid waste from a mine or quarry under s.31(3) of the 1974 Act;

(b)   that a water authority has unreasonably withheld consent to a discharge of trade or sewage effluent under s.34 of the 1974 Act;

(c)   that a water authority has unreasonably withheld consent to the applicant carrying out restricted or prohibited activities where these have been prescribed by the Secretary of State under s.31(5) of the 1974 Act;

(d)   that a water authority has given consent to a discharge of trade or sewage effluent under s.34 of the 1974 Act subject to conditions which are unreasonable;

(e)   that a water authority has issued a notice of revocation, or modification of consent under s.37 of the 1974 Act which is unreasonable;

(f)   that a water authority has specified an unreasonable period during which there will be no revocation or variation of a consent under s.38 of the 1974 Act.

There is no right of appeal to the Secretary of State if the initial determination regarding the consent was originally made by the Secretary of State exercising his powers under s.35 of the 1974 Act.

11.23 Deposits and Vegetation in Streams under s.49 of the Control of Pollution Act 1974

A provision of the Control of Pollution Act 1974 which is likely to be of direct relevance to riparian or fishery owners or angling associations conducting riverbed or bankside work is s.49 of the 1974 Act. This provides that if, without the consent of the relevant water authority, which shall not be reasonably withheld:

(a) a person removes from any part of the channel or bed of a stream a deposit accumulated by reason of any dam, weir or sluice holding back the water of the stream and does so by causing the deposit to be carried away in suspension in the water of the stream; or

(b) any substantial amount of vegetation cut or uprooted in a stream, or so near to the stream that it falls into it, is allowed to remain in the stream by the wilful default of any person,

then the person shall be guilty of an offence and liable on summary conviction to a fine not exceeding level 4 on the standard scale, presently equivalent to £1,000 (see para.1.12 on the standard scale of fines). This offence is made subject to the proviso that nothing under (a) is to apply to anything done in the exercise of statutory powers conferred by or under any enactment relating to land drainage, flood prevention or navigation (s.49(2) of the 1974 Act).

11.24 Miscellaneous Statutory Provisions

Alongside the Control of Pollution Act 1974 a number of miscellaneous statutory provisions remain in force governing water pollution brought about by particular kinds of polluting substances, or affecting particular kinds of water. One example of a measure of this kind is s.4 of the Salmon and Freshwater Fisheries Act 1975, which makes it unlawful to cause or permit poisonous or injurious matter to enter waters containing fish (discussed in paras.3.16 and 11.13). A discussion of other measures which regulate water pollution and may be of relevance to fisheries is given in the following paragraphs.

11.25 Diseased Animal Carcases

A specific offence is committed under s.35(4)(a) of the Animal Health Act 1981 if a person dumps a diseased animal carcase into a watercourse. The offence is committed where a person, without lawful authority or excuse, throws, places, causes, or suffers to be thrown or placed, into any river, stream, canal, navigation or other water, or the sea within three miles of the shore, the carcase of any animal which has died of disease or been slaughtered as diseased or suspected to be diseased. In such circumstances proof of lawful authority or excuse lies on the person who is charged with the offence (s.35(4) of the 1981 Act). 'Carcase' includes any part of a carcase (s.89(1) of the 1981 Act). 'Animal' is widely defined to include cows, sheep, goats, poultry and other farm animals (ss.87 and 89 of the 1981 Act). 'Disease' is defined to encompass an extensive collection of diseases (specified under ss.88 and 89 of the 1981 Act). A person convicted of this offence is, on summary conviction, liable to a maximum fine not exceeding level 5 on the standard scale, presently £2,000. In addition a fine not exceeding level 3 on the standard scale, presently £400, may be imposed in respect of every 508 kg in weight of the carcase (s.75(1) of the 1981 Act; and see para.1.12 on the standard scale).

11.26   Pollution by Gas Waste

A specific offence exists under s.68 of the Public Health Act 1875 in relation to the pollution of waters by persons engaged in the manufacture of gas. Section 68 of that Act provides that a person engaged in the manufacture of gas commits an offence if he:

(a)   causes or suffers to be brought or to flow into any stream, reservoir, aqueduct, pond or place for water, or into any drain or pipe communicating with it, any washing or other substance produced in making or supplying gas; or
(b)   wilfully does any act connected with the making or supplying of gas by which the water in any stream, reservoir, aqueduct, pond or place for water is fouled.

Discharges of this kind are now subject to the system of water authority consents provided for under s.34 of the Control of Pollution Act 1974 (discussed in para.11.21). Where the discharge has been authorised by consent, and any conditions subject to which the consent was given have been complied with, then no offence will be committed under s.68 of the Public Health Act 1875 (s.54, Control of Pollution Act 1974).

11.27   Pollution of Water Supplies

An offence of polluting water used for human consumption arises under s.21 of the Water Act 1945. This offence is committed if any person is guilty of any act or neglect by which any spring, well, borehole or adit, the water from which is used or is likely to be used for human consumption or domestic purposes, or for manufacturing food or drink for human consumption, is polluted or is likely to be polluted. The offence is made subject to two exceptions: (a) it does not apply to any method of cultivation of land which is in accordance with the principles of good husbandry; and (b) it does not apply to the reasonable use of oil or tar on any highway maintainable at the public expense, so long as the highway authority takes all reasonable steps for preventing the oil, tar, or any liquid or matter resulting from its use, from polluting any spring, well, borehole or adit. The offence is punishable, on summary conviction, by a fine not exceeding the prescribed sum, presently £2,000, and, in the case of a continuing offence, by a further fine not exceeding £50 for every day during which the offence is continued after conviction. On conviction on indictment the maximum penalty is a period of imprisonment not exceeding two years or a fine or both (s.99 and para.16 of Sch.2, Control of Pollution Act 1974).

11.28   Radioactive Pollution

The control of pollution by radioactive matter is governed by ss.6 and 7 of the Radioactive Substances Act 1960. This statute regulates the keeping and use of radioactive material and the disposal and accumulation of radioactive waste. It provides that no person may accumulate, on any premises used for an undertaking carried on by him, any radioactive waste with a view to its subsequent disposal without authorisation from the Secretary of State. 'Disposal' in this context includes the discharge of radioactive waste into water (s.19(1) of the 1960 Act). The disposal of radioactive waste from premises used by the Atomic Energy Authority or from premises on a site licensed under the Nuclear Installations Acts 1965 and 1969 must be authorised by both the Secretary of State and the Minister (ss.6 and 8 of the 1960 Act). Before authorisation of disposal is given, if disposal of waste requires any special precautions to be taken, the Secretary of State and the Minister are bound to consult local authorities, water authorities and other public authorities which they consider it proper to consult (s.9 of the 1960 Act). If the Secretary of State thinks that adequate facilities for disposal are not available, he may provide them (s.10 of the 1960 Act).

Discharges of radioactive matter are placed outside the scope of statutory provisions which would otherwise make them a legally actionable form of pollution. Section 9(1) of the Radioactive Substances Act 1960 stipulates that no account must be taken of any radioactivity possessed by any substance or article for the purposes of the exercise, performance or enforcement of any of the following provisions:

s.5 of the Sea Fisheries Regulation Act 1966;
s.4 and para.31 of Sch.3 Part II to the Salmon and Freshwater Fisheries Act 1975;
ss.27, 39, 48, 81, 82, 92, 108(2), 141, 259 and 261 of the Public Health Act 1936;
The Public Health (Drainage of Premises) Act 1937;
ss.17, 18 and 21 of the Water Act 1945;
ss.72, 74 and 76 of the Water Resources Act 1963.

The same prohibition applies to local enactments which prohibit or restrict the disposal of accumulation of waste or of any substances which are a nuisance or prejudicial to health or are noxious or polluting. Similarly, the prohibition applies to local enactments which confer or impose a power or duty on any local authority, water authority or other public authority to take any action for preventing, restricting or abating disposals or accumulations of waste or substances which are a nuisance or prejudicial to health or are noxious or polluting (ss.8, 9 and 10 of the 1960 Act). In effect, control over the disposal of radioactive substances is placed outside the general law on pollution and kept exclusively within the cognisance of the relevant Ministers.

11.29 Abandoned Vehicles and Litter

Although outside the ordinary sense of 'water pollution', abandoned vehicles, litter and other refuse are capable of being a considerable source of annoyance and visual disamenity when left on the banks or discarded in the waters of a fishery. A number of legal provisions create criminal offences in respect of discarding refuse which may be of relevance to fishery or riparian owners. Two of the most important of these are the Refuse Disposal (Amenity) Act 1978 and the Litter Act 1983.

Section 2(1) of the Refuse Disposal (Amenity) Act 1978 states that an offence is committed where any person, without lawful authority:

(a)   abandons on any land in the open air, or on any other land forming part of a highway, a motor vehicle or anything which formed part of a motor vehicle and was removed from it in the course of dismantling the vehicle on the land; or

(b)   abandons on any such land any thing other than a motor vehicle, being a thing which he has brought for the purpose of abandoning it there.

The maximum penalty for this offence, on summary conviction, is a fine not exceeding level 4 on the standard scale, presently set at £1,000 (see para.1.12) or imprisonment for a term not exceeding three months, or both. Section 2(2) of the 1978 Act stipulates that for the purposes of the offence a person who leaves any thing on any land in such circumstances, or for such a period, that he may reasonably be assumed to have abandoned it or to have brought it to the land for the purpose of abandoning it there shall be deemed to have abandoned it there or, as the case may be, to have brought it to the land for that purpose unless the contrary is shown. That is to say, the burden of proof is placed upon a person who leaves any thing on land in such circumstances, or for such a period, as to indicate an intention to abandon it there, to show that that was not his intention. Section 1(1) of the Litter Act 1983 states that it is an offence for any person to throw down, drop or otherwise deposit in, into or from any place in the open air to which the public are entitled or permitted to have access without payment, and to leave any thing whatsoever in such circumstances as to cause, or contribute to, or tend to lead to, the defacement by litter of any place in the open air. This offence is primarily concerned with the depositing of litter in public places, but will also cover a situation where litter is dropped, for example, on a public footpath alongside a river or lake and is blown or otherwise transported on to private land or water and left there. The offence is made subject to the proviso that the depositing and leaving is not authorised by law or done with the consent of the owner, occupier or other person or authority having control of the place in or into which the thing was deposited. The maximum fine which may be imposed for this offence is at level 3 on the standard scale, presently £400 (s.1(3) of the 1983 Act).

12

WATER ABSTRACTION

12.01   The Problem of Water Quantity

The counterpart of the need for water of a sufficient quality, considered in the last chapter, is the need for a sufficient quantity of water. In the case of any flowing watercourse a sustained flow is essential to maintain a habitat for fishlife, to carry away pollution which would otherwise accumulate, and, where populated by migratory fish, to permit passage to upstream spawning grounds. Low rates of flow in times of drought are a natural characteristic of almost all rivers, causing the dehydration of feeder streams and consequent fish mortality in extreme cases. Except in rivers where flow is artificially controlled this problem is unavoidable. Other causes of low flow in rivers are, however, a consequence of human interference, and contribute to the problem of low water flow at all times of the year. Large quantities of water are abstracted from many watercourses for industrial, agricultural and water supply purposes. Unless these abstractions are made in a controlled way, they are capable of having a devastating effect upon a fishery, and for this reason the law steps in to exercise control over the use of water resources and to regulate the abstraction of water in many circumstances.

A contributory factor to problems of water quantity is the drainage of land which tends to allow flood water to run off in a shorter period of time than would occur naturally. This, in turn, leads to rivers rising and falling in height more rapidly as a result of drainage, and water levels reaching higher and lower extreme levels than would otherwise be the case. This causes particular problems for migratory fish which have the task of ascending rivers in the shorter period during which spate conditions prevail. The law relating to land drainage is outside the scope of this work (the interested reader is referred to Fort and Brayshaw (1961) Ch.X; Wisdom (1966a); and Wisdom (1979) Ch.12).

12.02   Water Quantity Problems Relating to Fisheries

This chapter is confined to two areas of law that relate directly to water quantity as it concerns fisheries: first, the duties of water authorities with respect to water resources, and, second, the system of licensing control imposed upon the abstraction of water. Primarily these topics are governed by the Water Resources Act 1963 and the Water Act 1973. The former is referred to in this chapter as the 1963 Act, and the latter as the 1973 Act.

12.03   The General Obligations of Water Authorities with Regard to Water Resources

The Water Resources Act 1963 was enacted to promote measures for the conservation, augmentation and proper use of water resources in England and Wales, and to impose controls upon the abstraction of water. Subject to amendments made in subsequent Acts, these objectives are to be met by means of a number of measures administered by water authorities. The basic obligations of a water authority are now expressed in s.10(1) of the Water Act 1973. These are that every water authority is required to take such actions as it may from time to time consider necessary or expedient, or as directed, for the purpose of conserving, redistributing or otherwise augmenting water resources in its area, securing the proper use of water resources in its area, or transferring any such resources to the area of another water authority.

The central duty of water authorities with respect to water conservation, under s.10(1) of the Water Act 1973, involves the proper use of water resources in water authority areas. 'Water resources' are defined in relation to any area to mean the water which is for the time being contained in any source of supply in the area (s.2(1) of the 1963 Act). In turn, 'source of supply' is defined in relation to any area to encompass two kinds of waters: first, so much of any inland water as is situated in the area and discharges into other waters. This is specifically stated to exclude any inland water which is a lake, pond or reservoir which does not discharge into any other inland water, or which is one of a group of two or more lakes, ponds or reservoirs, whether near or distant from each other, and of watercourses or mains connecting them, where none of the inland waters in the group discharges into any inland water outside the group. The second kind of waters included in the definition of source of supply are any underground strata in that area. This includes water for the time being contained in a well, borehole or similar work, or in any excavation into underground strata where the level of water in the excavation depends wholly or mainly on water entering it from those strata (s.2 of the 1963 Act).

A number of other expressions used in the definition of source of supply are defined in s.135(1) of the Water Resources Act 1963. 'Inland water' is stated to mean any of the following:

(a) so much of any river, stream or other watercourse, whether natural or artificial and whether tidal or not, as is within any of the water authority areas;

(b) any lake or pond, whether natural or artificial, and any reservoir or dock, in so far as these do not fall within head (a) and is within any such area;

(c) so much of any channel, creek, bay, estuary or arm of the sea as does not fall within head (a) or head (b) and is within any such area.

'Watercourse' is stated to include all rivers, streams, ditches, drains, cuts, culverts, dykes, sluices, sewers and passages through which water flows, except mains and water fittings, local authority sewers and certain adits and passages. 'Underground strata' means strata subjacent to the surface of any land, and any reference to water contained in any underground strata is a reference to water so contained otherwise than in a sewer, pipe, reservoir, tank or other underground works constructed in any such strata (s.135(1), Water Resources Act 1963).

12.04   *Surveys, Plans and Programmes*

The obligation upon water authorities to make proper use of water resources involves their participation in a range of surveys, plans and programmes. In particular, as soon as practicable after 1 April 1965, each water authority, in consultation with any other authorities likely to be affected, was required to review three matters in connection with water resources in its area. The requirements were:

(a)   to carry out a survey of the water in its area, the existing management of the water, the purpose for which it was being used and its quality in relation to its existing and likely future uses, and to prepare a report on the results of the survey;

(b)   to prepare an estimate of the future demand for the use of the water over the next 20 years or such other period as the appropriate Minister or Ministers might direct;

(c)   to prepare a plan as to action to be taken during that period by the authority to secure more efficient water management, including meeting further demands for water and the use of water and restoring the wholesomeness of rivers and other inland coastal waters in its area (s.24(1) of the 1973 Act).

Each water authority must keep under review the particulars contained in any report, estimate or plan prepared by it and must periodically revise them, either by amendment or by taking fresh steps under heads (a) to (c) above, as it considers appropriate having regard to changes since the previous survey or revision (s.24(3) of the 1973 Act). In carrying out these duties a water authority must consult every local authority whose area is wholly or partly included in the area of the water authority and have regard to any structure plan, local plan and development plan prepared under the town and country planning legislation for any part of that area (s.24(8)(b) of the 1973 Act).

12.05   *Minimum Acceptable Flows*

The general duty placed upon water authorities to have regard to proper use of water resources impinges directly upon the interests of fishery owners in respect of water flow. Every water authority must consider for which inland waters in its area minimum acceptable flows ought to be determined. After appropriate consultation the water authority must then submit for ministerial approval a draft statement or series of draft statements indicating, with respect to each of the waters concerned, the control points at which the flow is to be measured, the method of measurement and the flow which is to be the minimum acceptable flow at each control point (s.19(3)(b) of the 1963 Act). Where the authority considers that it would be appropriate in the case of a particular inland water to measure the level or volume instead of or in addition to the flow, it may determine that the provisions are to apply similarly in respect of the level or volume (s.22(1) of the 1963 Act).

The submission of proposed water flows is made subject to a detailed procedure for publicisation and the registering of objections which allows those with an interest in water flow, such as fishery owners, to make their views known. Before submitting a draft statement relating to minimum acceptable flows the water authority must publish a notice stating its general effect, specifying a place where a copy with a map or plan may be inspected during the following 28 days and stating that within the period any person may object by written notice to the Secretary of State. Copies of the notice must be served on local authorities and others and the notice that the draft has been submitted must be published in the *London Gazette*. Where an objection is duly made and is not withdrawn, the Secretary of State must either hold a public inquiry or afford the objector and the authority an opportunity of being heard by a person appointed by him. Where the Secretary of State approves a statement he must give the authority notice of approval, specifying the date when the statement has effect. The authority must publish the notice and keep a copy of the approved statement available for free public inspection at all reasonable times (para.9, Sch.7 to the 1963 Act).

Unfortunately the requirement, under s.19(1) of the Water Resources Act 1963, that water authorities 'consider' determination of minimum acceptable flows has, as a matter of practice, amounted to no more than that. A recent consultation paper published by the Department of the Environment (1986) made the following comments on the establishment and observation of minimum acceptable flows in practice:

> Although the concept of formal minimum acceptable flows seems useful in principle, it is flawed in practice. Authorities claim that they do not have reliable long-term river flow data to determine flows accurately, and the question of what constitutes a minimum acceptable flow has never been satisfactorily resolved. The fact that resources have been managed satisfactorily for 23 years since the 1963 Act without formal determinations suggests that they are not essential for effective river management.

Nonetheless, water authorities are bound to have regard to the same considerations as would be relevant to the determination of minimum acceptable flows when deciding whether to grant a water abstraction licence (see para.12.09 below).

12.06   Records and Gauges

Another aspect of the duty of water authorities in respect of water resources, which may be of interest to those concerned with fisheries, relates to the records which authorities are bound to keep concerning water resources. Every water authority must provide reasonable facilities for the inspection of records kept by it of the rainfall, evaporation of water and the flow, level and volume of inland water and water in underground strata in its area. These facilities must be made available free of charge to all local authorities and internal drainage boards whose areas or districts are wholly or partly within the area of the water authority, and to all other persons on payment of such reasonable fees as the authority may determine (s.16(3) of the 1963 Act and para.77(2) of Sch.8 to the 1973 Act).

Any person other than a water authority who proposes to install a gauge for measuring and recording the flow, level or volume of certain inland water in a water authority area must notify the authority of his proposal, and having installed the gauge must notify the authority of where the records obtained are to be kept. A water authority is entitled at all reasonable hours to inspect and copy any records kept by any other person of the flow, level or volume of certain inland water in its area. Failure to give such notice or to permit inspection is an offence (s.17(3) of the 1963 Act). The general requirements with respect to gauges are qualified by a proviso in the Act to the effect that they do not apply to a gauge installed merely to indicate water levels for the benefit of fishermen, or a gauge removed within 28 days (s.17(1) of the 1963 Act).

12.07   *The Control of Water Abstraction*

Traditionally, the owner of the banks of a river had the right to make reasonable use of the water flowing past his land for domestic purposes, agricultural purposes such as watering of cattle, and generating water power where it was reasonable to do so. This was permitted even if the effect of abstraction was to reduce the flow of water passing to downstream riparian owners (*Miner* v *Gilmour* (1859)). These common law rights have now been superseded in most situations by a statutory system of licensing of water abstraction under the Water Resources Act 1963.

At the present time, the basic principle with respect to the abstraction of water is that no person is permitted to abstract water from any source of supply in a water authority area, or cause or permit it to be abstracted, except in accordance with a licence to abstract granted by a water authority (s.23(1) of the 1963 Act). Contravention of this, or non-compliance with a condition or requirement imposed by a licence, is an offence (s.49 of the 1963 Act). On summary conviction the maximum penalty for this offence is a fine not exceeding the prescribed sum, presently £2,000.

12.08   *Water Abstraction Exempted from Licensing*

The general requirement that abstraction of water is authorised by a licence from a water authority is made subject to a number of exceptions provided for under ss.24 and 25 of the Water Resources Act 1963. In so far as these apply to abstraction of water from inland waters they are as follows.

(a)   *Small abstractions*   An abstraction of water does not need to be authorised by licence if the quantity of water involved does not exceed 1,000 gallons and it does not form a part of a continuous operation or a series of operations by which an aggregate of more than 1,000 gallons is abstracted (s.24(1) of the 1963 Act).

(b)   *Domestic and agricultural purposes*   The licensing requirement for water abstraction does not apply to abstractions from inland waters by an occupier of land contiguous to the water at the point of abstraction, where the water is to be used on that land or other land held with it for the domestic purposes of the occupier's household or for agricultural purposes other than spray irrigation (s.24(2)(b) of the 1963 Act). 'Agriculture' is defined for this purpose to include horticulture, fruit growing, seed growing, dairy farming, the breeding and keeping of livestock (including any creature kept for the production of food, wool, skins or fur, or for the purpose of its use in the farming of land), the use of land as grazing land, meadow land, osier land, market gardens and nursery grounds, and the use of land for woodlands where such use is ancillary to the farming of land for other agricultural purposes (s.135(1) of the 1963 Act).

A notable consequence of this definition of agriculture is that fish farming, in so far as it involves the keeping of creatures for the production of food, will come within the definition. As a consequence of this fish farmers will be entitled to abstract water without the need for a licence, providing that they are able to satisfy the other requirements relating to water abstraction for agricultural purposes. Curiously, though, a fish farmer who is exempt from the licensing requirement for water abstraction will still require water authority consent to discharge water into the stream from which it has been removed (s.34 of the Control of Pollution Act 1974). As noted in para.11.21, this consent may stipulate a maximum quantity of water which may be discharged and a maximum rate of discharge. Unless a fish farmer has a means of storing a large quantity of water on his premises, as a practical matter, the consent which the water authority gives to a discharge will determine the amount of water which the farmer can abstract. It is doubtful whether the definition of agriculture extends to encompass persons rearing fish for ornamental purposes or even for purely sporting purposes, and therefore it is likely that such activities will be subject to the licensing requirement (see Ch.8 on fish farming).

'Spray irrigation' is defined to mean the irrigation of land or plants, including seeds, by means of water or other liquid emerging, in whatever form, from apparatus designed or adapted to eject liquid into the air in the form of jets or sprays (s.135(1) of the 1963 Act). The general position with respect to spray irrigation is that it remains subject to the licensing requirement. This is, however, subject to a statutory instrument which exempts the spraying of pesticides, nutrients, manure and certain other matters from the requirement (Spray Irrigation (Definition) Order SI 1965 No.1010).

(c) *Land drainage* The restriction on abstraction of water does not apply to the abstraction from a source of supply in the course of, or resulting from, land drainage operations (s.24(4)(a) of the 1963 Act). In this context 'land drainage' is defined to include the protection of land against erosion or encroachment of water, whether from inland waters or from the sea, and also includes warping and irrigation other than spray irrigation (s.40(2) and para.78 of Sch.8 to the 1973 Act).

(d) *Mining and other operations* Abstraction of water does not require to be licensed in so far as it is necessary to prevent interference with any mining, quarrying, engineering, building or other operations, or to prevent damage to works resulting from such operations (s.24(4)(b) of the 1963 Act). 'Engineering or building operations' are defined to include the construction, alteration, improvement or maintenance, closure or removal of any reservoir, watercourse, dam, weir, well, borehole or other works, the construction, alteration, improvement, maintenance or demolition of any building or structure and the installation, modification or removal of any machinery or apparatus (s.135(1) of the 1963 Act).

(e) *Water transfer*   The restriction on abstraction of water does not apply to any transfer of water from one inland water to another in the course of, or resulting from, any operations carried out by a navigation, harbour or conservancy authority in performing its duties as such (s.24(6) of the 1963 Act). Water transfer may be problematic for other reasons, though. Transfer of water of a different quality might amount to pollution in some circumstances (see para.11.03). Care would have to be exercised to ensure that the water did not contain fish or the spawn of fish since, without the permission of the water authority, this would constitute unlawful introduction of fish into an inland water contrary to s.30 of the Salmon and Freshwater Fisheries Act 1975 (see para.8.17).

(f) *Vessels*   The licensing requirement does not apply to abstractions by machinery or apparatus installed on a vessel where the water which is abstracted is for use on that or any other vessel (s.24(7) of the 1963 Act).

(g) *Fire fighting*   The restrictions do not apply to anything done for fire-fighting purposes or to test apparatus used for such purposes or training or practice in its use (s.24(8) of the 1963 Act).

(h) *Order of the Secretary of State*   Finally, it is possible for an order to be made by the Secretary of State under s.25 of the Water Resources Act 1963 excepting sources of supply within a water authority area from the licensing requirement. Such an order will be made where an application is made by the water authority, and the Secretary of State is satisfied that the restriction on abstraction is not necessary in relation to the source, or sources, of supply in question.

12.09   *Application for a Water Abstraction Licence*

Other than where a person is entitled to a licence by virtue of right (considered in para.12.11), a person who seeks to abstract water must apply to a water authority for permission to do so. In the first place the person seeking a licence must be a person who is either the occupier of land contiguous to inland water or he must satisfy the water authority that he has, or will have, a right of access to such land (s.27 of the 1963 Act).

Application for a licence to abstract is subject to a procedure for publication of the application set out in s.28 of the 1963 Act. This involves publication of a notice of the proposal in the *London Gazette* and for each of two successive weeks in one or more of the newspapers circulating in the locality of the proposed abstraction. The notice must give details of the intended abstraction and information as to where a copy of the application, and any map or plan or other document submitted by the applicant, can be inspected free of charge.

In determining whether to grant the licence the water authority must have regard both to any written representations which have been properly made concerning the application and to the reasonable requirements of the applicant (s.29(3) of the 1963 Act). Where the application relates to abstraction from an inland water for which a minimum acceptable flow has been determined, the authority is also bound to have regard to the need to secure that the flow will not be reduced, or further reduced, below the minimum (see para.12.05 on minimum acceptable flows). If no minimum acceptable flow has been determined for the water from which abstraction is proposed the authority must have regard to the matters to which it would be required to have regard in determining one (s.29(5) and (6) of the 1963 Act). Hopefully these matters would include the need to preserve a sufficient flow to permit the migration of migratory fish on those rivers with a stock of migratory fish.

If the water authority decides to grant the licence it must be in writing in a form deemed suitable by the water authority. In particular it must bear the name of the authority, the licence number, the name of the person to whom it is granted, the quantity of water authorised to be abstracted, the method of measuring or assessing it, the means of abstraction, the land on which and the purpose for which the water is to be used, and the duration for which it is to remain in force unless it is to remain in force until revoked (s.30 of the 1963 Act). If an applicant is dissatisfied with the decision of a water authority in determining an application for an abstraction licence he may appeal to the Secretary of State within three months of making the application, or within one month of notification of the water authority's decision, or any longer period allowed by the Secretary of State. A copy of the notice of the appeal must be served on the water authority and the applicant must provide the Secretary of State with all the relevant maps and particulars supplied to the authority. The Secretary of State may, and must if requested by the water authority or the applicant, hold a local inquiry or hearing before determining the appeal. The decision of the Secretary of State is final and where his decision is to grant, vary or revoke a licence, the decision will include a direction to the water authority accordingly (ss.39 to 41 of the 1963 Act).

12.10   *The Consequences of a Licence to Abstract Water*

The effect of a water authority granting a licence to abstract water is that, in any action brought against a person in respect of the abstraction of water from a source of supply, it is a defence to show that the water was abstracted in accordance with the provisions of a licence. This defence is not available in an action for negligence or breach of contract (s.31 of the 1963 Act).

In respect of a licence to abstract water, charges are payable to the water authority in accordance with a fixed scale made by the authority (s.30 of the 1963 Act). A person who is bound to pay such charges is entitled to apply to the water authority for a reduction in the charges or for total exemption from payment of charges for abstraction in lieu of any contribution made by the applicant towards fulfilling the functions of the water authority (see para.7.02 on the functions of water authorities); or financial assistance given by the applicant towards the water authority carrying out its functions; or any other material consideration. If the water authority refuses to make an agreement of this kind, or makes an agreement which the applicant considers to be unsatisfactory, the question may be referred by either party to the Secretary of State. The decision of the Secretary of State is final (s.60 of the 1963 Act). If charges payable under a licence are not paid within 14 days after written demand has been served on the licence-holder, the water authority may, after giving written notice, suspend the operation of the licence until the outstanding charges are paid (s.64 of the 1963 Act).

12.11   Licences of Right to Abstract Water

In addition to the normal procedure by which a person may apply for a licence to abstract water, another option is that the applicant may claim to be entitled to abstract by virtue of a protected right to abstract. Such 'licences of right' to abstract arise in two situations. The first is where by virtue of any statutory provision which was in force on 1 April 1965, other than the Water Act 1958, the applicant was entitled to abstract water from a source of supply in a water authority area (s.33(1)(a) of the 1963 Act). If this is the case, the terms of any licence which is issued to such an applicant must correspond as nearly as possible with the earlier statutory provision. Where the original authorisation does not specify or otherwise limit the quantity of water that may be abstracted the licence has to be limited by reference to the applicant's requirements as indicated by the amount of water abstracted by the applicant or his predecessors from time to time over the five year period up to 1 April 1965, or the period between the coming into operation of the provision and 1 April 1965, whichever is the shorter (s.24 of the 1963 Act).

The second situation in which a person may be granted a licence to abstract by virtue of a protected right is where he had abstracted water from a source of supply in a water authority area, otherwise than by virtue of a statutory provision, at any time within a five-year period ending with 1 April 1965 (s.33(1)(b) of the 1963 Act). If this can be established, the quantity of water which the licence of right will authorise to be abstracted will be determined by the requirements of the applicant. In particular, such requirements must be determined by reference to the quantities of water which are proved: first, to have been abstracted by the applicant or his predecessors from time to time during that five-year period or the period between the date on which he or his predecessors began to abstract and 1 April 1965, whichever is the shorter; and, second, to have been so abstracted for use on the same land, and for the same purposes, for which the licence is claimed (s.35(2) of the 1963 Act).

For an application for a licence of right to be successful, on either of the two grounds described in this paragraph, the application must have been made before 1 July 1965, since no licence of right can be granted unless the application was submitted in the proper form by that date (s.33(1) of the 1963 Act).

12.12   A Leading Case: Cargill v Gotts (1981)

Many of the legal principles relating to the abstraction of water under the Water Resources Act 1963 are illustrated by the decision of the Court of Appeal in the leading case of *Cargill* v *Gotts* (1981). In this case the occupier of a farm since 1928 had been in the practice of drawing water from a pond. The pond was near to, but not contiguous to, the farm. Originally the water was used for watering horses and cattle, but in later years the amount of water abstracted increased greatly when it was used to spray crops as well as watering cattle. In 1977 the ownership of the pond changed hands and the new owner took measures to prevent the farmer using the pond as a source of water. The self-help exercised by the new owner of the pond in preventing the farmer drawing water from the pond led to a civil action being brought between the parties to decide whether the farmer had any legal right to continue to use the pond as a source of water. This dispute, in turn, depended on whether the farmer could establish any right to draw water under the Water Resources Act 1963.

In the first place it was claimed on behalf of the farmer that he could rely on the exception for small abstractions under s.24(1) of the Water Resources Act 1963 permitting abstraction of water where the water abstracted did not exceed 1,000 gallons, and did not form a part of a continuous operation or of a series of operations whereby that amount was exceeded. In declining to accept this argument, the Court held that each abstraction made by the farmer using a 900 gallon water tanker formed a part of a series of operations the object of which was to help to meet the water requirements of the farm for agricultural purposes. The operations resulted in the abstraction of more than 1,000 gallons and so the farmer could not claim the benefit of the exception for small abstractions.

A second argument raised on behalf of the farmer was that his long use of the source of water supply would found a legal claim to continue to abstract the water as a common law prescriptive right (see para.11.09 on prescription). The court accepted that variations in the quantity of water which had been abstracted from time to time, attributable to changes in farming practice, did not detract from the prescriptive right to draw water from the pond, and a prescriptive right to draw the water was established at common law. This right was of no assistance to the farmer though, since the court held that the right could not be exercised without a water abstraction licence from the water authority and he did not hold any such licence. In effect, s.23(1) of the Water Resources Act 1963 makes all water abstraction unlawful unless it can be brought within one of the exceptions discussed in paragraph 12.08. Establishing a common law right to abstract water is no justification for failing to acquire a licence to authorise the abstraction under the 1963 Act.

A third point raised on behalf of the farmer was that under s.33 of the Water Resources Act 1963 he would have been entitled to a licence to abstract water because he had abstracted from the source of supply for a five-year period ending on 1 April 1965. This, it was claimed, entitled him to a licence of right under the Act (see para.12.11 on protected rights). Although the court accepted that he would have been entitled to a licence of right by virtue of exercising the right for five years before the Act came into effect, a licence of right could only be granted where an application for the licence had been made before 1 July 1965 (s.33(1) of the Water Resources Act 1963). The farmer had not applied for a licence of right within the period during which he was permitted to do so and had therefore forfeited his option to acquire a licence of right under the Act.

As a result of these findings the court determined that the farmer had acted illegally on every occasion when he abstracted water from the pond under s.23(1) of the Water Resources Act 1963. Nevertheless, the court noted that it was the duty of the water authority to enforce the provisions of the Act (s.118 of the 1963

Act) and the fact that the farmer had acted unlawfully did not entitle the owner of the pond to exercise self-help by forcibly preventing him from taking water (see para.11.10 on self-help, or 'abatement'). The proper course of action would have been for the owner of the pond to report the matter to the water authority rather than to take the matter into his own hands. Surprisingly, the court held that the owner of the pool had infringed the farmer's common law right to abstract water, even though it was illegal for the farmer to exercise the right without a licence. An award of damages was made against the owner for obstructing the farmer in drawing water. This reiterates the hazards of self-help remedies, but does not detract from the interpretation of the Water Resources Act 1963 provided by the court in deciding the case.

13
THE SALMON ACT 1986

13.01   Introduction: the Salmon Bill

When the detailed provisions of the Salmon Bill first appeared early in 1986 it was evident that the new legislation was concerned almost entirely with the Scottish law relating to salmon. With the exception of clauses concerning handling salmon in suspicious circumstances (see para.13.03) and removing differential penalties under the Salmon and Freshwater Fisheries Act 1975 (see para.13.06), the Bill made no changes to the law of England and Wales. In progressing through Parliament, however, important additions were made to the Anglo-Welsh part of the Bill. The House of Lords added further clauses extending dealer licensing in salmon to England and Wales (see para.13.02), modifying the requirement of water authority consent for fish to be introduced into fish farms (para.13.05), amending the rules regarding endorsement of commercial fishing licences (para.13.07), and requiring the Minister to conduct a review of salmon net fisheries (para.13.10). The House of Commons introduced clauses amending the law relating to the placing and use of fixed engines (para.13.04), giving powers to make byelaws under the Sea Fisheries Regulation Act 1966 to protect salmon (para.13.08) and making a minor amendment of the Diseases of Fish Act 1983 (see para.13.09). As a consequence of these additions, a Bill which had started life as a modest measure in relation to England and Wales has emerged from Parliament as a major collection of reforms of the Salmon and Freshwater Fisheries Act 1975.

The Salmon Act 1986 gained royal assent on 7 November 1986. In accordance with s.43(1) of the Act it will come into force on the expiry of a period of two months beginning with the date on which it was passed. Hence, although at the time of writing it is not yet in operation, the following paragraphs of this chapter describe the changes to the law of England and Wales to be brought about under the Act as if they are now in effect.

An initial point to note about the Salmon Act 1986 is that the title of the Act is something of a misnomer in suggesting that the Act is concerned only with salmon. Section 40(1), the interpretation section of the Act, makes it clear that 'salmon' means all migratory fish of the species *Salmo salar* and *S. trutta* and commonly known as salmon and sea trout respectively or any part of such fish. Consequently in the discussion of the Act which follows, 'salmon' must be understood to encompass sea trout unless the context requires otherwise.

Apart from miscellaneous provisions, the sections of the Salmon Act 1986 which deal with the law of England and Wales are contained in Part III of the Act, ss.31 to 38. These are:

s.31, dealer licensing in England and Wales;
s.32, handling salmon in suspicious circumstances;

s.33, placing and use of fixed engines;
s.34, introduction of fish into fish farms without consent;
s.35, removal of differential penalties under the Salmon and Freshwater Fisheries Act 1975;
s.36, servants and agents authorised by fishing licences;
s.37, byelaws under the Sea Fisheries Regulation Act 1966;
s.38, disclosure of information furnished under the Diseases of Fish Act 1983.

The following eight paragraphs are devoted to discussion of these sections, whilst the two final paragraphs of this chapter consider the review of certain salmon net fishing provided for under s.39 of the 1986 Act and certain miscellaneous reforms of the Salmon and Freshwater Fisheries Act 1975.

13.02   Section 31–Dealer Licensing in England and Wales

Throughout the parliamentary progress of the Salmon Bill minority support was given to a proposal put forward in a National Water Council Report of 1983 that a salmon tagging scheme should be introduced. The scheme envisaged was of the kind operated in Canada whereby all fish which are legitimately caught have an identificatory tag attached to them by the captor. Despite a number of advantages of tagging it was felt that, on balance, a scheme of this kind involved a number of major difficulties. The great majority of salmon which are sold in this country are either imported or farmed fish, and a tagging scheme would only be effective if coverage extended to these fish. When it is taken into account that the amount of fish produced from fish farms is approaching 10 times the amount produced by commercial fishing methods the scale of the problem is evident (see Ch.8 on fish farming). Ensuring that fish are appropriately tagged would place major administrative difficulties and burdens upon importers and salmon farmers. Moreover, further difficulties would be likely to arise because of the large number of fish tags involved and very strict controls would be required to prevent abuses. A black market in tags would allow them to fall into the hands of poachers, or dealers in illicit salmon, who would be able to use them to give apparent legitimacy to their activities. Because of these problems the proposal to introduce a salmon tagging scheme enjoyed only minority support in Parliament and, despite sustained lobbying, failed to pass into law.

The solution of the parliamentary majority to the problem of trade in unlawfully caught salmon was to introduce a system of dealer licensing whereby those trading in salmon would be required to possess a licence to do so. The idea of a system of dealer licensing for salmon had been proposed on several previous occasions. The Bledisloe Report (1961 para.306) recommended that salmon and trout should be dealt in only by those who hold a licence to deal in game as provided in the Game Act 1831. Licensed persons should keep a detailed record of their purchases and sales and these records should be open to inspection by persons authorised by river boards (now water authorities), the Fishmongers' Company, local authorities and local market authorities, and any police officer. Following similar lines, the Hunter Report on Scottish Salmon and Trout Fisheries (1965 paras 241 and 242) recommended that in Scotland any person who purchased salmon or trout other than from a licensed dealer would be required to hold a licence, and any person selling fish would have to be either a licensed dealer or the holder of an angling or commercial fishing licence. The cost of the licence would be no greater than necessary to cover the administrative expenses of the licensing authority, but if a dealer was found to have in his possession unrecorded fish, or to have purchased fish from a person who had no licence, or to have made a false record he would commit an offence and would be liable to a penalty and to the withdrawal of his licence. Although the Hunter Report had proposed that this scheme should operate in Scotland, it was suggested that it would be more effective if it extended to England as well.

Under the original Salmon Bill it was proposed to introduce dealer licensing for salmon only in Scotland, because of supposed administrative difficulties in giving effect to such a system in England and Wales. It was pointed out in the House of Lords debates on the Bill, though, that if such a limitation were to be imposed it would be a relatively simple matter to evade the system by taking salmon which had been illegally taken in Scotland, to be sold in England where licensing constraints did not apply. As a rhetorical threat Viscount Ridley asserted that if the original provision, applying licensing only to Scotland, passed into law he would set up in business as an unlicensed dealer in Berwick-upon-Tweed confident that by doing so he would be able to make a fortune purchasing salmon that had been caught illegally in Scottish waters! (House of Lords Debates Vol.469, col.1030.) In response to this kind of criticism the Bill was extended to allow dealer licensing to be introduced in England and Wales under subordinate legislation subject to the affirmative resolution of both Houses of Parliament. The problem of exporting salmon to evade dealer licensing does not arise in relation to Northern Ireland which already has a licensing scheme operated by the Northern Ireland Fisheries Conservancy Board.

The need for a comprehensive approach underlying the salmon dealer licensing scheme was a recurring theme in the parliamentary debates. As Lord Belstead announced in the third reading of the Salmon Bill in the House of Lords: 'The Government are on record as wishing to introduce a licensing scheme that will provide as strong a chain as possible, from the time when the salmon starts to change hands until it reaches the consumer [but] it has to be a matter now of consultation . . . with the interests concerned, as to where precisely the dealer licensing system ought to begin and end' (House of Lords Debates Vol.471, col.1011). In a similar vein, in the House of Commons, Mr Gummer (the Minister of State in the Ministry of Agriculture, Fisheries and Food) commented: 'We would envisage the licensing scheme in England and Wales as being extensive and it would deal with the vast majority of transactions. This would mean that many people who are now used to buying their salmon perfectly legally—perhaps at the back door of a hotel—will in future have to buy from a licensed dealer. This is necessary if we are to deal with poaching. We cannot have a half-baked scheme . . .' (House of Commons Debates Vol.93, col.283).

The machinery by which the dealer licensing system is to be operated has not yet been finalised, but the general assumption is that it will be placed in the hands of the water authorities. This may be unfortunate in that it places a new burden on the already stretched resources of water authorities especially in those areas where game fish are of minor importance. It is hoped that the authorities will be allocated additional resources to administer their new duties.

The dealer licensing scheme in England and Wales is provided for under s.31 of the Salmon Act 1986. The wording of s.31(1) authorises the Minister to make, by statutory instrument, an order prohibiting persons from:

(a)   dealing in salmon otherwise than under and in accordance with a licence issued in pursuance of the order by such person as may be so specified; or
(b)   buying salmon from a person who is not licensed to deal in salmon.

Two possible difficulties which may be anticipated under these provisions concern innocent purchasers and sales by fishermen. In the case of the innocent purchaser a difficulty which may arise is, for example, the situation of a housewife who buys a salmon from a person who appears to be a licensed dealer but later turns out to have no licence to deal in salmon or perhaps to have forgotten to renew his licence. Should the housewife be found guilty of buying a salmon from a person who is not licensed to deal in salmon? The probable answer to this is that the offence of buying salmon from an unlicensed dealer will require an intention to do so before the offence is committed. In the situation posed, the housewife has no intention to buy from an unlicensed dealer and consequently no offence will be committed. The position would be quite different where a person buys salmon at the back door of a hotel from a person known not to have a dealer's licence (see para.13.03).

A second possible difficulty concerns the sale of fish by a person having a fishing licence but no licence to deal in salmon. Since the licence to deal in salmon is quite separate from the system of licensing *fish* for salmon (see Ch.6), it follows from the wording of s.31(1)(a) of the 1986 Act that a licence to fish for salmon may not automatically authorise a fishing-licence-holder to sell his catch. 'Deal' in this context is defined to include the selling of salmon, whether by way of business or otherwise, and acting on behalf of a buyer or seller of salmon (s.31(6) of the 1986 Act). Unless the final ministerial order makes an exception to cover this situation, the effect of the new provisions is that commercial fishermen and anglers who wish to sell their catch will have to apply for a dealer's licence in order to do so. Another possibility is that special provision will be made for fishing-licence-holders to sell their catch. This could be brought about under s.31(3) of the Act which states that:

An order under this section may—
(a)   make different provision for different cases; and
(b)   contain such incidental, supplemental and transitional provision as appears to the Minister of Agriculture, Fisheries and Food and the Secretary of State to be necessary or expedient.

It remains to be seen what provisions will be made under this power and whether any exceptions will be made for fishing-licence-holders to sell salmon which they have caught.

Further indications as to the form which the eventual order under s.31(1) will take are given by a series of permissive provisions set out in s.31(2), which state that an order may:

(a)   prescribe the manner and form of an application for a licence to deal in salmon and the sum, or maximum sum, to be paid on the making of such an application;

(b)   specify the circumstances in which such an application is to be granted or refused and the conditions that may be incorporated in such a licence;

(c)   authorise the amendment, revocation or suspension of such a licence;

(d)   create criminal offences consisting in the contravention of, or failure to comply with, provisions made under this section;

(e)   .provide for matters to be determined for the purposes of any such provision by a person authorised by any such provision to issue a licence; and

(f)   make provision, whether by applying provisions of the Salmon and Freshwater Fisheries Act 1975 or otherwise, for the purpose of facilitating the enforcement of any provision made under this section.

The manner in which these powers are to be used is uncertain, but the Act incorporates two safeguards against their misuse. These are, first, that a statutory instrument relating exclusively to the sum, or the maximum sum, to be paid on the making of an application for a licence to deal in salmon shall be subject to annulment in pursuance of a resolution of either House of Parliament. Hence Parliament has the power to veto the amount to be charged for a salmon dealer's licence if it is thought to be excessive (s.31(5) of the 1986 Act). Second, in the case of other orders under s.31, no order is to be made unless a draft of the order has been laid before, and approved by a resolution of, each House of Parliament (s.31(4) of the 1986 Act).

Taken as a whole, the dealer licensing scheme looks to be a development which will prevent a substantial amount of trade in illicit salmon and in turn remove the commercial motive for taking salmon unlawfully. It would be premature to judge the effectiveness of the scheme in advance of the regulations which will determine its final shape, but it has been suggested by critics that despite the benefits of the scheme it will not prove fully adequate to counter the problems involved. In particular, it was suggested to the Standing Committee of the House of Commons considering the Bill that three major difficulties are retained by the dealer licensing scheme as it is likely to be finally formulated:

There is nothing in the enabling provisions in the Bill to require the licensed dealer to enquire as to the bona fide of the 'first seller' of salmon and therefore illegally caught fish could be lawfully disposed of via licensed dealers.

The dealer licensing scheme is clearly based on the sale of fish and therefore cannot cater for 'gifts' of fish—this being known to be a common practice and therefore likely to be a frequently encountered defence which evidently would be difficult to rebut.

The dealer licensing scheme will not enable the identification of individual fish. (Comments submitted by the Welsh Water Authority to House of Commons Standing Committee D (1986), col.571.)

Although the first of these criticisms may be met by the provision discussed in the next paragraph, the other two appear to be inherent faults in the dealer licensing scheme. It is to be hoped that even with these unavoidable imperfections the scheme brings about substantial improvements over the present situation.

13.03   Section 32–Handling Salmon in Suspicious Circumstances

Section 32 of the Salmon Act 1986 creates a new offence of handling salmon in suspicious circumstances. The offence is committed where a person believes, or it would be reasonable for him to suspect, that a 'relevant offence' has at any time been committed in relation to a salmon, and he receives that salmon, or undertakes or assists in its retention, removal or disposal by or for the benefit of another person, or if he arranges to do so (s.32(1) of the 1986 Act). A 'relevant offence' for these purposes is an offence which is committed either by taking, killing or landing a salmon, in England, Wales or Scotland, or where the salmon is taken, killed or landed, in England, Wales or Scotland, in the course of commission of the offence (s.32(2) of the 1986 Act). The underlying idea is that the 'offence' involved is an offence under the law applicable to the place where the salmon is taken, killed or landed, that is, an offence under English law if the fish is taken in England or Wales, or an offence under Scottish law if the fish is taken in Scotland (s.32(7) of the 1986 Act).

The requirement that the accused person must be shown to have a belief or reasonable suspicion that a relevant offence has taken place in relation to a salmon does not involve showing the accused person to have a belief or suspicion of a *particular* relevant offence to fall within the provision, since s.32(3) provides that: 'It shall be immaterial for the purposes [of the offence] that a person's belief or the grounds for suspicion relate neither specifically to a particular offence that has been committed nor exclusively to a relevant offence or to relevant offences.' That is to say, it will not be a defence for an accused person to maintain that his belief or suspicion did not relate to any particular relevant offence, nor that the belief or suspicion that he had was of a different relevant offence to that which had actually taken place. In effect, the belief or suspicion which must be shown by the prosecution is that of *any* relevant offence having taken place in relation to the salmon.

The new offence of handling salmon in suspicious circumstances is modelled on the offence of handling stolen goods under s.22(1) of the Theft Act 1968. The offence of handling stolen goods is committed where a person knowing or believing goods to be stolen, dishonestly undertakes or assists in their retention, removal, disposal or realisation by or for the benefit of another person, or arranges to do so. Although the two offences are closely related, the analogy between handling stolen goods and handling salmon in suspicious circumstances is an imperfect one for two main reasons: the first concerns the nature of the thing which is handled, and the second concerns the burden of proof involved.

The first difference between handling stolen goods and handling salmon in suspicious circumstances is that where a person is prosecuted under s.22(1) of the Theft Act 1968 for handling stolen goods the prosecution must show that the goods in question are in fact stolen. In *Anderton* v *Ryan* (1985) the accused was charged with handling a stolen video recorder and was found not guilty because the prosecution was unable to establish that the recorder in question had actually been stolen. Thus, unless the prosecution is able to show that the goods at issue have been stolen, an accused person cannot be convicted of handling stolen goods. On the other side of the analogy, if a conviction for handling salmon were to depend on the prosecution showing that the salmon had been unlawfully taken, then convictions would be very difficult to secure since it is almost impossible to distinguish a salmon which has been illegally taken from one which has been lawfully taken. For example, salmon which have been taken by means of a net are likely to bear the same marks whether the net used was lawful or unlawful. If the prosecution were given the task of showing that a particular salmon had been the subject of a relevant offence few prosecutions would succeed. Because of this difficulty, the formulation of the new offence of handling salmon in suspicious circumstances does not require it to be proved by the prosecution that the salmon in question has actually been the subject of a relevant offence. The offence is based on showing *belief or suspicion* that a salmon has been the subject of a relevant offence rather than proof that it has in fact been the subject of a relevant offence.

On the other hand, it would clearly be unjust if a person were to be convicted of handling salmon in suspicious circumstances if he could show that the fish in question had not actually been the subject of any relevant offence. To allow for this possibility, s.32(3) of the 1986 Act states that it shall be a defence in proceedings for an offence under the section to show that no relevant offence had in fact been committed in relation to the salmon in question. Hence an accused person could not be convicted of the offence of handling salmon in suspicious circumstances if he was able to establish, on the balance of probabilities, that the salmon at issue had never been the subject of a relevant offence, though for the reason stated above this defence may sometimes be difficult to establish.

The second major respect in which the offence of handling salmon in suspicious circumstances differs from handling stolen goods concerns the contrasting burdens of proof that are involved. If a person is to be convicted of handling stolen goods under s.22(1) of the Theft Act 1968 then it must be shown that he knew or believed the goods to be stolen. By contrast, where the offence is that of handling salmon in suspicious circumstances, it must be shown that the accused 'believes or it would be reasonable for him to suspect that a relevant offence has at any time been committed' in relation to the salmon. It is likely that in many cases this will be less difficult for the prosecution to establish than the corresponding requirements for the offence of handling stolen goods, and this has led to talk of 'a reversal of the normal burden of proof'. It is not clear, though, in what sense the new provision does in fact bring about a reversal of the burden of proof. Its effect was clearly expressed by Lord Belstead in the Report Stage of the Bill in the House of Lords:

> In proceedings under this clause and subsection the prosecution will have to prove certain basic facts; that the accused was in possession or was in some way handling the salmon in question; and that achieved, the prosecution must address the question of the defendant's attitude—what is called the mental

element—and must show that the defendant believed the salmon to be taken illegally, which would normally require an admission, or, more probably, that the circumstances were such that a reasonable man would have had reason to suspect that the fish were illegally taken. If the prosecution succeed in proving this to be the case the defendant would then be able to acquit himself only by proving that the salmon were not in fact illegally taken'. (House of Lords Debates Vol.471, col.372.)

On this account of the new offence, it is for the prosecution to show either that the accused believed the salmon in question to be unlawfully taken or that a reasonable person in the position of the accused would have suspected that the fish had been the subject of a relevant offence. That is to say, the circumstances must be viewed objectively in order to ascertain whether they were such as to make a reasonable person suspicious. Hence, other than where the accused admits his belief that the salmon at issue was unlawfully taken, the test is: would a reasonable person looking at the circumstances from the perspective of the accused have suspected that a relevant offence had been committed. The new offence falls well short of making the simple possession of salmon an offence or reversing the burden of proving lawful possession of salmon, but nonetheless it is likely to make proof of the offence easier to establish than is the case with the analogous offence of handling stolen goods.

Although the new offence is termed 'handling salmon in suspicious circumstances' in the marginal note to s.32 of the 1986 Act, the word 'handling' is not used in the wording of the section. The offence is said to be committed by a person who 'receives the salmon, or undertakes or assists in its retention, removal or disposal by or for the benefit of another person, or if he arranges to do so'. This wording makes it appear that many offences involving taking salmon which already exist under the Salmon and Freshwater Fisheries Act 1975 may now come within the terms of the new handling offence. This impression is countermanded, however, by an exception provided for under s.32(4) of the 1986 Act which states that no offence of handling salmon in suspicious circumstances is committed in respect of conduct which constitutes a relevant offence in relation to any salmon. This means that no offence of handling salmon in suspicious circumstances will be committed where the conduct in question already amounts to an offence involving the taking, killing or landing of a salmon. Consequently there is no overlap between the handling offence and those offences under the Salmon and Freshwater Fisheries Act 1975 which are concerned with taking, killing or landing fish. Nonetheless, there may be an overlap between the new handling offence and offences under the 1975 Act concerned with the sale and export of fish (see Ch.5).

Another exception to the offence of handling salmon in suspicious circumstances provided for in s.32(4) of the 1986 Act is in respect of anything done in good faith for purposes connected with the prevention or detection of crime or the investigation of disease. Remarkably, this exception makes no reference to purposes connected with artificial propagation of fish or scientific purposes.

The maximum punishment for a person found guilty of the offence of handling salmon in suspicious circumstances is, on summary conviction, imprisonment for a term not exceeding three months or a fine not exceeding the statutory maximum, or both, and on indictment, imprisonment for a term not exceeding two years or a fine or both (under s.32(5) of the 1986 Act). It is notable that, in so far as these punishments permit magistrates to give custodial sentences, they are more severe than those for offences under the Salmon and Freshwater Fisheries Act 1975 (contrast Sch.4 to the 1975 Act).

In order to harmonise the new offence with existing provisions under the Salmon and Freshwater Fisheries Act 1975, s.32(6) of the 1986 Act makes a number of changes to the 1975 Act. In s.31(1)(b) and (c) of the 1975 Act, relating to powers of search of water bailiffs, the references to fish taken in contravention of the 1975 Act includes a reference to a salmon in relation to which a relevant offence has been committed. In a number of places in the 1975 Act reference is to be made to s.32 of the 1986 Act. These are: in s.33(2), concerning warrants to enter suspected premises; in s.36(1), deeming water bailiffs to be constables for the purpose of enforcing the 1975 Act; in s.39(1), concerning border rivers; in para.39(1)(a) of Sch.3, regarding prosecution by water authorities; and Part II of Sch.4, dealing with procedure on prosecutions. The effect of these amendments is to extend the powers given to water bailiffs and others to enable them to enforce the 1986 Act on the same basis as the 1975 Act, without diminishing their powers under the 1975 Act.

13.04   Section 33–The Placing and Use of Fixed Engines

The difficulties underlying s.6(1) of the Salmon and Freshwater Fisheries Act 1975, concerning the placing and use of fixed engines, were discussed in para.4.09. Broadly stated, the re-enactment of the section in 1975 brought about a change in the law which had not been anticipated in that it made the placing of a fixed engine in inland or tidal waters an absolute offence, for which no intention to catch or obstruct salmon or migratory trout needed to be shown, as was held in *Champion* v *Maughan* (1984). This ruling caused considerable difficulties in that it had the effect of rendering unlawful a range of instruments, many of which were neither intended to catch or obstruct salmon or sea trout nor capable of doing so. As the Welsh Water Authority's *Report on Welsh Salmon and Sea Trout Fisheries* (1985 p.37) observed:

> The ruling has done much to facilitate enforcement in estuaries and along the coast: but it has also caused problems for the Authority in its relationships with sea fishing interests. While the Authority could, if it so wished, remove each and every fixed net along the entire Welsh coastline it recognises that some of these nets are worked by legitimate sea fishermen and that not all present problems in intercepting migratory fish. The Authority's approach has been that its powers to remove and destroy such nets should be exercised only where it is reasonable to believe that they are being fished deliberately to take migratory fish or where migratory fish are intercepted accidentally in significant numbers. The Authority has agreed to help legitimate sea fishermen by providing advice on where, when and how fixed nets can be

operated without damage to the resource and without fear of prosecution.

In a similar vein Mr MacKay, the Parliamentary Under-Secretary of State for Scotland, noted in the Standing Committee discussion on the Salmon Bill in the House of Commons:

> Since the ruling, the law has been enforced somewhat selectively to allow normal sea fishing practices to continue in circumstances where it is clear that salmon and sea trout are not at risk. While such local arrangements were necessary in the short term, it was obvious that section 6 [of the 1975 Act] must be set right substantively as soon as an opportunity arose.
>
> The answer . . . is to clarify the meaning of section 6(1) of the 1975 Act in the sense that the placing or use of unauthorised fixed engines is made illegal, but fixed engines may be authorised by byelaws made by either a sea fisheries committee or in areas where such committees do not operate, by a water authority. (House of Commons Standing Committee D (1986) Col.685.)

The legislative form taken by this answer to the problem is set out in ss.33 and 37 of the Salmon Act 1986. Section 33 amends s.6 of the 1975 Act with regard to the powers of water authorities, whilst s.37 extends the powers of local sea fisheries committees, formed under the Sea Fisheries Regulation Act 1966, to authorise the placing and use of fixed engines (s.37 is discussed in para.13.08).

Section 33 of the 1986 Act replaces s.6(1) of the 1975 Act by a new subsection which states that: 'Any person who places or uses an unauthorised fixed engine in any inland or tidal waters shall be guilty of an offence.' Technically this amounts to an extension of the law in that the *use* of an unauthorised fixed engine is at present only unlawful where it is for taking or facilitating the taking of salmon or migratory trout or for detaining or obstructing the free passage of salmon or migratory trout (s.6(1)(b) of the 1975 Act, see para.4.09). Since there are few types of unauthorised fixed engine which can be *used* without being *placed* unlawfully, the change is likely to make little difference in practice (see Ch.4 on the types of fixed engine).

Of greater significance is the extension of the meaning of 'authorised fixed engine' brought about by s.33(2) of the 1986 Act. This states that along with those instruments which are classified as authorised fixed engines by virtue of s.6(3) of the 1975 Act is to be included: 'a fixed engine the placing and use of which is authorised by byelaws made by a water authority under this Act [that is, the 1975 Act] or by byelaws made by a local fisheries committee by virtue of section 37(2) of the Salmon Act 1986'. The power of water authorities to make byelaws to authorise fixed engines is made explicit by a new paragraph to be interpolated amongst those which state the purposes for which water authorities may make byelaws (in Sch.3 to the 1975 Act). The new paragraph, para.21A, permits water authorities to make byelaws:

> 'authorising the placing and use of fixed engines at such places in the water authority area (not being places within the sea fisheries district of a local fisheries committee), at such times and in such manner as may be prescribed by

the byelaws and imposing requirements as to the construction, design, material and dimensions of such engines, including in the case of nets the size of mesh (s.33(3) of the 1986 Act).

As a matter of theory water authority fishery areas extend to a distance of six nautical miles from the baselines of the territorial sea, as was seen in para.1.04. As a matter of future practice, however, the power of water authorities to make byelaws authorising the placing and use of fixed engines will be greatly reduced by the exclusion of areas within the districts of local sea fisheries committees. Around many parts of the coast the excluded areas constitute the first three nautical miles from the coastline. Nonetheless, this limitation on the byelaw-making power of water authorities will be met by a corresponding increase in the powers given to sea fisheries committees to make byelaws authorising the placing and use of fixed engines within their areas (discussed in para.13.08).

13.05 Section 34–Introduction of Fish into Fish Farms without Consent

The 1981 Ministry of Agriculture, Fisheries and Food's *Review of Inland and Coastal Fisheries* proposed a number of new objectives in fish farming policies. Amongst these was the removal of unnecessary statutory or administrative restrictions which might impede the development of as economically viable a fish farming sector as possible (para.29). Pursuant to the implementation of this policy, s.34 of the 1986 Act brings about the relaxation of controls upon the introduction of fish into fish farms in inland waters in England and Wales. The new provision amends s.30 of the 1975 Act which prohibits the introduction of fish or the spawn of fish into an inland water without the written consent of the water authority for the area into which they are to be introduced. This is done by creating an exemption from the consent requirement in respect of certain fish farms. The exception is to the effect that the requirement of water authority consent will not apply where the introduction, or attempted introduction, of fish, or the spawn of fish, arises in relation to an inland water which consists exclusively of, or of part of, a fish farm which, if it discharges into another inland water, does so only through a conduit constructed or adapted for the purposes. The meaning of 'fish farm' in this context is the same as under the Diseases of Fish Act 1937 (see para.8.08).

Initially the proposal to relax the law governing the introduction of fish into fish farms by dispensing with the requirement of water authority consent gave rise to the concern that this might result in the spread of fish disease and consequent damage to existing fish populations and the general aquatic environment. In the early stages of the Salmon Bill the clause relating to introduction of fish into fish farms without water authority consent had allowed for a waiver of the requirement of consent for *any* fish farm in an inland water. In the later stages of the parliamentary proceedings, however, it became evident that the general government policy of deregulating fish farming might leave water authorities with insufficient powers to control the spread of disease. For this reason the original provision was modified to restrict the effects of the new clause to those fish farms which either do not discharge into another inland water, or do so by means of a specially constructed or adapted conduit. The purpose of these stipulations is to retain water authority control upon introduction of fish into fish farms in inland waters which are not insulated in some way from other inland waters. In practice this will mean that a minority of fish farmers will continue to require permission to introduce fish into fish farms consisting of cages or netted enclosures in inland waters. Nonetheless, the great majority of fish farmers will gain exemption from the requirement of water authority consent to introduce fish providing they are able to meet the requirements governing discharge conduits.

The new exemption under s.34 of the 1986 Act does not involve any slackening of the general regulations governing fish disease, and where notifiable fish disease is suspected or confirmed, controls upon movement of fish may be imposed under s.2 of the Diseases of Fish Acts (see para.8.08). Where such controls are imposed it will cease to be lawful to introduce fish into a fish farm, or to move fish eggs or foodstuff of fish into or out of the infected site, thereby limiting the spread of disease. In addition to this means of control, the requirements that all inland fish farms in Great Britain must be registered, must keep records of all movements of fish or eggs between sites, and must make annual returns of these movements, will enhance the ability of the Ministry of Agriculture, Fisheries and Food to monitor and apply fish disease control (see para.8.15).

13.06 Section 35–Removal of Differential Penalties under the Salmon and Freshwater Fisheries Act 1975

The table of penalties in Sch.4 to the Salmon and Freshwater Fisheries Act 1975 provides for different levels of punishments for certain offences according to whether persons act together or an individual acts alone. In particular, in the case of offences under s.1 of the Salmon and Freshwater Fisheries Act 1975 (using prohibited instruments) and offences under s.27 (unlicensed fishing), the table in Sch.4 to the 1975 Act provides that an offence is triable only summarily where committed by a person acting alone, but is triable either summarily or on indictment where the offence is committed by two or more persons acting together (see para.10.01). The maximum penalties which may be imposed on conviction of these offences where persons act together are correspondingly greater (see paras 3.18 and 6.10).

Under s.35 of the Salmon Act 1986 the distinction between offenders who act alone and those who act together is removed. This is for the reason that the distinction is no longer considered to be relevant to the seriousness of the offence which has been committed. Consequently, for offences under s.1 of the 1975 Act the seriousness of the offence, rather than the fact of collaboration, will in future determine the mode of prosecution. In respect of offences under s.27 of the 1975 Act, however, removal of the different provisions for offences committed alone and those committed by persons acting together would have the undesirable effect that minor but common offences such as fishing with a rod and line without a licence would become triable either summarily or on indictment. This would mean that it would not be possible for guilty pleas to be submitted by post, as is permitted for summary offences, where the accused is not liable to be sentenced to a term of imprisonment exceeding three months (s.12, Magistrates' Courts Act 1980). In the past the postal procedure has obviated the need for the accused person to appear in court and speeded up the work of the court considerably. For this reason it was considered that the postal procedure should be retained in respect of minor offences involving unlicensed fishing with rod and line. Thus where an offence of unlicensed fishing is committed by a person using a rod and line then the offence is only triable summarily and the postal procedure is retained. Other offences of unlicensed fishing become triable either way regardless of whether they are committed by a single person or by two or more persons acting together. Hence the provisions governing offences where persons act together are removed from the Salmon and Freshwater Fisheries Act 1975 and replaced by procedures and punishments which are intended to relate to the gravity of the offences committed rather than the fact of complicity.

Section 35 of the Salmon Act 1986 states that in the table in Part I of Sch.4 to the 1975 Act for the entries relating to sections 1 and 27 (being entries which make different provision according to whether the offender acted with another and do not provide for imprisonment on summary conviction) there are to be substituted the following entries:

Provision of Act creating the offence (1)	Description of offence (2)	Mode of prosecution (3)	Punishment (4)
'Section 1	Fishing with certain instruments for salmon, trout or freshwater fish and possessing certain instruments for fishing for such fish.	(a) Summarily	Three months or the statutory maximum or both.
		(b) On indictment	Two years or a fine or both.
Section 27	Fishing for fish otherwise than under the authority of a licence and possessing an unlicensed instrument with intent to use if for fishing.	(a) If the instrument in question, or each of the instruments in question, is a rod and line, summarily.	Level 4 on the standard scale.
		(b) In any other case—	
		(i) summarily	Three months or the statutory maximum or both;
		(ii) on indictment	two years or a fine or both.'.

Two points of note in respect of this amendment are, first, that in the case of both the offence under s.1 and the offence under s.27 (other than where the instrument used is a rod and line) the amendment brings about a substantial increase in the penalties which may be imposed on summary conviction since previously it had not been possible for magistrates to impose custodial sentences for these offences. A second point is that the new penalties are not to have retrospective effect, since s.35(2) of the 1986 Act stipulates that they are not to affect any proceedings in respect of, or the punishments for, an offence committed before the new penalties come into force.

13.07   *Section 36–Servants and Agents Authorised by Fishing Licences*

The detailed legal requirements concerning fishing licences for commercial fishing are set out in paras 9 to 14 of Sch.2 to the Salmon and Freshwater Fisheries Act 1975 and were discussed in para.6.06. Two features of contrast between rod and line fishing licences and commercial fishing licences which have been noted are that, first, in the case of a commercial fishing licence an amount of transferability of the licence is permitted in that persons other than the licence-holder, known as 'endorsees', are permitted to operate the licensed instrument as well as the licensed holder. A second point of contrast is that in the case of commercial fishing licences it is possible for a water authority to impose a limitation upon the number of licences that are issued for a particular type of instrument under s.26 of the 1975 Act (see para.6.07). Evidence presented in the parliamentary debates on the Salmon Bill suggested that where commercial fishing licence limitation orders were in effect the practice of endorsement had been subject to abuse. As Lord Belstead commented:

> Where licences are a scarce commodity, because on conservation grounds the number which may be issued is strictly limited by an order under section 26 of the 1975 Act, there have been reports of fishermen paying sizeable sums to be 'endorsed' on a licence and so have the right to use it in a manner which is, in effect, independent of the licence.
> In the case of the North-East drift net fishery, in particular, it was felt that this practice—which was clearly not envisaged when the provisions of the [1975] Act were originally drafted—was leading to excessive use of the licensed nets in a way which was contrary to the conservation considerations which caused nets to be limited. My honourable friend the Minister of Agriculture therefore announced last November that among the new measures to be introduced in the North-East fishery would be orders requiring the licensee to be present when the servants or agents—the 'endorsees'—were working the net, unless the licensee was sick or injured. (House of Lords Debates Vol.471, col.1014.)

The form which the new measures are to take is set out in s.36 of the 1986 Act. This section repeals the main provision relating to endorsement of commercial fishing licences, para.9 of Sch.2 to the 1975 Act, and replaces it with a new paragraph designed to prevent abuse of the endorsement procedure. The new paragraph provides that where an order under s.26 of the 1975 Act limiting the number of commercial fishing licences is in force, a person shall not be treated as a servant or agent (that is, an 'endorsee') of a licence-holder unless three conditions are satisfied:

(a)   his name and address are entered on the licence in accordance with the following provisions of Sch.2 to the 1975 Act; and
(b)   he is not himself the holder of a licence to use an instrument of that description in that area; and
(c)   he is accompanied by the licensee or has the consent of the water authority to his use of the instrument in the absence of the licensee.

The last of these conditions is the most significant change since its practical effect is that endorsees will no longer be able to make independent use of a licensed instrument. That is to say, an endorsee will only be able to operate the licensed instrument when the licence-holder is present. The exception to this is that a water authority is empowered to give consent to the independent use of the instrument under certain circumstances. These circumstances are limited by s.36(3) of the 1986 Act, so that water authority consent is not to be given except where the licensee is unable to accompany his endorsee through illness or injury. This amounts to a considerable curtailment of previous liberties afforded to endorsees and should result in the elimination of past malpractices in areas where net limitation orders are in effect.

In areas where a limitation order under s.26 of the 1975 Act is not in effect s.36(2) of the 1986 Act reimposes substantially the same conditions for endorsement as applied under para.9 of Sch.2 to the 1975 Act. These impose on the servant or agent three requirements:

(a)   his name and address are entered on the licence in accordance with the following provisions of Sch.2; or
(b)   he is accompanied by the licensee; or
(c)   he has the consent of the water authority to his use of the instrument otherwise than where there is compliance with paragraph (a) or (b) above.

These requirements are potentially less strict than those which apply where a limitation order is in effect, since s.36(3) of the 1986 Act provides that water authority consent may be given where it appears to the authority 'to be required by the special circumstances of the case'. It remains to be seen whether this phrase will be interpreted broadly or narrowly by the water authorities, but it appears to be capable of wider interpretation than the grounds for consent to an endorsement where a limitation order is in effect.

Finally, to ensure consistency between the reforms under s.36 of the 1986 Act and the 1975 Act, s.33(2)) of the 1986 Act provides that s.25(3) of the 1975 Act is to be amended. The part of s.25(3) of the 1975 Act which limited the number of licensees so as not to exceed the number permitted by para.13 of Sch.2 to the 1975 Act, is to be replaced by 'subject to the provisions of paragraphs 9 to 13 of Schedule 2 to this Act'. This takes account of the effects of the amendments brought about by s.36 of the 1986 Act and consequent tightening up of the endorsement procedure.

13.08   Section 37–Byelaws under the Sea Fisheries Regulation Act 1966

Although the fishery areas of water authorities extend to a distance of six nautical miles from the baselines from which the territorial sea is measured (see para.1.04), in many districts there is an overlap between the tidal and sea areas of water authorities and those areas managed by local sea fisheries committees (see Wisdom (1979) p.304). Local sea fisheries committees are established under the Sea Fisheries Regulation Act 1966 and provided with local regulatory responsibilities in respect of fishing around the coast for sea fish and shellfish to a distance of three miles from the baselines. The principal function of local fisheries committees is to enforce legislation relating to sea fisheries in their area, and in order to do this they are empowered to make byelaws restricting or prohibiting methods and instruments for fishing for sea fish (s.5, Sea Fisheries Regulation Act 1966). 'Sea fish' in this context is specifically defined to include fish of any description found in the sea, but to exclude salmon and trout which migrate to and from the sea (s.20(1), Sea Fisheries Regulation Act 1966). As a consequence of this', the sea fisheries committees are powerless to create byelaws within their area regulating improper fishing for salmon and sea trout.

On the other side of the division of responsibility for regulation of fishing in coastal waters, water authorities have experienced substantial difficulties in enforcing the Salmon and Freshwater Fisheries Act 1975 in many coastal waters because of the dichotomy of regulation. Methods which are in ostensible use for the purpose of catching sea fish in actual fact catch large numbers of salmon and sea trout, and yet the 1975 Act provides the water authorities with few powers to use the Act to prevent sea fishing methods being used to take migratory fish. The loophole in the law which has become apparent is that neither the water authorities nor the local sea fisheries committees possess adequate powers to regulate methods of fishing for sea fish which are actually used to take large numbers of salmon and sea trout.

The extent of exploitation of this loophole in the law was apparent in evidence heard by the House of Commons Standing Committee on the Salmon Bill, where one informant reported that: 'The most serious illegal fishing occurs in the Usk and Severn estuaries and the law is inadequate to control it. The degree of this poaching is apparent when I say that regularly on any day there are at least 25 boats at it and on occasions this number has risen to over 50. There are only eight boats licensed to fish legally for salmon.' (Letter from Sir Iwan Raikes, House of Commons Standing Committee D (1986) Col.689.) The unlicensed boats in this case were operating under the pretext of fishing for sea fish despite the small numbers of such fish in these waters (Welsh Water Authority (1985) p.39).

The legislative response to this state of affairs is s.37 of the Salmon Act 1986. This section gives effect to a proposal made in the Ministry of Agriculture, Fisheries and Food's *Review of Inland and Coastal Fisheries* (1981 para.11) that in those areas where salmon are to be found in coastal waters the responsibility for fisheries should be held jointly by local sea fisheries committees and adjacent water authorities. The sharing of regulatory responsibility for inshore fisheries is achieved by providing local fisheries committees with two new powers. The first of these powers, given by s.37(1) of the 1986 Act, permits local fisheries committees to make byelaws, under s.5 of the Sea Fisheries Regulation Act 1966, for the purpose of protecting salmon and preventing interference with their migration, so that references to 'sea fish' in s.5 of the 1966 Act shall be construed to include references to salmon. 'Salmon' are defined to mean fish of the salmon species and trout which migrate to and from the sea (s.37(4) of the 1986 Act). The second new power given to local fisheries committees permits them to make byelaws authorising the placing and use of fixed engines at such places in their sea fisheries district, at such times and in such a manner as may be prescribed by the byelaws, and impose requirements as to the construction, design, material and dimensions of such engines, including in the case of nets the size of mesh (s.37(2) of the 1986 Act). For these purposes 'fixed engine' is to have the same meaning as in s.41(1) of the Salmon and Freshwater Fisheries Act 1975 (see Ch.4).

On the other side of the new policy of collaboration between local sea fisheries committees and water authorities, s.37(3) of the Salmon Act 1986 prescribes that local fisheries committees shall not make byelaws for the two purposes authorised by s.37(1) and (2) of the Act without the consent of the appropriate water authorities. That is to say, if a sea fisheries committee wishes to enact a byelaw relating to salmon or the authorisation of fixed engines it must first obtain the permission of water authorities with fishery areas within the sea fisheries committee's district. Taken alongside the new power of water authorities to authorise the placing and use of fixed engines, discussed in para.13.04, the new collaborative policy should close the present loophole in the law with respect to 'sea fishing' for salmon and sea trout.

13.09   Section 38–Disclosure of Information under the Diseases of Fish Act 1983

In para.8.15, dealing with the scheme for registration of fish farms under the Diseases of Fish Act 1983, it was noted that information about fish farms communicated to the Minister in accordance with the registration scheme was of a confidential nature. In order to preserve this confidentiality, s.9 of the 1983 Act stipulates that such information is not to be disclosed except in specified exceptional situations. Along with the original situations where information may be disclosed, s.38 of the 1986 Act creates an additional exception permitting disclosure of information to enable a water authority to carry out any of their functions under the Diseases of Fish Act 1937. The new exception removes the incongruity by which water authorities were given duties under the Diseases of Fish Acts (see para.8.10) whilst being denied access to the information necessary to carry out those functions effectively. This is accomplished by the insertion of a new subsection, 9(1)(d), in the Diseases of Fish Act 1983 allowing information to be disclosed, 'for the purpose of enabling a water authority to carry out any of their functions under the 1937 Act'.

13.10   Section 39–Review of Certain Salmon Net Fishing and the Salmon Advisory Committee

The general background to the Salmon Act 1986 is that of increasing concern about the dramatic decline in stocks of the Atlantic salmon. In 1967 the world catch was about 10,400 metric tonnes but by 1984 this had diminished to 5,600 metric tonnes. This decline was due to a number of causes but not least significant amongst these was the increased effort and more efficient methods employed by netsmen, including those in the North-East of England drift-net fisheries. The methods used in these fisheries allow the interception of large numbers of fish migrating along the coastline to their spawning rivers resulting in a correspondingly lower number of fish returning to the rivers to breed (House of Lords Debates Vol.469, col.1004). It is incongruous that alongside a general trend of declining world catches of salmon the local catches of the North-East drift-net fisheries should be showing a substantial increase from just over 2,000 fish in the 1950s to 77,000 in 1984, and it was accepted that there was a need for review of these methods (House of Commons Standing Committee Col.644).

The general problems of conservation of the Atlantic salmon are not an easy topic on which to legislate given the range of factors involved and the poor state of knowledge on the optimum conservational policies to be pursued. For that reason the legislature declined the opportunity of the 1986 Act to translate into law a general policy for the conservation of salmon. Nonetheless, the need for better utilisation of the salmon as a resource was recognised by Parliament, and the indications are that at some time in the not-too-distant future a comprehensive approach to conservation and utilisation of the salmon resource must be adopted. With this in mind s.39 of the 1986 Act instructs the Minister of Agriculture, Fisheries and Food and the Secretary of State to prepare a report, as soon as practicable after the end of three years after the passing of the 1986 Act. The report is to be prepared in the context of the need to ensure:

(a)   that sufficient salmon return to spawn in the rivers wholly or partly situated in certain areas and districts; and

(b)   that fishing for salmon by means of nets is properly managed in those areas and districts,

and to review the nature and extent of all such fishing in those areas and districts. The areas and districts concerned are the areas of the Yorkshire and Northumbrian Water Authorities and the Scottish salmon fishery districts from the River Forth to the River Ugie, the River Tweed being deemed for the purposes of the section to be included in those areas and districts (s.39(3) of the 1986 Act). A copy of the report is to be laid before each House of Parliament (s.39(2) of the 1986 Act). The intention behind the order for this report is that the information which it provides will form the basis for a planned and coordinated approach to the problems of salmon conservation and the better future use of the resource.

Alongside the explicit provision for a review of salmon net fishing in s.39 of the 1986 Act, a further development intended to achieve a broader perspective upon salmon conservation was the announcement by the Minister of State in the Ministry of Agriculture, Fisheries and Food (Mr Gummer) that an advisory committee is to be established to examine and report on the conservation of salmon fisheries in Great Britain. The Salmon Advisory Committee, which is to be chaired by Professor George Dunnet, is to 'examine and report on those matters relating to salmon fisheries in Great Britain which are referred to it by fisheries Ministers'. In particular, at an early stage, the committee will be asked to examine:

(a) particular aspects of the availability of information on the status of salmon stocks; and
(b) the influences on the level of those stocks, including the effects of predators and of fishing at low water levels.

Subsequently, the committee will be asked to look at the effects of the measures contained in the Salmon Act 1986 to combat poaching in the light of experience of their operation. The precise membership of the committee has not yet been determined but it is proposed that it will be a representative body with membership including those who have knowledge of, and experience in, all the major aspects of salmon fisheries and conservation in Great Britain (House of Commons Debates, vol.161, col.1380, and Ministry of Agriculture, Fisheries and Food press release, 24 October 1986). Clearly it would be premature to judge the likely effectiveness of the committee at this stage, but it appears to provide a constructive step towards formulation of a national policy for salmon conservation. In the parliamentary debates it was generally assumed that the existence of such a policy is a prerequisite to a comprehensive approach to salmon conservation.

13.11   Miscellaneous Amendments

Section 41(1) of the Salmon Act 1986 states that the enactments mentioned in Sch.4 to the Act shall have effect subject to the amendments there specified. In respect of the Salmon and Freshwater Fisheries Act 1975, Sch.4 to the 1986 Act makes a minor amendment. This is that in s.39 of the 1975 Act, relating to the borders and the Solway Firth, there is to be added an additional subsection:

(5) Nothing in this section shall authorise a water authority to take legal proceedings in Scotland in respect of an offence against this Act.

To secure consistency between this amendment and s.43(3) of the 1975 Act, concerning its Scottish extent, s.43(3) is amended so that the new s.39(5) is recognised as a part of the Scottish extent of the Act. In respect of these changes Mr MacKay, the Parliamentary Under-Secretary of State for Scotland commented:

This is a technical amendment to make it clear and beyond any doubt that an English water authority cannot prosecute for 1975 Act offences in Scotland. In practice, it means that the North-West Water Authority should not be able to prosecute for offences on Scottish waters of the border Esk for which it is statutorily responsible. In fact, the North-West Water Authority does not prosecute in Scotland but does pass papers on to the procurator fiscal. (House of Commons Standing Committee D (1986) Col.678.)

APPENDIX 1   TEXT OF THE SALMON AND FRESHWATER FISHERIES ACT 1975

[To be read subject to the Salmon Act 1986]

Arrangement of Sections

Part I   Prohibition of Certain Modes of Taking or Destroying Fish, etc.

Section

Part IV Fishing Licences

Part V Administration and Enforcement

Regulation of fisheries etc.

Powers of water bailiffs etc.

Offences

Part VI Miscellaneous and Supplementary

1975, c. 51. An Act to consolidate the Salmon and Freshwater Fisheries Act 1923 and certain other enactments relating to salmon and freshwater fisheries, and to repeal certain obsolete enactments relating to such fisheries.

[Royal assent 1 August 1975]

Part I   Prohibition of Certain Modes of Taking or Destroying Fish, etc.

Prohibited implements

1.—(1)   Subject to subsection (4) below, no person shall—

(a)   use any of the following instruments, that is to say—

(i)   a firearm within the meaning of the Firearms Act 1968;
(ii)   an otter lath or jack, wire or snare;
(iii)   a crossline or setline;
(iv)   a spear, gaff, stroke-haul, snatch or other like instrument;
(v)   a light;

for the purpose of taking or killing salmon, trout or freshwater fish;
(b)   have in his possession any instrument mentioned in paragraph (a) above intending to use it to take or kill salmon, trout or freshwater fish; or
(c)   throw or discharge any stone or other missile for the purpose of taking or killing, or facilitating the taking or killing of any salmon, trout or freshwater fish.

(2)   If any person contravenes this section, he shall be guilty of an offence unless he proves to the satisfaction of the court that the act was done for the purpose of the preservation or development of a private fishery and with the previous permission in writing of the water authority for the area in which the act was done.
(3)   In this section—
   'crossline' means a fishing line reaching from bank to bank across water and having attached to it one or more lures or baited hooks;
   'otter lath or jack' includes any small boat or vessel, board, stick or other instrument, whether used with a hand line, or as auxiliary to a rod and line, or otherwise for the purpose of running out lures, artificial or otherwise;
   'setline' means a fishing line left unattended in water and having attached to it one or more lures or baited hooks;
   'stroke-haul or snatch' includes any instrument or device, whether used with a rod and line or otherwise, for the purpose of foul hooking any fish.
(4)   This section shall not apply to any person using a gaff (consisting of a plain metal hook without a barb) or tailer as auxiliary to angling with a rod and line or having such a gaff or a tailer in his possession intending to use it as aforesaid.

Roe, spawning and unclean fish, etc.
2.—(1)   Subject to subsection (5) below, any person who, for the purpose of fishing for salmon, trout or freshwater fish—

(a)   uses any fish roe; or
(b)   buys, sells, or exposes for sale, or has in his possession any roe of salmon or trout,

shall be guilty of an offence.

(2)   Subject to subsections (3) and (5) below, any person who—

(a)   knowingly takes, kills or injures, or attempts to take, kill or injure, any salmon, trout or freshwater fish which is unclean or immature; or

(b)   buys, sells, or exposes for sale, or has in his possession any salmon, trout or freshwater fish which is unclean or immature, or any part of any such fish,

shall be guilty of an offence.

(3)   Subsection (2) above does not apply to any person who takes a fish accidentally and returns it to the water with the least possible injury.

(4)   Subject to subsection (5) below, any person who, except in the exercise of a legal right to take materials from any waters, wilfully disturbs any spawn or spawning fish, or any bed, bank or shallow on which any spawn or spawning fish may be, shall be guilty of an offence.

(5)   A person shall not be guilty of an offence under this section in respect of any act, if he does the act for the purpose of the artificial propagation of salmon, trout or freshwater fish or for some scientific purpose or for the purpose of the preservation or development of a private fishery and has obtained the previous permission in writing of the water authority for the area.

Nets

3.—(1)   Any person who shoots or works any seine or draft net for salmon or migratory trout in any waters across more than three-fourths of the width of those waters shall be guilty of an offence.

(2)   Subject to subsection (3) below, any person who, except in a place where smaller dimensions are authorised by byelaw, takes or attempts to take salmon or migratory trout with any net that has a mesh of less dimensions than 2 inches in extension from knot to knot (the measurement to be made on each side of the square), or 8 inches measured round each mesh when wet, shall be guilty of an offence.

(3)   In subsection (2) above 'net' does not include a landing net in use as auxiliary to angling with rod and line.

(4)   The placing of two or more nets the one behind the other or near to each other in such manner as practically to diminish the mesh of the nets used, or the covering of the nets used with canvas, or the using of any other device so as to evade subsection (2) above, shall be deemed to be a contravention of that subsection.

Poisonous matter and polluting effluent

4.—(1)   Subject to subsection (2) below, any person who causes or knowingly permits to flow, or puts or knowingly permits to be put, into any waters containing fish or into any tributaries of waters containing fish, any liquid or solid matter to such an extent as to cause the waters to be poisonous or injurious to fish or the spawning grounds, spawn or food of fish, shall be guilty of an offence.

(2)   A person shall not be guilty of an offence under subsection (1) above for any act done in the exercise of any right to which he is by law entitled or in continuance of a method in use in connection with the same premises before 18th July 1923, if he proves to the satisfaction of the court that he has used the best practicable means, within a reasonable cost, to prevent such matter from doing injury to fish or to the spawning grounds, spawn or food of fish.

(3)   Proceedings under this section shall not be instituted except by the water authority for the area or by a person who has first obtained a certificate from the Minister that he has a material interest in the waters alleged to be affected.

Prohibition of use of explosives, poisons or electrical devices and of destruction of dams etc.
5.—(1)   Subject to subsection (2) below, no person shall use in or near any waters (including waters adjoining the coast of England and Wales to a distance of six nautical miles measured from the baselines from which the breadth of the territorial sea is measured) any explosive substance, any poison or other noxious substance, or any electrical device, with intent thereby to take or destroy fish.

[As amended by the Fishery Limits Act 1976, Sch.2, para.20.]

(2)   Subsection (1) above shall not apply to the use by a person of any substance or device—

(a)   for a scientific purpose, or for the purpose of protecting, improving or replacing stocks of fish; and
(b)   with the permission in writing of the water authority for the area;

but as respects the use of any noxious substance such permission shall not be given by a water authority otherwise than with the approval of the Minister.

(3)   No person shall, without lawful excuse, destroy or damage any dam, flood-gate or sluice with intent thereby to take or destroy fish.

(4)   A person who contravenes subsection (1) or (3) above or who, for the purpose of contravening subsection (1) above, has in his possession any explosive or noxious substance or any electrical device, shall be guilty of an offence.

(5)   The use of any substance in any waters for a purpose falling within paragraph (a) of subsection (2) above, and with the permission mentioned in paragraph (b) of that subsection, shall not constitute an offence under—

(a)   section 4 above;
(b)   any byelaws made under paragraph 31 of Schedule 3 below;
(c)   section 31(1)(a) of the Control of Pollution Act 1974; or
(d)   section 22(1)(a) of the Rivers (Prevention of Pollution) (Scotland) Act 1951.

[As amended by subsection (6) of this section. The Control of Pollution Act 1974, s.31, came into force on 31 January 1985; see SI 1985 No.70.]

(6)   On the coming into force of section 31 of the Control of Pollution Act 1974, subsection (5) above shall have effect as if the following paragraph were substituted for paragraph (c):—

'(c) section 31(1)(a) of the Control of Pollution Act 1974'.

Part II   Obstructions to Passage of Fish

Fixed engines

6.—(1)   Any person who—

(a)   places a fixed engine in any inland or tidal waters; or

(b)   uses an unauthorised fixed engine for taking or facilitating the taking of salmon or migratory trout or for detaining or obstructing the free passage of salmon or migratory trout in any such waters,

shall be guilty of an offence.

[See s.33(1) of the Salmon Act 1986.]

(2)   A person acting under directions to that effect given by the water authority for the area may take possession of or destroy an engine placed or used in contravention of this section.

(3)   In subsection (1) above 'unauthorised fixed engine' means any fixed engine other than—

(a)   a fixed engine certified in pursuance of the Salmon Fishery Act 1865 to be a privileged fixed engine; or

(b)   a fixed engine which was in use for taking salmon or migratory trout during the open season of 1861, in pursuance of an ancient right or mode of fishing as lawfully exercised during that open season, by virtue of any grant or charter or immemorial usage.

[See s.33(2) of the Salmon Act 1986.]

Fishing weirs

7.—(1)   No unauthorised fishing weir shall be used for taking or facilitating the taking of salmon or migratory trout.

(2)   Where a fishing weir extends more than halfway across any river at its lowest state of water, it shall not be used for the purpose of taking salmon or migratory trout unless it has in it a free gap or opening situated in the deepest part of the river between the points where it is intercepted by the weir, and—

(a)   the sides of the gap are in a line with and parallel to the direction of the stream at the weir; and

(b)   the bottom of the gap is level with the natural bed of the river above and below the gap; and

(c)   the width of the gap in its narrowest part is not less than one-tenth part of the width of the river.

(3)   A free gap need not be more than 40 feet wide and must not be less than 3 feet wide.

(4)   If any person uses a weir in contravention of this section or makes any alteration in the bed of a river in such manner as to reduce the flow of water through a free gap, he shall be guilty of an offence.

(5)   In subsection (1) above 'unauthorised fishing weir' means any fishing weir which was not lawfully in use on 6th August 1861, by virtue of a grant or charter or immemorial usage.

Fishing mill dams

8.—(1)   No unauthorised fishing mill dam shall be used for taking or facilitating the taking of salmon or migratory trout.

(2)   A fishing mill dam shall not be used for the purpose of taking salmon or migratory trout unless it has attached to it a fish pass of such form and dimensions as may be approved by the Minister, and unless the fish pass is maintained in such a condition and has constantly running through it such a flow of water as will enable salmon and migratory trout to pass up and down the pass.

(3)   If any person—

(a)   uses an unauthorised fishing mill dam as mentioned in subsection (1) above; or

(b)   uses or attempts to use a dam in contravention of subsection (2) above,

he shall be guilty of an offence.

(4)   If a fishing mill dam has not a fish pass attached to it as required by law, the right of using the fishing mill dam for the purpose of taking fish shall be deemed to have ceased and be for ever forfeited, and the water authority for the area may remove from it any cage, crib, trap, box, cruive or other obstruction to the free passage of the fish.

(5)   In subsection (1) above 'unauthorised fishing mill dam' means any fishing mill dam which was not lawfully in use on 6th August 1861, by virtue of a grant or charter or immemorial usage.

Duty to make and maintain fish passes

9.—(1)   Where in any waters frequented by salmon or migratory trout—

(a)   a new dam is constructed or an existing dam is raised or otherwise altered so as to create increased obstruction to the passage of salmon or migratory trout, or any other obstruction to the passage of salmon or migratory trout is created, increased or caused; or

(b)   a dam which from any cause has been destroyed or taken down to the extent of one-half of its length is rebuilt or reinstated,

the owner or occupier for the time being of the dam or obstruction shall, if so required by notice given by the water authority for the area and within such reasonable time as may be specified in the notice, make a fish pass for salmon or migratory trout of such form and dimensions as the Minister may approve as part of the structure of, or in connection with, the dam or obstruction, and shall thereafter maintain it in an efficient state.

(2)   If any such owner or occupier fails to make such a fish pass, or to maintain such a fish pass in an efficient state, he shall be guilty of an offence.

(3)   The water authority may cause to be done any work required by this section to be done, and for that purpose may enter on the dam or obstruction or any land adjoining it, and may recover the expenses of doing the work in a summary manner from any person in default.

(4)   Nothing in this section—

(a)   shall authorise the doing of anything that may injuriously affect any public waterworks or navigable river, canal, or inland navigation, or any dock, the supply of water to which is obtained from any navigable river, canal, or inland navigation, or any dock, the supply of water to which is obtained from any navigable river, canal or inland navigation, under any Act of Parliament; or

(b)   shall prevent any person from removing a fish pass for the purpose of repairing or altering a dam or other obstruction, provided that the fish pass is restored to its former state of efficiency within a reasonable time; or

(c)   shall apply to any alteration of a dam or other obstruction, unless—

(i)   the alteration consists of a rebuilding or reinstatement of a dam or other obstruction destroyed or taken down to the extent of one-half of its length, or

(ii)   the dam or obstruction as altered causes more obstruction to the passage of salmon or migratory trout than was caused by it as lawfully constructed or maintained at any previous date.

Power of water authority to construct and alter fish passes
10.—(1)   Any water authority may, with the written consent of the Minister, construct and maintain in any dam or in connection with any dam a fish pass of such form and dimensions as the Minister may approve, so long as no injury is done by such a fish pass to the milling power, or to the supply of water of or to any navigable river, canal or other inland navigation.

(2)   Any water authority may, with the written consent of the Minister, abolish or alter, or restore to its former state of efficiency, any existing fish pass or free gap, or substitute another fish pass or free gap, provided that no injury is done to the milling power, or to the supply of water of or to any navigable river, canal or other inland navigation.

(3)   If any person injures any such new or existing fish pass, he shall pay the expenses incurred by the water authority in repairing the injury, and any such expenses may be recovered by the water authority in a summary manner.

Minister's consents and approvals for fish passes
11.—(1)   Any approval or consent given by the Minister to or in relation to a fish pass may, if in giving it he indicates that fact, be provisional until he notifies the applicant for approval or consent that the pass is functioning to his satisfaction.

(2)   While any such approval or consent is provisional, the Minister may, after giving the applicant not less than 90 days' notice of his intention to do so, revoke the approval or consent.

(3)   Where the Minister revokes a provisional approval given to a fish pass forming part of or in connection with a dam or other obstruction, he may extend the period within which a fish pass is to be made as part of or in connection with the obstruction.

(4)   The Minister may approve and certify any fish pass if he is of opinion that it is efficient in all respects and for all purposes, whether it was constructed under this Act or not.

(5)   Where a fish pass has received the approval of the Minister, and the approval has not been revoked, it shall be deemed to be a fish pass in conformity with this Act, notwithstanding that it was not constructed in the manner and by the person specified in this Act.

Penalty for injuring or obstructing fish pass or free gap
12.—(1)   If any person—

(a)   wilfully alters or injures a fish pass; or

(b)   does any act whereby salmon or trout are obstructed or liable to be obstructed in using a fish pass or whereby a fish pass is rendered less efficient; or

(c)   alters a dam or the bed or banks of the river so as to render a fish pass less efficient; or

(d)   uses any contrivance or does any act whereby salmon or trout are in any way liable to be scared, hindered or prevented from passing through a fish pass,

he shall be guilty of an offence, and shall also in every case pay any expenses which may be incurred in restoring the fish pass to its former state of efficiency; and any such expenses may be recovered in a summary manner.

(2)   The owner or occupier of a dam shall be deemed to have altered it if it is damaged, destroyed or allowed to fall into a state of disrepair, and if after notice is served on him by the water authority in whose area the dam is or was situated he fails to repair or reconstruct it within a reasonable time so as to render the fish pass as efficient as before the damage or destruction.

(3)   If any person—

(a)   does any act for the purpose of preventing salmon or trout from passing through a fish pass, or takes, or attempts to take, any salmon or trout in its passage through a fish pass; or

(b)   places any obstruction, uses any contrivance or does any act whereby salmon or trout may be scared, deterred or in any way prevented from freely entering and passing up and down a free gap at all periods of the year,

he shall be guilty of an offence.

(4)   This section shall not apply to a temporary bridge or board used for crossing a free gap, and taken away immediately after the person using it has crossed.

Sluices

13.—(1)   Subject to subsection (3) below, unless permission in writing is granted by the water authority for the area, any sluices for drawing off the water which would otherwise flow over any dam in waters frequented by salmon or migratory trout shall be kept shut on Sundays and at all times when the water is not required for milling purposes, in such manner as to cause the water to flow through any fish pass in or connected with the dam or, if there is no such fish pass, over the dam.

(2)   If any person fails to comply with this section, he shall be guilty of an offence.

(3)   This section shall not prevent any person opening a sluice for the purpose of letting off water in cases of flood or for milling purposes or when necessary for the purpose of navigation or, subject to previous notice in writing being given to the water authority, for cleaning or repairing the dam or mill or its appurtenances.

Gratings

14.—(1)   Where water is diverted from waters frequented by salmon or migratory trout by means of any conduit or artificial channel and the water so diverted is used for the purposes of a water or canal undertaking or for the purposes of any mill, the owner of the undertaking or the occupier of the mill shall, unless an exemption from the obligation is granted by the water authority for the area, place and maintain, at his own cost, a grating or gratings across the conduit or channel for the purpose of preventing the descent of the salmon or migratory trout.

(2)   In the case of any such conduit or artificial channel the owner of the undertaking or the occupier of the mill shall also, unless an exemption is granted as aforesaid, place and maintain at his own cost a grating or gratings across any outfall of the conduit or channel for the purpose of preventing salmon or migratory trout entering the outfall.

(3)   A grating shall be constructed and placed in such a manner and position as may be approved by the Minister.

(4)   If any person without lawful excuse fails to place or to maintain a grating in accordance with this section, he shall be guilty of an offence.

(5)   No such grating shall be so placed as to interfere with the passage of boats on any navigable canal.

(6)   The obligations imposed by this section shall not be in force during such period (if any) in each year as may be prescribed by byelaw.

(7)   The obligations imposed by this section on the occupier of a mill shall apply only where the conduit or channel was constructed on or after 18th July 1923.

Power of water authority to use gratings etc. to limit movements of salmon and trout

15.—(1)   A water authority, with the written consent of the Minister—

(a)   may cause a grating or gratings of such form and dimensions as they may determine to be placed and maintained, at the expense of the authority, at a suitable place in any watercourse, mill race, cut, leat, conduit or other channel for conveying water for any purpose from any waters frequented by salmon or migratory trout; and

(b)   may cause any watercourse, mill race, cut, leat, conduit or other channel in which a grating is placed under this section to be widened or deepened at the expense of the authority so far as may be necessary to compensate for the diminution of any flow of water caused by the placing of the grating, or shall take some other means to prevent the flow of water being prejudicially diminished or otherwise injured.

(2)   If any person—

(a)   injures any such grating; or

(b)   removes any such grating or part of any such grating, except during any period of the year during which under a byelaw gratings need not be maintained; or

(c)   opens any such grating improperly; or

(d)   permits any such grating to be injured, or removed, except as aforesaid, or improperly opened;

he shall be guilty of an offence.

(3)   A water authority, with the written consent of the Minister, may adopt such means as the Minister may approve for preventing the ingress of salmon or trout into waters in which they or their spawning beds or ova are, from the nature of the channel or other causes, liable to be destroyed.

(4)   Nothing in this section shall—

(a)   affect the liability under this Act of any person to place and maintain a grating; or

(b)   authorise a grating to be so placed or maintained during any period of the year during which under a byelaw gratings need not be maintained; or

(c)   authorise any grating to be placed or maintained so as to obstruct any conduit or channel used for navigation or in any way interfere with the effective working of any mill;

and nothing in subsection (3) above shall authorise the water authority prejudicially to interfere with water rights used or enjoyed for the purposes of manufacturing or for milling purposes or for drainage or navigation.

Boxes and cribs in weirs and dams
16.—(1)   Any person who uses a fishing weir or fishing mill dam for the taking of salmon or migratory trout by means of boxes or cribs shall be guilty of an offence unless the boxes or cribs satisfy the requirements specified in subsection (2) below.

(2)   The requirements mentioned in subsection (1) above are—

(a)   the upper surface of the sill of the box or crib must be level with the bed

of the river;
(b)   the bars or inscales of the heck or upstream side of the box or crib—

(i)   must not be nearer to each other than 2 inches;
(ii)   must be capable of being removed; and
(iii)   must be placed perpendicularly;

(c)   there must not be attached to any such box or crib any spur or tail wall, leader or outrigger of a greater length than 20 feet from the upper or lower side of the box or crib.

Restrictions on taking salmon or trout above or below an obstruction or in mill races
17.—(1)   Any person who takes or kills, or attempts to take or kill, except with rod and line, or scares or disturbs any salmon or trout—

(a)   at any place above or below any dam or any obstruction, whether artificial or natural, which hinders or retards the passage of salmon or trout, being within 50 yards above or 100 yards below the dam or obstruction, or within such other distance from the dam or obstruction as may be prescribed by byelaw; or
(b)   in any waters under or adjacent to any mill, or in the head race or tail race of any mill, or in any waste race or pool communicating with a mill; or
(c)   in any artificial channel connected with any such dam or obstruction,

shall be guilty of an offence.

(2)   Nothing in this section shall apply to any legal fishing mill dam not having a crib, box or cruive, or to any fishing box, coop, apparatus, net or mode of fishing in connection with and forming part of such a dam or obstruction for purposes of fishing.
(3)   Where a fish pass approved by the Minister is for the time being attached to a dam or obstruction, this section shall not be enforced in respect of the dam or obstruction until compensation has been made by the water authority to the persons entitled to fish in the waters for that right of fishery.

Provisions supplementary to Part II
18.—(1)   If any person obstructs a person legally authorised whilst he is doing any act authorised by section 9, 10 or 15 above, he shall be guilty of an offence.
(2)   The Minister shall not give a water authority his consent—

(a)   to the construction, abolition or alteration of a fish pass or the abolition or alteration of a free gap in pursuance of section 10 above; or
(b)   to the doing of any work under section 15 above,

unless reasonable notice of the authority's application under the relevant section has been served on the owner and occupier of the dam, fish pass or free gap, watercourse, mill race, cut, leat, conduit or other channel, with a plan and specification of the proposed work; and the Minister shall take into consideration any objections by the owner or occupier, before giving his consent.

(3)   If any injury is caused—

(a)   to any dam by reason of the construction, abolition or alteration of a fish pass or the abolition or alteration of a free gap in pursuance of section 10 above; or

(b)   by anything done by the water authority under section 15 above,

any person sustaining any loss as a result may recover from the water authority compensation for the injury sustained.

(4)   The amount of any compensation under section 10, 15 or 17 above shall be settled in case of dispute by a single arbitrator appointed by the Minister.

(5)   In any case in which a water authority are liable to pay compensation under this Part of this Act in respect of injury or damage caused by the making or maintaining of any work, compensation shall not be recoverable unless proceedings for its recovery are instituted within two years from the completion of the work.

Part III   Times of Fishing and Selling and Exporting Fish

Close seasons and close times

19.—(1)   Schedule 1 to this Act shall have effect in relation to the close seasons and close times for the descriptions of fish there specified.

(2)   Subject to subsection (3) below, any person who fishes for, takes, kills or attempts to take or kill salmon—

(a)   except with a rod and line or putts and putchers, during the annual close season or weekly close time; or

(b)   with a rod and line during the annual close season for rod and line; or

(c)   with putts and putchers, during the annual close season for putts and putchers,

shall be guilty of an offence.

(3)   A person shall not be guilty of an offence under subsection (2) above in respect of any act done for the purpose of the artificial propagation of fish, or for some scientific purpose, if he has obtained the previous permission in writing of the water authority in whose area the act was done.

(4)   Subject to subsection (5) below, any person who fishes for, takes, kills or attempts to take or kill trout other than rainbow trout—

(a)   except with a rod and line, during the annual close season or weekly close time for trout; or

(b)   with a rod and line during the annual trout close season for rod and line,

shall be guilty of an offence.

(5)   A person shall not be guilty of an offence under subsection (4) above in respect of any act done for the purpose of the artificial propagation of fish or the stocking or restocking of waters, or for some scientific purpose, if he has obtained the previous permission in writing of the water authority in whose area the act was done.

(6)   Subject to subsection (8) below, any person who, during the annual close season for freshwater fish, fishes for, takes, kills, or attempts to take or kill, any freshwater fish in any inland water, or fishes for eels by means of a rod and line in any such water, shall be guilty of an offence.

(7)   Subject to subsection (8) below, any person who, during the annual close season for rainbow trout, fishes for, takes, kills or attempts to take or kill, any rainbow trout in any inland water, or fishes for eels by means of a rod and line in any such water, shall be guilty of an offence.

(8)   Subsections (6) and (7) above do not apply—

(a)   to the removal by the owner or occupier, from any several fishery where salmon or trout are specially preserved, of any eels, freshwater fish or rainbow trout not so preserved;

(b)   to any person fishing with rod and line in any such fishery with the previous permission in writing of its owner or occupier;

(c)   to any person fishing with rod and line for eels in any waters in which such fishing is authorised by a byelaw;

(d)   to the taking of freshwater fish or rainbow trout for scientific purposes;

(e)   to the taking of freshwater fish for bait—

(i)   in a several fishery with the permission in writing of its owner or occupier, or

(ii)   in any other fishery, unless the taking would contravene a byelaw.

Close seasons and close times—fixed engines and obstructions
20.—(1)   Subject to subsections (4) and (5) below, immediately after the commencement of the annual close season and the weekly close time, the occupier of any fixed engine for taking salmon or migratory trout shall cause it to be removed or rendered incapable of taking them or obstructing their passage.

(2)   Subject to subsections (4) and (5) below, where in pursuance of subsection (1) above a fixed engine has been rendered incapable (whether by removal or otherwise) of taking salmon or migratory trout or obstructing their passage, its occupier shall not replace it or otherwise render it capable of taking them or obstructing their passage until the end of the close season or close time.

(3)   If any person—

(a)   fails to comply with subsection (1) or (2) above; or

(b)   during the annual close season or weekly close time places any obstruction, uses any contrivance or does any act, for the purpose of deterring salmon or migratory trout from passing up a river,

he shall be guilty of an offence.

(4)   Subsections (1) to (3) above only apply to putts and putchers in relation to the close season for putts and putchers.

(5)   It shall be a defence for a person charged with an offence under subsection (3)(b) above to show that he placed the obstruction, used the contrivance or did the acts in question in the course of legally fishing for fish other than salmon or migratory trout.

(6)   In this section 'migratory trout' does not include rainbow trout.

Eel baskets etc.

21.—(1)   Subject to subsection (2) below, any person who—

(a)   before 25th June in any year, hangs, fixes or uses in any waters frequented by salmon or migratory trout any baskets, nets, traps or devices for catching eels, or places in any inland water any device whatsoever to catch or obstruct any fish descending the river; or

(b)   at any time places upon the apron of any weir any basket, trap or device for taking fish, except wheels or leaps for taking lamperns between 1st August and the following 1st March,

shall be guilty of an offence.

(2)   Subsection (1) above does not prohibit—

(a)   the use of eel baskets not exceeding in any part 10 inches in diameter constructed so as to be fished with bait, and not used at any dam or other obstruction or in any conduit or artificial channel by which water is deviated from a river; or

(b)   any device for taking eels in such places, during such time and subject to such conditions as may be authorised by the water authority for the area with the consent of the Minister.

Sale of salmon and trout

22.—(1)   Subject to subsections (2) and (3) below, any person who buys, sells, or exposes for sale or has in his possession for sale—

(a)   any salmon between 31st August and the following 1st February; or

(b)   any trout other than rainbow trout between 31st August and the following 1st March,

shall be guilty of an offence.

(2)   Subsection (1) above shall not apply to any person buying, selling or exposing for sale, or having in his possession for sale—

(a)   any salmon or trout which has been canned, frozen, cured, salted, pickled, dried or otherwise preserved outside the United Kingdom; or

(b)   any salmon which has been canned, frozen, cured, salted, pickled, dried or otherwise preserved in the United Kingdom between 1st February and 31st August; or

(c)   any trout which has been canned, frozen, cured, salted, pickled, dried or otherwise preserved within the United Kingdom between 1st March and 31st August; or

    (d)   any salmon or trout (other than an unclean salmon or trout) caught outside the United Kingdom; or

    (e)   any salmon or trout (other than an unclean or immature salmon or trout) caught within the United Kingdom, if its capture by any net, instrument or device was lawful at the time and in the place where it was caught.

    (3)   A person shall not be guilty of an offence in respect of trout under this section for any act done for the purpose of the artificial propagation of fish, or the stocking or restocking of waters, or for some scientific purpose.

    (4)   The burden of proving that any salmon or trout bought, sold, exposed for sale or in the possession of any person for sale between the dates mentioned in paragraph (a) or (b) of subsection (1) above is not bought, sold, exposed for sale or in the possession of that person for sale in contravention of this section shall lie on the person buying, selling or exposing it for sale, or having it in his possession for sale.

Export of salmon and trout

23.—(1)   No person shall export or enter for export any unclean salmon or trout or any salmon or trout caught during the time at which the sale of salmon or trout is prohibited where the salmon or trout was caught.

    (2)   All salmon or trout intended for export between 31st August and the following 1st May shall before shipment be entered for that purpose with the proper officer of Customs and Excise, at the port or place of intended export.

    (3)   If any salmon or trout is entered for export, or exported or brought to any wharf, quay or other place for export, contrary to this section, or is not entered as required by this section, the salmon or trout and any package containing it shall be deemed to be goods liable to be forfeited under the enactments relating to customs, and the person entering or exporting the salmon or trout, or bringing it for export, or failing to enter the salmon or trout as required by this section, shall be guilty of an offence.

    (4)   Any officer of Customs and Excise may, between 31st August and the following 1st May, open or cause to be opened any parcel entered or intended for export, or brought to any quay, wharf or other place for that purpose, and suspected by him to contain salmon or trout, and may detain or cause to be detained any salmon or trout found in the parcel until proof is given of the salmon or trout being such as may be legally exported; and if the salmon or trout becomes unfit for human food before such proof is given, the officer may destroy it or cause it to be destroyed.

    (5)   The burden of proving that any salmon or trout entered for export between 31st August and the following 1st May is not so entered in contravention of this section shall lie on the person entering it.

Consignment of salmon and trout

24.—(1)   A person who consigns or sends a package containing salmon or trout by any common or other carrier shall be guilty of an offence unless the outside of the package containing it is conspicuously marked 'salmon' or 'trout', as the case may be.

(2)   An authorised officer may open any package consigned or sent by a carrier, or brought to any place to be so consigned or sent, and suspected to contain salmon or trout.

(3)   If any such package is found to contain salmon or trout and is not marked in accordance with this section, or if there is reasonable cause to suspect that the salmon or trout contained in any marked package is being dealt with contrary to law, an authorised officer may detain the package and its contents until proof is given that the salmon or trout is not being so dealt with.

(4)   The power to detain salmon or trout conferred by subsection (3) above shall be exercisable also in relation to salmon or trout not packed in a package.

(5)   If any salmon or trout detained under this section becomes unfit for human food before the proof required by subsection (3) above is given, an authorised officer may destroy it or cause it to be destroyed.

(6)   If any person refuses to allow an authorised officer to exercise the powers conferred by this section, or obstructs such an officer in their exercise, he shall be guilty of an offence.

Part IV   Fishing Licences

Licences to fish

25.—(1)   A water authority shall by means of a system of licensing regulate fishing for salmon and trout in their area and, except so far as excused by the Minister, shall by such means regulate fishing for freshwater fish of any description or eels in their area.

(2)   Subject to the following provisions of this section, a licence granted for the purposes of this section (hereafter in this Act referred to as a 'fishing licence') shall entitle the person to whom it was granted and no others to use an instrument specified in the licence to fish for any fish of a description, in an area and for a period so specified.

(3)   A fishing licence for the use of an instrument other than a rod and line to fish for salmon or trout shall also authorise the use of the instrument for that purpose by the duly authorised servants or agents of the person to whom it was granted, but not exceeding the number permitted by paragraph 13 of Schedule 2 to this Act.

[See s.36(2) of the Salmon Act 1986.]

(4)   A fishing licence for the use of a rod and line shall entitle the licensee to use as ancillary to that use a gaff, consisting of a plain metal hook without a barb, or a tailer or landing net.

(5)   A fishing licence for the use of any instrument for fishing for salmon shall authorise the use of that instrument for fishing for trout.

(6)   A fishing licence in respect of any instrument for fishing for salmon or trout shall authorise the use of that instrument for fishing for freshwater fish and eels.

(7)   Any person or association entitled to an exclusive right of fishing in any inland waters may be granted a general licence to fish in those waters subject to any conditions agreed between the water authority and the licensee, and the licence shall entitle the licensee and, subject to paragraph 9 of Schedule 4 below, any person authorised by him in writing, or in the case of an association, by its secretary so to fish.

(8)   Schedule 2 to this Act shall have effect with respect to fishing licences.

(9)   Any licence in force under any provision of section 61 of the Salmon and Freshwater Fisheries Act 1923 immediately before 29th June 1972 shall be treated as having been granted under the corresponding provision of this section.

Limitation of fishing licences

26.—(1)   A water authority may by order confirmed by the Minister—

(a)   limit for a period not exceeding ten years from the coming into operation of the order the number of fishing licences to be issued in any year for fishing in any part of their area for salmon or trout other than rainbow trout with any instrument so specified other than rod and line; and

(b)   provide for the selection of the applicants to whom such licences are to be issued where the number of applications exceeds the number of licences which may be granted.

(2)   Where the Minister proposes to confirm an order under this section, he shall require the water authority to publish the order and notice of his intention to confirm it in such manner as he may require, together with a notification that within a period specified in the requirement written objections to the order may be made to him.

(3)   The Minister shall consider any such objections received by him within the said period, and—

(a)   if the number of licences as proposed to be limited by the order is less than the number of licences issued in any of the three years preceding the year in which the order is to come into operation; and

(b)   any such objection is made by any person who has during each of the two years preceding that year held a licence of the same description as the licences which it is proposed so to limit in number;

he shall cause a local inquiry to be held before confirming the order.

(4)   Subject to subsection (5) below, the Minister shall not confirm an order under this section unless he is satisfied that the terms of the order relating to the selection of applicants for licences are such as to secure that any person who during the year preceding that year held a fishing licence to use an instrument of any description and who is dependent on fishing for his livelihood will be able to obtain a fishing licence to use an instrument of that description.

(5)   If it appears to the Minister that the operation of subsection (4) above would be detrimental to the conservation of any fishery, he may direct that the subsection shall in its application to that fishery have effect with the substitution

for the words 'the year' of the words 'the two years' or, if in his opinion special circumstances justify it, 'the three years'.

(6)   The Minister may with the consent of the water authority vary an order submitted to him under this section before confirming it and may require the water authority to publish the terms of the proposed variation in such manner, if any, as he may specify in the requirement.

(7)   An order under this section may be revoked by the Minister, or by an order made by the water authority and confirmed by the Minister.

(8)   Any order limiting the number of licences in force in a water authority area under section 62 of the Salmon and Freshwater Fisheries Act 1923 immediately before 29th June 1972 shall be treated as having limited the number of licences in that area for a period of ten years from that date.

Unlicensed fishing
27.   A person is guilty of an offence if, in any place in which fishing for fish of any description is regulated by a system of licensing, he—

(a)   fishes for or takes fish of that description otherwise than by means of an instrument which he is entitled to use for that purpose by virtue of a fishing licence or otherwise than in accordance with the conditions of the licence; or

(b)   has in his possession with intent to use it for that purpose an instrument other than one which he is authorised to use for that purpose by virtue of such a licence.

Part V   Administration and Enforcement

Regulation of Fisheries etc.

General powers and duties of water authorities and Minister
28.—(1)   It shall be the duty of every water authority—

(a)   to maintain, improve and develop the salmon fisheries, trout fisheries, freshwater fisheries and eel fisheries in the area for which they exercise functions under this Act;

(b)   to establish advisory committees of persons who appear to them to be interested in any such fisheries in that area and consult them as to the manner in which the authority are to discharge their duty under paragraph (a) above.

(2)   The duty to establish advisory committees imposed by paragraph (b) of section (1) above is a duty to establish a regional advisory committee for the whole of the area mentioned in paragraph (a) of that subsection and such local advisory committees as the water authority consider necessary to represent the interests referred to in paragraph (b) of that subsection in different parts of that area.

(2A)   A water authority may pay to any member of an advisory committee established by it in accordance with paragraph (b) of subsection (1) above such allowances as may be determined by the Minister with the consent of the Treasury.

[Inserted by para. 4(1) of Sch. 4 to the Water Act 1983.]

(3)   Subject to subsection (4) below, the Minister may by statutory instrument make an order for the general regulation of the salmon, trout, freshwater and eel fisheries within an area defined by the order.

(4)   An order under subsection (3) above shall not apply to any waters in respect of which the Minister has granted a licence under section 29 below.

(5)   An order under subsection (3) above may amend or revoke any previous order made under that subsection or under section 38 of the Salmon and Freshwater Fisheries Act 1923 or any Act repealed by that Act.

(6)   Schedule 3 to this Act shall have effect in relation to the Minister's power to make orders under subsection (3) above, to the powers of water authorities under this Act and to byelaws.

(7)   Any person who contravenes or fails to comply with a byelaw shall be guilty of an offence.

(8)   Section 36(3) of the Water Act 1973 and Schedule 7 to that Act (byelaw procedure) shall have effect in relation to byelaws under this Act.

Fish rearing licences
29.—(1)   The Minister may grant a licence to carry on the business of artificially propagating or rearing salmon or trout in any waters.

(2)   Any such licence may be granted subject to such conditions (if any) as the Minister thinks fit, and may be revoked if he is of opinion that any condition has not been observed.

Introduction of fish into inland waters
30.   A person shall be guilty of an offence if he introduces any fish or spawn of fish into an inland water, or has in his possession any fish or spawn of fish intending to intoduce it into an inland water, unless he first obtains the written consent of the water authority within whose area any part of that water is situated.

[See s.34 of the Salmon Act 1986.]

Powers of Water Bailiffs etc.

Powers of search etc.
31.—(1)   Any water bailiff appointed by a water authority and any person appointed by the Minister—

(a)   may examine any dam, fishing weir, fishing mill dam, fixed engine or obstruction, or any artificial watercourse, and for that purpose enter on any land;

(b)   may examine any instrument or bait which he has reasonable cause to suspect of having been or being used or likely to be used in taking fish in contravention of this Act or any container which he has reasonable cause to suspect of having been or being used or likely to be used for holding any such instrument, bait or fish;

[See s.32(6)(a) of the Salmon Act 1986.]

(c)   may stop and search any boat or other vessel used in fishing in a water authority area or any vessel or vehicle which he has reasonable cause to suspect of containing—

(i)   fish which had been caught in contravention of this Act;

(ii)   any such instrument, bait or container as aforesaid;

[See s.32(6)(a) of the Salmon Act 1986.]

(d)   may seize any fish and any instrument, vessel, vehicle or other thing liable to be forfeited in pursuance of this Act.

(2)   If any person refuses to allow a water bailiff or a person appointed by the Minister to make any entry, search or examination which he is by this section authorised to make, or to seize anything which he is so authorised to seize, or resists or obstructs a water bailiff or person so appointed in any such entry, search, examination or seizure, he shall be guilty of an offence.

Power to enter lands
32.—(1)   Subject to subsection (2) below—

(a)   any water bailiff or other officer of a water authority, under a special order in writing from the authority, and
(b)   any person appointed by the Minister, under an order in writing from him,

may at all reasonable times, for the purpose of preventing any offence against this Act, enter, remain upon and traverse any lands adjoining or near to waters within a water authority area other than—

(i)   a dwelling-house or the curtilage of a dwelling-house, or
(ii)   decoys or lands used exclusively for the preservation of wild fowl.

(2)   An order under subsection (1) above shall not remain in force for more than 12 months.

Orders and warrants to enter suspected premises
33.—(1)   Where from a statement on oath of a water bailiff or any other officer of a water authority, or any person appointed by the Minister, it appears to any justice of the peace that the person making the statement has good reason to suspect that any offence against this Act is being or is likely to be committed on any land situate on or near to any waters, the justice may by order under his hand

authorise him, during a period not exceeding 24 hours to be specified in the order, to enter upon and remain on the land during any hours of the day or night for the purpose of detecting the persons committing the offence.

(2)   Any justice of the peace upon an information on oath that there is probable cause to suspect any offence against this Act to have been committed on any premises, or any salmon, trout, freshwater fish or eels to have been illegally taken, or any illegal nets or other instruments to be on any premises, by warrant under his hand and seal may authorise any water bailiff or other officer of a water authority, or any person appointed by the Minister, or any constable, to enter the premises for the purposes of detecting the offence or the fish, nets or other instruments, at such times of the day or night as are mentioned in the warrant, and to seize all illegal nets and other instruments and all salmon, trout, freshwater fish or eels suspected to have been illegally taken that may be found on the premises.

[See s.32(6)(b) of the Salmon Act 1986.]

(3)   A warrant under subsection (2) above shall not continue in force for more than one week.

Power to apprehend persons fishing illegally at night

34.   If any person, between the end of the first hour after sunset on any day and the beginning of the last hour before sunrise on the following morning, illegally takes or kills salmon, trout, freshwater fish or eels, or is found on or near any waters with intent illegally to take or kill salmon, trout, freshwater fish or eels, or having in his possession for the capture of salmon, trout freshwater fish or eels any instrument prohibited by this Act, a water bailiff or a person appointed by the Minister, with any assistants, may seize him without warrant and put him as soon as may be into the custody of a police officer.

Power to require production of fishing licences

35.—(1)   A water bailiff appointed by the water authority for the area, or any constable, may require any person who is fishing, or whom he reasonably suspects of being about to fish or to have within the preceding half hour fished in a water authority area, to produce his licence or other authority to fish and to state his name and address.

(2)   A person holding a fishing licence for any water authority area may, on production of his licence, require any person who is fishing in that area to produce his licence or other authority to fish and to state his name and address.

(3)   If any person required to produce his fishing licence or other authority or to state his name and address fails to do so, he shall be guilty of an offence; but if within seven days after the production of his licence was so required he produces the licence or other authority at the office of the water authority he shall not be convicted of an offence under this section for failing to produce it.

Provisions supplementary to sections 31 to 35

36.—(1)   A water bailiff and a person appointed by the Minister shall be deemed to be a constable for the purpose of the enforcement of this Act, or any order or byelaw under it, and to have all the same powers and privileges, and be subject to the same liabilities as a constable duly appointed has or is subject to by virtue of the common law or of any statute.

[See s.32(6)(b) of the Salmon Act 1986.]

(2)   The production by a water bailiff or a person appointed by the Minister of evidence of his appointment shall be a sufficient warrant for him exercising the powers conferred on him by this Act.

(3)   A police constable whose services are provided under paragraph 39(1)(c) of Schedule 3 below shall have all the powers and privileges of a water bailiff.

Offences

Prosecution etc. of offences
37.   Parts I and II of Schedule 4 to this Act shall have effect with regard to the prosecution and punishment of offences against this Act and the procedure on such prosecutions.

Part VI   Miscellaneous and Supplementary

Works below high water mark
38.—(1)   Any works proposed to be constructed under this Act on, over or under tidal lands below high-water mark of ordinary spring tides shall be constructed only in accordance with such plans and sections and subject to such restrictions and regulations as the Secretary of State approves in writing before they are commenced.

(2)   Any alteration or extension of any such works shall be subject to the like approval.

(3)   If any such work is commenced or completed contrary to this section, the Secretary of State may abate and remove it and restore its site to its former condition at the cost of the person who commenced or executed it, or (if he is not the owner of the work) of the owner, and the cost shall be summarily recoverable by the Secretary of State.

(4)   This section is in addition to and not in derogation of any local Act.

Border rivers and Solway Firth
39.—(1)   This Act—

(a)   does not apply to the River Tweed, but

(b)   applies to so much of the River Esk, with its banks and tributary streams up to their source, as is situated in Scotland,

and in this subsection 'the River Tweed' means 'the river' as defined by the Tweed Fisheries (Amendment) Act 1859 and any byelaw amending that definition.

[See s.32(6)(b) of the Salmon Act 1986.]

(2)   Where the minimum size of mesh of nets used for taking salmon prescribed by any provision of this Act or by any byelaw in force in any part of the Solway Firth within England is greater than that which may be lawfully used in the part of the Solway Firth within Scotland, the provision or byelaw shall have effect as if the minimum size of mesh so prescribed in relation to the part of the Solway Firth within England were such as may be so lawfully used as aforesaid in the part of the Solway Firth within Scotland.

(3)   The limits of the Solway Firth for the purposes of this section shall be determined by the Minister.

(4)   Nothing in this Act shall authorise a water authority to acquire compulsorily under this Act any land in Scotland.

[See para. 13 of Sch. 4 to Salmon Act 1986.]

40.   This Act applies to the dams constructed by the Severn Commissioners under the Severn Navigation Act 1842 and the Severn Navigation Act 1853 and now vested in the British Waterways Board, and to all fish passes in those dams; and it shall accordingly be the Board's duty, subject to the provisions of this Act and to section 23 of the Severn Navigation Act 1881 (by virtue of which they have power to stop up the passes with the agreement of the water authority for the area) to maintain those passes in an efficient state.

Interpretation
41.—(1)   In this Act, unless the context otherwise requires—
　　'authorised officer' means—

　　　(a)   any officer of a water authority acting within the water authority area;
　　　(b)   any officer of a market authority acting within the area of the jurisdiction of that authority;
　　　(c)   any officer appointed by the Minister;
　　　(d)   any officer appointed in writing by the Fishmongers Company, or
　　　(e)   any police officer;

　　'byelaw' means a byelaw under this Act;
　　'dam' includes any weir or other fixed obstruction used for the purpose of damming up water;
　　'eels' includes elvers and the fry of eels;
　　'fishing licence' has the meaning assigned to it by section 25(2) above;
　　'fishing mill dam' means a dam used or intended to be used partly for the purpose of taking or facilitating the taking of fish, and partly for the purpose of supplying water for milling or other purposes;
　　'fishing weir' means any erection, structure or obstruction fixed to the soil either temporarily or permanently, across or partly across a river or branch of a river, and used for the exclusive purpose of taking or facilitating the taking of fish;
　　'Fishmongers Company' means the wardens and commonalty of the

Mystery of Fishmongers in the City of London;

'fixed engine' includes—

(a)   a stake net, bag net, putt or putcher;

(b)   any fixed implement or engine for taking or facilitating the taking of fish;

(c)   any net secured by anchors and any net or other implement for taking fish fixed to the soil, or made stationary in any other way; and

(d)   any net placed or suspended in any inland or tidal waters unattended by the owner or a person duly authorised by the owner to use it for taking salmon or trout, and any engine, device, machine or contrivance, whether floating or otherwise, for placing or suspending such a net or maintaining it in working order or making it stationary;

'foreshore' includes the shore and bed of the sea and of every channel, creek, bay, estuary and navigable river as far up it as the tide flows;

'freshwater fish' means any fish living in fresh water exclusive of salmon and trout and of any kinds of fish which migrate to and from tidal waters and of eels;

'general licence' means a licence granted under section 25(7) above;

'grating' means a device approved by the Minister for preventing the passage of salmon or trout through a conduit or channel in which it is placed;

'immature' in relation to salmon means that the salmon is of a length of less than 12 inches, measured from the tip of the snout to the fork or cleft of the tail, and in relation to any other fish means that the fish is of a length less than such length (if any) as may be prescribed by the byelaws applicable to the water in which the fish is taken;

'inland water' has the same meaning as in the Water Resources Act 1963;

'market authority' includes any corporation, local authority, body of trustees or other persons having power to maintain or regulate any market;

'migratory trout' means trout which migrate to and from the sea;

'mill' includes any erection for the purpose of developing water power, and 'milling' has a corresponding meaning;

'the Minister' means, subject to subsection (2) below, the Minister of Agriculture, Fisheries and Food;

'occupier' in relation to a fishery or premises includes any person for the time being in actual possession of the fishery or premises;

'owner' includes any person who is entitled to receive rents from a fishery or premises;

'river' includes a stream;

'rod and line' means single rod and line;

'salmon' means all fish of the salmon species and includes part of a salmon;

'trout' means any fish of the salmon family commonly known as trout, including migratory trout and char, and also includes part of a trout;

'unclean' in relation to any fish means that the fish is about to spawn, or has recently spawned and has not recovered from spawning.

(2)   In the following provisions of this Act, namely—

Part IV;

section 28(3);

paragraph 2 of Schedule 1;

paragraphs 5 to 11 and Part II of Schedule 3; and Schedule 2,
any reference to the Minister shall be construed, in relation to water authority areas wholly or partly in Wales, as a reference to the Minister and the Secretary of State jointly.

(2A) In section 28(2A) above, the reference to the Minister shall be construed, in relation to the Welsh Water Authority, as a reference to the Secretary of State.

[Inserted by para. 4(2) of Sch. 4 to the Water Act 1983.]

(3) Except so far as provision is made by paragraph 13 of Schedule 3 below, nothing in this Act shall be construed as authorising a water authority or any other person to take or use land or other property belonging to the Crown.

(4) In any byelaw made under an enactment repealed by the Salmon and Freshwater Fisheries Act 1923 'salmon' and 'trout' have the meaning assigned to them by subsection (1) above.

Repeals etc.
42.—(1) The enactments specified in Schedule 5 to this Act are hereby repealed to the extent specified in the third column of that Schedule.

(2) In section 18(1) of the Sea Fish (Conservation) Act 1967 (enforcement of orders in relation to salmon and migratory trout) for paragraph (a) there shall be substituted the following paragraph:—

'(a) section 31(1)(d) of the Salmon and Freshwater Fisheries Act 1975 (which confers power of seizure) shall apply as if the reference in it to that Act included a reference to this Act, and sections 36(1) and (2) of that Act, and paragraph 8 of Schedule 4 (all of which contain ancilliary provisions), shall be construed accordingly as including references to that Act applied by this subsection;'.

(3) In so far as any instrument made or other thing whatsoever done under any enactment repealed by this Act could have been made or done under a corresponding enactment in this Act, it shall not be invalidated by the repeal of that enactment but shall have effect as if made or done under that corresponding enactment; and for the purposes of this provision anything which under section 93(2) of the Salmon and Freshwater Fisheries Act 1923 had effect as if done under any enactment in that Act shall, so far as may be necessary for the continuity of the law, be treated as done under the corresponding enactment in this Act.

(4) Any enactment or other document referring to an enactment repealed by this Act or by the Salmon and Freshwater Fisheries Act 1923 shall, so far as may be necessary for preserving its effect, be construed as referring, or as including a reference, to the corresponding enactment in this Act.

(5) Nothing in this Act shall affect the admissibility in evidence of any

instrument made under the Salmon Fishery Act 1865.

(6)   Section 254(2)(c) of the Local Government Act 1972 (power of Secretary of State to amend, etc., enactments by order) shall apply to this Act as if it had been passed before 1st April 1974.

(7)   The Water Act 1973 shall have effect as if the functions conferred on water authorities by section 28(1) and (2) above were conferred by it.

(8)   Nothing in this Act shall affect the legal right of any conservators, directors, commissioners, undertakers or other persons to dredge, scour, cleanse or improve any navigable river, canal or other inland navigation.

(9)   Nothing in this Act shall be taken as prejudicing the operation of section 38 of the Interpretation Act 1889 (which relates to the effect of repeals).

Citation etc.
43.—(1)   This Act may be cited as the Salmon and Freshwater Fisheries Act 1975.

(2)   Subject to section 39 above and subsection (3) below, this Act extends only to England and Wales.

(3)   The following provisions of this Act, namely—
section 28(1) and (2) above,
section 39(1) and (4) above,
section 42(1) above, so far as it relates to the repeal of section 15 of the Salmon and Freshwater Fisheries Act 1972 and section 18 of the Water Act 1973,
paragraph 3 of Schedule 4 below,
extend to Scotland.

[See para. 14 of Sch. 4 to the Salmon Act 1986.]

(4)   This Act shall come into force on 1st August 1975.

Schedule 1   Close Seasons and Close Times

1.   It shall be the duty of every water authority to make byelaws fixing for their area or the respective parts of it, subject to paragraph 3 below, the annual close season and weekly close time for fishing by any method for salmon and trout other than rainbow trout.

2.   If a water authority have not before the commencement of this Act made any such byelaws for a part of their area, the Minister may make such byelaws for that part of that area with or without a local inquiry.

3.   The minimum close seasons and close times are specified in the following Table (subject to the power to dispense altogether with a close season for freshwater fish or rainbow trout conferred by paragraph 20 of Schedule 3 below).

Table

Minimum duration

1.	Salmon close season	153 days
2.	Close season for fishing for salmon with rod and line	92 days
3.	Close season for fishing for salmon or trout with putts and putchers	242 days
4.	Weekly close time for salmon	42 hours
5.	Trout close season	181 days
6.	Close season for fishing for trout with rod and line	153 days
7.	Weekly close time for trout	42 hours
8.	Close season for freshwater fish or rainbow trout	93 days

4.   If byelaws neither specify nor dispense with an annual close season for freshwater fish, the annual close season for such fish shall be the period between 14th March and 16th June.

5.   The annual close season for rainbow trout for any waters is that fixed for those waters by byelaws.

6.   Subject to any byelaws under this Act or the Salmon and Freshwater Fisheries Act 1923—

   (a)   for salmon—

   (i)   the annual close season shall be the period between 31st August and the following 1st February;
   (ii)   the close season for rods shall be the period between 31st October and the following 1st February;
   (iii)   the close season for putts and putchers shall be the period between 31st August and the following 1st May; and
   (iv)   the weekly close time shall be the period between 6 a.m. on Saturday and 6 a.m. on the following Monday; and

   (b)   for trout—

   (i)   the annual close season shall be the period between 31st August and the following 1st March;
   (ii)   the annual close season for rod and line shall be the period between 30th September and the following 1st March; and
   (iii)   the weekly close time shall be the period between 6 a.m. on Saturday and 6 a.m. on the following Monday.

Schedule 2 Licences

Duty on Licences

1.—(1) Subject to sub-paragraph (2) below, there shall be payable in respect of a fishing licence a duty fixed in accordance with this Schedule by the water authority.

(2) The water authority may in special cases grant an exemption from the duty.

2. Different duties may be fixed under paragraph 1 above for different instruments, different periods, different parts of the water authority area, different descriptions of fish and different classes of licence holder.

3. A water authority shall at least one month before fixing or altering a duty for the use of any instrument in any part of their area, except a duty payable in respect of a temporary licence, publish in one or more newspapers circulating in that part of their area notice of their intention to do so.

4. If during the month immediately following the publication of a notice under paragraph 3 above a written objection to the proposed duty is made to the Minister by any interested person, the water authority shall not fix or alter the duty without the approval of the Minister.

5. The Minister, with or without a local inquiry, may refuse to approve any duty submitted by a water authority for his approval under paragraph 4 above or may approve the duty with or without modifications; and the authority, if so directed by the Minister, shall cause notice of any proposed modification to be given in accordance with the direction.

6. No duty fixed under the foregoing provisions of this Schedule shall take effect until the beginning of the year following that in which it is fixed or, in the case of a duty required to be approved by the Minister, in which it is approved by him.

7. A water authority may grant a temporary licence, that is to say, a licence authorising the use of an instrument for fishing in circumstances specified in the licence during a period not exceeding 14 days, and may charge in respect of that licence a duty less than the duty fixed for the use of that instrument under the foregoing provisions of this Schedule.

8. There shall be payable in respect of a general licence such sum as may be agreed by the water authority and the licensee.

Net etc. Licences for Salmon and Trout Fishing

9. A person shall be treated for the purposes of section 25(3) above as the duly

authorised servant or agent of the holder of a licence to use an instrument of any description only in the following cases—

(a)   in an area in which there is in force an order under section 26 above limiting the number of licences for fishing with instruments of that description, if his name and address are entered on the licence in accordance with the following provisions of this Schedule and he is not the holder of another licence to use an instrument of that description in that area;

(b)   in any other area, if his name and address are so entered or when using the instrument to which the licence relates he is accompanied by the licensee; or

(c)   in the case of any area, if the water authority direct that owing to special circumstances he is to be so treated.

[See s.36(1) of the Salmon Act 1986.]

10.   The name and address of a servant or agent may be entered on a licence by an employee of a water authority authorised to do so or by the licensee or an agent who has been appointed by the licensee to act for the purposes of this paragraph and whose appointment, together with his name and address, has been notified to the water authority.

11.   The date of entry in the licence shall be stated in the licence at the time of the making of the entry, and within twenty-four hours of the making of an entry by a licensee or his agent a copy shall be sent to the water authority, together with a fee of 20p for every name and address entered.

12.   The name and address of a servant or agent may be removed from, or inserted in, a licence on payment of a fee of 20p for each removal or insertion or, where a name and address are inserted in substitution for a name and address removed, for each substitution.

13.   The number of servants or agents whose names may at any time be entered on a licence shall not exceed twice the number of persons who in the opinion of the water authority are required to work at one time the instrument to which the licence relates or, where the applicant for the licence notifies the authority at the time of the application that he proposes to take part in working the instrument, one less than twice that number.

14.   Any person who, with intent to deceive, enters on a licence more names than are permitted by paragraph 13 above or states falsely the date of entry in a licence is guilty of an offence.

Miscellaneous

15.   Subject to section 26 above, a fishing licence shall be granted by the water authority to every applicant who is at the time of the application not disqualified from holding a fishing licence, on payment of the duty in respect of the instrument to which the licence relates.

16.   A fishing licence shall not confer any right to fish at a place or a time at which the licensee is not otherwise entitled to fish.

17.   A fishing licence shall not authorise the erection of any structure or the use of any installation or instrument for or in connection with fishing the erection or use of which would otherwise be illegal.

18.   The production of a printed copy of a statement purporting to be issued by a water authority as to a licence duty fixed and, if it be the case, approved by the Minister under this Schedule shall be prima facie evidence that the licence duty was fixed or approved as there mentioned and of the amount of the duty, and without proof of the handwriting or official position of any person purporting to sign the statement.

Schedule 3   Administration

Part I   Orders

Scope

1.   An order may provide—

(a)   for the imposition, collection and recovery by a water authority of contributions assessed on several fisheries regulated by the order or on the owners and occupiers of such fisheries;

(b)   for enabling the water authority with the approval of the Minister, but subject to paragraphs 2 and 3 below, to erect and work by themselves or their lessees any fixed engine for catching salmon or migratory trout within the area within which the order is to apply;

(c)   for modifying in relation to the fisheries within the area any of the provisions of this Act which relate to the regulation of fisheries, or of any local Act relating to any fishery within the area.

2.   An order shall not authorise a fixed engine to be worked for a period exceeding five years unless authorisation is from time to time extended by licence of the Minister for such term as may be specified in the licence and not exceeding at any one time five years.

3.   The Minister shall not grant a licence until he has inquired into the effect of the working of the engine on the salmon or trout fisheries within the area.

4.   An order may contain any incidental, consequential or supplemental provisions, including provisions for payment of compensation to persons injuriously affected by the order, which may appear to be necessary or proper for the purposes of the order.

Procedure

5.   An application for an order may be made by any of the following, namely—

(a)   a water authority;

(b)   a county or metropolitan district council;

(c)   persons who in the opinion of the Minister are the owners of one-fourth at least in value of the several fisheries proposed to be regulated or constitute a majority of the persons holding licences to fish in public waters within the area of the proposed order;

(d)   any association of persons which in the opinion of the Minister is sufficiently representative of fishing interests within that area.

[As amended by the Local Government Act 1985, Sch. 8, para. 20.]

6.   The applicant for an order shall give such security for the Minister's expenses as the Minister may require.

7.   Before making an order the Minister shall cause notice of the intention to make the order and of the place where copies of the draft order may be inspected and obtained, and of the time within and manner in which objections to the draft order may be made, to be published in the London Gazette and in such other manner as he thinks best adapted for informing persons affected.

8.   Before making an order the Minister shall consider any objections which may be duly made to the draft order, and may cause a public local inquiry to be held with respect to any such objections.

9.   After an order has been settled and made by the Minister it shall be published in such manner as he thinks best adapted for informing persons affected with notice that the Minister has settled the order, and that the order will become final unless within such period, not being less than 30 days, as may be stated in the notice, a memorial is presented to the Minister by a water authority, local authority or other person or association affected by it, praying that it shall be subject to special parliamentary procedure.

10.   If within such period, not being less than 30 days, as may be stated in the notice so published, no memorial against the order is presented to the Minister by any water authority, local authority or other person or association affected by the order, or if any such memorial so presented is withdrawn, the Minister may confirm the order, but if any such memorial is presented and is not withdrawn, the order shall be subject to special parliamentary procedure.

11.   The making and confirmation of an order shall be prima facie evidence that all the requirements of this Act in respect of proceedings required to be taken previously to the making and confirmation of such an order have been complied with.

12.   The Minister may by statutory instrument make regulations in relation to the publication of notices and advertisements and the holding of and procedure at public local inquiries under this Part of this Schedule, and the payment of

expenses of and incidental to such inquiries and to any other matters of procedure respecting the making of orders.

13.   Where—

(a)   any fishery, land or foreshore proposed to be comprised in an order; or
(b)   any fishery proposed to be affected by any order; or
(c)   any land over which it is proposed to acquire an easement under an order,

belongs to Her Majesty in right of the Crown or forms part of the possessions of the Duchy of Lancaster or the Duchy of Cornwall, or belongs to or is under the management of any government department, the Minister may make the order if he has previously obtained—

(i)   in the case of any foreshore under the management of the Crown Estate Commissioners, or of any fishery or land belonging to Her Majesty in right of the Crown, the consent of those Commissioners;
(ii)   in the case of any foreshore or fishery or land forming part of the possessions of the Duchy of Lancaster, the consent of the Chancellor of the Duchy;
(iii)   in the case of any foreshore, fishery or land forming part of the possessions of the Duchy of Cornwall, the consent of the Duke of Cornwall, or the persons for the time being empowered to dispose for any purpose of the land of the Duchy;
(iv)   in the case of any foreshore or fishery or land which belongs to or is under the management of a government department, the consent of that government department.

Part II   Byelaws

General

14.   Subject to Schedule 1 above, the power to make byelaws shall be exercisable by water authorities.

15.   Byelaws may be made for any of the purposes mentioned in paragraphs 19 to 36 below.

16.   A byelaw may be made to apply to the whole or any part or parts of a water authority area or to the whole or any part or parts of the year.

17.   If at any time before the end of 12 months after the confirmation of a byelaw made for the purpose specified in paragraph 21 or 25 below the owner or occupier of any fishery within the water authority area, by notice in writing to the water authority, claims that the fishery is injuriously affected by the byelaw, the claim and the amount of compensation to be paid, by way of annual payment or

otherwise, for the damage (if any) to the fishery shall be determined, in default of agreement, by a single arbitrator appointed by the Minister.

18.   When the compensation is payable under any award by way of an annual payment, the water authority or the person entitled to the annual payment may at any time after the end of 5 years from the date of the award require it to be reviewed by a single arbitrator appointed by the Minister, and the compensation to be thenceforth paid shall be such, if any, as may be determined by that arbitrator.

Purposes for Which Byelaws May be Made

19.   Fixing or altering, subject to paragraph 3 of Schedule 1 above, any such close season or close time as is mentioned in that paragraph.

20.   Dispensing with a close season for freshwater fish or rainbow trout.

21.   Specifying the nets and other instruments (not being fixed engines) which may be used for taking salmon, trout, freshwater fish and eels and imposing requirements as to their construction, use, design, material and dimensions, including in the case of nets the size of mesh.

[See s.33(3) of the Salmon Act 1986.]

22.   Requiring and regulating the attachment to licensed nets and instruments of marks, labels or numbers, or the painting of marks or numbers or the affixing of labels or numbers to boats, coracles or other vessels used in fishing.

23.   Prohibiting the carrying in any boat or vessel whilst being used in fishing for salmon or trout of any net which is not licensed, or which is without the mark, label or number prescribed by the byelaws.

24.   Prohibiting or regulating the carrying in a boat or vessel during the annual close season for salmon of a net capable of taking salmon other than a net commonly used in the area to which the byelaw applies for sea fishing if carried in a boat or vessel commonly used for that purpose.

25.   Prohibiting the use for taking salmon, trout, or freshwater fish of any instrument (not being a fixed engine) in such waters within the water authority area and at such times as may be prescribed by the byelaws.

26.   Prohibiting the taking or removal from any water without lawful authority of any fish, whether alive or dead.

27.   Determining for the purposes of this Act the period of the year during which gratings need not be maintained.

28.   Prohibiting or regulating the taking of trout or any freshwater fish of a size less than such as may be prescribed by the byelaw.

29.   Prohibiting or regulating the taking of fish by any means within such distance as is specified in the byelaw above or below any dam or any other obstruction, whether artificial or natural.

30.   Prohibiting or regulating fishing with rod and line between the end of the first hour after sunset on any day and the beginning of the last hour before sunrise on the following morning.

31.   Regulating the deposit or discharge in any waters containing fish of any liquid or solid matter specified in the byelaw which is detrimental to salmon, trout or freshwater fish, or the spawn or food of fish, but not so as to prejudice any powers of a local authority to discharge sewage in pursuance of any power given by a public general Act, a local Act or a provisional order confirmed by Parliament.

32.   Requiring persons fishing for salmon, trout or freshwater fish to send to the water authority returns, in such form, giving such particulars and at such times as may be specified in the byelaws, of any such fish which they have taken, or a statement that they have taken no such fish.

33.   Regulating the use in connection with fishing with rod and line of any lure or bait specified in the byelaw.

34.   Determining the time during which it shall be lawful to use a gaff in connection with fishing with rod and line for salmon or migratory trout.

35.   Authorising fishing with rod and line for eels during the annual close season for freshwater fish.

36.   The better execution of this Act and the better protection, preservation and improvement of any salmon fisheries, trout fisheries, freshwater fisheries and eel fisheries in a water authority area.

Part III   Miscellaneous

37.   Without prejudice to paragraph 2 of Schedule 3 to the Water Act 1973 (general power of water authorities to do anything which in their opinion is calculated to facilitate or is conducive or incidental to the discharge of any of their functions), it is hereby declared that the powers conferred by Part VI of the Water Resources Act 1963 (which relates to land and works) include power for a water authority to purchase or take on lease (either by agreement or if so authorised compulsorily)—

(a)   any dam, fishing weir, fishing mill dam, fixed engine or other artificial obstruction and any fishery attached to or worked in connection with any such obstruction;

(b)   so much of the bank adjoining a dam as may be necessary for making or maintaining a fish pass for the purposes of section 10 above; and

(c)   for the purpose of erecting and working a fixed engine under paragraph 1(b) above, any fishery land or foreshore specified in the relevant order under that paragraph together with any easement over any adjoining land necessary for securing access to the fishery land or foreshore so acquired.

38.   Without prejudice to the said paragraph 2, a water authority may either alter or remove an obstruction acquired in the exercise of the powers mentioned in paragraph 37 above, or may by themselves or their lessees use or work in any lawful manner the obstruction for fishing purposes and exercise the right conferred by any fishery so acquired, subject in the case of an obstruction or fishery acquired by way of lease to the terms of the lease.

39.—(1)   Without prejudice to the said paragraph 2, a water authority—

(a)   may take legal proceedings in respect of any offence against this Act, or for the enforcement of the provision of this Act or for the protection of the fisheries in their area from injury by pollution or otherwise;

[See s.32(6)(b) of the Salmon Act 1986.]

(b)   may purchase or lease by agreement any fishery, fishing rights, or any establishment for the artificial propagation or rearing of salmon, trout or freshwater fish, and may use, work or exercise the same by themselves, their lessees, or any person duly authorised by them in writing; and

(c)   may obtain the services of additional constables under section 15 of the Police Act 1964.

(2)   Nothing in this paragraph shall authorise anything to be done which may injuriously affect any navigable river, canal, or inland navigation.

Schedule 4   Offences

Part I   Prosecution and Punishment

1.—(1)   Column 2 of the Table below gives a description of the offences against the provisions of this Act specified in column 1 of the Table, and in relation to any such offence—

(a)   column 3 shows whether the offence is punishable summarily (that is to say, on summary conviction) or on indictment or either in one way or the other; and

(b)   column 4 shows the maximum punishment by way of fine or imprisonment which may be imposed on a person convicted of the offence in the way specified in column 3 (that is to say, summarily or on indictment), any reference in column 4 to a period of years or months being construed as a reference to a term of imprisonment for that period.

(2)   A person guilty of an offence against any provision of this Act not specified in the Table shall be liable on summary conviction to a fine not exceeding level 4 on the standard scale.

Table

Provision of Act creating the offence	Description of offence	Mode of prosecution	Punishment
(1)	(2)	(3)	(4)
Section 1	Fishing with certain instruments for salmon, trout or freshwater fish and possessing certain instruments for fishing for such fish.	(a) If not acting with another, summarily. (b) If acting with another—	Level 4 on the standard scale; or in the case of a second or subsequent conviction level 4 on the standard scale.
		(i) summarily	£100; or in the case of a second or subsequent conviction £200.*
		(ii) on indictment	Two years or a fine or both.
Section 4	Discharging poisonous or injurious matter into waters containing fish or spawn.	(a) Summarily	£400* and £40 for each day on which the offence continues after a conviction thereof.
		(b) On indictment	Two years or a fine or both.
Section 5(1)	Using explosives, poisons, noxious substances or electrical devices to take or destroy fish.	(a) Summarily	£200; or in the case of a second or subsequent conviction £400.*
		(b) On indictment	Two years or a fine or both.
Section 5(3)	Destroying or damaging dams etc., to take or destroy fish.	(a) Summarily	£200; or in the case of a second or subsequent conviction £400.*
		(b) On indictment	Two years or a fine or both.
Section 19(2)	Fishing for salmon during the annual close season or weekly close time.	Summarily	Level 4 on the standard scale; or in the case of a second or subsequent conviction level 4 on the standard scale.
Section 19(4)	Fishing for trout during the annual close season or weekly close time.	Summarily	Level 4 on the standard scale; or in the case of a second or subsequent conviction level 4 on the standard scale.

Provision of Act creating the offence	Description of offence	Mode of prosecution	Punishment
(1)	(2)	(3)	(4)
Section 19(6)	Fishing for freshwater fish during the annual close season for freshwater fish and fishing for eels by means of a rod and line during that season.	Summarily	Level 4 on the standard scale; or in the case of a second or subsequent conviction level 4 on the standard scale.
Section 19(7)	Fishing for rainbow trout during the annual close season for rainbow trout and fishing for eels by means of a rod and line during that season.	Summarily	Level 4 on the standard scale; or in the case of a second or subsequent conviction level 4 on the standard scale.
Section 21	Prohibition on use of certain devices at certain times.	Summarily	Level 4 on the standard scale; or in the case of a second or subsequent conviction level 4 on the standard scale.
Section 27	Fishing for fish otherwise than under the authority of a licence and possessing an unlicensed instrument with intent to use if for fishing.	(a) If not acting with another, summarily.	Level 4 on the standard scale; or in the case of a second or subsequent conviction level 4 on the standard scale.
		(b) If acting with another—	
		(i) summarily	£100; or in the case of a second or subsequent conviction £200.*
		(ii) on indictment	Two years or a fine or both.

[As amended by the Criminal Law Act 1977, Sch. 6, and the Criminal Justice Act 1982, s.46.]
[*By virtue of the Magistrates' Courts Act, s.32(2) and (3), the maximum fine is now the prescribed sum (£2,000) irrespective of whether the conviction is a first, second or subsequent one.]
[See s.35 of the Salmon Act 1986.]

(3)   A person shall be treated as acting together with another for the purposes of the above Table if both are engaged in committing an offence against section 1 or 27 above, other than one committed by means of a rod and line or without any instrument, or one is aiding, abetting, counselling or procuring the commission of such an offence by the other.

Part II   Procedure

2.   Any offence against this Act committed on the sea-coast or at sea beyond the ordinary jurisdiction of a court of summary jurisdiction shall be deemed to have been committed in any place abutting on that sea-coast or adjoining that sea, and may be tried and punished accordingly.

3.   Offences against this Act committed in Scotland shall be proceeded against and punished in Scotland.

4.   A justice of the peace shall not be disqualified from hearing any case under this Act by reason only of being a subscriber to any society for the protection of fish, but a justice shall not be entitled to hear any case in respect of an offence committed on his own land or in relation to any fishery of which he is owner or occupier.

5.   The court by which a person is convicted of an offence against this Act may order the forfeiture of—

   (a)   any fish illegally taken by him or in his possession at the time of the offence;
   (b)   any instrument, bait or other thing used in the commission of the offence;
   (c)   in the case of an offence of unlawful possession of any substance or device in contravention of section 5 above, that substance or device; and
   (d)   on conviction on indictment, any vessel or vehicle used in or in connection with the commission of the offence or in which any substance or device unlawfully in his possession was contained at the time of the offence;

and may order any object so forfeited to be disposed of as the court thinks fit.

6.   Schedule 3 to the Customs and Excise Management Act 1979 (provisions relating to the forfeiture of things seized under that Act) shall apply in relation to any vessel or vehicle liable to forfeiture under paragraph 5 above as it applies in relation to anything liable to forfeiture under that Act, but in its application in relation to any such vessel or vehicle shall have effect subject to the following modifications:—

   (a)   paragraphs 1(2) and 5 shall be omitted;
   (b)   for references to the Commissioners of Customs and Excise there shall be substituted references to the water authority within whose area the offence in question was committed; and
   (c)   the court shall not condemn a vehicle or vessel as forfeited under paragraph 6 of that Schedule if satisfied by its owner that that offence was committed without his knowledge and that he could not have reasonably foreseen that it would be used as mentioned in paragraph 5(d) above;

and where notice of claim in respect of anything is duly given in accordance with paragraphs 3 and 4 of that Schedule, as applied by this paragraph, the court shall not exercise its power of ordering forfeiture of the vessel or vehicle under paragraph 5 above.

In this paragraph 'owner', in relation to a vessel or vehicle which is the subject of a hire-purchase agreement, means the person in possession of the vehicle under that agreement.

[As amended by para. 12 of Sch. 4 to the Customs and Excise Management Act 1979.]
[See s.32(6)(b) of the Salmon Act 1986.]

7.   An authorised officer may seize any salmon, trout or freshwater fish bought, sold or exposed for sale by, or in the possession for sale of, any person in contravention of this Act.

8.   Where any fish or any other thing of a perishable nature is seized as liable to forfeiture under paragraph 5 above, the person by whom it is seized may sell it, and the net proceeds of sale shall be liable to forfeiture in the same manner as the fish or other thing sold, and if and so far as not forfeited shall be paid on demand to the owner; but no person shall be subject to any liability on account of his neglect or failure to exercise the powers conferred on him by this paragraph.

9.   If a person is convicted of an offence against this Act and is subsequently convicted of any such offence, the court may order that any fishing or general licence held by him shall be forfeited, and that he shall be disqualified from holding and obtaining a fishing or general licence or for fishing in a water authority area by virtue of a fishing or general licence for such period not exceeding one year as the court thinks fit.

10.   A person who is prosecuted for an offence against this Act and who is the holder of a fishing or general licence shall either—

(a)   cause it to be delivered to the clerk of the court not later than the day before the date appointed for the hearing, or
(b)   post it, at such a time that in the ordinary course of post it would be delivered not later than that day, in a letter duly addressed to the clerk and either registered or sent by the recorded delivery service, or
(c)   have it with him at the hearing;

and if he is convicted of the offence and the court makes an order under paragraph 9 above the court shall order the licence to be surrendered to it; and if the offender has not posted the licence or caused it to be delivered as aforesaid and does not surrender it as required then he shall be guilty of an offence and the licence shall be revoked from the time when its surrender was ordered.

11.   Where a court orders a fishing or general licence to be surrendered to it under paragraph 10 above, or where by an order of a court under paragraph 9

above a person is disqualified from holding or obtaining a licence, the court shall—

(a)   send notice of the order to the water authority within whose area the offence was committed, unless the authority prosecuted in the case;

(b)   if the licence has been so surrendered, retain it and forward it to that authority, who may dispose of it as they think fit.

12.   Where any person is convicted of an offence against this Act, the clerk of the court before whom he is convicted shall, within one month of the date of conviction, forward a certificate of the conviction to the water authority for the area in which the offence was committed.

13.   A certificate under paragraph 12 above shall be receivable in evidence in all legal proceedings.

Schedule 5   Repeals

Chapter	Short title	Extent of repeal
13 & 14 Geo. 5. c. 16.	The Salmon and Freshwater Fisheries Act 1923.	The whole Act.
19 & 20 Geo. 5. c. 39.	The Salmon and Freshwater Fisheries (Amendment) Act 1929.	The whole Act.
25 & 26 Geo. 5. c. 43.	The Salmon and Freshwater Fisheries Act 1935.	The whole Act.
1963 c. 38.	The Water Resources Act 1963.	In section 71(6), the words 'the Salmon and Freshwater Fisheries Act 1923 or by'. In section 126(1), the words 'the Salmon and Freshwater Fisheries Act 1923 to 1972, and'.
1965 c. 56.	The Compulsory Purchase Act 1965.	In Schedule 6, the entry relating to the Salmon and Freshwater Fisheries Act 1923.
1965 c. 68.	The Salmon and Freshwater Fisheries Act 1965.	The whole Act.
1972 c. 37.	The Salmon and Freshwater Fisheries Act 1972.	The whole Act.
1973 c. 37.	The Water Act 1973.	Section 18. Section 40(4)(c). In Schedule 8, paragraphs 1 to 19 and paragraphs 95 to 97.
1974 c. 40.	The Control of Pollution Act 1974.	In Schedule 3, paragraph 5.

APPENDIX 2 OTHER STATUTORY PROVISIONS RELATING TO FISHERY LAW

The Theft Act 1968

Basic definition of theft

1.—(1) A person is guilty of theft if he dishonestly appropriates property belonging to another with the intention of permanently depriving the other of it; and 'thief' and 'steal' shall be construed accordingly.

(2) It is immaterial whether the appropriation is made with a view to gain, or is made for the thief's own benefit.

(3) The five following sections of this Act shall have effect as regards the interpretation and operation of this section (and, except as otherwise provided by this Act, shall apply only for purposes of this section).

'Dishonestly'

2.—(1) A person's appropriation of property belonging to another is not to be regarded as dishonest—

(a) if he appropriates the property in the belief that he has in law the right to deprive the other of it, on behalf of himself or of a third person; or

(b) if he appropriates the property in the belief that he would have the other's consent if the other knew of the appropriation and the circumstances of it; or

(c) (except where the property came to him as trustee or personal representative) if he appropriates the property in the belief that the person to whom the property belongs cannot be discovered by taking reasonable steps.

(2) A person's appropriation of property belonging to another may be dishonest notwithstanding that he is willing to pay for the property.

'Appropriates'

3.—(1) Any assumption by a person of the rights of an owner amounts to an appropriation, and this includes, where he has come by the property (innocently or not) without stealing it, any later assumption of a right to it by keeping or dealing with it as owner.

(2) Where property or a right or interest in property is or purports to be transferred for value to a person acting in good faith, no later assumption by him of rights which he believed himself to be acquiring shall, by reason of any defect in the transferor's title, amount to theft of the property.

'Property'

4.—(1)   'Property' includes money and all other property, real or personal, including things in action and other intangible property.

(2)   A person cannot steal land, or things forming part of land and severed from it by him or by his directions, except in the following cases, that is to say—

(a)   when he is a trustee or personal representative, or is authorised by power of attorney, or as liquidator of a company, or otherwise, to sell or dispose of land belonging to another, and he appropriates the land or anything forming part of it by dealing with it in breach of the confidence reposed in him; or

(b)   when he is not in possession of the land and appropriates anything forming part of the land by severing it or causing it to be severed, or after it has been severed; or

(c)   when, being in possession of the land under a tenancy, he appropriates the whole or part of any fixture or structure let to be used with the land.

For purposes of this subsection 'land' does not include incorporeal hereditaments; 'tenancy' means a tenancy for years or any less period and includes an agreement for such a tenancy, but a person who after the end of a tenancy remains in possession as statutory tenant or otherwise is to be treated as having possession under the tenancy, and 'let' shall be construed accordingly.

(3)   A person who picks mushrooms growing wild on any land, or who picks flowers, fruit or foliage from a plant growing wild on any land, does not (although not in possession of the land) steal what he picks, unless he does it for reward or for sale or other commercial purpose.

For purposes of this subsection 'mushroom' includes any fungus, and 'plant' includes any shrub or tree.

(4)   Wild creatures, tamed or untamed, shall be regarded as property; but a person cannot steal a wild creature not tamed nor ordinarily kept in captivity, or the carcase of any such creature, unless either it has been reduced into possession by or on behalf of another person and possession of it has not since been lost or abandoned, or another person is in course of reducing it into possession.

'Belonging to another'

5.—(1)   Property shall be regarded as belonging to any person having possession or control of it, or having in it any proprietary right or interest (not being an equitable interest arising only from an agreement to transfer or grant an interest).

(2)   Where property is subject to a trust, the persons to whom it belongs shall be regarded as including any person having a right to enforce the trust, and an intention to defeat the trust shall be regarded accordingly as an intention to deprive of the property any person having that right.

(3)   Where a person receives property from or on account of another, and is under an obligation to the other to retain and deal with that property or its proceeds in a particular way, the property or proceeds shall be regarded (as against him) as belonging to the other.

(4)   Where a person gets property by another's mistake, and is under an

obligation to make restoration (in whole or in part) of the property or its proceeds or of the value thereof, then to the extent of that obligation the property or proceeds shall be regarded (as against him) as belonging to the person entitled to restoration, and an intention not to make restoration shall be regarded accordingly as an intention to deprive that person of the property or proceeds.

(5)   Property of a corporation sole shall be regarded as belonging to the corporation notwithstanding a vacancy in the corporation.

'With the intention of permanently depriving the other of it'
6.—(1)   A person appropriating property belonging to another without meaning the other permanently to lose the thing itself is nevertheless to be regarded as having the intention of permanently depriving the other of it if his intention is to treat the thing as his own to dispose of regardless of the other's rights; and a borrowing or lending of it may amount to so treating it if, but only if, the borrowing or lending is for a period and in circumstances making it equivalent to an outright taking or disposal.

(2)   Without prejudice to the generality of subsection (1) above, where a person, having possession or control (lawfully or not) of property belonging to another, parts with the property under a condition as to its return which he may not to be able to perform, this (if done for purposes of his own and without the other's authority) amounts to treating the property as his own to dispose of regardless of the other's rights.

32.—(1) . . . the provisions in Schedule 1 to this Act (which preserve with modifications certain offences under the Larceny Act 1861 of . . . taking or destroying fish) shall have effect as there set out.

Schedule 1

[As amended by the Criminal Justice Act 1982, ss. 35, 38 and 46.]

Taking or Destroying Fish

2.—(1)   Subject to subparagraph (2) below, a person who unlawfully takes or destroys, or attempts to take or destroy, any fish in water which is private property or in which there is any private right of fishery shall on summary conviction be liable to imprisonment for a term not exceeding three months or to a fine not exceeding level 3 on the standard scale or to both.

(2)   Subparagraph (1) above shall not apply to taking or destroying fish by angling in the daytime (that is to say, in the period beginning one hour before sunrise and ending one hour after sunset); but a person who by angling in the daytime unlawfully takes or destroys, or attempts to take or destroy, any fish in water which is private property or in which there is any private right of fishery shall on summary conviction be liable to a fine not exceeding level 1 on the standard scale.

(3)   The court by which a person is convicted of an offence under this

paragraph may order the forfeiture of anything which, at the time of the offence, he had with him for use for taking or destroying fish.

(4)   Any person may arrest without warrant anyone who is, or whom he, with reasonable cause, suspects to be, committing an offence under subparagraph (1) above, and may seize from any person who is, or whom he, with reasonable cause, suspects to be, committing any offence under this paragraph anything which on that person's conviction of the offence would be liable to be forfeited under subparagraph (3) above.

[As amended by the Criminal Justice Act 1982, s. 46.]

The Import of Live Fish (England and Wales) Act 1980

[As amended by s. 37 of the Fisheries Act 1981.]

1980, c.27. An Act to restrict in England and Wales the import, keeping or release of live fish or shellfish or the live eggs or milt of fish or shellfish of certain species.
[Royal assent 15 May 1980]

Power to limit the import etc. of fish and fish eggs
1.—(1)   Without prejudice to section 1(1) of the Diseases of Fish Act 1937 and subject to subsection (2) below, the Minister may by order forbid either absolutely or except under a licence granted under this section, the import into, or the keeping or the release, in any part of England and Wales of live fish, or the live eggs of fish, of a species which is not native to England and Wales and which in the opinion of the Minister might compete with, displace, prey on or harm the habitat of any freshwater fish, shellfish or salmon in England and Wales.

(2)   Before determining whether or not to make an order under this section, the Minister shall consult the Nature Conservancy Council and any other person with whom the Minister considers that consultation is appropriate.

(3)   The Minister may, subject to such conditions as he thinks fit, grant a licence to any person to import, keep or release live fish, or the live eggs of fish, of a species specified in an order under this section and the Minister may revoke or vary any such licence.

(4)   An order under this section may, with the consent of the Treasury, authorise the making of a charge for a licence under this section and shall specify a maximum charge.

(5)   The power conferred by this section to make orders shall be exercisable by statutory instrument, which shall be subject to annulment in pursuance of a resolution of either House of Parliament.

Powers of entry and inspection
2.—(1)   While an order under section 1 of this Act is in force any officer commissioned by the Commissioners of Customs and Excise, or a person duly authorised by the Minister may at all reasonable times, on production of his authority if so required, enter and inspect any land occupied by a person holding

a licence granted under that section and any other land upon which he has reason to believe that live fish, or the live eggs of fish, of the species specified in the order are being kept or may be found.

(2)   In this section 'land' includes land covered with water but does not include a dwelling-house.

Offences etc.

3.—(1)   Subject to subsection (2) below, any person who—

(a)   imports or attempts to import into, or keeps or releases, in any part of England and Wales any live fish, or the live eggs of fish, of a species specified in an order under section 1 of this Act—

(i)   in a case where the order forbids absolutely such import, keeping or release;

(ii)   without having a valid licence granted under the said section 1 authorising such import or keeping or release, in a case where the order forbids the import or keeping or release except under such a licence;

(b)   being the holder of a licence granted to him under the said section 1, acts in contravention of or fails to comply with any term of the licence;

(c)   obstructs any person from entering or inspecting any land in pursuance of section 2 of this Act;

shall be guilty of an offence under this Act and shall be liable on summary conviction to a fine not exceeding level 4 on the standard scale.

(2)   A person shall not be guilty of an offence under this Act in respect of any act if he does the act for some scientific or research purpose authorised by the Minister.

(3)   The Court by whom any person is convicted of an offence under paragraph (a) or (b) of subsection (1) above may order any fish or eggs in respect of which the offence was committed to be forfeited and destroyed.

(4)   Any person who is empowered to enter land under section 2 of this Act may seize any fish or eggs with respect to which he has reason to believe that an offence under paragraph (a) or (b) of subsection (1) above has been committed, and may detain them pending the determination of any proceedings to be instituted under the said paragraph (a) or (b), or until the Minister is satisfied that no such proceedings are likely to be instituted.

[As amended by the Criminal Justice Act 1982, s.46.]

Interpretation

4.   In this Act—

'eggs' include milt;

'fish' includes shellfish;

'freshwater fish' means any fish living in fresh water including eels and the fry of eels, but excluding salmon;

'Minister' means

(a)   in relation to England, the Minister of Agriculture, Fisheries and Food; and

(b)   in relation to Wales, the Secretary of State for Wales;

'salmon' includes all migratory fish of the species Salmo salar and Salmo trutta commonly known as salmon and sea trout respectively;

'shellfish' includes crustaceans and molluscs of any kind and any spat or spawn of shellfish.

Short title and extent

5.—(1)   This Act may be cited as the Import of Live Fish (England and Wales) Act 1980.

(2)   This Act extends to England and Wales only.

The Fisheries Act 1981

Part IV   Fish Farming

Financial assistance

31.—(1)   The Ministers may, in accordance with a scheme made by them with the approval of the Treasury, make such grants as appear to them to be desirable for the purpose of reorganising, developing or promoting fish farming in Great Britain.

(2)   In this section 'fish farming' means the breeding, rearing or cultivating of fish (including shellfish) for the purpose of producing food for human consumption.

(3)   A scheme under this section may be confined to the making of such grants as appear to the Ministers to be requisite for enabling persons to benefit from any Community instrument which provides for the making of grants by a Community institution where such grants are also provided by a member State.

(4)   A scheme under this section may extend to the whole of Great Britain, to England, Wales or Scotland only or to any two of those countries.

(5)   In this section 'the Ministers' means—

(a)   in relation to a scheme extending to the whole of Great Britain, the Minister of Agriculture, Fisheries and Food and the Secretaries of State respectively concerned with fisheries in Wales and Scotland;

(b)   in relation to a scheme extending to England only or to England together with Wales or Scotland, that Minister or, as the case may be, that Minister and the Secretary of State concerned with fisheries in Wales or Scotland;

(c)   in relation to a scheme extending to Wales or Scotland only or to both of those countries, the Secretary of State concerned with fisheries in Wales or Scotland or, as the case may be, the Secretaries of State respectively concerned with fisheries in each of those countries;

but a scheme made by two or more Ministers may provide for payments under the scheme to be made by any of them.

(6)   A scheme under this section shall be laid before Parliament after being made and shall cease to have effect (without prejudice to anything previously done thereunder or to the making of a new scheme) after the expiration of the period of forty days beginning with the day on which it is made unless within that period it has been approved by a resolution of each House of Parliament.

(7)   In reckoning any period under subsection (6) above no account shall be taken of any time during which Parliament is dissolved or prorogued or during which both Houses are adjourned for more than four days.

(8)   Section 17 above shall have effect in relation to a scheme under this section as it has effect in relation to a scheme under Part II of this Act.

Research, development and advice

32.—(1)   The Minister of Agriculture, Fisheries and Food and the Secretaries of State respectively concerned with fisheries in Scotland and Wales may each carry out research and development for the purpose of promoting the breeding, rearing or cultivating of fish (including shellfish) for the purpose of producing food for human consumption.

(2)   Each of those Ministers may provide scientific, technical and other advice and instruction on matters relating to the breeding, rearing or cultivating of fish (including shellfish) whether or not for the purpose of producing food for human consumption.

(3)   Fees may be charged for any advice or instruction provided under this section.

Exclusion of offences under conservation legislation

33.—(1)   A person shall not be guilty of an offence mentioned in Part I of Schedule 4 to this Act by reason of anything done or omitted by him in the course of fish farming if it is done or omitted under the authority of an exemption conferred by the Minister and in accordance with any conditions attached to the exemption.

(2)   The Minister may by regulations confer general exemptions for the purposes of subsection (1) above, and such regulations may—

(a)   make different provision for different methods of fish farming and for other different circumstances; and

(b)   specify conditions to which the exemptions are subject.

(3)   Regulations under subsection (2) above shall be made by statutory instrument which shall be subject to annulment in pursuance of a resolution of either House of Parliament.

(4)   In the application of subsections (1) and (2) above to offences under the Salmon and Freshwater Fisheries Act 1975, 'the Minister' means, in relation to the area of the Welsh Water Authority, the Secretary of State and, in relation to other areas to which the Act applies, the Minister of Agriculture, Fisheries and Food; and in the application of those subsections to offences under enactments relating to sea fishing, 'the Minister' means, in relation to England, the Minister of Agriculture, Fisheries and Food, and, in relation to Wales or Scotland, the

Secretary of State concerned with fisheries in that country.

(5)   It shall be a defence for a person charged with an offence mentioned in Part II of Schedule 4 to this Act to show that he believed on reasonable grounds that the fish with respect to which the offence is alleged to have been committed were produced by fish farming.

(6)   In this section 'fish farming' means the breeding, rearing or cultivating of fish (incuding shellfish) whether or not for the purpose of producing food for human consumption; but the reference in subsection (5) above to fish produced by fish farming does not include fish bred, reared or cultivated in captivity which have later been released to the wild.

Schedule 4   Exemptions for Fish Farming

Part I   Offences to Which Section 33(1) of This Act Applies

Offences under the Salmon and Freshwater Fisheries Act 1975

1.   Any offence under section 2(2)(a) of the Salmon and Freshwater Fisheries Act 1975 (taking, killing or injuring or attempting to take, kill or injure, unclean or immature fish).

2.   Any offence under section 3 of that Act (restriction on shooting or working seine or draft net in certain waters and prohibition on use of certain nets).

3.   Any offence under section 5(1) of that Act (prohibition on use of explosives, poison or electrical devices to take or destroy fish) relating to the use of a noxious substance or electrical device, and any offence under section 5(4) of that Act relating to the possession of such a substance or device.

4.   Any offence under section 19 of that Act (fishing for, taking or killing or attempting to take or kill fish during close seasons or close times).

5.   Any offence under section 27 of that Act (fishing for or taking fish without a licence or possession of equipment with intent to use it for an unlicensed purpose).

6.   Any offence under section 28(7) of that Act (infringement of byelaws) consisting of a contravention of a byelaw made for a purpose mentioned in any of the following paragraphs of Schedule 3 to that Act—

   (a)   paragraph 21 or 25 (descriptions of nets and other instruments which may be used for taking fish and restrictions on their use);
   (b)   paragraph 23 or 24 (restrictions on carrying of certain nets);
   (c)   paragraph 26 (taking or removing fish from water without lawful authority);
   (d)   paragraph 28 (taking fish of less than prescribed size).

Part II   Offences to Which Section 33(5) of This Act Applies

Offences Relating to Freshwater Fish and Salmon

26.   An offence under section 2(2)(b) of the Salmon and Freshwater Fisheries Act 1975 (buying, selling, exposure for sale or possession of unclean or immature fish or parts of such fish).

27.   Any offence under section 22(1) of that Act (buying, selling, exposure for sale or possession for sale of fish at prohibited times of year).

28.   Any offence under subsection (3) of section 23 of that Act of entering for export or exporting fish contrary to subsection (1) of that section (unclean fish and fish caught at a time when their sale is prohibited).

The Diseases of Fish Act 1937

[As amended by the Diseases of Fish Act 1983. Throughout this Act the term 'water authority' has been substituted for 'fishing board' by virtue of the River Boards Act 1948, Sch. 3, para. 7, the Water Resources Act 1963, Sch. 3, paras 3 and 4, and the Water Act 1973, s. 9.]

Restriction on importation of live fish and eggs of fish
1.—(1)   Subject to subsection (6) of this section it shall not be lawful to import or bring into Great Britain any live fish of the salmon family.

(2)   It shall not be lawful to import or bring into Great Britain any live freshwater fish or live eggs of fish of the salmon family, or of freshwater fish, unless the fish or eggs are consigned to a person licensed under this section and the licence is produced at the time of the delivery under the enactments for the time being in force relating to customs or excise of the entry of the consignment.

[As amended by para. 12 of Sch. 4 to the Customs and Excise Management Act 1979.]

(3)   The Minister may grant a licence to any person to have consigned to him such fish or eggs as are mentioned in the last foregoing subsection, and the following provisions shall have effect in relation to such licences, that is to say:—

(a)   a licence may be granted subject to such conditions as the Minister thinks fit as to the quantities or kinds of fish or eggs which may be imported or brought in under the licence, as to the disposal, transport, inspection, cleansing and disinfection of the fish or eggs and of the containers or other vessels in which they are to be transported or kept and otherwise as to the precautions which are to be taken for avoiding the spreading of disease among salmon and freshwater fish;

(b)   a licence may be granted for any period not exceeding twelve months but may be suspended or revoked by the Minister at any time during the currency thereof;

(c)   there shall on the grant of a licence be paid by the person applying therefor to the Minister such fee not exceeding 25p as the Minister may, with the consent of the Treasury, determine.

[As amended by virtue of the Decimal Currency Act 1969, s. 10(1).]

(4)   If any person in contravention of the provisions of this section imports or brings or procures to be imported or brought into Great Britain any live fish or eggs of fish or, being the holder of a licence under this Act, contravenes any condition subject to which the licence was granted, he shall be guilty of an offence; and any officer of police, officer of Customs and Excise, or inspector may seize any fish or eggs with respect to which he has reason to believe that such an offence has been committed and may detain them pending the determination of any proceedings instituted under this Act in respect of that offence or until the Minister is satisfied that no such proceedings are likely to be instituted.

(5)   Notwithstanding the foregoing provisions of this section where it is shown to the satisfaction of the Commissioners of Customs and Excise that any live fish or eggs of fish, of which the importation or bringing into Great Britain is prohibited or restricted by this section, are being imported or brought solely with a view to the re-exportation thereof after transit through Great Britain or by way of transhipment, the Commissioners may, subject to such conditions as they think fit to impose for securing the re-exportation of the goods, allow the fish or eggs of fish to be imported or brought as if the prohibition or restriction did not apply thereto.

(6)   Subsection (1) of this section shall not apply to any fish of a description specified in an order made by the Minister under this subsection.

(7)   The description may be made by reference to species, place of origin or any other factor.

(8)   Where an order under subsection (6) of this section has effect in relation to any fish, subsections (2) to (5) of this section shall have effect as if it were a freshwater fish.

(9)   The power to make an order under subsection (6) of this section shall be exercisable by statutory instrument, and no such order shall be made unless a draft of the order has been laid before and approved by resolution of each House of Parliament.

(10)   An order under subsection (6) of this section may be varied or revoked by a subsequent order made under that subsection.

Power to designate areas
2.—(1)   If, at any time, the Minister has reasonable grounds for suspecting that any inland or marine waters are or may become infected waters, he may by order designate the waters and such land adjacent to them as he considers appropriate in the circumstances; and in the following provisions of this section 'designated area' means anything designated by an order under this section.

(2)   The Minister may, to such extent as he considers practicable and desirable for the purpose of preventing the spread of infection among fish, by the same or a subsequent order—

(a)   prohibit or regulate the taking into or out of the designated area of such of the following (or of such description of them) as may be specified in the order, namely, live fish, live eggs of fish and foodstuff for fish;
(b)   regulate the movement within the area of such of those things (or of such description of them) as may be specified in the order.

(3)   Any person who is the occupier of any inland waters in a designated area, or carries on the business of fish farming in any marine waters in such an area, shall be entitled, on application, to be supplied by the Minister free of charge with a report of the evidence on which the order was made.
This subsection does not apply to Scotland.
(4)   In Scotland any person who—

(a)   is the occupier of any inland waters;
(b)   carries on the business of fish farming in any marine waters;
(c)   has a right to fish for salmon in any marine waters; or
(d)   has a right of fishing in any private non-navigable marine waters,

which are in a designated area, shall be entitled, on application, to be supplied by the Secretary of State free of charge with a report of the evidence on which the order was made.
(5)   Any order under this section shall be published in the prescribed manner and may be varied or revoked by a subsequent order made under this section.
(6)   If any person intentionally contravenes any provision of an order under this section he shall be guilty of an offence.

Designated areas: direction to remove fish
2A.—(1)   Where an order is in force under section 2 of this Act, the Minister may serve a notice in writing on—

(a)   any occupier of inland waters situated in the designated area (that is, the area designated by the order);
(b)   any person carrying on the business of fish farming in marine waters situated in the designated area.

(2)   A notice served on a person under subsection (1)(a) of this section may direct him to take such practicable steps as are specified in the notice to secure the removal of dead or dying fish from the waters concerned, and may regulate the manner in which any fish removed from the waters, and any parts of such fish, are to be disposed of.
(3)   A notice served on a person under subsection (1)(b) of this section may direct him to take such practicable steps as are specified in the notice to secure the removal of dead or dying fish from any cage which is owned or possessed by him,

is used for the purposes of the business and is situated in the waters concerned, and may regulate the manner in which any fish removed from such a cage, and any parts of such fish, are to be disposed of.

(4)   No notice may be served under subsection (1)(a) of this section in respect of waters in the area of a water authority, not being a fish farm.

(5)   If the Minister is satisfied that a direction contained in a notice served under this section has not been complied with within the time specified in the notice, he may authorise an inspector to carry out the direction, and any expenses reasonably incurred by the inspector in so doing shall be recoverable by the Minister from the person upon whom the notice was served; and if any person intentionally does any act which is prohibited by such a notice, he shall be guilty of an offence unless he shows that he did not know that the act was so prohibited.

Designated areas: authority to remove fish

2B.—(1)   Where an order is in force under section 2 of this Act, the Minister, if he is satisfied that for the protection against disease of the stock of fish in any waters it is necessary to do so, may by a notice served under section 2A of this Act or otherwise in writing give authority falling within subsection (2) or (3) of this section; and in those subsections 'the designated area' means the area designated by the order.

(2)   Authority falling within this subsection is authority to any occupier of inland waters situated in the designated area to remove, notwithstanding anything in any agreement to the contrary, any fish (or any fish of a description specified in the authorisation) from the waters, and to do so by such agents and by such methods (including methods otherwise illegal) as the Minister considers to be most expedient for the purpose.

(3)   Authority falling within this subsection is authority to any person carrying on the business of fish farming in marine waters situated in the designated area to remove, notwithstanding anything in any agreement to the contrary, any fish (or any fish of a description specified in the authorisation) from any cage which is owned or possessed by him, is used for the purposes of the business and is situated in the waters, and to do so by such agents and by such methods (including methods otherwise illegal) as the Minister considers to be most expedient for the purpose.

(4)   No authority may be given as mentioned in subsection (2) of this section in respect of waters in the area of a water authority, not being a fish farm.

(5)   Where a person has in pursuance of an authority under this section removed any fish, he shall comply with any directions given to him by the Minister as to the manner in which the fish, and any parts of such fish, are to be disposed of; and, if he intentionally fails to comply with any such directions, he shall be guilty of an offence.

Powers and duties of water authorities

3.—(1)   Any water authority who have reasonable ground for suspecting that any inland waters, not being a fish farm, are infected waters, shall forthwith report the facts to the Minister, and may take any practicable steps for securing the removal of dead or dying fish from the waters.

The Minister on receiving any such report as aforesaid with respect to any inland waters, shall forthwith cause an investigation to be made as to whether they are infected waters.

(2)   Where an order is in force in relation to an area under section 2 of this Act, the Minister may authorise any water authority to remove any fish (or any fish of a description specified in the authorisation) from any inland waters in that area (not being a fish farm) and to do so by such agents and by such methods (including methods otherwise illegal) as he considers to be most expedient for the purpose.

(3)   Every water authority—

(a)   shall destroy or otherwise properly dispose of all fish removed under any powers conferred on them by or under this section; and

(b)   shall at such times as the Minister may direct send to him a return stating the number of fish so removed.

Preliminary precautions: inland waters

4.—(1)   If an inspector has reasonable grounds for suspecting that any inland waters which are the waters of any fish farm are infected waters, he may serve the prescribed notice upon the occupier of the fish farm and (if the inspector serves such a notice) he shall report the facts to the Minister.

(2)   Where a notice has been served under subsection (1) of this section—

(a)   no live fish and no live eggs of fish shall, without the permission of the Minister, be taken into or out of the fish farm, and

(b)   no foodstuff for fish shall, without the permission of the Minister, be taken out of the fish farm,

until after the expiration of thirty days from the service of the notice, unless before the expiration of that period the occupier receives from the Minister a written intimation that such permission is no longer required.

(3)   Where a notice has been served upon an occupier under subsection (1) of this section, the Minister may if he thinks it desirable authorise an inspector to serve a further prescribed notice upon the occupier so long as no written intimation under subsection (2) above has been given to the occupier; and if the inspector does so before the expiration of thirty days from the service of the first notice, that subsection shall have effect in relation to the fish farm concerned as if for 'thirty' there were substituted 'sixty'.

(4)   A person who intentionally takes any fish, eggs or foodstuff into or out of a fish farm while the taking is prohibited by this section shall be guilty of an offence, unless he shows that he did not know that the taking was prohibited.

(5)   If any person entitled to take fish from any inland waters, or employed for the purpose of having the care of any inland waters, has reasonable grounds for suspecting that the waters are infected waters, it shall be his duty forthwith to report the facts in writing to the Minister or, if the waters are not a fish farm, to the water authority in whose area the waters are situated; and if without reasonable excuse he fails to do so, he shall be guilty of an offence.

Preliminary precautions: marine waters

4A.—(1)   If an inspector has reasonable grounds for suspecting that any marine waters are infected waters—

(a)   he may serve, upon any person who owns or possesses a cage which is situated in the waters and is used by him for the purposes of a business of fish farming carried on by him, the prescribed notice specifying the waters suspected to be infected waters, and

(b)   if the inspector serves such a notice, he shall report the facts to the Minister,

and in the following provisions of this section 'the farmer' means the person so served.

(2)   Where a notice has been served under subsection (1) of this section—

(a)   no live fish and no live eggs of fish shall, without the permission of the Minister, be taken into or out of any cage which is situated in the waters specified in the notice and is used by the farmer for the purposes of a business of fish farming carried on by him, and

(b)   no foodstuff for fish shall, without the permission of the Minister, be taken out of any such cage,

until after the expiration of thirty days from the service of the notice, unless before the expiration of that period the farmer receives from the Minister a written intimation that such permission is no longer required.

(3)   Where a notice has been served upon a farmer under subsection (1) of this section, the Minister may if he thinks it desirable authorise an inspector to serve a further prescribed notice upon the farmer so long as no written intimation under subsection (2) above has been given to the farmer; and if the inspector does so before the expiration of thirty days from the service of the first notice, that subsection shall have effect in relation to any cage concerned as if for 'thirty' there were substituted 'sixty'.

(4)   A person who intentionally takes any fish, eggs or foodstuff into or out of a cage while the taking is prohibited by this section shall be guilty of an offence, unless he shows that he did not know that the taking was prohibited.

(5)   If any person who—

(a)   owns or possesses a cage which is situated in marine waters and is used by him for the purposes of a business of fish farming carried on by him, or

(b)   is employed for the purpose of having the care of a cage so situated and used for the purposes of a business of fish farming,

has reasonable grounds for suspecting that the waters in which the cage is situated are infected waters, it shall be his duty forthwith to report the facts in writing to the Minister; and if without reasonable excuse he fails to do so, he shall be guilty of an offence.

Duty of Minister to examine waters on demand of a water authority or occupier
5.   It shall be the duty of the Minister, on the demand of any water authority, or of an occupier of any inland waters, to cause an inspector to make an examination of any waters within their area, or in his occupation, as the case may be, with a view to discovering whether or not they are infected waters, and to cause a report of the result of the examination to be furnished to the said water authority or occupier free of charge; and if at any such examination the waters are found to be infected waters, the Minister shall cause an inspector to make a further examination thereof when required so to do by the water authority or occupier, as the case may be:

Provided that the Minister shall not be bound to cause an examination to be made of any waters if the period which has elapsed since the conclusion of any previous examination of those waters undertaken in accordance with a demand made under this section is so short that in his opinion a further examination is not yet necessary.

Powers of entry on land and inspection
6.—(1)   Any justice of the peace, upon an information on oath that there is reasonable cause to suspect an offence under this Act to have been committed, may, by warrant under his hand authorise any person named in the warrant to enter on any land mentioned in the warrant at such times as are so mentioned and to seize any fish, eggs of fish, or foodstuff or article which that person suspects to have been imported or brought into Great Britain, removed or otherwise dealt with, or to be about to be removed or otherwise dealt with, in contravention of this Act or of any licence granted, order made, or notice served thereunder:

Provided that a warrant under this subsection shall not continue in force for more than one week from the date of the granting thereof.

The preceding provisions of this subsection shall have effect for the purpose of authorising the boarding of and entry into a cage situated in marine waters and used for the purposes of a business of fish farming as they have effect for the purpose of authorising entry on land.
(2)   Any inspector shall have power (to the extent that he does not have it apart from this subsection)—

(a)   to inspect any inland waters in which fish or the eggs of fish or foodstuff for fish are likely to be found, and to take therefrom samples of any fish or of any such eggs or foodstuff or of water, mud, vegetation or other matter;
(aa)   to inspect any cage situated in marine waters and used for the purposes of a business of fish farming, and to take therefrom samples of any fish or of any eggs of fish or of foodstuff for fish or of water or other matter;
(ab)   to inspect any marine waters in which fish of the salmon family or freshwater fish or the eggs of such fish or foodstuff for fish are likely to be found, and to take therefrom samples of any such fish, eggs or foodstuff or of water, mud, vegetation or other matter;

(b)   for the purpose of exercising any powers or performing any duties under this Act, to enter, upon production on demand of his authoirity, on any land;

(c)   for the purpose of exercising any powers or performing any duties under this Act, to board and enter, upon production on demand of his authority, any cage situated in marine waters and used for the purposes of a business of fish farming,

and any person who refuses to admit or intentionally obstructs an inspector in the exercise or performance of any of the said powers and duties shall be guilty of an offence.

(3)   If in any sample of fish taken from any inland waters by an inspector under the powers conferred by the last foregoing subsection none is found to be infected, the Minister shall pay to the occupier of the waters, or where there is more than one occupier of the waters, to such of the occupiers as he considers equitable, a sum equal to the market value of the fish taken in that sample.

(3A)   If in any sample of fish taken from a cage by an inspector under the powers conferred by subsection (2)(aa) of this section none is found to be infected, the Minister shall pay to the person who owns or possesses the cage and uses it for the purposes of a business of fish farming carried on by him a sum equal to the market value of the fish taken in that sample.

(4)   Any person authorised in writing in that behalf by a water authority may, for the purpose of performing any duties imposed on him by the water authority in exercise of their functions under this Act, enter, upon production on demand of his authority, on any land situate within the area of the water authority not being part of a fish farm, and any person who refuses to admit him or intentionally obstructs him in the carrying out of any of those duties shall be guilty of an offence.

(5)   Any person exercising powers conferred on him by or under this section on land owned or used for the purposes of any railway or canal undertaking shall conform to such reasonable requirements of the undertakers as are necessary to prevent obstruction to, or interference with, the working of the traffic on their railway or canal, as the case may be, and the undertakers shall not be liable for any accident or injury happening to any person while exercising such powers—

(a)   in the case of a railway undertaking, upon any railway or land carrying a railway belonging to them; and

(b)   in the case of a canal undertaking, upon any canal or reservoir or the banks of any canal or reservoir belonging to them.

Service of notices, and authority of agents
7.—(1)   Any notice required or authorised to be served for the purposes of this Act upon an occupier of any inland waters may be served by delivering it to him, or to any servant or agent employed by him for the purpose of having the care of any of the waters, or by sending it by registered post to the usual or last-known address of the occupier, or, if his address is not known and cannot reasonably be ascertained, by exhibiting the notice addressed to him in some conspicuous place

at or near the waters, and, where the identity of the occupier of the waters cannot reasonably be ascertained, the notice, if so exhibited as aforesaid, shall be deemed to be addressed to every person who is an occupier of the waters if it is addressed 'The Occupier' without further name or description.

(1A)   Any notice required or authorised to be served for the purposes of this Act upon a person carrying on the business of fish farming in marine waters may be served by delivering it to him or by sending it by registered post to his usual or last-known address.

(2)   Where a notice requiring anything to be done by an occupier of any inland waters has been served under this section by delivering it to a servant or agent having the care of any of the waters, that servant or agent shall be deemed to have authority from that occupier to do on his behalf and at his expense whatever is required by the notice to be done in relation to any of the waters.

Penalties and legal proceedings

8.—(1)   Any person guilty of an offence under this Act shall be liable on summary conviction to a fine not exceeding level 4 on the standard scale (as defined in section 75 of the Criminal Justice Act 1982); and the court by whom any person is convicted of an offence under this Act may order to be forfeited any fish, eggs of fish, foodstuff or article in respect of which the offence was committed.

(2)   In England and Wales a water authority shall have power to take legal proceedings to enforce provisions of this Act as respects inland waters in their area.

[As amended by the Water Act 1973, Sch. 8, para. 43.]

(3)   Offences against this Act committed in Scotland (including offences committed in waters with respect to which functions under this Act are exercisable by the North West Water Authority) shall be prosecuted and fines recovered in manner directed by the Salmon Fisheries (Scotland) Act 1868.

[As amended by the Water Act 1973, Sch. 8, para. 43.]

(4)   For the purposes of and incidental to the jurisdiction of any magistrates' court or, in Scotland, of the sheriff, any offence under this Act committed in the territorial sea adjacent to Great Britain shall be taken to have been committed in any place in which the offender may for the time being be found.

Power to make regulations

9.   The Minister may make regulations for giving effect to the provisions of this Act and in particular for prescribing—

(a)   the form of licences to be granted under this Act and the manner in which application is to be made for such licences;

(b)   the manner in which orders made under this Act (other than those made under section 1(6) or 13) are to be published;

(c)   the form of notice to be served by an inspector upon the occupier of any waters where the inspector has reasonable grounds for suspecting that the waters are infected waters;

(d)   the manner in which any fish, eggs of fish, foodstuff or articles seized or forfeited under this Act are to be dealt with.

Interpretation
10.—(1)   In this Act, unless the context otherwise requires, the following expressions have the meanings hereby respectively assigned to them, that is to say:—

'business of fish farming' means business of keeping live fish (whether or not for profit) with a view to their sale or to their transfer to other waters;
'cage' means any structure for containing live fish;
'district board' has the same meaning as in the Salmon Fisheries (Scotland) Acts 1828 to 1868;
'fish' does not include shellfish but otherwise means fish of any kind;
'fish farm' means any pond, stew, fish hatchery or other place used for keeping, with a view to their sale or to their transfer to other waters (including any other fish farm), live fish, live eggs of fish, or foodstuff for fish, and includes any buildings used in connection therewith, and the banks and margins of any water therein;
'fish of the salmon family' includes all fish of whatever genus or species belonging to the family Salmonidae;
'foodstuff for fish' means any substance used, or intended or likely to be used, as food for fish, including natural food;
'freshwater fish' does not include fish of the salmon family, or any kinds of fish which migrate to and from tidal waters, but save as aforesaid includes any fish living in fresh water;
'infected' means, in relation to fish, infected with any of the diseases respectively known as bacterial kidney disease (BKD), furunculosis of salmon, infectious haematopoietic necrosis (IHN), infectious pancreatic necrosis (IPN), spring viraemia of carp (SVC), viral haemorrhagic septicaemia (VHS) and whirling disease (*Myxosoma cerebralis*);
'infected waters' means waters in which any of the diseases mentioned in the definition of the expression 'infected' exists among fish, or in which the causative organisms of any of those diseases are present;
'inland waters' means waters within Great Britain which do not form part of the sea or of any creek, bay or estuary or of any river as far as the tide flows;
'inspector' means a person authorised by the Minister to act as an inspector under this Act, either generally or for the particular purpose in question;
'land' includes land covered with inland waters.
'marine waters' means waters (other than inland waters) within the seaward limits of the terrritorial sea adjacent to Great Britain;
'the Minister' means—

(a)   in relation to England, and any marine waters adjacent to England, the Minister of Agriculture, Fisheries and Food;

      (b) in relation to Wales, and any marine waters adjacent to Wales, the Secretary of State;

      (c) in relation to Scotland (including the marine waters thereof), the Secretary of State;

    'occupier' means in relation to any inland waters a person entitled, without the permission of any other person, to take fish from the waters;

    'prescribed' means prescribed by regulations made under this Act;

    'shellfish' includes crustaceans and molluscs of any kind;

    'waters' means any waters (including any fish farm) which are frequented by, or used for keeping, live fish, live eggs of fish, or foodstuff for fish, and includes the banks and margins of any such waters and any buildings used in connection therewith.

[As amended by SI 1973 No. 2093 and SI 1984 No. 301.]

    (2) Notwithstanding anything in the foregoing definition of the expression 'occupier', where the persons entitled without the permission of any other person to take fish from any inland waters are so entitled only by reason of their membership of a club or association, the person having the management of the waters on behalf of the club or association shall, to the exclusion of any members of the club or association (other than himself if a member), be deemed to be the occupier of the waters; and where a person is entitled, without the permission of any other person, to take fish from any inland waters only by virtue of a right acquired for a period not exceeding one year, not he, but the person from whom the right was acquired, shall be deemed to be the occupier of the waters.

    (3) For the purposes of this Act, the Commissioners appointed under the Tweed Fisheries Act 1857, shall be deemed to be a water authority, and the river as defined by the Tweed Fisheries (Amendment) Act 1859, and any byelaw amending that definition shall be deemed to be their area.

11.   In the application of this Act to Scotland, for references to a water authority there shall be substituted references to a district board.

Expenses of Minister

12.   Any expenses incurred by the Minister in connection with the execution of this Act, or in connection with any arrangements made by him with the consent of the Treasury for the carrying on of scientific investigation, or laboratory diagnosis as to diseases affecting fish of the salmon family or freshwater fish, shall be defrayed out of moneys provided by Parliament.

Power to amend definition of 'infected'

13.—(1)   The Minister may by order add to or remove any disease for the time being set out in the definition of 'infected' in section 10(1) of this Act.

    (2) The power to make an order under this section shall be exercisable by statutory instrument subject to annulment in pursuance of a resolution of either House of Parliament.

Short title, commencement and extent
14.—(1)   This Act may be cited as the Diseases of Fish Act 1937.

(2)   [Subsection (2) repealed by the Statute Law Revision Act 1953.]

(3)   This Act shall not extend to Northern Ireland.

The Diseases of Fish Act 1983

Information About Fish Farming

Power to require information
7.—(1)   If it appears to the Minister necessary to do so for the purpose of obtaining information with a view to preventing the spread of disease among fish, he may make an order under this section.

(2)   An order under this section may require any person who occupies an inland fish farm for the purposes of a business of fish farming carried on by him (whether or not for profit)—

(a)   to register the business in a register kept for the purpose by the Minister,

(b)   to furnish in writing to the Minister such information as may be specified in the order in relation to the farm and to fish, eggs of fish and foodstuff for fish,

(c)   to compile such records as may be so specified in relation to the matters mentioned in paragraph (b) above, and

(d)   to retain for such period (not exceeding 3 years) as may be so specified any records compiled in accordance with paragraph (c) above.

In this subsection 'fish' does not include shellfish.

(3)   An order under this section may require any person who owns or possesses any cage, pontoon or other structure which is anchored or moored in marine waters and is used by him for the purposes of a business of fish farming carried on by him (whether or not for profit)—

(a)   to register the business in a register kept for the purpose by the Minister,

(b)   to furnish in writing to the Minister such information as may be specified in the order in relation to any such cage, pontoon or other structure and to fish, eggs of fish and foodstuff for fish,

(c)   to compile such records as may be so specified in relation to the matters mentioned in paragraph (b) above, and

(d)   to retain for such period (not exceeding 3 years) as may be so specified any records compiled in accordance with paragraph (c) above.

In this subsection 'fish' does not include shellfish.

(4)   An order under this section may require any person who carries on a business of shellfish farming (whether or not for profit)—

(a)   to register the business in a register kept for the purpose by the Minister,

(b)   to furnish in writing to the Minister such information as may be specified in the order in relation to any activity carried on (whether in marine or inland waters or on land) for the purpose of cultivating or propagating shellfish in the course of the business, and in relation to shellfish deposited in or on or taken from such waters or land in the course of the business,

(c)   to compile such records as may be so specified in relation to the matters mentioned in paragraph (b) above, and

(d)   to retain for such period (not exceeding 3 years) as may be so specified any records compiled in accordance with paragraph (c) above.

(5)   An order under this section may require any person registering a business as mentioned in subsection (2)(a), (3)(a) or (4)(a) above to pay to the Minister in respect of each registration such fee (complying with subsection (6) below) as may be specified in the order.

(6)   The fee shall be such as the Minister may determine with the Treasury's approval but shall not exceed the cost to the Minister of effecting the registration.

(7)   Any person authorised by the Minister may, on producing on demand evidence of his authority, require the production of, and inspect and take copies of, any records which a person is required to retain by virtue of an order under this section.

(8)   In this section—

'fish farming' means the keeping of live fish with a view to their sale or to their transfer to other waters;

'inland fish farm' means any place where inland waters are used for the keeping of live fish with a view to their sale or to their transfer to other waters (whether inland or not);

'inland waters' means waters within Great Britain which do not form part of the sea or of any creek, bay or estuary or of any river as far as the tide flows;

'marine waters' means waters (other than inland waters) within the seaward limits of the territorial sea adjacent to Great Britain;

'the Minister' means—

(a)   in relation to England, and any marine waters adjacent to England, the Minister of Agriculture, Fisheries and Food;

(b)   in relation to Wales, and any marine waters adjacent to Wales, the Secretary of State;

(c)   in relation to Scotland (including the marine waters thereof), the Secretary of State;

'shellfish' includes crustaceans and molluscs of any kind, and includes any brood, ware, half-ware, spat or spawn of shellfish;

'shellfish farming' means the cultivation or propagation of shellfish (whether in marine or inland waters or on land) with a view to their sale or to their transfer to other waters or land.

(9) The power to make an order under this section shall be exercisable by statutory instrument subject to annulment in pursuance of a resolution of either House of Parliament.

Information: enforcement

8.—(1) Any person who—

(a) fails without reasonable excuse to comply with a requirement of an order under section 7 above (other than a requirement mentioned in subsection (5) of that section), or

(b) in purported compliance with a requirement of an order under section 7 above knowingly furnishes any information or compiles a record which is false in a material particular, or

(c) knowingly alters a record compiled in compliance with a requirement of an order under section 7 above so that the record becomes false in a material particular, or

(d) fails without reasonable excuse to comply with a requirement imposed by virtue of section 7(7) above, or

(e) intentionally obstructs a person in the exercise of his powers under section 7(7) above,

shall be guilty of an offence and liable on summary conviction to a fine not exceeding level 4 on the standard scale (as defined in section 75 of the Criminal Justice Act 1982).

(2) Where an offence under this section which has been committed by a body corporate is proved to have been committed with the consent or connivance of, or to be attributable to any neglect on the part of, a director, manager, secretary or other similar officer of the body corporate, or any person who was purporting to act in any such capacity, he, as well as the body corporate, shall be guilty of that offence and shall be liable to be proceeded against and punished accordingly.

(3) For the purposes of and incidental to the jurisdiction of any magistrates' court or, in Scotland, of the sheriff, any offence under this section committed in, or in relation to anything in, the territorial sea adjacent to Great Britain shall be taken to have been committed in any place in which the offender may for the time being be found.

Disclosure of information

9.—(1) Information (including information in records) obtained by any person in pursuance of section 7 above or an order under that section shall not be disclosed except—

(a) with the written consent of the person by whom the information was provided, or

(b) in the form of a summary of similar information obtained from a number of persons, where the summary is so framed as not to enable particulars

relating to any one person or business to be ascertained from it, or
    (c) for the purpose of any criminal proceedings or for the purpose of a report of any such proceedings.

[See s. 38 of the Salmon Act 1986.]

    (2) Any person who discloses any information in contravention of subsection (1) above shall be guilty of an offence and liable on summary conviction to a fine not exceeding level 4 on the standard scale (as defined in section 75 of the Criminal Justice Act 1982).
    (3) In this section 'the Minister' has the same meaning as in section 7 above.

General

Finance
10.   There shall be paid out of money provided by Parliament—

    (a) the expenses of any Minister of the Crown incurred in consequence of this Act;
    (b) any increase attributable to this Act in the sums so payable under any other Act.

Short title, etc.
11.—(1) This Act may be cited as the Diseases of Fish Act 1983.
    (2) This Act (except this section) shall come into force on such day as the Minister of Agriculture, Fisheries and Food and the Secretary of State acting jointly may by order made by statutory instrument appoint, and an order under this subsection may appoint different days for different provisions or different purposes.

[The Act was brought into force on 1 April 1984 by SI 1984 No. 302.]

    (6) This Act does not extend to Northern Ireland.

The Salmon Act 1986

Part III   Provisions Applying to England and Wales

Dealer licensing in England and Wales
31.—(1) The Minister of Agriculture, Fisheries and Food and the Secretary of State may by order made by statutory instrument make provision for the purpose of prohibiting persons, in such cases as may be specified in the order, from—

    (a) dealing in salmon otherwise than under and in accordance with a licence issued in pursuance of the order by such person as may be so specified; or
    (b) buying salmon from a person who is not licensed to deal in salmon.

(2)   Without prejudice to the generality of subsection (1) above, an order under this section may—

(a)   prescribe the manner and form of an application for a licence to deal in salmon and the sum, or maximum sum, to be paid on the making of such an application;

(b)   specify the circumstances in which such an application is to be granted or refused and the conditions that may be incorporated in such a licence;

(c)   authorise the amendment, revocation or suspension of such a licence;

(d)   create criminal offences consisting in the contravention of, or failure to comply with, provisions made under this section;

(e)   provide for matters to be determined for the purposes of any such provision by a person authorised by any such provision to issue a licence; and

(f)   make provision, whether by applying provisions of the Salmon and Freshwater Fisheries Act 1975 or otherwise, for the purpose of facilitating the enforcement of any provision made under this section.

(3)   An order under this section may—

(a)   make different provision for different cases; and

(b)   contain such incidental, supplemental and transitional provision as appears to the Minister of Agriculture, Fisheries and Food and the Secretary of State to be necessary or expedient.

(4)   Except in the case of an order to which subsection (5) below applies, no order shall be made under this section unless a draft of the order has been laid before, and approved by a resolution of, each House of Parliament.

(5)   A statutory instrument containing an order under this section which relates exclusively to the sum, or maximum sum, to be paid on the making of an application for a licence to deal in salmon shall be subject to annulment in pursuance of a resolution of either House of Parliament.

(6)   In this section 'deal', in relation to salmon, includes selling any quantity of salmon, whether by way of business or otherwise, and acting on behalf of a buyer or seller of salmon.

Handling salmon in suspicious circumstances
32.—(1)   Subject to subsections (3) and (4) below, a person shall be guilty of an offence if, at a time when he believes or it would be reasonable for him to suspect that a relevant offence has at any time been committed in relation to any salmon, he receives the salmon, or undertakes or assists in its retention, removal or disposal by or for the benefit of another person, or if he arranges to do so.

(2)   For the purposes of this section an offence is a relevant offence in relation to a salmon if—

(a)   it is committed by taking, killing or landing that salmon, either in England and Wales or in Scotland; or

(b)   that salmon is taken, killed or landed, either in England and Wales or in Scotland, in the course of the commission of the offence.

(3)   It shall be immaterial for the purposes of subsection (1) above that a person's belief or the grounds for suspicion relate neither specifically to a particular offence that has been committed nor exclusively to a relevant offence or to relevant offences; but it shall be a defence in proceedings for an offence under this section to show that no relevant offence had in fact been committed in relation to the salmon in question.

(4)   A person shall not be guilty of an offence under this section in respect of conduct which constitutes a relevant offence in relation to any salmon or in respect of anything done in good faith for purposes connected with the prevention or detection of crime or the investigation or treatment of disease.

(5)   A person guilty of an offence under this section shall be liable—

   (a)   on summary conviction, to imprisonment for a term not exceeding three months or to a fine not exceeding the statutory maximum or to both;

   (b)   on conviction on indictment, to imprisonment for a term not exceeding two years or to a fine or to both.

(6)   The Salmon and Freshwater Fisheries Act 1975 shall have effect as if—

   (a)   in section 31(1)(b) and (c) (powers of search of water bailiffs), the references to a fish taken in contravention of that Act included references to a salmon in relation to which a relevant offence has been committed; and

   (b)   in sections 33(2) (warrants to enter suspected premises), 36(1) (water bailiffs to be constables for the purpose of enforcing Act) and 39(1) (border rivers) and in paragraph 39(1)(a) of Schedule 3 (prosecution by water authorities) and Part II of Schedule 4 (procedure on prosecutions), the references to that Act included references to this section.

(7)   In this section 'offence', in relation to the taking, killing or landing of a salmon either in England and Wales or in Scotland, means an offence under the law applicable to the place where the salmon is taken, killed or landed.

Placing and use of fixed engines
33.—(1)   For subsection (1) of section 6 of the Salmon and Freshwater Fisheries Act 1975 (under which is it an offence to place a fixed engine in any inland or tidal waters or to use an unauthorised fixed engine for specified purposes) there shall be substituted the following subsection—

   '(1)   Any person who places or uses an unauthorised fixed engine in any inland or tidal waters shall be guilty of an offence.'.

(2)   In subsection (3) of the said section 6 (definition of unauthorised fixed engine), at the end of paragraph (b) there shall be inserted '; or

   (c)   a fixed engine the placing and use of which is authorised by byelaws made by a water authority under this Act or by byelaws made by a local fisheries committee by virtue of section 37(2) of the Salmon Act 1986.'.

(3) In Part II of Schedule 3 to the said Act of 1975 (byelaws), after paragraph 21 there shall be inserted the following paragraph—

'21A. Authorising the placing and use of fixed engines at such places in the water authority area (not being places within the sea fisheries district of a local fisheries committee), at such times and in such manner as may be prescribed by the byelaws and imposing requirements as to the construction, design, material and dimensions of such engines, including in the case of nets the size of mesh.'.

Introduction of fish into fish farms without consent

34. In section 30 of the Salmon and Freshwater Fisheries Act 1975 (prohibition of introduction of fish into inland waters without the consent of the water authority), at the end there shall be added the words 'or the inland water is one which consists exclusively of, or of part of, a fish farm and which, if it discharges into another inland water, does so only through a conduit constructed or adapted for the purpose.

In this section "fish farm" has the same meaning as in the Diseases of Fish Act 1937.'.

Removal of differential penalties under Salmon and Freshwater Fisheries Act 1975

35.—(1) In the Table in Part I of Schedule 4 to the Salmon and Freshwater Fisheries Act 1975 (mode of prosecution and punishment for offences), for the entries relating to sections 1 and 27 (being entries which make different provision according to whether the offender acted with another and do not provide for imprisonment on summary conviction) there shall be substituted the following entries, respectively—

Provision of Act creating the offence (1)	Description of offence (2)	Mode of prosecution (3)	Punishment (4)
'Section 1	Fishing with certain instruments for salmon, trout or freshwater fish and possessing certain instruments for fishing for such fish.	(a) Summarily	Three months or the statutory maximum or both.
		(b) On indictment	Two years or a fine or both.
Section 27	Fishing for fish otherwise than under the authority of a licence and possessing an unlicensed instrument with intent to use if for fishing.	(a) If the instrument in question, or each of the instruments in question, is a rod and line, summarily.	Level 4 on the standard scale.
		(b) In any other case—	
		(i) summarily	three months or the statutory maximum or both;
		(ii) on indictment	two years or a fine or both.'.

(2)   Subsection (1) above shall not affect any proceedings in respect of, or the punishment for, an offence committed before that subsection comes into force.

Servants and agents authorised by fishing licences
36.—(1)   For paragraph 9 of Schedule 2 to the Salmon and Freshwater Fisheries Act 1975 (persons treated as servants and agents of licensee for the purpose of being entitled to use an instrument under the authority of the licence) there shall be substituted the following paragraph—

'9.—(1)   A person who uses an instrument of any description for fishing in an area in relation to which an order under section 26 above limiting the number of licences for fishing with instruments of that description is in force shall not be treated for the purposes of section 25(3) above as the duly authorised servant or agent of any holder of a licence to use an instrument of that description unless, at the time that person uses the instrument—

(a)   his name and address are entered on the licence in accordance with the following provisions of this Schedule; and
(b)   he is not himself the holder of a licence to use an instrument of that description in that area; and
(c)   he is accompanied by the licensee or has the consent of the water authority to his use of the instrument in the absence of the licensee.

(2)   A person who uses an instrument of any description for fishing in an area in which no such order as is mentioned in subparagraph (1) above is in force shall not be treated for the purposes of section 25(3) above as the duly authorised servant or agent of any holder of a licence to use an instrument of that description unless, at the time that person uses the instrument—

(a)   his name and address are entered on the licence in accordance with the following provisions of this Schedule; or
(b)   he is accompanied by the licensee; or
(c)   he has the consent of the water authority to his use of the instrument otherwise than where there is compliance with paragraph (a) or (b) above.

(3)   The consent of a water authority shall not be given under this paragraph except—

(a)   in the case of a consent for the purposes of subpargraph (1)(c) above, in relation to a period which appears to the water authority to be a period throughout which the licensee will be unable through illness or injury to accompany his servant or agent;
(b)   in the case of a consent for the purposes of subparagraph (2)(c) above, where the giving of the consent appears to the water authority to be required by the special circumstances of the case.'.

(2)   Accordingly, in section 25(3) of that Act, for the words from 'not

exceeding' onwards there shall be substituted the words 'subject to the provisions of paragraphs 9 to 13 of Schedule 2 to this Act'.

Byelaws under Sea Fisheries Regulation Act 1966

37.—(1) Subject to subsection (3) below, the power of a local fisheries committee to make byelaws under section 5 of the Sea Fisheries Regulation Act 1966 shall be exercisable for the purposes of protecting salmon and of preventing any interference with their migration and shall be so exercisable as if the references in that section to sea fish included references to salmon.

(2) Subject to subsection (3) below, the power of a local fisheries committee to make byelaws under the said section 5 shall also include power to make byelaws which for the purposes of section 6 of the Salmon and Freshwater Fisheries Act 1975 authorise the placing and use of fixed engines at such places in their sea fisheries district, at such times and in such manner as may be prescribed by the byelaws and impose requirements as to the construction, design, material and dimensions of such engines, including in the case of nets the size of mesh.

(3) A local fisheries committee shall not make byelaws for any purpose mentioned in subsection (1) or (2) above unless the water authority whose area for the purposes of functions relating to fisheries includes the whole or any part of the committee's sea fisheries district have consented to byelaws being made by the committee for that purpose.

(4) For the purposes of any byelaws made by virtue of this section the references to sea fish in sections 10(2)(c) and 12 of the said Act of 1966 (which include provision with respect to the seizure of, and searches for, sea fish taken in contravention of byelaws) shall be deemed to include references to salmon.

(5) In this section—

'fixed engine' has the same meaning as in the Salmon and Freshwater Fisheries Act 1975; and
'salmon' means fish of the salmon species and trout which migrate to and from the sea.

Disclosure of information furnished under the Disease of Fish Act 1983

38.   In subsection (1) of section 9 of the Diseases of Fish Act 1983 (disclosure of information obtained in pursuance of section 7 of that Act), after paragraph (c) there shall be inserted the words 'or
(d)   for the purpose of enabling a water authority to carry out any of their functions under the 1937 Act'.

Part IV   Miscellaneous

Review of certain salmon net fishing

39.—(1)   The Minister of Agriculture, Fisheries and Food and the Secretary of State shall, as soon as practicable after the end of the period of three years beginning with the passing of this Act, prepare a report which, in the context of the need to ensure—

(a)   that sufficient salmon return to spawn in the rivers wholly or partly situated in the areas and districts specified in subsection (3) below; and

(b)   that fishing for salmon by means of nets is properly managed in those areas and districts,

reviews the nature and extent of all such fishing in those areas and districts.

(2)   A copy of the report prepared under subsection (1) above shall be laid before each House of Parliament.

(3)   The areas and districts referred to in subsection (1) above are the areas of the Yorkshire and Northumbrian water authorities and the salmon fishery districts from the River Forth to the River Ugie, the River Tweed being deemed for the purposes of this section to be included in those areas and districts.

Interpretation

40.—(1)   In this Act, unless the context otherwise requires—

. . .

'inland waters' has the same meaning as in the Salmon and Freshwater Fisheries (Protection) (Scotland) Act 1951;

. . .

'River Tweed' means 'the River' as defined by the Tweed Fisheries Amendment Act 1859, as amended by the byelaw made under section 4 of the Salmon Fisheries (Scotland) Act 1863;

. . .

'salmon' means all migratory fish of the species *Salmo salar* and *Salmo trutta* and commonly known as salmon and sea trout respectively or any part of any such fish;

. . .

Amendments and repeals

41.—(1)   The enactments mentioned in Schedule 4 to this Act shall have effect subject to the amendments there specified (being minor amendments or amendments consequential on the preceding provisions of this Act).

. . .

Citation, commencement and extent

43.—(1)   This Act, which may be cited as the Salmon Act 1986, shall . . . come into force on the expiry of the period of two months beginning with the date on which it is passed.

. . .

(3)   The provisions of this Act modifying or repealing other enactments except section 38 have respectively the same extent as those other enactments.

(4)   Subject to the application of section 39(1) of the Salmon and Freshwater Fisheries Act 1975 (border rivers) in relation to section 32 of this Act and the enactments amended by sections 33 to 36 of this Act, sections 31 to 38 of this Act extend to England and Wales only.

Schedule 4   Minor and consequential amendments

Salmon and Freshwater Fisheries Act 1975

13.   In section 39 of the Salmon and Freshwater Fisheries Act 1975 (Border rivers and Solway Firth), after subsection (4) there shall be added the following subsection—

'(5)   Nothing in this section shall authorise a water authority to take legal proceedings in Scotland in respect of an offence against this Act.'.

14.   In section 43(3) of that Act (Scottish extent), for the words 'and (4)' there shall be substituted the words '(4) and (5)'.

BIBLIOGRAPHY

Ben Yami, M. (1976) *Fishing with Light*. Fishing News Books.
Bledisloe (1961) *Report of the Committee on Salmon and Freshwater Fisheries*. Command Paper 1350.
Calderwood, W.L. (1931) *Salmon Hatching and Salmon Migration*. E. Arnold & Co.
Command Paper (1986) *Privatisation of the Water Authorities in England and Wales*. Cmnd 9734.
Corrie, J. (1979) *Fish Farming in Europe*. European Conservative Group.
Davis, F.M. (1958) *An Account of the Fishing Gear of England and Wales* (4th edn). Ministry of Agriculture & Fisheries.
Department of the Environment (1986) *Water and Sewage Law* (consultation paper).
De Smith, S.A. (1985) *Constitutional and Administrative Law* (5th edn). Penguin.
Forrest, D.M. (1976) *Eel Capture, Culture, Processing and Marketing*. Fishing News Books.
Fort, R.S., and Brayshaw, J.D. (1961) *Fishery Management.* Faber & Faber.
Garner, J.F. (1975) *Control of Pollution Act 1974*. Butterworths.
Gregory, M. (1974) *Angling and the Law* (2nd edn). C. Knight.
Hale, Sir M. (1736) *A History of the Pleas of the Crown*.
Hale, Sir M. (1787) *De Jure Maris* (Hargrave's Law Tracts).
Hall, R.G. (1875) *Hall's Essay on the Rights of the Crown in the Sea Shores of the Realm* (2nd edn., Loveland).
Harrison, L. (1984) *Commercial Eel Capture*. Institute of Fisheries Management.
Hartley, G. (1979) *Salmon and Sea Trout Fishing*. (ed A. Wrangles). Davis-Poynter.
Hawkins (1716) *Pleas of the Crown*.
Hickley, P. (1985) *Electric Fishing*. Institute of Fisheries Management.
Houghton, W. (1879) *British Fresh-Water Fishes* (reprinted 1981). Webb & Bower.
Hughes, A.J. (1986) *Environmental Law*. Butterworths.
Hunter (1965) *Report on Scottish Salmon and Trout Fisheries*. Cmnd 2691.
Jenkins, J.G. (1974) *Nets and Coracles*. David & Charles.
Law Commission (1965) *Law Commission Report No. 32—Civil Liability for Dangerous Activities and Things*.
Leigh, L.H. (1985) *Police Powers in England and Wales* (2nd edn). Butterworths.
Lewis, M.R. (1984) *Fish Farming in the United Kingdom*. Univ. of Reading, Dept. of Agric. Econ. & Mgmt.
Maxwell, H. (1904) *British Fresh-Water Fishes*. Hutchinson & Co.
McLoughlin, J. (1972) *The Law Relating to Pollution.* University of Manchester.
Millichamp, R.I. (1976) *Fishing Methods*. Institute of Fisheries Management.

Millichamp, R.I. (1982) *Implementation and Enforcement of Fisheries Law by Bailiffs and Keepers.* Institute of Fisheries Management.

Mills, D.H. (1978) *Fisheries Management.* Institute of Fisheries Management.

Ministry of Agriculture, Fisheries and Food (1981) *Review of Inland and Coastal Fisheries.*

Ministry of Agriculture, Fisheries and Food (1983) *Fish For Food and Sport.*

Moore, S.A., and Moore, H.S. (1903) *The History and Law of Fisheries.* Stevens & Haynes.

National Water Council (1983) *Salmon Conservation — a new approach.*

Newsom, G. and Sherratt, J.G. (1972) *Water Pollution.* Sherratt.

Oke, G.C. (1884) *Fishery Laws* (2nd edn by Willis Bund; (other edns 1862, 1878, 1903, and 1924). Butterworths.

Okun, D.A. (1977) *Regionalization of Water Management.* Applied Science Publishers.

Parry, M.L. (1976) *Institute of Fisheries Management Training Course Part I: Legal.*

Paterson, J. (1873) *A Treatise on the Fishery Laws of the United Kingdom* (2nd edn). Shaw & Sons.

Pollock, F. (1884) *Fisheries Exhibition Literature Volume I: The Fishery Laws.*

Pryce-Tannatt, T.E. (1938) *Fish Passes.* E. Arnold & Co.

Roberts, R.J. and Shepherd, C.J. (1986) *Handbook of Trout and Salmon Diseases* (2nd edn). Fishing News Books.

Sedgwick, S.D. (1982) *The Salmon Handbook.* Deutsch.

Sedgwick, S.D. (1985) *Trout Farming Handbook* (4th edn). Fishing News Books.

Seymour, R. (1970) *Fishery Management and Keepering.* C. Knight.

Smith, J.C. and Hogan, B. (1983) *Criminal Law* (5th edn). Butterworths.

Spillett, P. (1985) *Lead Poisoning in Swans.* Institute of Fisheries Management.

Stone's Justices' Manual (1986) (ed J. Richman and A.T. Draycott). Butterworths.

Telling, A.E. (1974) *Water Authorities.* Butterworths.

Templeton, R.G. (ed) (1984) *Freshwater Fisheries Management*, Fishing News Books.

Thomas, D.A. (1979) *Principles of Sentencing* (2nd edn). Heinemann Educational.

Turing, H.D. (1952) *River Pollution.* E. Arnold & Co.

Vibert, R. (ed) (1967) *Fishing with Electricity: its applications to biology and management.* Fishing News Books.

Walker, A. (1979) *The Law of Industrial Pollution Control.* George Godwin.

Water Authorities Association (1985) *Waterfacts.*

Water Authorities Association (1986) *Who's Who in the Water Industry 1986.*

Welsh Water Authority (1985) *Welsh Salmon and Sea Trout Fisheries.*

Wheeler, A. (1969) *Fishes of the British Isles and North-West Europe.*

Williams, G.L. (1982) *Learning the Law* (11th edn). Stevens.

Winfield and Jolowicz (1984) *Tort* (12th edn by H. Rogers). Sweet & Maxwell.

Wisdom, A.S. (1966a) *Land Drainage.* Sweet & Maxwell.

Wisdom, A.S. (1966b) *The Law Relating to Pollution of Waters* (2nd edn). Shaw.

Wisdom, A.S. (1979) *The Law of Rivers and Watercourses* (4th edn). Shaw.

Wisdom, A.S. (1982) *Aspects of Water Law.* B. Rose.

Wisdom, A.S., and Skeet, J.L.G. (1981) *The Law and Management of Water Resources and Supply*. Shaw.

Wrangles, A. (ed) (1979) *Salmon and Sea Trout Fishing.* Davis-Poynter (Chs. 1 and 3 by **G. Hartley**.)

Zander, M. (1985) *The Police and Criminal Evidence Act 1984*. Sweet & Maxwell.

INDEX